THE STONES CRY OUT
SWEDEN'S RESPONSE TO THE PERSECUTION OF THE JEWS 1933–1945

Steven Koblik

**Documents translated by
David Mel Paul and Margareta Paul**

**Holocaust Library
New York**

Library of Congress Catalogue Card Number 87-81218

ISBN: 0-89604-118-2 (cloth)
0-89604-119-0 (softcover)

Cover design by The Appelbaum Company

Printed in the United States of America

THANKS TO SCANDINAVIA records its gratitude to the following whose significant financial contributions made possible the research, writing and publication of this work:

SANNA & VICTOR BORGE
THE CROWN FAMILY
ALAN C. GREENBERG
CHRIS & BERNARD MARDEN
ALICE & RICHARD NETTER
BARBARA & EDWARD NETTER
THE ROSENSTIEL FOUNDATION
NELL & HERBERT M. SINGER
MARIANNE & JOHN H. SLADE

and

Eleanor & Mel Dubin
in tribute to the name and memory of
NINA MICHELLE DUBIN

and

SAS
in tribute to the name and memory of
S. RALPH COHEN

Holocaust Library

Statement of Purpose

The Holocaust spread across the face of Europe almost fifty years ago. The brutality then unleashed is still nearly beyond comprehension. Millions of innocents — men, women and children — were consumed by its flames.

The goal of Holocaust Library, a non-profit organization founded by survivors, is to publish and disseminate works on the Holocaust. These will include survivors' accounts, testimonies and memoirs, historical and regional analyses, anthologies, archival and source documents and other relevant materials that will help shed light on this cataclysmic era.

These books and studies will be made available to the general public, scholars, researchers, historians, teachers and students. They will be used in Holocaust Resource Centers, libraries and schools, synagogues and churches. They will help foster an increased awareness of the Holocaust and its implications. They will help *to preserve the memory* for posterity and to enable this awesome time to be better understood and comprehended.

Thanks To Scandinavia

Until the founding of Thanks To Scandinavia in June of 1963, America was unaware of the singular acts of humanity and bravery of Denmark, Finland, Norway and Sweden in rescuing persons of the Jewish faith from the Holocaust. During the war years, the mass media featured major battles and armed struggle; but there was no way that information about the Scandinavian Rescue could have filtered out of occupied Europe. When the war was over and we learned the full horror of Hitler's "final solution," we still knew very little about those quiet heroes of the Rescue.

Against the Nazis, who were the perpetrators of such incomprehensible evil, most of the world made no decisive effort to rescue the persecuted and doomed victims. Fear, complacency and disinterest outweighed the sense of responsibility.

Since 1963, in devoted effort to honor the people, the governments and the churches of Denmark, Finland, Norway and Sweden, Thanks To Scandinavia has been raising money to provide "thank you" scholarships and fellowships to Scandinavians at American universities and medical centers. Grants for the fiscal year 1987/88 will exceed $200,000 and efforts continue to enlarge our capital funds (now over $2,250,000) to extend these educational opportunities in perpetuity.

Since 1963, the rescue activities of Denmark have been the subject of books (three funded by Thanks To Scandinavia), magazine articles and film documentaries. However, with the exception of brief chapters in Philip Friedman's book "Their Brothers' Keepers" and the literature of Thanks To Scandinavia, little has been printed in the English language about the rescue activities in Finland, Norway and Sweden.

For historical purposes, and to provide long overdue recognition of the rescue efforts made by the citizens of the three overlooked Nordic countries during the Holocaust, Thanks To Scandinavia has undertaken to publish authoritative and fully documented books by Dr. Hannu Rautkallio on Finland, Professor Samuel Abrahamsen on Norway and Professor Steven Koblik on Sweden.

Inquiries concerning the scholarship fund may be addressed to Thanks To Scandinavia, 745 Fifth Avenue, New York, New York, 10151. Telephone: (212) 486-8600.

We will indeed appreciate support in this honorable endeavor.

RICHARD NETTER   VICTOR BORGE
President   *National Chairman*

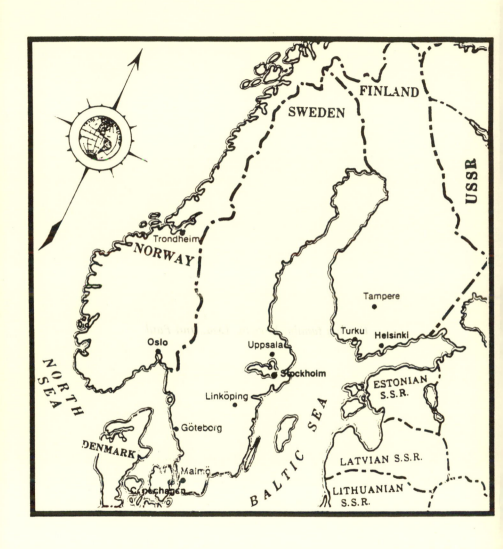

Contents

Foreword

Between 1939 and 1945, over six million Jews died as a result of the policies of Nazi Germany and its allies. What began as a desire to rid Germany of its Jews by forced emigration led to a systematic, industrialized campaign to exterminate Europe's Jews. Of all the developments related to Adolf Hitler's rise to power and the subsequent coming of the Second World War, no other episode has concerned scholars and the general public as much as the Final Solution. Winston Churchill was not alone in thinking that German policy toward the Jews constituted the greatest crime in the history of mankind.[1]

Churchill's conclusions might seem overstated, applying as they do to a history of mankind that stretches over millennia and encompasses horrors and massacres of virtually unimaginable proportions. Yet Churchill's reaction depended to a great extent on his belief that Western man had historically advanced the level of civilized man from barbarism to a culture based on humanistic and Judeo-Christian values. Churchill recognized that Germany represented a highly civilized land which utilized the most modern of scientific techniques and bureaucratic tradition for the basest of goals. The deeds of Germany undermined a fundamental aspect of Western culture — its belief in man's progress.

When the Western public finally comprehended the complete nature of the Final Solution, there was a desperate need to blame it on someone or group of persons. Hitler and the men who ran the death camps became the criminals who were held responsible for their crimes. Even today, we witness the efforts of various groups to bring to trial those who

---

1. Great Britain, Public Records Office, PREM 4 51/10, note by Winston Churchill to Anthony Eden on materials on the extermination of Hungarian Jews sent by Archbishop William Temple, July 11, 1944.

1

directly participated in the murders. Historians, however, have not been as prone to examine the Final Solution simply in terms of its immediate perpetrators. Instead they have also sought to explain how such a monstrous crime could have been successfully managed. In their studies, no group in the West has been left untouched: the Jews themselves, the occupied states, Germany's allies, the neutrals, and the United Nations. The extent of the Final Solution meant that passive as well as active participation was necessary in order for it to have had such an extensive impact on Europe's Jews.

This book is part of that historical effort to understand how the Final Solution occurred. It examines the country of Sweden and its response to German persecution of the Jews. This is the first time that any scholar has tried to present a study of Swedish policy toward the "Jewish Question." Sweden was an important country in the context of the Final Solution. As a neutral during the war, it could receive Jewish immigrants and try to offer its diplomatic protection to them in other countries. Denmark's Jews found a safe haven in Sweden. Swedish protective passes and the work of men such as Raoul Wallenberg in Budapest saved tens of thousands of lives. The specific organization of this volume is dependent on a presumption that most readers are unfamiliar with the history of Sweden.

Therefore, the first chapter is an introduction into Swedish history in the thirties and the war period. No understanding of the Holocaust is possible without recognition of the way in which the war influenced responses to persecution of the Jews. In the case of Sweden, there were historical factors that both encouraged a passive response to German activities and an activist policy to help Jews. Chapter 2 is an overview of Swedish policy toward the Jews in the 1933-1945 period. It allows the reader the opportunity to see the whole picture. The Jewish Question was never uppermost in the minds of Swedish policy-makers, but sometimes it attracted considerable attention. Chapter 3 offers an examination of one Swedish institutional response to the Holocaust: that of the Swedish Lutheran Church, which is the state church of Sweden.

To understand the Swedish response to the persecution of the Jews, it is not sufficient to study government policy. Swedish businessmen, journalists, church officials, and simply private individuals came into contact with developments transpiring on the continent. How they responded affected directly the way in which the government behaved. In this volume, the church is used as an example of an institutional response partially because church officials had such close ties with fellow Lutherans in Germany and therefore knew of the Final Solution earlier than most other people. There was also the moral issue which German persecution posed for Christians. The dilemmas which faced the Swedish church had a character familiar to all Christian groups; the Swedish response was not different from a number of prominent church institutions on the continent.

Chapter 4 is a case study of a rescue mission, the Red Cross efforts of 1945. Sweden partook in four major successful rescue efforts and at least one unsuccessful one. Each experience deserves careful consideration on its own merits. The Red Cross mission has been selected here because it was the largest rescue effort of the war within Germany proper. Over 20,000 people were taken from concentration camps and brought to Sweden in March–April 1945. The experience demonstrated some of the possibilities for rescue, the limitations, and the political factors that produced them. Historical studies of this particular set of developments have been either skewed by personal partisanship related to those involved in the mission itself or ignored by most scholars of the war.

Chapter 5 is an essay that examines the questions: Could the Swedes have done more to help Jews on the continent, and if so, why was it not done? That more could have been done to help Jews is clear. Sweden's restrictive immigration policy in the late thirties, like so many other countries', blocked Jewish refugees from seeking safe haven when Germany still permitted or encouraged Jews to leave Germany. At times during the war, Sweden stood prepared to act more positively. German officials were not deaf to international pressure. The Swedish government needed encouragement and some guarantees. The Western powers were slow in making them.

Following Chapter 5 is a relatively large collection of documents pertinent to the issues examined in the first part of the study. They are organized chronologically. They are intended to provide the reader with an opportunity to examine primary materials. A certain amount of editing was unavoidable, both in terms of selection of the documents and within the documents themselves. An attempt was made to take the most significant and typical documents and to provide the reader with as much material as space would allow. It is our hope that a second volume on this topic will be forthcoming to allow for the study of other issues raised in Chapter 2 not examined in detail here and to present additional documents.

The availability of source materials deserves special comment. The Swedish government and the state church have cooperated fully with the author in allowing full access to all their materials. King Carl Gustaf has also shown generosity in opening Gustaf V's archive. Unfortunately, much material in this archive has been destroyed. In addition, other potentially important private archives have either been damaged or are not available to independent scholarship. Among the most important missing materials, the archives of Erik Boheman (lost in a fire after the war), of the Wallenberg family (closed to scholars), and Gunnar Josephson (deliberately destroyed after the war) deserve mention. It is possible to imagine that sometime in the future new materials will be released that will allow us a more comprehensive understanding of the response of Swedes and Sweden.

Many individuals and institutions have provided encouragement and support for this study. *The Thanks to Scandinavia Foundation* and the Mrs. Mary E. LaFetra research awards at Pomona College provided most of the funding. The generosity of others — archivists, librarians, and historical colleagues — made the work possible. I would like to thank each of them individually, especially Professor Franklin Scott, Dr. Krister Wahlbäck, Professor Sven Lundkvist, Mr. Svante Hansson, Mrs. Mary E. LaFetra, and Mr. Gustaf Olivecrona, whose help was so much appreciated. They of course bear no responsibility for the final form of the study which is solely my own.

The topic under study in this book is not only an important one, it is also a sensitive and highly emotional issue. It is difficult to maintain a reasonable balance and perspective. It is my view that there is no value in simply pointing one's finger at individuals or states arguing that "you could have done more." Rather, our pressing need is to understand how this horrible event could have occurred. And in our understanding be determined never to allow it to be repeated . . . to Jews and/or any other ethnic, religious, or racial group.

Steven Koblik
March 1987
Claremont, California

Chapter 1

Domestic Challenges and Foreign Threats 1932–1945

"National independence," "sovereignty," "freedom" are all relative terms. No state can maintain absolute freedom or national independence. There exist limits on all states' sovereignty. The size of the country, its general level of economic development and its specific nature, its location, the attitudes of neighbors and major trading partners, all affect the ability of a single country to maximize control over its own affairs. Some states are, however, more sensitive to outside influences than others. Sweden during the interwar period, for example, was highly dependent upon external forces for its domestic well-being and international position.[1]

Small states naturally tend to depend more on the actions of other states than large ones do. Between 1890 and 1920, Sweden enjoyed a period of rapid industrialization and improvement in the standard of living. By the twenties, Swedish industrial development had integrated into the larger international marketplace. The ability of Sweden to continue to progress economically relied on the international competitiveness of Swedish business and manufacturing and the general health of the capitalist world's economy. Most of Sweden's industrial giants had

---

1. The classic study of Sweden during the interwar period is Herbert Tingsten, *The Debate on the Foreign Policy of Sweden, 1919–1939* (London, 1949). See also Thomas Munch-Petersen, *The Strategy of Phony War, Britain, Sweden, and the Iron Ore Question, 1939–1940* (Stockholm, 1981); Erik Lönnroth, *Den svenska utrikespolitikens historia V, 1919–1939,* (Stockholm, 1959); and works produced at the University of Gothenburg in the economic history project, "Under Pressure from Abroad — Sectors of the Swedish Economy, 1933–1945," including Martin Fritz, *German Steel and Swedish Iron Ore, 1939–1945* (Gothenburg, 1974).

become multinational and therefore highly sensitive to fluctuations in the international marketplace. The stock market crash in New York in 1929, the failure of major German and Austrian banks, and the precipitous decline in international trade produced serious problems in Sweden. How to respond to the Depression became the first challenge for Sweden in the thirties.

The impact of the Depression on Sweden, while quite severe, was comparatively brief. During the winter of 1930–1931, unemployment began to rise and wages fell. It was the latter phenomenon which led to a series of labor conflicts in the spring of 1931 and an outbreak of violence on May 14, 1931, when five workers were killed in Ådalen in Northern Sweden. This incident shocked the country which, while used to labor conflict, had not experienced loss of life in such matters. A second critical experience came in September 1931, when Sweden followed Britain's decision to go off the gold standard. In March 1932, Sweden's most spectacular and best known businessman, Ivar Kreuger, committed suicide in Paris. His financial empire lay in ruins as a result of his own questionable transactions and the collapse of the international monetary system. A number of important Swedish industries, including L. M. Ericsson and Swedish Match Company, were directly threatened because of Kreuger's death. By March 1933, unemployment reached a new height. No less than 186,000 workers were out of work, which represented nearly 8 percent of the total workforce. By the end of 1934, however, the worst of the Depression had passed, and Sweden appeared to be on the road to recovery.[2]

The economic difficulties between 1929 and 1933 led to a significant shift in the political life of the country. Beginning with elections for the upper house of the Swedish parliament in 1930–1931, the Social Democrats began a steady rise in their popularity from a 37 percent voter support in 1929 to a total in 1940 of 53.8 percent.[3] As a result of the September 1932 lower house elections, the Social Democrats built a minority government. The most important members of the cabinet were the party chairman, Per Albin Hansson, prime minister; Ernst Wigforss, minister of economics; Gustav Möller, minister of social welfare; and Rickard Sandler, minister of foreign affairs. With the exception of a three-month period in 1936, the Social Democrats would sit in the gov-

---

2. Sten Carlsson, *Svensk Historia*, v. II, (Stockholm, 1961) pp. 682–684.
3. Dankwart A. Rustow, *The Politics of Compromise* (Princeton, 1955), pp. 242–250.

ernment, sometimes alone, sometimes in coalition, for the next 44 years, the longest continuous experience in governing power of any party in the democratic West.

In 1932 it was not clear, however, that Sweden stood at the dawn of a new age of political stability. Sweden's democracy had only been fully established in 1918 and had been plagued during the twenties by a series of minority governments. There had been nine different governments between 1920 and 1932, the last of which had only 28 of 230 and 24 of 150 seats in the two houses. The prime minister in this government, C. G. Ekman, had been implicated in the scandals following Kreuger's suicide and resigned in disgrace. The king, Gustaf V, tried after the elections of 1932 to build a government based on a broad coalition, as Britain had done to meet the economic crisis. He failed and had to turn to the Social Democrats, who held 162 of the 380 seats in both houses. The Social Democrats argued during the 1932 campaign that the government must adopt an "expansive" economic and fiscal policy to stimulate Swedish economic recovery. They did not receive support for this policy from any other party. It did not seem likely in 1932 that the new Hansson government would be much more successful than the ones that had preceded it.

Their comparatively rapid recovery from the Depression influenced the Swedes in a number of ways. Domestically, the Social Democrats claimed credit and their popularity continued to grow. Internationally, Sweden became an object of attention as a model for democracy. In 1936, Marquis Childs published a book, Sweden: The Middle Way.[4] It became a best seller and was reprinted many times in the thirties and as late as 1961. Childs suggested that Sweden offered the world an alternative to what he called unfettered capitalism (the United States) and totalitarian regimes (the Soviet Union and Nazi Germany). Childs's analysis emphasized the role cooperatives played in the Swedish economy and the spirit of pragmatism that marked the political arena. Childs overestimated the influence of the cooperatives and did not understand that the spirit of cooperation and pragmatism that he observed was something new and in the process of being created.[5]

---

4. Marquis Childs, Sweden: The Middle Way (New Haven, 1937).

5. See Sven Anders Söderpalm "The Crisis Agreement and the Social Democratic Road to Power," in S. Koblik, Sweeden's Development From Poverty to Affluence, 1750-1959 (Minnesota, 1975) and B. von Sydow, "Krisuppgörelsen: man måste betona förändringarna," Politisk Tidskrift, Nos. 1–2, 1983.

The first major change that the new government managed in 1933 was to build a reliable political base of support in parliament. While the Social Democrats wanted to adopt a more aggressive role for the government in the economy, they had set their classical Marxism to one side and were attempting to develop an alternative economic policy that stimulated economic growth through expansive fiscal policies. Ernst Wigforss deserved much of the credit for these policies which later would be identified with the liberal English economist John Maynard Keynes. In order to adopt such a program as well as emergency measures to meet the rising unemployment, the Social Democrats needed allies in the parliament. Per Albin Hansson took the lead in building bridges into the non-socialist majority.

Coalitions within the parliament were hardly a new phenomenon. The parliament had witnessed a series of floating coalitions during the twenties which had been responsible for the frequent changes in government. Politicians who represented small political parties, or factions within parties, thus had the opportunity to play important roles in the political life of the country because they were able to tip the political balance in the parliament. Ekman, who led a small Liberal Party, was something of a master at this game. Hansson and many others felt that the inability to have a stable governmental system was a threat to democracy as a whole. He was acutely aware of the collapse of German democracy and the coming to power of Adolf Hitler in January 1933. Hansson sought at the same time both to build a solid political base for his government and to demonstrate the efficacy of democratic governments. Similar efforts were being made in Denmark and Norway.

In 1932–1933 Swedish political parties were not finely organized, hierarchical, disciplined institutions. Individual members of parliament maintained considerable freedom from party whips, and the leadership of the three major non-socialist parties had lost much of its influence vis-à-vis its own members in parliament. Given the general strength of the Social Democrats in the new parliament, Hansson had an excellent opportunity to build a parliamentary coalition. Making an agreement with two leaders of the Farmers' Party, Axel Pehrsson i Bramstorp and K. G. Westman, Hansson was able to establish a solid working majority in parliament. The agreement depended upon the willingness of the Social Democrats to support the Farmers' Party's program to aid agricultural production and of the willingness of the Farmers to accept the Social Democratic economic program. Labeled at the time as the "barn-

yard coalition" and seen later as the historic mo~~
established a stable parliamentary system, the coalitio~~
tenuous, and the Farmers' Party refused to join the go~~
Social Democrats maintained their minority government u~~
ally it resigned when the three non-socialist parties voted agai~~
their proposals in 1936.

Contemporary debate as well as historical interpretations have~~
been able to create a consensus on the amount of credit the governmen~~
can rightfully claim for the turnaround in the Swedish economy during
1934–1936.[6] The Social Democrats believed that it was their new economic program that was most effective, especially a new budgetary
technique which allowed the government to spend more money in the
short term (one to three years) than it collected in taxes as long as a long-
term budget was balanced. By unbalancing the budget, the government
could develop a number of expansionist programs including public
works and increased aid to the unemployed without increasing taxation
of individuals or companies. Many economists maintain that the effect of
such measures were dependent on the role the international
marketplace played in the Swedish recovery. In particular, the decision
by the Ekman government to go off the gold standard in 1931 and
Germany's own economic recovery after 1933 provided opportunities
for Swedish industry to sell its products abroad and lead Swedish economic expansion at home. Without these fortuitous developments, the
Social Democrats would not have been as effective as they were. In
addition, there were some important political ramifications of the initial
successes of the Hansson government.

By building a much more stable parliamentary coalition than had
existed in the twenties, Hansson's activities encouraged internal consol-
idation within all the political parties. In the years 1934–1936, a dramatic reorganization of the party structure occurred. In 1934, the Conservatives unified themselves and prepared for a new generation of
leaders headed by Gösta Bagge. In 1935, the Liberal factions reunited
in a single party. Pehrsson/Bramstorp and Westman extended their
authority in the Farmers' Party. Individual members of parliament
slowly began to lose their importance. If the leadership of the Social
Democrats and the Farmers, for example, agreed on a particular bill in

---

6. See Arthur Montgomery, *How Sweden Overcame the Depression* (Stockholm, 1938); Leif Lewin, *Planhushållnings Debatten* (Stockholm, 1967).

›re the case, then the debate and
ic show and foregone conclusion.
ıl leaders as the political system

derwent a slow metamorphosis.
t decreased, the authority of the
ınd the power of the various cabi-
own areas of competence. There
specialization among the politi-
ing Social Democrats. Hansson
...tyle of operating within the gov-
ernment. He gave great leeway and authority to individual members of
the cabinet, providing them with his support when necessary. A mod-
ernization within the Swedish bureaucracy also moved in the same
direction. In the Foreign Office, for example, Rickard Sandler was left
quite free to develop a foreign policy that bore his own personal stamp.
His main advisers were the permanent staff of the Foreign Office. They
in turn had ceased to be a kind of social elite and play area for the Swedish aristocracy. While the aristocracy continued to dominate the ranks of
the foreign service, the quality of work improved, and Sweden found
itself with a competent set of foreign service officers when the crisis of
the late thirties broke over Europe. The parliament's influence in foreign policy was negligible.

Hansson still had to face the problem of the reliability of his parliamentary partners. In a number of areas — defense, social welfare,
industrial policy, for example — little agreement or cooperation existed.
As the likelihood of war increased in the middle thirties as a direct result
of Hitler's policies, the defense issue became the most troublesome.
Not only did the Social Democrats have a strong pacifist tradition within
their ranks, but defense was the one issue where the non-socialist parties would most likely unite, thereby producing a governmental crisis.
Hansson tried to steer a middle ground between the extreme elements
in his own party and the demands of the non-socialists. In the spring of
1936 the issue had to be decided. Hansson tied large-scale concessions
from the Social Democrats on defense spending to a proposal to increase
significantly the general pension program. He was defeated and
resigned. A caretaker government took over for the three months prior
to the election of the lower house in September 1936.

As an election strategy, Hansson's maneuver was close to brilliant.

He could come forward as a full supporter of Swedish rearmament and at the same time as the protector of the welfare of the little people. The election campaign was hotly contested. The turnout of voters was higher than in 1932. The big winner was the Social Democrats, who gained twelve seats, while the losers were the Conservatives, who lost twenty. The Farmers won ten new seats. The policy of cooperation had appeared to triumph, and Hansson was able to build a new Social Democrat-Farmer coalition government with an operating majority in the parliament. Sweden had a majority government for the first time since 1920.

The tendencies already noted toward the centralization of power continued as a result of the creation of the new government. Decisions now became more an issue of negotiations between the governing parties and within the committees of the parliament. Neither the leaders of the Farmers' Party nor Per Albin wanted to isolate themselves; a spirit of cooperation evolved within the committee structure. Yet major new directions in domestic policy did not occur immediately.

Childs and others liked to refer to Sweden's New Deal. Such comparisons were more an attempt to justify Roosevelt's administration than an attempt to understand Swedish experiences. The American New Deal was far more radical in the context of American experience and far less carefully developed than Sweden's own programs. Ideologically, the Swedish Social Democrats were to the left of FDR but in the sense of governance, Hansson was far more judicious. Considerable social reform occurred, but the most radical ideas either became the focus of further study (and postponed until after 1945) or were ignored, such as the committee on nationalization of Swedish industry.

The most dramatic new direction of social policy came in the area of support for families. As a result of widespread concern for Sweden's nativity rate, the parliament adopted programs to improve the quality of life for families and provide free prenatal, hospitalization, and postnatal care for mothers. A government allowance was created to pay mothers to help meet the cost of raising children. Most of these programs had the support of not only the governing parties but the other non-socialist parties as well. There were also improvements in old age and disability benefits, broadened price supports for agriculture, and extension of the eight-hour workday to a variety of groups heretofore ignored. Perhaps the most important new development occurred in labor relations and outside the parliament's purview.

Both organized labor and organized entrepreneurs feared that the growing power of government might lead to new political interventions in the labor market. The parliament did repeal the Åkarp Law, which had prevented unions from utilizing secondary boycotts and was seen as the symbol of traditional governmental hostility to the rights of working-men. But there existed no guarantee that at some later time a government less friendly to labor would restore it or something like it. Union leaders and the leading figures in Swedish industry preferred to negotiate directly without the threat of government intervention. These same officials also had observed the growing tendency in Swedish politics toward centralization and the rising authority of political and bureaucratic elites. They wanted to accomplish similar positions of authority within their own institutions.[7]

Upon this background, labor and business leaders met in the Stockholm suburb of Saltsjöbaden in 1938 and signed the first Basic Agreement. This document established the parameters for labor negotiation in Sweden. It identified acceptable and unacceptable methods of conflict between the two labor market partners, legitimized the authority and power of the unions and the employers' federation, and established a method of arbitration. The key to the agreement was that it insured that labor market relations would be controlled by two great organized blocs, the unions and the employers' federation, and negotiations would occur directly between the leaders of the two groups. At one time, the authority of the labor market leadership dramatically increased, and the government was removed from the labor market field in a general sense. What had heretofore been an area of considerable conflict in Swedish history quickly became a symbol of cooperation and consensus. It would be difficult to exaggerate the importance of this agreement for postwar Swedish development.

If Sweden's political experiences were less dramatic than those of the American New Deal, in the area of cultural development the thirties were a period of considerable awkwardness for Sweden. Sweden had been part of the German cultural sphere since the mid-nineteenth century. The German language, German technology and education, German music and art — all exercised greater influence on Sweden than did the culture of any other foreign country. Especially among the well-educated and upper classes of Sweden, Germany represented the finest

7. See Sven Anders Söderpalm, *Direktörsklubben* (Stockholm, 1976); Ragnar Casparsson, *LO under fem årtionden* (Stockholm, 1948).

traditions of Western culture. What German culture represented in a broad and simplified sense was a combination of order, achievement, symmetrical forms, respect for the past, and Christian (Lutheran) tradition. It stood in contrast to either Western culture or the Bolshevik menace. Bolshevism was not only the latest version of the traditional Russian threat to Sweden, but it was godless, dictatorial, totalitarian, and lacking in humanism. England and especially France in a cultural sense stood for experimentation, democracy, and chaos. While the influence of Western culture spread in the thirties, not the least by the introduction of popular talking films, German values remained preeminent. When Hitler took power, traditionalist Swedes faced a problem.

When Adolf Hitler assumed the chancellorship on January 30, 1933, it was not clear either inside Germany or to knowledgeable international observers exactly what would be the ramifications of his coming to power. After all, Hitler's success depended to a considerable extent on the support he had received from traditional, influential conservatives in Germany. Many believed that the conservative coalition that Hitler headed would reaffirm the values for which German culture stood and reestablish proper order. The rapidity of the Hitler revolution — the creation of a one-party state, the introduction of anti-Semitic laws, and the establishment of concentration camps — left few doubts in Sweden that events in Germany had taken a radical turn.

As the true nature of the Hitler regime became known, reactions in Sweden varied. The most common response was undoubtedly negative. Whatever sympathy Germany had earned because of the popular belief that she had been unfairly treated at the end of the Great War dissipated when faced with the militancy of the new regime. Liberals such as newspaper editor Torgny Segerstedt and Social Democrats perceived early that Hitler not only had destroyed democracy in Germany but threatened it everywhere. Segerstedt's newspaper, *Göteborgs Handelstidning*, became the most outspoken critic of Hitler and frequently embarrassed the government. At the other political extreme, there was a small group of people attracted to National Socialism. They came primarily from traditional elements of Swedish society — some Conservatives, some Farmers, and a handful of Liberals and socialists.

The Swedish national socialists were never of any consequence to Sweden's domestic or international policy.[8]

The group whose position had become most awkward because of events in Germany was the upper class, educated elites who suddenly had to confront a Germany different from their preferences. The King, for example, a well-established Germanophile, felt that he must protest to President Hindenburg about the ill effects that Hitler's anti-Semitism was having on Germany's reputation abroad. He visited Hindenburg in May 1933 to voice his feelings.[9] Other important traditionalists, including Archbishop Erling Eidem and a leading literary critic and professor of literature, Fredrik Böök, made similar pilgrimages. Needless to say, Hitler was not amused by such criticism. These individuals learned — perhaps Sweden's famous explorer, Sven Hedin, clearest of all — that Hitler's anti-Semitism was a fundamental part of his political beliefs.[10] Most shared either a traditional Christian hostility to Judaism and/or accepted contemporary race theory which was a guise for anti-Semitism; yet Hitler's policies went beyond what they could support, even in the beginning. For most of the thirties, they tried to sustain their belief in the supremacy of things German without succumbing to the obvious crassness of the regime. After all, Germany overcame the Depression, demonstrated renewed vitality, removed the shackles of Versailles, and reestablished herself as the preeminent European state. It was a balancing act that became all the more difficult as the thirties progressed.

The advent of Hitler created a new set of problems for Swedish foreign policy. With the formation of the League of Nations at the end of the Great War, Sweden decided to give up formally its traditional neutrality and join the League. The decision underscored the perception in Sweden that as a small state Sweden could gain much from organized international institutions and also that Sweden should play an active role in international affairs. Sweden contributed continuously to the work of the League and allowed it to arbitrate the border dispute between

8. See Ulf Lindström, *Fascism in Scandinavia, 1920–1940* (Stockholm, 1985); and E. Wärenstam, *Fascismen och nazismen i Sverige, 1920–1940* (Uppsala, 1970).

9. Sweden, Riksarkivet, Gustaf V Privata Samling, v. 80, Wirsén Uppteckning, April 29, 1933. See Documents Collection.

10. Sweden, Uppsala länsarkivet, Erling Eidems arkiv, Sven Hedin to Erling Eidem, April 2, 1943. See Documents Collection. Archbishop Eidem visited Hitler in May 1934.

Sweden and Finland on the issue of the Åland Islands.[11] The League decided against Sweden and part of Sweden's willingness to abide by the decision was based in the desire to strengthen the authority of the League and the notion of binding arbitration or adjudication in disputes between states. Despite the series of Swedish regimes during the twenties and early thirties, Swedish foreign policy remained consistently supportive of collective security through the League. As for Sweden's relations with its Nordic neighbors, the foreign ministers of Finland, Denmark, Norway, and Sweden met for the first time in ten years in January 1932. Increased Nordic cooperation became one of the main trends in Rickard Sandler's foreign policy in the ensuing years.

Swedes did not view the rearmament of Germany under Hitler in a positive light but found themselves in an awkward position. During the twenties, Sweden had been used by German companies and the German government to avoid some of the military limitations of the Versailles treaty. The German Krupp concern had established a very close working relationship with Sweden's largest arms manufacturer, Bofors, including considerable ownership in it, and German capital also controlled AB Flygindustri in Malmö. The Swedish economy obviously benefited from German arms expenditures. Nonetheless, in 1934 a series of parliamentary decisions forced changes in the relations between German and Swedish arms producers and ended their close cooperation.

Sweden tried to support the League in its life struggles over Manchuria and Ethiopia. Sweden wanted to sustain collective security in the face of increasing threats from aggressive, fascist regimes. Hitler had reportedly said in 1934 that eventually Sweden should become part of Greater Germany.[12] In some future war, the German chancellor saw no place for neutrals. In 1935, Sweden accepted the decision of the League to apply sanctions to Italy as a result of Italy's invasion of Ethiopia. However, the perfidious behavior of Britain and France in the Ethiopian crisis undermined much of the hope in Sweden that the League could provide adequate security for Sweden and maintain a stable international order. The outbreak of the Spanish Civil War in 1936 quickly led to a circumstance where the war took on an international significance. Italy and Germany aided the rebels, while the Soviet

---

11. See Tingsten, and Lönnroth, op. cit.
12. Norman Rich, *Hitler's War Aims* (New York, 1973) pp. 123–135.

Union and volunteers from the Western democracies supported the Spanish government. Approximately six hundred Swedes joined the international brigade; nearly two hundred were killed. The government decided to follow the lead of Britain and France and joined the Anti-intervention League in September 1936. As the likelihood of war grew and the League became moribund, the choices for Sweden were not many.

Sweden had a long historical tradition of non-participation in European conflict. The last war in which Sweden partook ended in 1815. The success of Swedish neutrality during the Great War reinforced Swedish reservations about any great power. The behavior of the great powers in the interwar period provided no reason to reexamine the near-universally held opinion in Sweden that small powers in alliance with great powers are often ignored or sacrificed in the larger designs of the great powers. Plenty of recent examples existed to reaffirm this view. Swedes held an intuitive distrust of all great powers. Therefore, the thought of some form of alliance with any great power, either during the latter half of the thirties or during the war, was never seriously considered. Swedish instinct, as with the other European small states (Switzerland, Holland, Belgium, Denmark, Norway, and Finland), was to look toward neutrality in case of a great power war. By 1937, Sweden announced that it would no longer be bound by those clauses of the League's constitution which forbade neutrality. The other small states took the same position. Could Sweden do anything else to avoid a coming conflict?

Geographically, Sweden has had an advantageous position. Situated on the extreme northern portion of the European continent, Sweden did not provide a likely battlefield for European great powers. Her security has depended to a large extent on the balance of great power interests in the Baltic, Three great powers — Britain, Germany, and Russia (U.S.S.R.) — had primary concerns in the area. Scandinavia protects the approaches to Leningrad. Britain used the Baltic to project its military authority and to secure vital trade routes, both with Sweden and Russia. During the Great War, no great power had strategic designs on Sweden, and Swedish neutrality guaranteed an open trading policy that each of the great powers appreciated. Nonetheless, these historical experiences were no guarantee for the next conflict. The growth of German power and the decline of British authority in the Baltic potentially created a new situation. The purges of the Soviet military leadership in

1937–1938 appeared to foreign observers to weaken seriously the ability of the Soviet Union to provide a balance to growing German strength. The only possible thing that Sweden could do to reinforce its desire to remain outside a future conflict would be to try to increase cooperation between all the Nordic states having the same perception and thereby remove the entire region from conflict.

Nordic cooperation became the pressing issue in Swedish foreign policy between 1937 and the outbreak of the Winter War in late November 1939. In one sense, cooperation between the Nordic states was like motherhood — everyone favored it, yet at another level, enormous problems existed which could not be easily overcome. Each of the Nordic countries had its own special security problems. Denmark, for example, shared a common and disputed border with Germany. Denmark held no illusions that the other Nordic countries would come to its defense if Germany attacked Denmark. Therefore, in 1937 Denmark cut its defense expenditures and began the process that would lead during the war to the "policy of accommodation." Finland also shared a border with a great power. The Finnish-Russian border was within easy artillery range of the Soviet Union's second largest city, Leningrad. Finnish-Soviet relations had been troubled throughout the twenties and thirties. Finland had the largest and most significant fascist movement of any of the Scandinavian states. The Finnish and German militaries had close contact and relationships. Swedish Foreign Office officials appreciated that the Soviet Union was suspicious of the possibility of Finland serving as a staging ground for an attack on the Soviet Union. The challenge for Sweden, then, was to strengthen its relationship with Finland, thereby guaranteeing both the Soviet Union and Germany that the Finns would remain neutral. Norway had other problems: its coastline served as the winter sea lanes to the Soviet Union and for Swedish iron ore to Germany. The fjords were perfect hiding places for German submarines and heavy cruisers. Whoever controlled Norway would have significant advantages in the battle over the North Atlantic. Norway opted to try to maintain an impartial neutrality without being involved in the problems of the other Nordic states. Norway supported Scandinavian cooperation but did not play an active part in the efforts to solidify Nordic relations.[13]

Within the context of Nordic cooperation, Sweden's relationship with

---

13. Henrik S. Nissen, ed., *Scandinavia during the Second World War* (Minneapolis, 1983), pp. 48–50; and Johannes Andenæs, O. Riste, and M. Skodvin, *Norway and the Second World War* (Oslo, 1966).

Finland became the key question. Serious divisions existed in Sweden about how far Sweden should go with regard to Finland. There were some politicians fearful of the Soviet Union, primarily within the Conservative Party, who argued that Sweden and Finland should form a defensive military alliance. At the other extreme, other politicians, including members of all the political parties but concentrated in the Liberal, Farmers', and Social Democratic Parties, wanted to maintain Sweden's non-belligerency if at all possible. They feared that a defense alliance with Finland might draw Sweden into a war unnecessarily, and many of them were suspicious of the intent of Finnish policy-makers. Ernst Wigforss, minister of finance in the coalition government, became the most important person to hold these views, but his influence on this question did not become influential until 1939. The majority within the government found themselves somewhere in between these two extreme positions. Sweden's Finnish policy evolved during the two years prior to the war but never took complete form. The man who initially controlled the policy was the foreign minister, Rickard Sandler.

Given Hansson's propensity to permit individual ministers great freedom, it was hardly surprising that Sandler exercised great influence over the shape of Swedish foreign policy. Rickard Sandler was quite a unique figure in modern Swedish history and a person who has received much criticism from postwar historians. Not only have his Finnish policies been described as foolish, risky, dangerous, and adventuresome, but he has been labeled as haughty, arrogant, reserved, ideological, and gauche.[14] In addition, he has the remarkable distinction to have served as the prime minister of a minority Social Democratic government for only one year — 1925-1926. No historian has studied Sandler carefully. He actually played an important role in the development of Sweden from the middle of the second decade of the twentieth century well into the decade of the sixties. His constant criticism of government foreign policy after November 1939 as well as his own policies in 1939 made him an attractive target for postwar scholars anxious to defend the govern-

---

14. W. M. Carlgren, *Swedish Foreign Policy During the Second World War* (London, 1977), p. 25. The Swedish version of this work, *Svensk utrikespolitik 1939–1945* (Stockholm, 1973) is the standard study of Swedish foreign policy during the war. Carlgren was head of the Archives of the Swedish Foreign Office. See also, Alf W. Johansson, *Per Albin och Kriget* (Stockholm, 1984), pp. 40, 50, 79; and Gunnar Hägglöf, *Det kringrända Sverige* (Stockholm, 1983), pp. 151–154.

ment's policies. Skiöld once remarked that he differed in temperament from his socialist colleagues, especially Per Albin Hansson.[15] Sandler tended to identify problems and try to solve them; Hansson was often willing to wait for a problem to disappear or to ripen. In the dark days of the late thirties, Sandler was called an activist, while Per Albin was said to be patient.

Sandler wanted to ensure that Sweden remained a non-belligerent. The greatest danger to Swedish neutrality lay in Finland. It was too tempting a target both for the Soviet Union and for Germany. This analysis was also shared by the permanent staff of the Foreign Office, including the Secretary General of the Foreign Office, Erik Boheman. Sandler believed in 1938–1939 that Sweden should seek to find ways to guarantee Germany and Russia that Finland would not act against either's interest. The Finns themselves were anxious to make such assurances. Discussions went back and forth during 1938 as the drama of Czechoslovakia, a small state who had tied itself to the Great Powers and paid the price, unfolded.

By the spring of 1939, negotiations between Finland and Sweden had become more confined: the remilitarization of Åland. A joint occupation of the islands was agreed upon, and the two states sought the acceptance of the other signatories of the Åland agreements. The Soviet Union refused. To the shock of the refusal of the international community to allow for a joint occupation came in the summer of 1939 news of the Nazi-Soviet pact of August 23 and the outbreak of World War II in the first week of September. The exact nature of the German-Russian agreement was unclear, but Sandler and others feared for Finland's independence and the subsequent threat to Sweden. What was abundantly clear to all was that there no longer existed a great power balance in Northern Europe. Russia and Germany were allies, and the Western powers did virtually nothing to help Poland. Sweden found itself isolated and threatened.

A deep division developed within the Social Democratic-Farmers coalition. The Farmers' Party, particularly K. G. Westman, wanted Hansson to form a broad coalition government. He also was suspicious of Sandler's policies and those who argued for either a joint Swedish-Finnish occupation of the islands or unilateral action.[16] More impor-

---

15. K. G. Westman, *Politiska anteckningar september 1939–mars 1943* (Stockholm, 1981), p. 36.
16. Ibid., pp. 56 ff.

tantly, Ernst Wigforss, second in power and influence in the government and the Social Democratic Party, also exhibited a deep distrust of
his party colleague, Sandler. Sandler and Per Edvin Sköld argued that
something must be done to demonstrate to the Soviet Union that
Sweden would not sit idly by and watch Finland once again become part
of Russia. Their position, however, was quite tenuous. Both understood
that a military alliance was out of the question, and that there was a
growing feeling within the government that doing neither was better
than doing something that might turn out to be wrong. The crisis
focused upon two issues: military occupation of Åland and mining of the
Gulf of Bothnia. Intensive discussions between Sweden and Finland
continued throughout October and November. Wigforss threatened to
resign, knowing that he would bring the whole governnment down with
him. Hansson, who had sided with Sandler until September, slid cautiously into Wigforss's camp. Hansson wrote the Finnish prime minister, who was also a Social Democrat, that Sweden would not partake in
any unilateral or joint occupation of Åland. He said, in a rather unusual
personal letter, that Sweden was too peaceloving and not energetic
enough to get involved with such activities. Now Sandler and Sköld
offered to resign. Wigforss eventually won out, and Hansson became
convinced that with the Russian attack on Finland on November 30,
Sweden needed a coalition government.

On December 13, the composition of the new four-party government
— Social Democrats, Farmers, Liberals, and Conservatives — was
announced. The Social Democrats held four of the thirteen minister
posts. The most important positions were: Per Albin Hansson, prime
minister; Ernst Wigforss, minister of finance; Per Edvin Sköld, minister
of defense; K. G. Westman, minister of justice; Gösta Bagge, minister of
education; Gustav Möller, minister of social welfare; and Christian Günther, minister for foreign affairs (plus a number of other less critical min-
istries). The purpose of the government was to present a unified front to
the rest of the world, to attempt to protect Swedish neutrality, and to
avoid internal conflict. Most of all, the establishment of the coalition
government represented an agreement to opt for a foreign policy that
took the least possible risks. Per Edvin Sköld noted on December 5: "a
shift in our policy to a more moderate, and a more modest, attitude than
previously."[17]

---

17. Carlgren, op. cit., p. 27.

Sandler's removal from the foreign ministry was the symbol of this change. Günther was a career diplomat who had most recently been serving as Swedish ambassador in Oslo. He was one of the more professional diplomats that had begun to rise within the foreign service. His interest in helping Sweden's Scandinavian neighbors was genuine and did not differ in principle from Sandler as much as was suggested by government critics during the war or many scholars after the war. The real difference between the two men was temperament and sensitivity toward Germany. Günther, for example, advocated in April 1940 Swedish participation in the defense of the Åland Islands. Throughout the war, he looked constantly toward Finland and attempted to insinuate Sweden as mediator between the Soviet Union and Finland in order to bring peace to the Baltic. He also showed great sympathy toward Denmark and Norway in the last year of the war.

Public opinion in Sweden over the formation of the new government and Sandler's replacement was mixed. There was broad public sympathy for Finland as it fought alone against the Russian aggressor. A considerable portion of the populace wanted Sweden to intervene directly in the conflict on Finland's side. The slogan, "Finland's cause is ours," reflected the deep concern in Sweden for Finland, but one should be careful not to overestimate the nature of the support. The government steered a careful policy through the 3½ month-long conflict.

Hansson stated in December: "We will try to help Finland as far as we can without directly involving ourselves."[18] Sweden avoided making a formal declaration of neutrality and made available to Finland Swedish military supplies including rifles, artillery, and airplanes. Sweden also provided credits and allowed over 8,000 volunteers to join the Finnish army. The heart of the government's policy was to end the war as quickly as possible and to try to avoid further great power complications. Both belligerents eventually showed a willingness to negotiate, and Sweden served as mediator. The peace that ended the war in March 1940 was harsh. Finland lost much of its Eastern province of Karelia which lay so close to Leningrad. It also lost the economic resources of the Northern region of Petsamo. Many in Finland were critical of the role Sweden had played. The Hansson government had showed itself unwilling to go any further with regard to increasing the number of volunteers, and, it was claimed, had applied pressure on Finland to resign

---

18. Johansson, op. cit., p. 103.

itself to defeat. These criticisms have little basis. Finland simply found itself in an untenable situation, a small state at war with a great power, and had to extricate itself as graciously as possible. Sweden provided an opportunity to do so. At the same time that the peace negotiations evolved, Germany, France, and Britain prepared to enter Scandinavia militarily and threatened to draw Sweden into the war.

Hitler adopted a passive attitude toward the Finno-Russian war. Hitler was, however, vitally interested in Scandinavia and warned Sweden to avoid taking an anti-German position. German pressure on Sweden not to involve itself directly in the war and to show more sympathy for Nazi Germany in general remained at high levels. The Swedish minister in Berlin, Arvid Richert, a friend of Günther, warned Stockholm to be more sensitive about German feelings. A major point of distraction, Richert suggested, was the behavior of the Swedish press which Germany complained was too hostile to the Hitler regime.

The behavior of the Swedish press during the war caused much concern both within the Swedish government and within Swedish-German relations. Contemporary critics of the Hansson government's foreign policy often used its press policy as the best example of how the Swedish government had lost its own sense of democratic values and had bent over backwards to please Germany. Press policy is worth a more careful analysis.

Sweden's constitution guaranteed freedom of the press. Such freedom was seen as the most fundamental of Sweden's democracy. By the 1930s, there existed a large number of daily newspapers as well as weekly and monthly journals whose political views spanned the entire spectrum of Swedish politics. A few newspapers, however, had national circulation while others enjoyed only a local impact. Ownership also varied: many papers were owned by the political parties, others by individuals, while still others were controlled by foreign governments. One family, the Bonniers, who owned one of the national newspapers, *Dagens Nyheter*, attracted special attention.

The Bonniers were seen by anti-Semites in Germany and Sweden alike as the example of "Jewish control" of the Swedish media. The Bonniers not only owned *Dagens Nyheter* but also one of the largest publishing companies which produced weekly and monthly journals as well as books. What is interesting is that the "Jewishness" of the Bonniers is not at all clear. The family certainly originally came from Jewish stock, but by the time of the thirties, the family had had over a

100-year opportunity to assimilate into Swedish society. Bonniers married non-Jews and Jews alike; many of the family converted to Lutheranism; and the family played no role in the Jewish temple in Stockholm. Further, the editorial staff of *Dagens Nyheter* operated quite independently from the family and in no way provided an outstanding example of anti-Hitler propaganda or hostility to the government during the war.

Criticism of Hitler came most consistently from Segerstedt in Göteborg. During the war, Ture Nerman, a Social Democrat, published *Trots Allt!*, which also adopted an extreme anti-Hitler, pro-Allied position. Quite early in the thirties, the German government complained about the attitudes of the Swedish press toward Hitler and Germany. This complaining became a constant line from the German ministers in Stockholm and from the German Foreign Office to Swedish diplomats in Berlin. Initially the Swedish government tended to ignore German remarks; however, as the stability of the international system weakened, the attitude of the cabinet changed.

As early as 1938, Sandler and Hansson warned Swedish newspaper editors that the freedom of the press was not absolute. Any story or issue which endangered the ability of Sweden to maintain its neutrality or security was liable for confiscation. The authority granted the government to protect Swedish security thus limited freedom of the press. The government, however, was reluctant to use its power, and instead relied upon informal pressure and the "good sense" of Swedish editors. Most Swedish journalists responded patriotically; the few that didn't caused great distress in the government. Segerstedt in particular was viewed by some, including Gustaf V, as capable of dragging Sweden into the war against Germany on the strength of his anti-Hitler campaign.

Torgny Segerstedt no doubt was the most prominent anti-Hitler publicist in Sweden. Segerstedt was praised and damned during the war and afterwards. As recently as the mid-seventies, Tage Erlander, prime minister from 1946 to 1968 and prominent Social Democrat politician during the war, felt it necessary in his memoirs to criticize Segerstedt and argue that Segerstedt had little support among the Swedish people.[19] Others claim that Segerstedt represented the soul of Sweden during the war. The King pleaded directly with Segerstedt in 1940 to cease and desist from his attacks on Hitler. K. G. Westman, minister of justice during the period and therefore responsible for any action against the

---

19. Tage Erlander, *1940–1949* (Stockholm, 1973), p.20.

independence of the press, recorded in his diary a macabre explanation of Segerstedt's un-Swedish behavior: "His Jewish mistress has removed his soul and replaced it with a Jewish one."[20] Westman advocated an active policy against the overly critical Swedish press, and in November 1939 got the government's permission to confiscate an issue of *Trots Allt!*

Swedish press policy became an interesting barometer of Swedish foreign policy. Although no formal censorship was ever established, a Board of Information was created in 1940 to facilitate control over the type of information Swedish press received and to check what they printed. On occasion, certain issues were confiscated by the Board. In reality, an informal censorship operated quite effectively. Editors of the larger papers met regularly to receive information and discuss issues with officials of the government. The government was, therefore, able to explain its policy and appeal for self-censorship. The editors rarely failed to comply. The issues confiscated therefore were relatively few. Individual journalists, however, might have found their freedom quite restricted.[21]

The major Swedish newspapers had correspondents stationed in Berlin. These journalists became after 1941 one of the few independent sources of news from German-controlled areas. They also had opportunities to travel to German-occupied areas both in the East and the West. No scholar has examined systematically what these correspondents sent to Stockholm in contrast to what was eventually printed; nor has anyone examined the pressure that they faced in Sweden and their own self-censorship. More than one of them published books about their Berlin years that were frank in their appraisals. Indeed, a careful reading of the Swedish press provides a remarkable range of contemporary information about developments in German-controlled Europe. It was not, however, always displayed in prominent places in the press and probably was not noticed to the degree scholars after the war would judge it. British and American newspapers received considerable information from these reports, as did the intelligence agencies of the same governments. Unfortunately, it is very difficult to judge the relationship between what appeared in the press and public opinion and public

---

20. Westman, op. cit., p. 123.

21. See Arvid Fredborg, *Bakom Stålvallen* (Stockholm, 1943), and *Destination: Berlin* (Stockholm, 1985). Also, Jarl Torbacke, *Dagens Nyheter och demokratins kris 1937–1946* (Stockholm, 1972).

knowledge. Only rarely did it become clear where public opinion in Sweden lay. That the public felt sympathy for Finland during the Winter War and therefore had mixed feelings toward the government's policies was apparent. There was, however, virtually no awareness of a growing threat to drag Sweden into the war.

British and French help to their ally, Poland, was negligible. The Winter War offered new opportunities for action when Finland appealed for their help. For the Western powers, the Finnish appeal had a number of attractions, at least if it was met with military action through Norway and Sweden. The only transit route for a potential Western action in Finland was through the Norwegian port of Narvik, across Northern Sweden to Finland. This very route also happened to be the route of most of Sweden's iron ore exports to Germany. A Western action would have the multiple positive effect of securing control of the Norwegian leads, thereby denying the area to German ships, and gaining control of the Swedish iron ore fields. Such an action was also likely to drag Sweden into the war, a prospect that did not disturb London or Paris.[22] The Swedish government had a different perspective. Information about the planned Western intervention reached Stockholm in January. Peace negotiations between Finland and the Soviet Union were reaching a climax. Sweden rejected the Western power request for transit; so, too, did Norway. The peace negotiations were concluded before any military action could be undertaken. A recent study of Swedish foreign policy during the war concludes: "The air of self-satisfaction that had characterized Swedish policy since the outbreak of the war in September had changed to a situation where the government not only was faced with the question whether Sweden should involve itself in the Finnish-Russian conflict but also whether Sweden was threatened to be drawn into a great power war, something which had seemed very distant in September 1939."[23]

The growing sense of helplessness increased as intelligence reports reached Stockholm of a German military buildup in Northern German ports and staging areas. At the same time, relations between Britain and Norway continued to deteriorate as Britain unilaterally tried to exercise increasing control over Norwegian territorial waters. Hitler warned

---

22. Carlgren, op. cit., pp. 32–33, 55–59. See also Per G. Andreen, *De Mörka Åren* (Stockholm, 1971), and Munch-Petersen, op. cit.

23. Johansson, op. cit., pp. 137–138.

Sven Hedin that "one thing you in Sweden must be quite clear about and that is that the moment British and French troops set foot on Swedish soil, Germany will instantly intervene."[24] The great power race for control of Scandinavia was on: Germany struck first.

On April 9, Germany simultaneously attacked Denmark and Norway. Denmark capitulated almost at once and reorganized itself as a "model protectorate." Norway resisted, and British units arrived shortly thereafter — Britain had intended to invade Norway itself but now could be cast as its liberators. The war in Norway, in which Germany had the upper hand from the beginning, dragged on for nearly three months. The Swedish government found itself in an almost untenable situation. At no time did Sweden come closer to entering the war than in the last days of the struggle in Norway.

The Swedish government had received reliable intelligence before April 9 of Germany's plans and the fact that Sweden would be left untouched. Sweden passed the information along to the Norwegians but decided against any other decisive policy steps. It was decided, for example, not to mobilize the Swedish military forces for fear of a German response. Only 50,000 of the possible 400,000 Swedish troops were in place when the attack occurred. They were neither well trained nor well equipped. Sweden would not have been a consequential opponent for the German army. The Swedish general staff, particularly the chief of staff, Olof Thornell, had no illusions about Swedish preparedness, and an air of defeatism emanated from these quarters until well into the war. As the war dragged on, new and difficult questions arose.

Germany had hoped that their surprise attack would carry Norway before the English arrived and be capable of holding it against Britain. The logistical problems facing the German army in Norway would be considerable, if not impossible, in the long run. Britain controlled the sea lanes. Inside Norway, there were few roads or rail lines; it was impossible to provide reinforcements or provisions by ground to the German division in the area of Narvik. The only way to reach them was via the Swedish rail system. As the fighting continued and grew most intensive just in the Narvik area, Germany requested permission to transit troops to the north. It was an impossible request for Sweden to meet.

A wave of sympathy and horror broke out in Sweden among the pub-

---

24. Carlgren, op. cit., p. 50.

lic when they learned of the German attack. Anti-German feeling
increased, yet few advocated actively aiding their Scandinavian brothers. A sense of helplessness and of dependence on government leadership was clear. A spirit of togetherness began to develop that had been
missing in the earlier phases of the war. Segerstedt and others continued to use harsh language to attack Hitler, but a growing majority
including many previously critical of the government rallied to Hansson
and his colleagues in this critical hour. The government was unsure
what to do.

Norwegian requests of various kinds came in steadily. Sweden
refused the kind of aid that it had offered Finland months previously.
While condemning the German action, Sweden opted to declare its
neutrality. Sweden chose to take as distant a stance as possible. Even
the Norwegian request that the King be granted temporary sanctuary in
Sweden if he had to go into exile in Britain caused considerable
discussion in the cabinet, and Hansson initially proposed that when the
Norwegian King crossed the Swedish border, he be interned. This idea
did not sit well with Gustaf V. On May 10, the war in Norway undecided, Germany attacked in the West.

Toward the end of May, British troops succeeded in driving the German army out of Narvik. 4000 German soldiers stood between the
advancing English and the Swedish border. If the British troops crossed
into Sweden, the Swedes could either defend their border, or give up
their neutrality by allying with one of the two belligerents, a hopeless
choice from Sweden's perspective. Sweden even proposed to occupy
Narvik as a neutral zone. What saved Sweden was the disaster on the
Western front for the Western powers and the determination of the
German soldiers in the Narvik area. The British withdrew their troops
in early June after Dunkirk and in anticipation of an invasion of England.
Official Norwegian resistance ceased, and the King and his government
went into exile in London. In the name of caution, Sweden refused to
grant full diplomatic status to the Norwegian government-in-exile's representative in Stockholm. The German request for transit could be
examined more directly.

On June 15, Germany made a formal request to transit replacement
troops and matériel through Sweden to Norway. Within the government, there was no consequential opposition; only in the Social Democratic parliamentary group were voices raised against acceptance.
Rickard Sandler and Östen Undén, a former foreign minister, opposed a

positive response. Hansson presented the issue as one between peace and war, not as a change in the direction of Swedish policy. On June 18, Sweden agreed to Germany's request. In principle, the agreement was to cover only replacements and be strictly enforced. In actuality, Germany operated with little restraint from Sweden. Between 1940 and 1943, ten percent of all Swedish rail facilities were utilized in this traffic. Over 650,000 soldiers were transshipped. The transit agreement was the first of a series of accommodations made to Germany.

A complete public announcement of the agreement was not made. Of course, its terms in general were publicized. The traffic could not have been kept secret in any case. Segerstedt and a few others lambasted the agreement and concluded that Sweden had lost its soul and had become a lackey of Germany. The September 1940 elections to the lower house gave an opportunity to evaluate the public's response. The campaign itself was quite muted, but to a large extent was seen as a vote of confidence for Per Albin Hansson and his policies. The results were incontrovertible. The Social Democrats received the largest percentage of votes (53.8 percent) of any single party in Swedish history. Hansson remarked, "My responsibility is heavy these days, not the least because the election is seen as a personal vote of confidence for me."[25]

As a result of the election, the Social Democrats now had an absolute majority in the parliament and could have chosen to govern alone. Hansson never seriously considered it. The continuance of the coalition guaranteed Sweden domestic tranquility. A purely Social Democratic government would have both given the non-socialists an opportunity to criticize government policy and thereby weaken Sweden's relations internationally and would have brought back into the government some of the most consistent critics of the government's foreign policies. Hansson personally remained committed to a broad coalition government. As his public image as leader of his country in wartime grew more popular, Hansson began to see himself more as the people's choice. His commitment to be a statesman grew, while his interest in the Social Democratic Party remained relatively constant. Even after the war, he preferred the continuation of the coalition government. He believed that it provided a stable base for Swedish development.

Internationally, a certain stability existed in the Baltic during the nine

---

25. Sweden, Arbetarrörelsens arkiv, Per Albin Hanssons Samling, Minnesanteckningar 1940, September 15, 1940.

months between September 1940 and June 1941. Sweden found itself within the German sphere of influence without the possibility of help from the West. Swedish policy reflected the lack of international balance to Germany's hegemony. Control of the anti-German press in Sweden was hardened. Within the government, there was widespread fear that the greatest danger of a German attack came from hostility of the Swedish press to Germany. Günther and Gösta Bagge argued during this period that a more openly friendly policy toward Germany would improve Sweden's security and allow Sweden to aid Finland. Beside the transit agreement, Sweden permitted Germany to utilize its airspace and domestic shipping lanes regularly. Sweden also refused to permit ten Norwegian ships at anchor in Göteborg to leave the country for Britain. None of these policies conformed to the particular vision of neutrality that Sweden claimed prior to the war. In the minds of the Swedes, they represented concessions to Germany to keep Sweden out of the war. The Western powers appreciated Sweden's awkward position and were cautious in their criticisms of Swedish behavior. Germany seemed to approve, too; after all, most of the Swedish concessions had come without undue or ugly pressure. The Swedes demonstrated an anxiousness in this period to please the Germans.[26]

There were, however, limits to Sweden's accommodations. Control of the press was at best inconsistent. No complete censorship as existed in the belligerent countries developed. Proposals to ban the Communist Party were discussed at length, but nothing was ever done. Trade agreements between Sweden and the Western powers allowed Sweden to maintain contact with the West. The next crisis came when the Swedes learned that Germany planned to attack its erstwhile ally, the Soviet Union.

As early as February 1941, Günther learned of Germany's intentions via Swedish banker Jacob Wallenberg. As the spring progressed, a growing anxiety existed within the government. What would be Finland's role in a German attack on Russia? What place would a democratic Sweden have in a totally dominated Germanic Europe? There was little hope that the Soviet Union could withstand what France and Britain had failed to do a year earlier. Besides, many Swedes including part of the government wanted to see the destruction of the Soviet Union.

---

26. See Andreen, op. cit., among others.

On June 22, Germany launched its attack. The same day, it requested Swedish permission to transfer an armed division from Northern Norway to Finland to aid the joint Finnish-German effort on the northern sector of the struggle. Finland had decided to attack the Soviet Union simultaneously, and in concert with Germany. Sweden failed to convince the Finns that such an enterprise was fraught with danger. The German request for transit of the Engelbrecht division led to a new domestic crisis: the so-called midsummer crisis.

For two days, the government, the members of the parliament, and the King considered Germany's request. On June 24, Sweden acceded to a one-time transfer of German troops through Northern Sweden. What Sweden had refused the Western powers in 1940, she now granted to Germany. Historical debate about how this decision was reached has been the most discussed aspect of Swedish foreign policy during the entire war. All scholars agree that the King, Günther, the Conservatives, and the Farmers all favored acceptance. A majority of the Liberals did, too. The Social Democrats were badly divided, but a majority of the parliamentary group led by Sandler, Wigforss, and Undén stood in opposition. Hansson's attitude and activities are the focal point for much of the debate.

Hansson did not want to accede to the German request, but he saw little choice. His behavior during the two days seemed more directed toward building as broad a consensus for the decision as possible and toward isolating any potential critics. He insisted that all the parliamentary parties discuss and approve the decision. He knew that the greatest difficulty lay with his own party. A solid core within the Social Democratic parliamentary group not only opposed this newest German request but questioned the wisdom of much of what the government had done after April 1940. A certain frustration existed within the group over the failure of the government, especially its Social Democratic members, to consult more frequently with the parliament. In this particular sense, the majority party had effectively been kept at arm's length from governmental decisions.

Two votes were taken in the Social Democratic party group. The first, a vote on acceptance, was overwhelmingly rejected. The second, a willingness to accept if all the other parties did, was approved by a solid majority. Since the other parties had accepted, Hansson in effect had unanimous approval from all the coalition parties. During the discussions within the Social Democratic group, Hansson argued that it was critical for Swedes to remain united and that the King had intimated that a refusal to accept would lead to his abdication. As Gustaf V had become, along with Hansson, a rallying point for Swedes during the war, such a threat posed serious problems. In actuality, it is unclear whether Gustaf made the threat; he certainly wanted approval of the German request. Nor is it clear how important Hansson's claim vis-à-vis Gustaf's position was for the actual decision. Although certain governmental ministers — Wigforss, Möller, and Sköld — opposed acceptance, none of them threatened to resign, as had been the case in earlier crises, if their views did not triumph.[27]

The midsummer crisis appears more as a crisis of self-image than of policy. Hansson did not want Sweden to think of itself as entirely subservient to Germany. On the decision itself, there was little choice this time, but Hansson assured both his party brothers and the Germans it was a one-time action. A second request the following month was rejected. One historian called the decision "a victory in defeat for the majority of the Social Democrats."[28] This view is overly optimistic. Had the war developed differently, new concessions would have been forthcoming. Indeed, it should be noted that the German request was not accompanied by hints or threats of German military or economic retaliation if Sweden said no to the transit of the Engelbrecht division. Some of the critical Social Democrats had argued that the concession should only be made when the Germans made a clear threat. Government policy for the time being was a positive accommodation whenever it appeared necessary and possible.

The midsummer decision represented no new direction for Swedish policy. Segerstedt and others, of course, criticized the decision, arguing once again that the government had sold Sweden's soul to the devil. The position of the government with the public did not waver; indeed, if anything, it seemed to grow stronger. There were no signs that any significant segment of the population wanted a dramatically different policy than that offered by the government. One must be careful, however, from drawing too many conclusions from public acquiescence. A trust in government lay deep in the political nature of Swedes. Their knowledge

---

27. The literature on the midsummer crisis is large. The most interesting debate occurred in the early 1970s when Göran B. Nilsson applied decision-making models to the crisis. Krister Wahlbäck, among others, disagreed with his interpretations. See *Historisk Tidskrift*, 1971:1, 1973:1,2, 1974:1.

28. Johansson, op. cit., p. 270.

and involvement in foreign policy were minimal. Swedes wanted to avoid the war. They obviously sympathized with the democratic powers and felt deep bitterness over the treatment of Norway and Denmark. Yet they trusted the government to manage the details of foreign policy. There is no reason to believe that public opinion supported either a more accommodating policy or a less accommodating one. After the war, Swedes would feel embarrassed and critical of the midsummer decision. It was and remains a question of self-image.

The German campaign went forward but did not totally destroy the Soviet Union. Indeed, the failure of Germany to crush its opponent led some Swedes to feel that the tide of the war had begun to turn. Günther continued to argue for greater accommodations to Germany, but Hansson resisted. His policy could best be described as watchful waiting. In December 1941, the United States entered the war. Hope for the democratic states increased.

Still, Germany presented the only immediate threat to Swedish security. Relations between the two states had deteriorated somewhat in the fall-winter 1941–1942. Sweden had refused additional requests for concessions. The Allies had raided Norwegian territorial waters, causing anxiety in Berlin. The failure of the Russian offensive led Hitler to be more openly critical of Swedish neutrality. Germany strengthened its Norwegian defenses. Sweden mobilized additional troops in February 1942. The King, worried by the growing tension, wrote Hitler personally that Sweden would defend its neutrality. The chancellor responded in assuring tones: Germany respected Swedish neutrality. Sweden cautiously moved toward a more even-handed neutrality.

The one issue that had soured Swedish relations with Britain and its Allies was the continued refusal of the Swedes to allow the Norwegian ships to leave Göteborg. In late March, Sweden permitted the ten ships to depart. Three were sunk by the Germans; three destroyed themselves rather than permit German capture; two made it to England; and two, *Lionel* and *Dicto*, returned to Göteborg. Sweden was shocked to learn that the boats had been armed during their stay in Göteborg. The Allies demanded that *Lionel* and *Dicto* be allowed to leave port at the first opportunity. Sweden refused until January 1943. The breakout failed again, but in 1943 Germany retaliated by closing the normal Swedish-Allied trading routes. Relations with the West were acceptable, but the Western powers showed growing impatience with the reluctance of Sweden to move more rapidly toward a pro-Allied position.

The international events that touched Sweden most directly during the first three quarters of 1942 were those in Norway. Norwegian resistance to the occupying forces spread, and German hostility hardened. Some Norwegian labor leaders were executed. Other resistance figures were sent to concentration camps in Germany. The Swedish press followed events in Norway closely and critically. Swedish public opinion grew ever more hostile to Germany. The Swedish Foreign Office warned Germany of the potential consequences to German-Swedish relations if the problems continued. Little effect of the Swedish warnings can be found in German policy in Norway. The culmination of deteriorating relations over Norway came in November, when Germany applied the Final Solution to Norway's Jews (see Chapter 2). The Norwegian bishops protested despite the fact that some were being held under house arrest. A storm of public opinion broke loose in Sweden led by the church and the press.

Events in Norway and the public response in Sweden were difficult for the Swedish government to handle. Official Norwegian-Swedish relations were poor in 1942. The Norwegian government-in-exile had considerable doubt about Swedish behavior in 1940–1941 and resented the cautiousness of Swedish policy on Norway.[29] Officials in the Swedish Foreign Office were sympathetic to Norway's plight but more sensitive to Germany's potential displeasure. Hansson privately criticized Norwegian labor and political leaders for their open resistance. In this case, however, the government understood that the Swedish public wanted to help. An offer was made to Germany in December 1942 to take all of Norway's remaining Jews and intern them in Sweden. Although the offer was rejected, Sweden eventually provided a safe haven for half of Norway's Jews, just as it offered refuge to other Norwegians. The progress of the war was moving Swedish policy away from Germany.

Any doubts about the eventual outcome of the war in the minds of Swedish policy-makers disappeared after November 1942. The Allied

---

29. See Olav Riste, *London Regjeringa. V. 1, 1940–1942: Prøvetid* (Oslo, 1973). The Swedish government's recognition of Norway's attitudes led to a series of white papers being published after the war. See among others, *Frågor i samband med norska regeringens vistelse utanför Norge 1940–1943* (Stockholm, 1947), and *Sveriges förhållande till Danmark och Norge under krigsåren* (Stockholm, 1945).

victories at Stalingrad and El Alamein sealed a conviction already held
that the issue was not so much whether Germany would lose the war but
under what conditions. The prospects were not encouraging. First, the
issue of Finland was troublesome. Sweden wanted Finland out of its
"continuation war" with the Soviet Union. The longer that war continued, the closer Finland and Germany drew together, the greater the
danger was that an eventual Russian victory would lead to the loss of
Finnish independence. More critically, the disappearance of a sover-
eign Finland meant that Russia would be Sweden's neighbor and occupy
"the gun pointed at Sweden's heart," the Åland Islands. A neutralized
Finland, whatever the price, was a better alternative. The Swedish Foreign Office watched events in Finland carefully and whenever possible
tried to encourage Finland to remove itself from the war. Eventually,
Sweden renewed its mediator role between Finland and Russia to end
their war in 1944.

A second problem revolved around the nature of Germany's eventual
defeat. What Sweden preferred was the reestablishment of a great
power balance in the Baltic area. The replacement of German hegemony with Soviet control was viewed as highly unattractive. The ability
and interest of the Western democracies to inject themselves into the
area was unclear. Indeed, if they did involve themselves militarily, their
actions might provoke a German response.

The fear of a possible German attack on Sweden did not disappear,
despite the real improvement of Sweden's defenses and the absence of
any military preparations in Germany. As Germany's armies met defeat,
Günther, Hansson, and others worried that Hitler might irrationally
strike out at Sweden if Sweden drew too close to the Allies. Hitler's dislike of Sweden had been confirmed from many different sources. His
interventions in Italy in 1943 and Hungary in 1944, as well as the Battle
of the Bulge in the winter 1944–1945, were seen as proof that when
Hitler decided to act, he could and would do so without much consequence for the costs. While some members of the cabinet argued for a
more activist, pro-democratic policy, Hansson and Günther resisted.
Their fear of German reprisals and a firmly-established reluctance to
take any dramatic steps led the prime minister and his foreign minister
to take the position that no concessions should be made to the Western
powers without sufficient pressure from London and Washington. Their
policy offers an interesting contrast to the earlier concessions to
Germany.

Sweden's relations with Britain and the United States had two primary components: political affinity and economics. The levels of sympathy for the Western powers might vary within the Swedish government,
but everyone hoped for an Allied victory. The real question for Swedes
was what was their responsibility to the forces of democracy in their life-
and-death struggle with fascist dictatorships? In the thirties, under
Sandler's tutelage, Sweden had supported sanctions under the guise of
collective security against those who broke the peace. The critics of wartime foreign policy wanted Sweden to continue this tradition without
taking Sweden into the war. They did not believe that Sweden needed
to make so many concessions to Germany and conversely suggested that
Sweden go a considerable distance to support the Allies and the resistance groups in Norway and Denmark. These critics were not a uniform
group; they existed within the government, within the foreign ministry,
as well as in the parliament and the press. Their strength grew as a general fear of Germany declined. Yet Hansson in particular preferred
extreme caution.

The economic relationship with the West had two components: a
short-term, wartime part and a postwar concern. The former issue was
resolved through a series of trade agreements. Each time trade agreements between Sweden and the Western powers had to be negotiated, a
relatively clear picture of their broader relationship emerged. The first
agreements in the early part of the war sought only to reaffirm the economic relationship, to maintain a modicum of trade. By 1943, however,
the Western powers took a more demanding position; they wanted to
limit and eventually cut off Sweden's trade with Germany. Led by Günther and Hansson, Sweden showed great reluctance to alter too quickly
its trade relationship with Germany.

British and American attitudes toward Sweden in the period
1942–1945 remained steady. No serious interest developed in these
countries to create a new theater of war in the north. While they would
have preferred to see Sweden militarily engage itself on the Allies' side
— Sweden's army, now over 400,000 men and well prepared, would
have forced a major German commitment — there was no doubt in
London and Washington that Sweden would not voluntarily take such
action. Therefore, the Western powers' primary interest was to eliminate or to cut severely the amount of trade between Sweden and
Germany. Much has been written about Swedish iron ore and ball-
bearing trade with Germany. Both goods were significant to German

war production, particularly the latter when the Allied bombing campaign concentrated on German production of the same item. Swedish trade with Germany grew in the years 1940–1944. It was highly profitable, and Sweden avoided the problem of offering credit to the Nazis.[30] The Allied desire to limit or stop the Swedish-German traffic had both political and economic consequences. A balance to this close Swedish-German economic relationship was Sweden's postwar economic and political concerns.

The Swedish government recognized quite early, late 1942/early 1943, that Sweden must begin preparing its postwar strategies. Issues such as Sweden's role in postwar European reconstruction, the proposed United Nations, and a strengthening of ties with the United States became the subject of study and discussion. Quite perceptibly, Swedish officials recognized the coming Pax Americana. A powerful governmental committee composed of leading businessmen, academics, and governmental officials, chaired by Erik Boheman, was appointed in February 1943 to examine Sweden's "transoceanic" relationships and to prepare a series of proposals. Many Swedes feared that an insensitive wartime Swedish policy would have serious consequences for postwar relationships. The task of Swedish foreign policy in the last years of the war, therefore, was to balance the resistance of Günther-Hansson to radical changes in Swedish-German relations with concerns to build closer ties with the West and to the Soviet Union, for which Möller and Wigforss among others spoke.

The first area where Sweden could adapt to the changed international balance of power was with regard to the special services Sweden had provided Germany in the earlier part of the war: transit, use of Swedish air space, and use of Swedish territorial waters. The transit traffic in particular was of particular embarrassment to the government; it was so visible to Swedish citizens. The Allies demanded during trade negotiations in May–June 1943 both an end to the transit traffic and strict limitations of Swedish-German trade. When the cabinet learned of the Western demands, there was an interesting psychological response — complaints that the Western powers were pressing Sweden harder and more unfairly than Germany had ever done.

This sense of outrage reflected a combination of a narrow perspective

---

30. See Martin Fritz, "A Question of Practical Policies. Economic Neutrality During the Second World War," in *Revue Internationale d'Histoire Militaire*, No. 57, 1984.

on the war and a pent-up frustration with the perceived limitations of Swedish policy. The Swedish negotiators, Gunnar Hägglöf in particular, warned Stockholm that the failure to accept the trade agreement might lead to harsher Western policies. The discussions in the cabinet revolved around the economic losses the agreement symbolized, the fear of German reaction, and the need to placate the Allies. By July, the government decided to announce the end of the transit traffic on August 1 and reject in principle the trade agreement but in practicality accept it. The agreement was signed on September 23.

In this way, the government tried to maintain the fiction that it alone had decided to end the transit agreement, thereby deflecting the expected German response. An additional mobilization occurred in late July just prior to notification of the Germans. The rejection of the trade agreement in principle also attempted to underline Sweden's independence and willingness to refuse what it judged too harsh or unfair demands of the Allies. Here, too, the possible interpretations of Germany weighed heavily. But the actual signing of the agreement also demonstrated Sweden's sacrifices to meet Allied interests. A diminution of trade with Germany hurt Sweden economically and allowed the Allies to think that they could bargain Sweden into a more pro-Allied position.

A similar round of negotiations occurred in 1944. This time Allied interests focused on the ball-bearing traffic and a desire to stop completely Swedish-German trade. The American government in particular was more frank in warning the Swedes of possible consequences of a negative response from Stockholm. A suggestion was even made that an American air raid on the main facilities of SKF, the Swedish Ballbearings Company, at Göteborg might occur "accidentally." An outpouring of rage burst forth from Stockholm over the American threat. Britain and later the United States retreated. Sweden once again refused to accept in principle but allowed the United States to negotiate directly with SKF, thereby guaranteeing that the ball-bearing traffic would cease in 1945. Sweden maintained its dignity but thought that the Allies should be satisfied.

A second area where Sweden changed its policies was with regard to its Scandinavian neighbors. The Finnish question remained uppermost in the minds of the government ministers. The many twists and turns in Finnish-Soviet relations need not be covered here; what was important from a Swedish point of view was to end the war as soon as possible and with the best result under the circumstances. Sweden took large numbers of Finnish children to Sweden in 1943–1944, as well as a few other Finnish refugees. Once the basis for a Finnish-Soviet agreement was fixed — a peace harsher than that of 1940 yet one which maintained Finnish independence — Sweden urged Finnish compliance. With the successful withdrawal of Finland from the war in late 1944, Sweden's eastern boundary was secure. Its attention could focus on its Western neighbors.

Sweden's relations with Denmark and Norway improved in the second half of 1943. In August 1943, Germany proclaimed martial law in Denmark, thereby destroying the basis for cooperation between the Danish elite and the occupying forces. The Danish resistance increased its activities, although its general effectiveness was marginal.[31] Almost immediately it was clear that the first group of Danes threatened by the end of the "model protectorate" was the Jews, approximately 8,000 people. German authorities in Denmark warned both Danish and Swedish officials of the coming application of the Final Solution to Denmark's Jews. When the attempted roundup of Jews began on October 1, the Jews went underground, aided by the spontaneous response of their fellow Danes. Sweden opened its borders to the Jews. German officials in Denmark turned their backs. The result was that nearly 95 percent of the Danish Jews found a safe haven in Sweden (see Chapter 2). The increased resistance activity meant an increase in the number of Danes that fled the country. Sweden became a general refuge for the Danish underground.

As for Norway, Sweden finally accredited the Norwegian minister in Stockholm on December 15, 1943. This act made public an increasing willingness on the part of the Swedish government to aid Norway. Norwegians in large numbers already used Sweden as a refuge. In 1944, Niels Christian Ditleff began to plan for the rescue of Norwegians held in German concentration camps. He received enthusiastic support from the Swedish Foreign Office, especially from Günther. His initiative eventually led to the Red Cross expedition in 1945, the largest successful rescue mission in Germany during the entire war (see Chapter 4).

The most awkward issue with regard to Denmark and Norway was the

31. See Jørgen Hæstrup, *Secret Alliance*, 3 volumes, (Odense, 1976–77) and *Den gang i Danmark* (Odense, 1982). Also, Ole Kristian Grimnes, "The Beginnings of the Resistance Movement," in Nissen, op. cit.

likely violence in those countries at the end of the war. What would the German occupying troops do in each of the countries? Would they continue to fight even after a surrender on the main fronts? Would the Allies intervene? If so, which Allies would intervene where? The Swedes did not want Russians in Northern Norway. Should Sweden use its military forces for a short-term occupation and/or action against the German troops stationed in those countries? Should Sweden allow Denmark and Norway to build military forces in Sweden to be used at the end of the war?

These questions dominated Swedish policy in the last months of the war. Considerable differences of opinion existed within the government about how to respond to them. Great uncertainty existed about the behavior of the great powers and their soldiers. An agreement to allow the training of Norwegian and Danish "police forces" was reached. The capabilities of these groups in terms of military action was left unsettled. Hansson, most importantly, resisted the temptations to adopt a more active Scandinavian policy. His strategy was to maintain options but give no clear indication of a Swedish willingness to move its troops. One option was to try to guarantee that the war in the north would end peacefully.

Sweden permitted itself to be used by Himmler and others in attempts to reach a separate peace with the Western powers. The main conduit for these efforts at the end of the war was Count Folke Bernadotte, who was in Germany leading the Red Cross rescue mission. The Swedes harbored no illusions about the likely results of Himmler's efforts but used them to serve their own purposes of rescuing victims of the concentration camps and securing promises that German troops would surrender to native officials in Denmark and Norway once a general truce had been reached. The rescue effort succeeded well beyond the imagination of almost everyone. The German troops surrendered in Scandinavia with the end of the war. Swedish fears that a last-minute involvement in the war might be necessary proved groundless.

A third area where Swedish policy shifted at the end of 1942 was in the area of "humanitarian" efforts. This term "humanitarian," which was what the foreign office used, can be confusing. In one sense, humanitarian is appropriate. It refers to the services offered by Sweden to various victims of the war, especially the "innocent civilians." In another sense, it is highly misleading. It suggests a policy based solely on the goodwill of Sweden and the needs of the victims. In fact, Swedish "humanitarian

efforts" were calculated policy whose purposes were not simply to serve
the victims of a terrible war but also to meet the security and economic
needs of Sweden. How could it have been otherwise? The numbers of
victims in the war totaled in the millions, and Sweden had an established hierarchy of foreign policy concerns. This is not to deny the
genuine commitment of Swedish organizations such as the Red Cross to
relief work nor the importance of the help that was actually provided.
Rather, it is necessary to examine why the government permitted
and/or encouraged certain kinds of "humanitarian efforts" and resisted
others.

During the war, Sweden's "humanitarian efforts" followed closely the
contours of Swedish security policy. Five major areas of activity can be
noted: aid to Greece; refuge for Baltic peoples; aid to fellow Scandinavians; conduit for exchange of wounded prisoners of war between
Germany and the Allies; and the rescue of the Jews. Aid to Greece
began quite early and lasted throughout the war. Germany obviously
did not object, and the Allies were appreciative. The Baltic peoples
were a more difficult issue. A variety of Balts found refuge in Sweden:
some anti-Communist, some anti-German, and some descendants of
Swedish emigration to Estonia. This aid began to be criticized already in
1944 as highly insensitive to the Soviet Union. Charges were made by
Russia that Sweden was providing safe havens for Baltic fascists. Jewish
groups in Sweden noted that almost none of the post-1941 Baltic refugees were Jewish despite the fact that large numbers of Jews were in
hiding in the Baltic states and in extreme danger. More serious still,
after the war a new Hansson government decided to return a number of
the Baltic refugees to the Soviet Union. Östen Undén, the foreign minister, has been blamed for these deportations. The fault lay elsewhere.
Undén often opposed government policy during the war and favored a
more active neutrality. He was, however, expected as the new foreign
minister to continue the policies of his predecessors, at least on this
issue. Hansson simply did not want to risk Soviet ire on the issue of a few
hundred refugees.[32] Swedish "humanitarian efforts" had real limits, not
just with regard to the Balts.

Perhaps the most consistent aid programs Sweden managed were

---

32. Karl Molin, "Winning the Peace: Vision and Disappointment in Nordic Security
Policy, 1945–49," in Nissen, op. cit., pp. 340-341. See also Per Olot Enqvist,
Legionäverna (Stockholm, 1968).

with regard to fellow Scandinavians. This aid, however, was not without concerns related to larger security issues. The question of internment of Scandinavian refugees for the duration of the war reflected the Swedish desire to assure Germany that Swedish refugee policy would not damage Germany's interests. Although internment in fact was rejected by the government, it can be found prominently amidst discussions about how Sweden should behave. For example, Sweden's initial offer to Germany to take all of Denmark's Jews in late September 1943 was accompanied by a promise to intern all the Jews and keep them quiet for the duration of the war. Nor were the Swedes willing to take all Scandinavians at all times. Known communists were interned. Finnish requests for refuge for Jews in Finland, the number of whom was approximately 200, were not received positively until late in 1943. In addition, Sweden rarely took any initiatives. They provided help — a great deal, to be exact — but it generally came in response to efforts either by the countries concerned or by citizens of those countries. The Red Cross expedition was a good example of Swedish support for a Norwegian initiative.

These comments are not intended as criticism of Swedish behavior. Rather, it is important to realize that there was an overarching continuity in Swedish foreign policy that also affected "humanitarian efforts," a reluctance toward adopting an active foreign policy. "Humanitarian efforts" were not only limited by assuming strong, negative German and Soviet responses; they were also part of the policies gauged to demonstrate to the Western powers the value of Swedish neutrality.

Sweden was anxious to justify its policies to the Western democracies. The role Sweden played in serving as the locale for exchange of wounded prisoners of war was used as one example of how Swedish neutrality benefited the West (as well as Germany). As a neutral, Sweden could represent the interests of the belligerents in hostile countries and offer the opportunity for contact and discussion between the belligerents. In addition, Sweden's willingness to aid Jews after 1942 depended considerably on the belief in the Swedish foreign ministry that such aid benefited Sweden in the United States and Great Britain. Examples of this can be most clearly seen in the cases related to the Adler-Rudel scheme to rescue Belgian and French Jewish children, the appointment of Raoul Wallenberg, and the help to Jews provided in 1945, both immediately before the end of and after the war (see Chapter 2). The policy gained considerable attention, too, in the West. Newspaper sto-

ries, editorials, and large public meetings congratulated Sweden for the
work it was doing to help the Jews. What impact the policy had on the
Western governments was another question; none of the Allies showed
enormous concern to help persecuted Jews.

The issue of whether Sweden could have done more and under what
circumstances will be examined in Chapter 5. At this point, it is more
important to note that the level of "humanitarian activities" increased
dramatically as the war progressed. It was an area where Swedes could
affirm their democratic and humanistic principles and where Germany
demonstrated a high degree of tolerance. Indeed, there was little criticism from Berlin about such activities even after the rescue of the Danish Jewry, a fact which contrasted with the continuing German protests
about anti-German articles in the Swedish press. The Allies, except for
the Soviet Union and the Baltic refugee question, could hardly criticize
the humanitarian activities.

Swedish foreign policy after 1942 became more evenhanded. Some
Swedish historians have suggested that Swedish policy in 1944–1945
was as favorable to the West as Swedish policy had benefited Germany
between 1940 and 1942.[33] Such an interpretation is not convincing.
What is striking about Swedish policy during the war is the sensitivity
shown Germany throughout the conflict and the relative slowness to
concede to Western concerns.

There was nothing of similar importance done in favor of Western
interests compared with the transportation services provided to
Germany. Sweden was also quite slow in revoking those privileges. The
German response to the ending of the transit traffic in August 1943 was
mild. Air and sea traffic was not stopped until 1944. In contrast, Swedish
artillery batteries had instructions until late in 1944 to shoot down Allied
bombers that might stray into Swedish air space. The concessions made
by Sweden on trade certainly benefited Western interests against
Germany's and had some negative effect on Sweden's economy. The
real impact, however, was far less than the terms of the trade agree-

---

33. Carlgren characterized Swedish foreign policy as one dependent upon the evolution of the war with Sweden becoming "*de facto* involved in the Western powers' war on
Germany" by the end of 1944, p. 227. Sweden's reluctance to become too pro-Western
was not based as Johansson has argued on principles of neutrality. pp. 412–413. *Realpolitik*
within the limits of a small power motivated Swedish policy. Sweden wanted to survive the
war as an independent non-belligerent, and to do as much as possible to insure a peaceful
and free Northern Europe after the war.

ments. Swedish-German trade remained quite high, and profitable, until the end of 1944.

Yet it would be wrong to conclude that the biases in Swedish neutrality were caused by a pro-German attitude in the Swedish coalition government. This simply did not exist. Cultural preferences for Germany were shared by a number of leading Swedes, including Gustaf V. But Hansson and the majority of the cabinet and the Foreign Office were convinced that Sweden's independence and democracy rested fully on the ability of the Western powers to win the war, and the peace. Hansson's views, more than any other person's, were implanted upon Swedish foreign policy during the war. By temperament and preference, Hansson opted for a passive foreign policy.

Sweden's geography placed it into a German area of dominance. The evolution of the war isolated Sweden from the West and exposed it to the struggles between Germany and the Soviet Union. The complete victory of one or the other of these belligerents would bring with it great risks for Swedish sovereignty. The Swedish government chose to take as few chances as possible. What future did a small state have in a great power conflict? The concessions to Germany were perceived as necessary. Under Hitler, Germany was an aggressive, ambitious, and irrational state. Sweden should not provoke Germany into military action against Sweden. When the likelihood of such action decreased, Hansson among others showed reluctance to shift Swedish policy quickly.

Neither Hansson nor Günther believed that Sweden was well served by a foreign policy that appeared to change as quickly as the winds of war blew in another direction. They felt that such rapid changes in Swedish policy would undermine confidence in Sweden, both domestically and internationally. Therefore, they took the position that Sweden should only concede to the Western powers in terms of favors and services which appeared necessary after pressure had been applied from the West. They were lucky that each of the three great powers of the United Nations had such limited goals in Scandinavia. Only in the area of "humanitarian activities" and military intelligence did the Swedish government demonstrate an unxiousness to meet Allied interests in an active way. In particular, Swedish policy toward the Jews after 1942 reflected a general concern about Swedish-Western powers relations. Sweden's Jewish policy 1942–1945 cannot be examined in isolation. There were other factors than simply great power considerations that affected it.

Chapter 2

Sweden and "The Jewish Problem," 1933–1945

"The Jewish problem," as it was called in Swedish documents after January 1933, developed as a direct consequence of Adolf Hitler's assumption of power in Germany. Anti-Semitism held a prominent place in the political program of the National Socialists. Soon after he became chancellor, Hitler announced new measures to limit and eventually eliminate Jewish influence in Germany. His actions received widespread attention in the international press. In Sweden, not only did anti-Hitler journalists such as Torgny Segerstedt protest, so did traditionally pro-German figures like King Gustaf V and Professor Fredrik Böök.

Swedish responses to German persecution of Jews can be divided into four periods: 1933–1938, 1938–1939, 1939–1942, and 1942–1945. In the first period, persecution of the Jews did not directly affect Sweden. The responses to Germany's policies were grounded in concerns removed from Swedish interests. In the second period, "the Jewish problem" became activated in Sweden by a sudden interest in Sweden by Jewish refugees, particularly those in Austria and Czechoslovakia. In the third period, all foreign policy issues including policy with regard to Jews were overwhelmed by Sweden's struggle to avoid participation in the war. Christian Günther wrote in February 1940: "Sweden's primary goal must be to avoid entanglement in the World War, and all questions must be regarded with that overriding consideration in mind."[1]

The fourth period, 1942–1945, brought a very different kind of

---

1. Christian Günther to MacMillan, February 23, 1940, in Carlgren, *Svensk Utrikespolitik 1939–1945*, pp. 86–87.

response from Sweden. Sweden slowly activated itself to help the Jews. This aid took the form first of being a refuge from Nazi persecution. Next, Sweden negotiated with Germany for the release of thousands of Jews. Then Sweden took steps to intervene in other countries, such as Hungary, to try to protect Jews. Finally, Sweden launched a rescue mission directly into Germany, the purpose of which partially was to take Jews in concentration camps to Sweden. The evolution of Swedish policy stemmed partially from the changing war conditions and partially from the general values and attitudes held by Swedes.

Anti-Semitism was hardly a unique German phenomenon. Hostility toward Judaism was a fundamental aspect of most Christian sects. In the nineteenth century, a new form of hatred of Jews took shape in the form of pseudo-Darwinian race theory. This anti-Semitism differed in a variety of ways from earlier forms of anti-Jewish hostility because it emphasized biological factors rather than religious ones as the basis of Jewishness. With the earlier forms of prejudice, a Jew could always convert to escape persecution. Anti-Semitism offered no escape. Moreover, it was unclear with anti-Semitism how exactly to identify a Jew. Was it someone who anywhere in his past had Jewish ancestors, or was it necessary to have two Jewish parents, four grandparents, etc.? Anti-Semitism was vacuous but vicious; it could be used against virtually anyone. The impact of Darwinism on the study of biology gave anti-Semitism an air of legitimacy. Professors of race biology sprung up throughout Europe, including Sweden.

Anti-Semitism existed in Sweden. It is difficult to judge how widespread it was. Much of the literature of the last part of the nineteenth century and the early twentieth century used Jewish characters in traditional anti-Jewish fashion — as moneylenders, exploitive capitalists, etc. The popularity of race biology strengthened the conviction that Jews were a race apart from European peoples. For example, Fredrik Böök, professor of Swedish literature and the most influential literary critic of the interwar period in Sweden, combined anti-Semitism with a desire to see the Jews establish their own state in Palestine.[2] The most vulgar forms of anti-Semitism can be found in the propaganda of the Swedish National Socialist Party.

The Swedish Nazis were never an important element in Swedish politics. Nonetheless, they were a visible feature of the politics of the

---

2. See Fredrik Böök, *Resa Till Jerusalem 1925* (Lund, 1977), pp. 205–252.

thirties and a potential element of discord had the Swedish economy soured or Germany occupied Sweden after 1940. In their first party program (1933), the"Jewish Question" was identified as Sweden's, and Europe's, most critical problem. Jews, it was claimed, had destroyed the Swedish state and enslaved the people through modern democracy, capitalism, and Marxism. Jews had managed these feats by control of the banks, the newspapers, radio, and other forms of public opinion. The Swedish Nazis wanted Sweden Jew-free and proposed a series of policies to accomplish this goal.[3]

If the Swedish Nazis expressed anti-Semitism in its most vulgar form, there seems little doubt that a widespread, almost intuitive anti-Semitism existed, especially among well-educated upper-class Swedes. K.G. Westman's diaries provide ample evidence of anti-Semitism. Westman was one of Sweden's most prominent politicians: a leading figure in the Farmers' Party; a member of the Hammarskjöld government, 1914–1917; a member of the two governments, 1936–1944, in which he served as minister of justice; and a professor of legal history. Westman's wartime diaries, published in 1981, contain many anti-Semitic slurs. He exhibited his criticisms of Swedish foreign policy by blaming it on the "Jewish blood" of Erik Boheman. Boheman had one grandparent who was Jewish. Westman was not alone within the government in sometimes ascribing to Boheman's behavior his "Jewishness." Westman offered similar explanations when the Crown Prince opposed policies advocated by Westman. As mentioned previously, the worst example was his explanation for Torgny Segerstedt's opposition to government policy: "His Jewish mistress has removed his soul and replaced it with a Jewish one."[4] How extreme Westman's anti-Semitism was in comparison to a broader public opinion is impossible to gauge. Many in the Swedish Jewish community of the thirties thought it not atypical.

The Jewish community in Sweden prior to the war was quite heterogeneous. After the establishment in the eighteenth century of the rights of Jews to reside in Sweden and practice their religion, the Jewish population grew until by the late thirties it probably numbered slightly over 7,000. This figure did not, of course, include those Swedes who, only according to German race laws and anti-Semites, were Jews. There

---

3. Nationalsocialistiska Arbetarepartiet, *Den svenska nationalsocialismens Program* (Göteborg, 1933), pp. 7, 29–30. Also, Ulf Lindström, op. cit.

4. Westman, op. cit., p. 123.

were three main congregations: Stockholm, Göteborg, and Malmö. The Stockholm congregation was the largest and most influential. It was also dominated by Jews well assimilated into Swedish society and contained comparatively less early twentieth century, East European immigrants or refugees from Hitler's Germany. The occupational and economic distribution of Jews in Sweden has not yet been established, but scattered evidence suggests a broad range of activities and financial stability. The most recent immigrants were most likely to be the poorest and most unprepared to participate in Swedish life. Yet some Jews had achieved positions of distinction in academic and professional life. They were also prominent in industrial and financial circles as well as in publishing. In none of these areas save the latter could it be claimed that Jews held a monopoly or anything remotely approaching one.

In the publishing field, one family, the Bonniers, had a dominant place. They controlled a major portion of the book publishing business as well as produced a significant number of the weekly and monthly magazines and owned one of the largest daily newspapers, *Dagens Nyheter*. Ownership did not, however, mean active direction of these enterprises by family members for political purposes. In addition, the "Jewishness" of the family was questionable. The Bonniers had arrived in Sweden early in the nineteenth century and had intermarried with non-Jews from the beginning. They were not active in the Jewish community and exactly how many were still practicing Jews was unclear. Still, they were used by anti-Semites both in Sweden and in Germany as examples of the "Jewish influence" in Sweden. During the war, the family kept a low profile. *Dagens Nyheter* operated independently of their influence.[5]

The Stockholm congregation was the important Jewish organization. Whenever the government wanted an opinion on matters related to Jews, leaders of the Stockholm congregation were questioned. In this fashion, the Stockholm Jewish leaders represented the others. Their views were believed by the government to be the official "Jewish view." In fact, the Stockholm congregation was itself seriously divided on nearly every issue and did not reflect well the attitudes of other Jewish congregations in Sweden.

Politically, all the major parties were represented in the Stockholm congregation. On the question of Palestine, there existed strong groups

---

5. See Torbacke, op. cit.

both for and against Zionism. The rabbi, Marcus Ehrenpreis, chief rabbi of Sweden, sided with the Zionists on questions related to Palestine but otherwise had to be careful not to antagonize the various groups. The committee established to help refugees from Hitler in the thirties was chaired by Gunnar Josephson, owner of one of the best book stores in Sweden, and an example of an assimilated Jew. Josephson's wife was the sister of Erik Boheman. Josephson's views were an important influence on government policy regarding the Jews.

Josephson and other well placed Jews feared for a rise of anti-Semitism in Sweden. The greatest danger for such a development might be caused by a new, large influx of Jews in the thirties. For nearly two hundred years, Sweden had experienced little immigration, only emigration. Those few immigrants who came to Sweden found a society difficult to penetrate and often openly hostile to foreigners. Jews who had successfully assimilated did not want to jeopardize their positions in Swedish life, especially for the sake of uneducated, East European Jews.

Josephson and his committee found themselves in the position of having the power of approval for every Jew who applied for the right to live in Sweden. They exercised care in selecting Jews, most of whom were well educated and reasonably solvent.[6] The Jewish community also bore financial responsibility for these new immigrants. Criticism of the conservativeness of the policy existed within the Stockholm congregation and even more vocally in other Jewish groups. Some wanted a more active refugee policy and were willing to risk the consequences of a rise in anti-Semitism. Even after the war began and persecution of Jews turned to murder, the divisions continued.

Josephson remained skeptical of the viability of Sweden as a major depot of Jewish refugees. He put little pressure on the government to act forcefully. Non-Swedes, such as Jewish Agency representative Saloman Adler-Rudel or War Refugee Board representative Iver Olsen, registered dismay as late as 1943–1944 that the Stockholm Jewish com-

---

6. Hugo Valentin, "Rescue and Relief Activities on Behalf of Jewish Victims of Nazism in Scandinavia," *YIVO Annual of Jewish Social Science*, v. VIII, 1953, pp. 224–225. Valentin suggested that the policy of financial guarantees "greatly obstructed and limited the activities on behalf of the Jewish refugees." He also argued that "the leaders of the Jewish communities, without exception, made it their business to induce their governments to act more generously toward the refugees," and that there was "no foundation" to rumors from abroad of an "unfriendly position" toward the refugees. Valentin did admit that he had "misgivings" about whether Josephson's group had shown "sufficient energy."

munity showed so little interest in rescue efforts to help Jews on the Continent.[7] Critics of the establishment's policies led to the formation of other groups.

One center of activity was within the pro-Zionist groups. They had a journal, *Judisk Krönika*, founded in 1932, that publicly tried to change the official congregation policy and influence the larger Swedish community. The journal developed close contacts in Eastern Europe, especially Poland, and provided some of the best information on the extent of the Final Solution found in any Western publication. The journal also became a source of information for other non-Jewish publications.[8]

Other organizations had international ties. In 1942, a small group of individuals within the Stockholm congregation organized what became officially in 1944 the Swedish branch of the World Jewish Congress. The leading figure of this group was Gillel Storch, a recent refugee from the Baltic area with considerable financial resources. Storch and his associates probably represented the furthest extreme from Josephson's group. They constantly devised schemes to rescue Jews. Their activities reflected a sense of desperation quite justified by actual circumstances on the Continent. They were often criticized in turn for being unrealistic by other organizations involved in rescue efforts.

In 1943, the American Jewish Joint Distribution Committee established a section in Stockholm, headed by a lawyer, Ragnar Gottfarb. The Joint Committee was the largest and most powerful international Jewish organization trying to aid Jewish victims of German policies. One of the committee's European field officials, Laura Margolin, visited Stockholm in the fall of 1944, and her reports reflected both criticisms of the Jewish establishment (". . . at no time was the congregation ready or helpful in making the immigration of refugees into Sweden a possibility") and Storch ("a completely disorganized person," who proposed "fantastic rescue schemes").[9] Storch's group also ran afoul of the War Refugee Board.

The War Refugee Board was established by Franklin Roosevelt in

---

7. United States, War Refugee Board (Hyde Park-FDR Library), Iver Olsen to John Pehle, August 10, 1944; and Box 35, Report of Laura Margolin, November 20, 1944.

8. *Svenska Israelsmissionens Tidning* frequently cited *Judisk Krönika*. Other Swedish newspapers and journals did so less often. Remarkable information can be found on the pages of *JK* including a November 1943 story identifying Auschwitz as a major killing center and including statistics for numbers killed and country of origin.

9. United States, Franklin D. Roosevelt Library (Hyde Park, New York), War Refugee Board papers, Box 45, Report from Laura Margolin, November 20, 1944.

January 1944 to aid Jews and to circumvent the procrastinating bureaucracy of the State Department. A Treasury official attached to the American legation in Stockholm, Iver Olsen, was appointed as the representative of the WRB in Stockholm. Olsen spent six months actively promoting various rescue operations, the most spectacular of which was the placement of Raoul Wallenberg, who received $100,000 from the Joint Committee via Olsen for his activities, in Budapest. Olsen, too, reported both the reluctance of the Stockholm congregation to aid him and the problems that he was having with Storch. In particular, Storch criticized Olsen for his lack of activities to help Baltic Jews. Margolin supported Olsen's position.[10]

All these examples underline the division within the Jewish community. In retrospect, it appears easy to criticize Josephson and his committee. Yet they spent enormous amounts of energy and time as well as money trying to help Jewish refugees. How many refugees could a community of 7,000 Jews support? Why didn't the Swedish state accept broader financial responsibility as it was to do with Scandinavian refugees during the war? Fear of growing anti-Semitism combined with the apparent financial limitations of the Swedish Jewish community created a conservatism within the official refugee committee that was to prove disastrous to many Jews who sought asylum in Sweden. The criticism within the Jewish community of their approach was much more muted in the period 1933–1938 than it was thereafter.

Indeed, this first period is of interest because the "Jewish problem" appeared not to concern Sweden and Swedish institutions directly. The most fascinating aspect of the Swedish response initially was the vigor with which the traditional pro-German upper class elements protested Hitler's anti-Semitic policies. Gustaf V, for example, on his way home from Italy, stopped in Berlin to complain of the damage Hitler's anti-Semitism had on Germany's international reputation.[11] Gustaf voiced his views to Hitler in the presence of President von Hindenburg; the whole experience must have been discomforting for the ex-corporal and dictator-in-the-making. Fredrik Böök made similar appeals, as did Archbishop Erling Eidem. The criticisms were not so much of the existence of anti-Semitism but that Hitler chose to make it such a prominent aspect of his government's policy. Many conservative Swedes, without

---

10. Ibid.
11. Gustaf V Privata Samling, Wirsén Uppteckning.

identifying themselves as Nazis, approved of Hitler's successes in restoring the power and authority of the German state. Sven Hedin, world-famous explorer, defended the new order in Germany and showed great sympathy for its anti-Semitism. Even at the end of the war, Hedin continued to voice positive views of Hitler, although he no longer supported the Jewish policies of the Third Reich.[12]

If conservative reaction was mixed in this first period, liberals and socialists condemned Hitler's action. Individuals like Torgny Segerstedt attacked Hitler and his regime from its outset. Anti-Semitism was a symbol for them of his dictatorial propensities and lack of Christian humanism. Segerstedt's ideological hostility never wavered; his paper ran story after story on the brutality of the Hitler regime.[13] Other newspapers followed suit. Information about the progress of Germany's anti-Semitism abounded in the Swedish press.

The issue as far as the government was concerned remained quite muted. Jewish refugees rarely sought to immigrate into Sweden in this period. The most concrete issues were related to attempts by Germany to stop trade between Swedish firms with Jewish managers and German companies and pressure on Sweden to change a number of their honorary consuls in Germany who happened to be Jewish. The latter phenomenon was corrected, but Sweden resisted German demands to rid their major corporations of Jewish executives. Sandler, the foreign minister, and his top aides not only rejected Hitler's overtures but sought to help those who were being displaced by his policies.

Sandler supported collective security through the League of Nations.[14] He also showed considerable interest and sympathy for League attempts to define the "refugee problem," which was the euphemism used by the League in discussing Hitler's attempts to drive Jews from Germany. Despite extensive activities by various commissions, nothing of consequence was accomplished. Swedish diplomatic officials reported to Stockholm that the "Jewish problem" was not simply a German one. Erik Boheman, for example, in a long report from Warsaw observed that anti-Semitism was more widespread in Poland and that

---

12. Eidems arkiv, Hedin to Eidem, April 2, 1943.
13. Ingrid Segerstedt Wiberg, *Torgny Segerstedt* (Stockholm, 1955). Also, Klas Åmark, *Makt eller moral* (Stockholm, 1973). A collection of Segerstedt's editorials was published: Torgny Segerstedt, *Idag* (Stockholm, 1945). Henrik Sandblad, *GHT och Hitlerregimen* (Göteborg, 1960).
14. Hägglöf, op. cit., p. 151.

any successful international effort to care for German Jews would immediately bring demands from other countries to take their Jews.[15] Swedish policy seemed to recognize the international character of the "Jewish
problem" and was willing to participate in a multinational resolution of
it. However, Sweden did not offer itself as an appropriate place for large
numbers of Jewish immigrants and felt that the best solution was a "non-
European" one, perhaps, but not necessarily, in Palestine.

Between 1938 and 1940, Sweden no longer could maintain the luxury
of responding to persecution of the Jews on a diplomatic level. A sudden
change in the patterns of Jewish immigrants led Sweden to take decisive
action. The immediate cause of this change was Germany's occupation
and annexation of Austria. Jews in Vienna, and somewhat later in
Prague, crowded into the Swedish legations to get visas to travel to
Sweden. The Swedish minister in Prague wrote that the legation was
being inundated by Jews who were trying to leave Czechoslovakia like
"rats leaving a sinking ship."[16] The government and parliament had to
decide how to respond to this wave of would-be immigrants.

Swedish immigration laws had been partially rewritten in 1937.[17]
They were not particularly hospitable to any potential immigrant. A
broad consensus in the parliament viewed immigrants as threats to
Swedish workers and a possible burden on the financial resources of the
state. The new laws in effect made immigration into Sweden more difficult, but the Jews presented a special problem. After the *Anschluss*,
Austrians received German passports. At this time, it was not necessary
for bearers of German passports to have a visa in order to travel to
Sweden. This meant, as government officials realized, that German and
Austrian Jews could come to Sweden without any formal Swedish
approval; however, once in Sweden, Germany refused to allow the Jews
to return to their homes. Switzerland faced the same problem. Both
countries warned Germany that if Germany did not distinguish a Jew in
their German passport, Switzerland and Sweden would establish new
regulations for visas and apply them to all Germans. The German

---

15. Sweden, Riksarkivet, Utrikesdepartementets arkiv, 1920 års (known hereafter as
UD 1920), HP 1049, Erik Boheman to Rickard Sandler, November 25, 1935. See Documents Collection.

16. Ibid., Folke Malmar to the Swedish Foreign Office, April 4, 1938.

17. See Hans Lindberg, *Svensk flyktingpolitik under internationellt tryck 1936–1941*
(Stockholm, 1973). Statens Offentliga Utredningar (SOU), *Parlamentariska
Undersökningskommissionen Angående Flyktningsärenden och Säkerhetstjänst*, vol. 1,
Flyktningars Behandling (Stockholm, 1946).

response was the creation of the so-called "J-passport." A large letter "J"
was stamped into German Jewish passports. Swiss and Swedish customs
officials could then take action to stop Jews from entering their countries.

There was one potential opportunity for Jews to emigrate to Sweden
— if they were classified as refugees from political persecution. Swedish
law gave the government some flexibility in the definition of a "political
refugee" and how many to accept into the country. Sweden decided not
to accept Jews as "political refugees" on the simple basis of their religious affiliations. This policy meant that Sweden could allow certain
Jewish refugees into the country but for reasons other than their religion. For example, a number of Czech Jewish labor leaders were
granted permission to enter the country in 1938 and 1939 but not on the
basis of their religion. In September 1938, Sigfrid Hansson, brother of
the prime minister, issued instructions to customs officials to turn back
all Jews who attempted to enter the country.[18]

News of the order leaked out. What was the public response? A small
minority of the parliament — primarily Social Democrats and Liberals
— questioned the government's policy. A broad majority supported it.
In the fall of 1938 and winter-spring of 1939, a fear grew that Sweden
was about to be overwhelmed by a massive wave of Jewish immigration.
Swedish doctors protested and demanded protection from the import of
Jewish colleagues. A large, well-publicized student meeting in Uppsala
demanded that the government keep Jews out of the country. A counter
pro-refugee meeting received less attention. Some speeches in the parliament were openly anti-Semitic, especially from a few Farmers' Party
parliamentarians.[19] Most of the country's newspapers supported the
government's policy. Even many Jewish groups accepted the restrictive
policy.

The actual selection of which refugees would be permitted into

---

18. UD 1920, P 1349, Memorandum of Sigfrid Hansson to all border stations, September 9, 1938. See Documents Collection. Lindberg, op. cit., p. 167, cited Gösta Engzell in
a dispatch to Malmar, "Naturallly we are very restrictive in accepting Jewish emigrants."
See also, Göte Friberg, Stormcentrum Öresund (Borås, 1978), p. 35.

19. Riksdagens Protokoll vid Lagtima Riksmötet År 1939 Andra Kammarens, nummer
12, debate of February 22, 1939, pp. 19–53. Among other comments: "Jews have avoided
productive work for hundreds of years . . .", and "the Asiatic race does not belong with our
respectable Swedish race." Riksdagens Protokoll vid Lagtima Riksmötet År 1939, Första
Kammaren, first volume, nrs. 1–23, sessions of January 18, 1939, and February 22, 1939,
see especially K.G. Westman's speech of January 18 on pp. 79–81.

Sweden was managed through a consultation process in which a number of refugee committees had certain quotas of individuals assigned to them. Josephson's committee represented the Jewish community. It made no demands to increase the number of Jews being granted entrance into the country. Their passiveness was cited by Foreign Office officials as proof that the government's policy was correct.[20] Those Jewish groups that advocated a more permissive policy had no impact on the government or, indeed, the general public.

How can this broad hostility to Jewish immigration be explained? In these years, it was not possible to blame external factors on Swedish response. All the great powers would have been pleased if Sweden had adopted a more open-handed policy. Some argued that a primary motivation was economic. Sweden's recent experience with large-scale unemployment left many Swedes terrified that a large group of refugees would take their jobs and leave them without work. Swedish labor unions, normally a progressive force in Swedish politics, favored a restrictive policy. A traditional dislike of foreigners of all sorts also contributed to the feeling. Nonetheless, it was difficult at the time, and now, not to conclude that the fundamental source of the negative attitude was anti-Semitism.

Approximately 3,000 Jews were permitted to settle in Sweden prior to the war. This represented far less proportionally than those accepted by other countries such as Holland, Belgium, France, and Great Britain.[21] In 1944, Sweden would care for over 175,000 refugees. The economic capacity of Sweden to absorb far more immigrants in 1939 than was actually permitted was pointed out in parliamentary debate at the time by two future Nobel Prize-winning economists, Gunnar Myrdal and Bertil Ohlin. Had economics been the primary factor, the debate would have had a different character. These years reinforced the views of Stockholm's assimilated Jews that Sweden was not ready for an influx of Jewish refugees. Pro-refugee cabinet members like Gustav Möller shared their views with considerable resignation.[22] The out-

20. UD 1920, P 61, Engzell Memorandum, April 21, 1939. See Document Collection.

21. UD 1920, P 50, Swedish Legation (London) to Swedish Foreign Office, February 23, 1940.

22. See *Riksdagens Protokoll*, op. cit. Lindberg suggested that after the war began, "The government's treatment of the Jewish refugee problem became obviously even more sporadic and limited to individual cases." Günther reportedly did not want to be bothered, pp. 280–281.

break of war in September 1939 relieved the immediate pressure of Jewish immigrants.

Although Sweden felt secure for the first four months of the war, that
security collapsed in the wake of the Finnish-Soviet war and the opening of hostilities in Denmark and Norway in April 1940. Sweden felt
threatened and isolated. For the next two years, all foreign policy concerns would be subjected to keeping Sweden out of the war. Jewish
requests for visas slowed. In 1941, Germany's policies took a new, much
more destructive turn. As German armies swept across eastern Poland
and Russia after June 1941, special SS-units were assigned to slaughter
Jews.

The evolution of German policy toward the Jews remains a source of
controversy. A traditional view has been that a kind of natural progres-
sion from an idea to make Germany Jew-free by emigration became a
policy to exterminate all of Europe's Jews as Germany established control over much of the Continent in the period 1939–1942. Others suggest that certain Nazi leaders, including Hitler, desired the destruction
of all things Jewish from the outset and only the realities of the thirties
hindered them from a more radical policy initially. Once the war began,
these barriers disappeared and the true intention of the Nazis' anti-
Semitism could be realized.[23] Swedish policy-makers and those Swedes
involved with German developments during the war seemed to com-
bine these two interpretations. They identified some Nazi leaders as
"radical" on the Jewish Question (Hitler, Goebbels, Heydrich, among
others) and others as opportunistic (Göring, Himmler, Best, etc.).
Whether or not their interpretations conform precisely with the latest
historiographical views is less important than the fact that contemporary
Swedes observed a changing German policy toward the Jews.

Sometime in the summer of 1941, Hitler decided upon a policy of
extermination of all Jews within Germany's control. A policy of
liquidating large numbers of Jews in the wake of German military
advances on the Eastern front was initiated. Experimentation and
planning for a more coordinated effort to murder systematically the
Jews of Western Europe took more time. By January 1942, a meeting of
German bureaucratic officials at Wannsee finalized the technical details

---

23. Literature on "the Final Solution" continues to grow. The classic study remains
Raul Hilberg, *The Destruction of the European Jews* (Chicago, 1967). See Gerald Flem-
ing, *Hitler and the Final Solution* (Berkeley, 1984); Martin Gilbert, *The Holocaust* (New
York, 1985).

of the mass extermination program. Within a few weeks, the specially-created Jewish ghettos of Poland began to be emptied into newly-created killing centers. All the killing centers — Auschwitz, Belsec, Chelmno, Majdanek, Sobibor, and Treblinka — were established in Poland. A systematic, technologically efficient method of killing and disposing of the Jews and their bodies was developed. An integrated and coordinated bureaucratic effort had to be mounted in the midst of the world war in order to accomplish the "Final Solution." Only such an advanced Western country as Germany could have managed such a task.

Reports of Germany's continued and stepped-up persecution of the Jews reached Stockholm in 1941. Swedish businessmen, reporters, and diplomats moved about in occupied Eastern Europe. The mail continued to function, and censored private letters traveled between Sweden and Poland. The censorship exercised by Germany did not attempt to hide the increasing harsh fate that awaited Jews, but the specific details were eliminated, or at least attempts to eliminate them were made. Still, it was apparent in Stockholm that conditions for the Jews had changed dramatically in the summer of 1941 and, as Swedish state church publications noted, Jews awaited a certain death. Such reliable sources as the Swedish minister in Berlin, Arvid Richert, reported an eyewitness account of the activities of special SS-units.[24] Information about the killing centers came to Sweden in the summer of 1942.

No evidence has yet been discovered to indicate that anyone in Sweden was aware of the Wannsee conference. The first mention of an extermination campaign came from London via the press and diplomatic reports in conjunction with a press conference held jointly by the British Ministry of Information and the Polish government-in-exile in early July.[25] The Poles had also produced a book on the German atrocities in Poland, including descriptions of the use of gas in the killing of Jews and other Poles. Immediately after the press conference in London, five Swedish businessmen were arrested in Poland by Germany and accused of conducting espionage and sabotage against German interests.

These "Warsaw Swedes" had participated in anti-German activities

---

24. UD 1920, 590 Diverse, Richert Memorandum, October 26, 1941. See Document Collection.

25. UD 1920, HP 485, Speech of General Sikorski, June 9, 1942. Ibid., Pressarkiv, v. 394, *The Times* (London), July 10, 1942; and *Göteborgs Handels- och sjöfartstidning*, July 11, 1942. See Documents Collection.

by serving as couriers from the Polish underground to the Polish legation in Stockholm ever since the occupation of Poland.[26] They represented a number of Sweden's largest companies and had excellent contacts within the Swedish government, especially the foreign office.
There exist a number of reports from them in the Foreign Office files,
including detailed descriptions of the establishment of the Warsaw
ghetto. Much of the intelligence information sent to the Polish
government-in-exile in London went via Stockholm. How much of that
information various levels of the Swedish government got remains
unclear.[27] Minister Richert guessed in July 1942 that the reason why the
Swedes were arrested was because of the release in London of the information on the extermination campaign against the Jews.[28]

The first direct accounts of the new policy from diplomatic sources
came on August 20 from the Swedish consul general in Stettin. The document described in chilling detail how Jews were assembled, stripped,
gassed, and cremated. Its author had no doubts about the accuracy of
the information.[29] Two days later, a young Swedish diplomat, Göran
von Otter, returning from an interview with the jailed "Warsaw
Swedes" in Poland, met accidentally a German SS officer, Kurt
Gerstein, who had the responsibility to transport poison gas to the killing centers. For five hours, Gerstein told von Otter all that he knew
about the extermination campaign.[30]

On the morning of August 23, von Otter reported this information to
the acting head of the Swedish mission in Berlin, Eric von Post. What
later happened to the von Otter report is still not clear. That Richert

26. See Jozef Lewandowski, *Swedish Contribution to the Polish Resistance Movement
during World War II (1939–1942)* (Uppsala, 1979); and Wilhelm Carlgren, *Svensk
Underrättelsetjänst 1939–1945* (Stockholm, 1985).

27. Carlgren's study of Sweden's secret service leaves many questions unanswered
including who within the government received what information. Carlgren indicates that
Sweden broke the code used by the Polish government-in-exile to send messages from
Stockholm to London in August 1942, yet he gives no indication of what was done with the
information. See Riksarkivet, Sven Grafström's diary, August 17, 1942. Grafström apparently received the intelligence, but did he receive it regularly? See also, UD arkiv,
Herman Eriksson papper, anteckning, January 27, 1943.

28. Sweden, Riksarkivet, Statens Informations Styrelsen, v. 89, Richert to
Hallenberg, July 22, 1942.

29. UD 1920, HP 324. K.Y. Vendel Memorandum, August 20, 1942, sent by von Post
to Kumlin, August 22, 1942. See Document Collection.

30. Saul Friedlander, *Kurt Gerstein: The Ambiguity of Good* (New York, 1969). Interviews with Göran von Otter, spring 1982. See also, UD 1920, HP 1052, Aide-Mémoire,
August 7, 1945.

learned of the report when he returned to Berlin in late August seems certain. Von Otter also had time to confirm Gerstein's information with other established resistance figures. No document has been found in Stockholm to prove that the Berlin legation forwarded the details of the von Otter-Gerstein meeting. In September, Richert was highly concerned about Swedish press criticism of Germany and was trying to get the government to take a more restrictive policy. He viewed information about persecution of the Jews as a well-proved source of irritation between Sweden and Germany. Throughout the fall, Richert failed to confirm other reports emanating from all over Europe that a deadly new campaign against the Jews had begun.[31] The von Otter information was most likely passed on to a few Foreign Office officials verbally and not necessarily in the specific detail that Gerstein had intended. If in fact this was the case, the most concrete and damaging evidence available at the time about the Final Solution was lost.

Other reports of a European-wide campaign streamed into Stockholm in the fall. Among responsible Foreign Office officials, there was little doubt that the purpose of the campaign was to kill Europe's Jews. Among the rest of the government and the Swedish public, understanding was less precise. The Swedish press had published reports of the intensified persecution of the Jews. While the Board of Information stopped circulation of a Swedish version of Poland's book on German atrocities, the English copy circulated freely.[32] What was difficult to comprehend was that a civilized country such as Germany was systematically murdering all of Europe's Jews. Even after the publication of the Allied announcement of December 17 of the existence of such an effort and additional information in the Swedish press, much of the Swedish public could not grasp the reality of the situation. The government did not have the same luxury. In late November 1942, the Final Solution was applied to Norway. Could and should Sweden help its Scandinavian brother?

The case of the Norwegian Jews was a pivotal point for Swedish policy. It was the beginning of a learning process stretching into October 1943, during which time the Swedish government discovered that it had the possibility to help Jews in ways heretofore believed impossible. The

---

31. Ibid., HP 1589, Richert to Kumlin, November 18, 1942. Richert certainly must bear responsibility for the failure to send a written report on the Gerstein-von Otter meeting.

32. Statens Informationsstyrelsen, v. 459, Propaganda Report #5, July 31, 1942, p. 51.

arrest, detention, and transportation of Norway's Jews in November 1942 caught Swedes unprepared, but caused a massive public protest. The departure of the ship that carried half of Norway's Jews (approximately 700 people) to Poland and their death was reported in all Swedish newspapers and on the radio. Public meetings were held to show solidarity for Norway's Jews. Many pastors gave sermons condemning Germany's policy toward the Jews, and all the bishops of Sweden issued a joint declaration protesting Germany's racial activities. A Gallup poll taken in mid-December indicated that 25 percent of the respondents named persecution of the Jews in Norway as the event they would most remember from 1942. Stalingrad was a distant second at 12 percent.[33]

Pressure from individuals and interest groups, especially the Swedish church, prevailed upon the government to take some action to aid the Jews. Prime Minister Hansson wanted to make some effort to help the Norwegians.[34] Although he had opposed any Swedish activities that might endanger Sweden's non-belligerency, he and his top advisers recognized that Stalingrad, El Alamein, and the American landings in North Africa represented a turning point in the war. His willingness to initiate a more openly anti-German policy increased slowly but perceptibly after November 1942 — as long as it did not drag Sweden into the war. Hansson's dilemma was how to find a method that would be effective and that would not prompt a preemptive action on the part of Germany. The Swedish government had no preconceived plan. It made two parallel attempts.

Diplomatically, Günther instructed Arvid Richert to inquire at the German Foreign Office if Germany would permit Sweden to offer the remaining Norwegian Jews (approximately 750) residence in Sweden. Simultaneously, the government asked Prince Carl, head of the Swedish Red Cross, to ask his counterpart in Norway if Norway would release the Jews to Sweden.[35] The former approach received a quick and decisive negative response. Throughout the war, Richert and his staff were to remain critical of this type of diplomatic activity and pessimistic about its likely outcome. The Norwegians were apparently caught unprepared by the Swedish request and their negative response was slower in com-

---

33. *Dagens Nyheter*, December 31, 1942, p. 1.
34. Eidems arkiv, P.A. Hansson to Eidem, December 7, 1942.
35. PRO, FO 188–390, Minute by Pollock, December 28, 1942. UD 1920, HP 1070, Cabinet to Swedish Legation, Berlin, December 3, 1942; and Westring to Engzell, December 12, 1942.

ing. Most importantly, although both approaches received negative replies, Sweden was in fact able to provide refuge for most of Norway's remaining Jews — over half the prewar population.[36]

The Norwegian Jews were saved by the same method as other Norwegian refugees who had found a haven in Sweden. Sweden accepted all Norwegians who got across the border. The border is extremely long and unguarded over much of that length. Equally critical was the fact that the Swedish government deliberately kept quiet about their activities. Swedish newspapers that knew what had happened were encouraged not to print stories.[37]

At the same time that Sweden involved itself in efforts to help Norway's Jews, public pressure in Britain and the United States grew for the Allied powers to intervene on behalf of the Jews. The Allied protest in December had confirmed the worst fears of Western Jewish leaders and given legitimacy to demands for some sort of new, positive Allied policy. Neither the British nor American governments were anxious to meet these demands. Eventually they would hold a special conference in Bermuda in April, the purpose of which was to defuse the public pressure rather than try to develop a new policy. Among the possible policy alternatives suggested by those concerned for the plight of Jews was the suggestion that the Allies use the good offices of the neutrals, particularly Sweden and Switzerland, to help Jews directly. In January–February 1943, one such plan materialized.

The Jewish Agency of Palestine, which was the political organization of Jewish residents of the British mandate, decided in January 1943 to try to rescue Jewish children via Sweden. One of its agents, Saloman Adler-Rudel, was commissioned to carry out the mission. First he needed, and received, permission from the British to travel to Sweden to negotiate with the Swedish government. Arriving in Stockholm, Adler-Rudel found "little enthusiasm in Jewish circles" for the scheme to bring 20,000 French and Belgian Jewish children to Sweden.[38] "Jewish circles" probably referred to Rabbi Ehrenpreis and Josephson's refu-

---

36. Statens Informationsstyrelsen, v. 106, Günther speech, February 27, 1943.

37. UD 1920, HP 1070, Thorsing to Westring, December 29, 1942. See also *Dagens Nyheter*, December 20, 1942, p. 3, editorial.

38. PRO, FO 371, Mr. Liston (Jewish Agency for Palestine-London) to Alan Walker, January 5, 1943. FO 188, 405, Minute to Mallet, March 11, 1943, and Minute of April 15, 1943. See also Great Britain, Lambeth Palace, William Temple papers, v. 55, Memorandum of May 5, 1943. It is interesting to note that British church officials remained very active in this scheme.

gee committee. Apparently, Storch and other individuals were more receptive. They introduced him to Gustav Möller, minister of social welfare, who liked the idea and promised to take the proposal to the cabinet.[39]

The cabinet meeting of April 15, 1943, which discussed the Adler-Rudel scheme, was apparently the only time when the full government discussed a rescue effort before it had begun. In the case of later efforts, such as with Denmark, Hungary, etc., the decisions were taken usually between the foreign minister and the prime minister and then the cabinet was simply informed. Perhaps the use of Möller as the channel to the government necessitated a cabinet decision — Möller had been critical of the Günther–Hansson policies toward Germany in 1941–1942. But it is quite clear that the Foreign Office liked the idea as much as Möller did. Even the Conservative leader, Gösta Bagge, had no objection to an attempt to realize the scheme.[40] Had there been a change in the attitude of the government, and if so, why?

---

39. PRO, FO 188, 405, Minute to Mallet, March 11, 1943.
40. Riksarkivet, Gösta Bagges anteckningar, April 15, 1943, p. 840. Formal minutes are not kept of Swedish cabinet meetings. Bagge, the Conservative Party chairman, kept the most extensive notes on the war cabinet's meetings. He reported that Möller had argued for the Adler-Rudel scheme "with the motivation that we would thereby win good will with England and America." Hansson was dubious about the likely results. Bagge commented, "the Jewish question was Hitler's bee in the bonnet. . . ." The cabinet's agreement to approve the Adler-Rudel scheme should be contrasted with an on-going discussion in the cabinet about bringing 100 plus Jewish refugees from Finland to Sweden. In the February 3, 1943, cabinet meeting, Günther announced that Sweden had warned Finland not to deport the refugees to Poland as Germany had requested as "such action would make a bad impression not only in Sweden but also in America." Bagge complained, "We are completely overrun by refugees in the country especially Norwegians." Ibid., pp. 779–781. No policy decision was taken and the issue dragged on through the late spring and summer. UD 1920, HP 1589, Beck-Friis to Söderblom, March 15, 1943, and Thyberg to Beck-Friis, March 23, 1943. Hansson even wrote a memorandum dated March 22, 1943, in which he first denied that he had encouraged the Finns to send the Jews to Sweden and then said that they might be allowed to enter the country but that Sweden would not be responsible for them economically. Ibid., HP 119, P. A. Hansson Memorandum, March 22, 1943. By June, Sweden had decided to allow "a certain limited number of Jewish refugees to move to Sweden as an exception to general policy on general humanitarian grounds. . . ." Ibid., Beck-Friis Memorandum, June 30, 1943. Why did Sweden so readily agree to seek 20,000 Jewish children from Belgium and France and behave so reluctantly with regard to a few Jewish refugees in Finland? The most likely answer is to be found in Hansson's belief that the Adler-Rudel scheme would not work but as Möller said, it would be good propaganda for Sweden in the Western capitals. The reluctance with regard to the Finnish Jewish refugees reflects a continuing fear of German response — although this seems unlikely. Bagge recorded of the cabinet discussion of May 18, 1943 on the Finnish question: "Günther had the view that it was unsuitable from a Swedish view-

The cabinet accepted the Adler-Rudel scheme with three conditions:

1. The United States and Britain would carry the costs for the 20,000 children while in Sweden.
2. The United States and Britain would allow for an increase in food imports from the West to feed the children.
3. The United States and Britain would promise to remove the children "immediately" after the war.

Sweden, in effect, offered to serve as a temporary haven for the Jewish children. But the Swedes insisted that the Western powers provide guarantees both for the maintenance of the children and their removal at the earliest possible time. The limitations placed on Swedish policy suggest that while Sweden was willing to help Jews, it did not want to be a permanent refuge for them. Moreover, by demanding guarantees, Sweden wanted formal concessions from the Western powers. These must be appreciated from the perspective of a growing recognition within the Swedish Foreign Office and the cabinet that Swedish ties with the Western powers had to be improved. The Swedish response to the Adler-Rudel plan was part of an effort to demonstrate to the Western powers the value of Sweden's neutrality.[41]

The continued evolution of the idea also shed interesting light on the relative importance that the Western powers and Sweden placed on the proposal. Sweden immediately embarked upon diplomatic negotiations with Germany for release of the children. The British and Americans procrastinated on the issues of guarantees. The Swedish-German negotiations eventually failed because of Germany's refusal to offer "adequate transport." After the collapse of the negotiations and eight months after the initial proposal, the Western powers gave the requested guarantees. They were of no consequence.[42]

Less spectacular Swedish diplomatic efforts in Berlin met with a simi-

---

point to take too many of these Jews as that would suggest that Sweden was willing to be some kind of general evacuation place for the Jews . . . ", and Dagger added, "I emphasized the need to maintain a restrictive policy so that we would not be overrun with Jews in the country." Ibid., p. 854.

41. The British in particular indicated their appreciation of Sweden's action. UD 1920, HP 1589, "Aide Mémoire" from British Legation-Stockholm, May 22, 1943. See also, Eidem arkiv, Archbishop of Canterbury to Eidem, May 7, 1943: ". . . it is the initiative of Sweden that has given us any hope."

42. PRO, FO 188, 405, Minute of August 2, 1943, and Mallet to Randall, August 5, 1943.

lar fate. There were 30–40 Jews in Germany with either Swedish citizenship or married to Swedish citizens. They had remained in Germany at the outset of the war and now found themselves caught in the Final Solution. Some were "mischlinge" — of mixed Christian-Jewish ancestry — who mistakenly believed that the anti-Semitic policies would not touch them.

Germany's discovery that Sweden had naturalized some Jews without proper procedures only reinforced official German policy. There were, however, a few cases where individual Jews escaped from the Continent to Sweden. In at least one case, Jacob Wallenberg, a powerful Swedish businessman, intervened directly in Germany to help a Jewish counterpart without using the offices of the Swedish government.[43] Sweden's Berlin legation spent many fruitless hours trying to accomplish similar tasks. The second major crisis for Sweden came with the declaration in Denmark on August 27, 1943, of martial law and the resignation of the Danish government. Swedish officials immediately understood that application of the Final Solution to Denmark was now only a matter of time.

Denmark had been a "model protectorate."[44] The Danes had for the most part cooperated with the Germans on the understanding that Danish law would be maintained. Any action against Denmark's 8,000 Jews, the German authorities had been told, would lead to an immediate rise in the Resistance movement. Nonetheless, no plans had been made to get Danish Jews to Sweden in case the Germans changed their policies. The first three weeks after August 27 witnessed an increasing number of Danish Jews applying at the Swedish legation in Copenhagen for permission to move to Sweden.

Sweden was willing to take all Danish Jews, but records of the foreign office indicated a continued pessimism about Sweden's ability to do anything for those Jews who had no direct connection with Sweden. There-

---

43. UD 1920, HP 1050, Richert to Hallenborg, August 3, 1943.

44. Denmark decided prior to the outbreak of war not to oppose militarily a German invasion because of overwhelming German military power. The Danish government and King remained in the country after the occupation, and adopted the policy of passive collaboration as long as Germany respected Danish law and the authority of the Danish government. See the works of Jørgen Hæstrup, op. cit. Swedish fear of German action against Danish Jews can be found as early as March 1943. UD 1920, HP 1056, Swedish Legation (Copenhagen) to Hallenborg, March 29, 1943. After the declaration of August 27, the Swedish Foreign Office indicated a willingness to help the Jews including the use of "provisional passes." Ibid., Engzell to von Dardel, August 31, 1943.

fore, the warning from the second-ranking German civilian authority in Denmark on September 25 that a roundup of all Danish Jews was scheduled for the night of October 1–2 only caused further gloom in the Swedish government and brought about a determination to try again to circumvent German policy.

Instructions from Stockholm to Minister Richert stated that Richert was to make a formal démarche (the Norwegian case had been handled informally) to the effect that Sweden was willing to receive all Danish Jews and that Sweden would intern them for the length of the war so that they would cause no discomfiture for Germany. Richert responded by saying that the effort was doomed to failure and that Stockholm would be well advised to cancel these instructions.[45] The government held firm; the démarche was delivered. The Germans did not answer it. Events in Denmark outran the diplomatic efforts.

The German roundup failed. Hours before the Germans struck, Danish Jews went underground and were protected by their fellow Danes. On October 3, Sweden announced publicly that all Danish Jews were welcome in Sweden — no mention was made of detention camps. A trickle of refugees soon became a flood. Nearly 7,500 of the 8,000 Danish Jews made the hazardous journey across the Sound. The Swedish government, individuals, and private institutions provided food and housing and encouraged the refugees to find employment. The success of the rescue operation surprised the Swedish government, which concluded that the critical factor for success was the willingness of German officials in Denmark to let "Jews slip through their fingers."[46]

---

45. Ibid., Richert to Günther, September 30, 1943. See also Riksarkivet, Sven Grafströms anteckningar, October 2, 1943. Grafström suggested that it was primarily on the initiative of the Swedish Foreign Office — Söderblom and himself — that Günther approved the public pronouncement of October 3 which offered Danish Jews protection in Sweden. Grafström noted that Niels Bohr was in conference with Günther when Grafström got approval. At the cabinet meeting of October 2, Günther announced — but did not discuss — the decision to offer the Danish Jews a safe haven. Bagges anteckningar, October 2, 1943, p. 950. Bagge complained that the cabinet had not been informed before the decision was taken. Leni Yahil in *The Rescue of the Danish Jewry* (Philadelphia, 1969) suggested that Sweden would not have made a public pronouncement except for pressure from Bohr and Ebbe Munck, p. 330. There is little material in Swedish archives to confirm Yahil's interpretation.

46. UD 1920, HP 1057, Richert to Grafström, October 14, 1943; and HP 1589, Günther speech, October 31, 1943. Another interesting element of the rescue of the Danish Jews was the question of who should pay for them during their stay in Sweden. The Danish minister in Washington, Henrik Kauffmann, offered as early as September 29 to pay their

The Danish episode showed Swedish officials that German authorities were not uniformly willing to enforce the Final Solution. Furthermore, it demonstrated that at least in 1943, not even Hitler would threaten Swedish security when Sweden acted in favor of the Jews, as long as Sweden remained relatively silent about what it was doing. The experience also gave Sweden much good will in the West.[47] Jewish organizations lionized the Swedish action, Western governments commended Sweden, and Sweden's value as a non-belligerent was further illustrated. The Swedish government sought new areas for a more active foreign policy.

Most important among Sweden's efforts were the attempts to establish peace between the Finns and the Russians. Sweden constantly sought ways to remove Finland from the war. But the longer Finland participated in a war against the U.S.S.R., the more the Swedes feared an extension of Soviet authority. While humanitarian efforts, including aid to Jews, were of less import, they still remained a part of a coherent policy to remain outside the conflict. The Swedes saw less reason to hide their Western biases, even if they still demonstrated great self-restraint.

As for aid to Jews, by 1944 much of Europe's Jewry had already been destroyed. The one major concentration of Jews in German hands was in Hungary. Nearly 800,000 remained in Hungary in the early spring of 1944. World attention focused on the plight of the Hungarian Jews in a way that it had not when the Jewish populations of Germany, the Low Countries, France, Austria, and Poland were sent to death. Even the American government had finally committed itself to aiding the Jews.

Secretary of the Treasury Henry Morgenthau was responsible for the establishment of the War Refugee Board in January 1944. Special agents, such as Iver Olsen, were appointed to initiate action. The WRB was probably more important as a signal to other nations than for the work it actually carried out. Its activities were always hamstrung by an administration that put "winning the war" above saving Jews.

Those authors who suggest Sweden's activities in Hungary were the direct product of WRB policy or international Jewish pressure are incorrect. Swedish policy depended primarily on Swedish initiatives and changing circumstances in Hungary. The Swedish goverment followed

---

costs. The Swedish government decided, however, to foot the entire bill themselves. PRO, FO 371, 36744, Expulsion of the Danish Jews, November 1943.

47. Ibid., FO 371, 37080, Note by Nutting [?], October 29, 1943, and 42752, Selbourne to Prytz, January 19, 1944.

events there with a grim fascination, and when opportunities arose, Swedish representatives in Budapest were quick to act. An activist Swedish policy was in effect long before Raoul Wallenberg set foot in Hungary.

The pattern of developments in Hungary was too complex to be covered fully here.[48] A simple outline of the chronology of events should underscore the three critical periods in 1944–1945: March–June; July–October 15; and October 15–January. In the first period, the Final Solution under Adolf Eichmann's direction was ruthlessly applied to Hungary. The second period witnessed a brief interlude when Hungary, under the leadership of Admiral Horthy, stopped the deportations. The third period began with a coup engineered by a fascist group, the Arrow Cross, and ended with the liberation of Budapest by the Soviet army. In each case, treatment of the remaining Jews of Budapest became a central issue. The end of the horrors of 1944 for Hungary's Jews came only with the liberation of Hungary by the Soviet armies. Additionally, as the year progressed, normal order was replaced by growing chaos. It was during the chaos of the fall that Raoul Wallenberg demonstrated his remarkable courage. Swedish policy, however, had begun to operate in May.

News of Eichmann's activities spread quickly around the world. The question was what to do to stop him. Few countries were capable of direct military intervention. Those who were — the United States and the Soviet Union — refused to commit needed manpower and materials. Roosevelt, for example, would not bomb the rail networks and facilities at Auschwitz despite good intelligence on the role of the camp.[49] In the first ten weeks of Eichmann's campaign, in April, May, and June, 600,000 Jews perished, mostly at Auschwitz. Alternatives to military intervention were unclear. Could outside pressure be brought to bear on the Hungarian government?

The Swedish Foreign Office records contain extensive details of events in Hungary. Of equal significance, both the prime minister and

---

48. See Randolph L. Braham, *The Politics of Genocide*, v. 2 (New York, 1981).

49. See Martin Gilbert, *Auschwitz and the Allies* (New York, 1981). Gilbert's view that the Allies did not understand that Auschwitz was a killing center is incorrect. Information about the killing process at Auschwitz began to reach the West in early 1943 and was continually reported from various sources until the complete documentation of the camp in the form of the "Auschwitz protocols" came to London in June 1944. The full story of Auschwitz and the Allies remains to be told.

Gustaf V read most of the important dispatches. Their "marks" can be found on nearly all the critical documents. The collection also indicates that the initiative for Swedish policy in Hungary was primarily, but not exclusively, in Budapest. Legation officials and a Swedish academic, Valdemar Langlet, tended to respond to conditions and opportunities as they found them. The Foreign Office served to approve and encourage their activities. In a couple of cases, the government in Stockholm took its own initiative. At the end of the year, the Foreign Office refused one important request of Minister Ivan Danielsson, who was head of the Swedish legation in Budapest.

Danielsson and Per Anger were the key figures representing Sweden in Hungary. Anger was the more energetic and imaginative of the two. As early as June, the Swedish legation began to use immigration visas and "protective passes" in attempts to provide some aid to persecuted Jews. Anger requested that Stockholm send additional personnel — a request that coincided with the appointment of Raoul Wallenberg.[50] Communication between Budapest and Stockholm frequently was slow. Legation officials had to act quickly. Sometimes considerable disparity existed between the official policy of Sweden and the actions of Swedish representatives in Hungary. Langlet, who ran an aid program for the Swedish Red Cross, took independent action including production of his own "protective passes" that the legation chose to honor. The friction that existed — in Budapest between various Swedes — and between Stockholm and Hungary — had little impact on the success of Sweden in helping Jews. At the outset, however, it was not clear that anyone could or would do anything to protect Hungary's Jews.

In the first period, Swedish policy took two different directions: experiments in devising documents to protect individual Jews; and initiation of a joint neutral rescue effort. This latter activity began as early as the first part of May. The initiative came from Budapest, but it also received strong support in Stockholm and other Western capitals. Likewise, the World Jewish Congress and other Jewish organizations encouraged all constructive efforts. The pace of action was terribly slow, and hundreds of thousands of Jews died.

By mid-June, little concrete action had been taken. International activity had focused on the Hungarian government and the hope that it could be encouraged to stop the German atrocities. With the govern-

---

50. UD 1920, HP 1095, Cabinet to Swedish Mission – Budapest, June 21, 1944.

ment's approval, King Gustaf sent a personal telegram to Admiral Horthy in late June pleading with him to stop the persecutions.[51] The action apparently stemmed from a reading of the now-famous "Auschwitz Protocols," which reached Stockholm on June 28. In early July, the Hungarian government halted the destruction of the Hungarian Jews. Most scholars have credited Gustaf's telegram as being of considerable importance in encouraging a change in Hungarian policies.

Given the warnings on the part of the United States and other belligerents to the Hungarian government, why would the appeal of a relatively powerless and aged king have any effect? The primary leverage that Sweden had in Hungary was the fact that Sweden represented Hungarian interests in many areas of the world during the war. Sweden had also helped Hungary in similar fashion in the Great War of 1914–1918. Relations between the two countries had often been intimate, and Hungary placed considerable weight on maintaining a good relationship. Furthermore, Gustaf had prestige among old-fashioned, conservative Europeans. Horthy appreciated Gustaf's appeal to a higher morality. There seems little doubt that Horthy, while no lover of Jews, repudiated German policy personally and wanted to maintain Hungarian independence in the face of increasing pressure from both Germany and Russia. He took a great risk in stopping the persecutions.

By July, only the approximately 200,000 Jews of Budapest remained in the country. In July and August, the attitude of the Hungarian government offered the neutrals — Sweden, Switzerland, Spain, Portugal, and the South American neutrals — an opportunity to act. The Hungarians indicated a willingness to respect virtually any document that purported to be a foreign passport or statement of responsibility. Under these conditions, pressure quickly mounted to inflate the number of such documents.

The Swedish experience is probably not dissimilar to the experience of the Swiss and other neutrals. The Swedes took the lead in most cases. The Swedish archives do not give the picture of a conscious policy slowly being put into place. Instead, the beginnings were quite exploratory. Legation officials first offered documents to individual applicants with identifiable connections, usually through family, with Sweden. Each application was sent to Stockholm for confirmation. Additionally, lists of

---

51. Ibid., HP 1095, Cabinet to Swedish Mission – Budapest, June 30, 1944. See Document Collection.

individuals were being sent from Stockholm — often from Swedish citizens. The process was slow and ineffectual, given the circumstances. The legation requested and was given permission to offer immigration visas and protective passes to certain categories of applicants. Later the categories were extended. By August, Stockholm officials worried primarily about the total number of documents. They believed that overly zealous activity to aid the Jews would lead to devaluation of the Swedish documents. Langlet had also designed his own documents and was busy helping people.[52] The legation, after the fact, had to confirm the legitimacy of his papers. In addition, as conditions deteriorated, special houses were established under Swedish "protection" to care for Jews. Neither in the cases of the documents nor the protected houses did Sweden have any idea whether its acts would be respected. A change in the Hungarian cabinet in late August seemed to Swedish diplomats a threat to all of Sweden's (and the other neutrals') work. For a few days, even Wallenberg feared his work would be undone.[53]

Raoul Wallenberg arrived in Budapest on July 9, 1944. His appointment was the product of the combined activities of the WRB, some key people in Stockholm, and the commitment of the Foreign Office and the government to give the Budapest mission new help. What Wallenberg provided was remarkable knowledge of Hungary, complete dedication, and a willingness to try almost anything if the situation demanded it. Wallenberg spoke Hungarian and German and had been active in business in the area. Educated in the United States, he belonged to Sweden's most influential banking family. When Wallenberg arrived in Budapest, the Swedes were already deeply involved in aid activities. He designed a more official-looking protective document, but most important, he provided renewed vigor and determination. He established a section of the consular division that became legendary in Budapest. Most of his immediate aides were volunteer Hungarian Jews. His first goal was to awaken the Jews to the possibilities of rescue and to break their lethargy, a task that he felt he had accomplished by late August.

A change in the Hungarian cabinet in late August seemed to endanger

---

52. See Valdemar Langlet, *Verk och dagar i Budapest* (Stockholm, 1946), Nina Langlet, *Kaos i Budapest* (Vällingby, 1982). Langlet began his activity in early May as had Swedish officials at the Budapest legation. See also UD 1920, HP 1096, Hellstedt to Danielsson, August 8, 1944; and Per Anger arkiv–Stockholm, Prince Carl to Langlet, August 17, 1944, and Prince Carl to Danielsson, August 29, 1944.

53. UD 1920, HP 1097, Danielsson to Swedish Foreign Office, August 28, 1944.

all Budapest Jews, regardless of whether they carried a foreign passport or lived in a "protected" house. The new government initially refused to recognize either the documents or the right of neutral missions to extend their territoriality. Both practices, incidentally, have little basis in international law. The Swedes, however, proved to be effective negotiators with the new government.

One of the main goals of the new Hungarian cabinet was international recognition. The willingness of the neutrals, and especially Sweden, to recognize the new government was a key to the establishment of their credibility. Danielsson advised Stockholm not to recognize the new government if it did not promise to accept the validity of all Swedish documents issued to Jews in Hungary. Stockholm concurred and Danielsson was able to get the new government to promise, in exchange for Swedish recognition, to leave "Swedish Jews" untouched.[54] This agreement made it possible for Wallenberg and Langlet to continue to operate effectively. It did not guarantee the safety of the Jews under Swedish protection, who by this time numbered close to 20,000, but it gave them hope.

After a reasonably quiet September, the situation once again deteriorated substantially. The Arrow Cross organization staged a coup, seized power, and tried to meet the demands of Germany to complete the Final Solution in Hungary. By this time Soviet troops were nearing Budapest and the whole situation was a race against time. Danielsson and his colleagues hoped to continue the same policy that they had pursued in August, i.e., an exchange of recognition for protection of "Swedish Jews." The Foreign Office refused, however, to give permission to recognize the new government. In fact, it indicated that it would not recognize the Arrow Cross regime. The situation for the mission in Budapest was further complicated by the Hungarian demand to move the legation personnel as the Russian troops neared the city. Stockholm issued instructions to Danielsson that the mission was to refuse to leave Budapest, that Sweden would not recognize the Hungarian government, and that Danielsson and his staff were to do everything in their power to help the Jews.[55]

---

54. Anger Arkiv, Danielsson to Engzell, September 14, 1944. UD 1920, HP 1092, Cabinet to Swedish Legation – Budapest, October 19, 1944.

55. Ibid., Cabinet to Swedish Mission–Budapest, November 16, 1944, and Swedish Foreign Office to Swedish Mission–Budapest, December 5, 1944, and von Post to Danielsson, December 13, 1944.

At first glance, the Stockholm instructions appear to be an exercise in futility. How could the legation protect its Jews if it had nothing to bargain with? The Foreign Office believed, however, that the term of the new regime would be brief, that it would be eager enough to deal with mission officials on a semi-official basis, and that it would not violate Sweden's diplomatic immunity. The policy perhaps made sense politically and intellectually, but legation officials had to deal with the growing violence against "Swedish Jews."

Bands of Hungarian thugs and German officials began to round up Jews for shipment to Auschwitz. The struggle to protect them was carried on at two levels: diplomatically and in the streets. In the streets Wallenberg demonstrated his mettle. Numerous incidents occurred where he bluffed various groups out of taking Jews away. He also traveled to places where Jews were being detained, and in some cases to the actual railway cars, to save the "Swedish Jews." He was remarkably successful in his brazen acts and undoubtedly encouraged others to protect "their" Jews. Rumor had it that Eichmann ordered Wallenberg's assassination.[56]

Danielsson's hands were tied but the members of the legation, and Wallenberg in particular, continued to function effectively. Wallenberg's most spectacular contributions came in November and December. He succeeded in rescuing Jews already in the clutches of the Arrow Cross and the Germans. He also established contact with the new regime and attempted to impress upon it that the world would judge it on how it treated its Jews. The Swedes succeeded in the main in protecting their Jews until the Russians liberated Budapest in January 1945. Some 20,000 Jews were directly under Swedish protection — half, approximately, carrying papers issued by Wallenberg's operation at the mission, and half under Swedish Red Cross auspices, led by Langlet and Asta Nilsson. Probably tens of thousands of other Jews were saved by Swedish action.

When the Russian troops arrived in Budapest, Raoul Wallenberg went with his chauffeur to meet with them. They were arrested on January 17, 1945, and Wallenberg's fate has been unclear since. The Soviet Union claimed first that he had been killed shortly thereafter; later, they suggested that he died in prison in 1948. Survivors of the Soviet gulag released into the West have brought information that suggest that nei-

---

56. Ibid., Danielsson to Swedish Foreign Office, December 15, 1944.

ther Soviet version was correct. Swedish, American, and Jewish demands that the Soviet Union clarify Wallenberg's fate have been met by Russian refusals. Wallenberg has become a symbol and a hero both as a non-Jew who made every conceivable effort to help Jews and as an innocent victim of Soviet policy. Despite a remarkably large outpouring of popular literature in recent years, many critical details of Wallenberg's mission in Hungary remain unexamined.

Who had the idea to send Wallenberg to Budapest? The earliest document related to sending a special emissary to Hungary to help Jews is a letter from Norbert Masur to Rabbi Ehrenpreis, dated April 18, 1944. Masur was a leading figure in the Stockholm congregation, a founding member of the Swedish section of the World Jewish Congress, and a German Jewish refugee. His proposal was to find "a personable, intelligent, reputable, non-Jew" who would be willing to travel both to Rumania and Hungary and to lead a rescue operation of Jews. Masur noted that a "few hundred Jews" could be saved if the right man could be found, if the mission have the support of the Swedish Foreign Office, and if proper economic resources were provided. He estimated the last item the least difficult because of aid from the United States. He also doubted there would be any difficulty with the Swedish Foreign Office and even conceived of the possibility of a "limited number of provisional passports" being issued to Jews. The most critical thing, according to Masur, was time.[57]

This letter provides clear indication that the idea of a rescue mission took form remarkably early in the context of Eichmann's application of the Final Solution to Hungary. Apparently Masur was dissuaded from pursuing the plan in April by "some very influential politicians" and instead sought the aid of Archbishop Erling Eidem to have an appeal of the Swedish Lutheran Church sent to its Hungarian counterpart. The request for an appeal was denied.[58] In early May, Koloman Lauer, a Hungarian Jewish businessman resident in Stockholm, asked the Swedish Foreign Office to rescue his parents. Lauer's partner was Raoul Wallenberg; Lauer also served on a refugee committee with Norbert Masur. The Lauer-Wallenberg firm was located in the same building where Iver Olsen, the War Refugee Board representative, had his office.

---

57. Sweden, Mosaiskt Församlingsarkiv, Marcus Ehrenpreis samling, Norbert Masur to Marcus Ehrenpreis, April 18, 1944.

58. WRB, 34, Hungary 1, Memorandum of July 1944, unsigned but probably written by Gillel Storch or Norbert Masur. See Document Collection.

In late May, Olsen asked the Swedish Foreign Office for assistance in aiding Jews in Hungary. He received a positive reply, although it is unclear from the documents exactly why Olsen made the proposal at this particular time. It appears as though he had an idea to send a "Swedish businessman" in a "private capacity" to rescue Jews. Circumstantial evidence indicates that he had already fixed upon Raoul Wallenberg.[59] It seems likely that Lauer and Masur had suggested Wallenberg to Olsen.[60]

On June 9, Olsen met with Secretary General Boheman and suggested that Sweden increase its diplomatic staff in its Budapest legation in order to save Jews and gather more information. Boheman agreed. Two days later, Olsen had dinner with Wallenberg "for purposes of exploring the possibilities and to ascertain in some measure his capabilities along those lines." Wallenberg's name was then forwarded to the Foreign Office by Sven Salén, an influential businessman.[61] Wallenberg was officially appointed on June 20. What were his instructions?

Although the Swedish government appointed Wallenberg, they did not provide him with any clear instructions as to what he should do beyond some general commitment to help Jews. Obviously, Lauer had made some suggestions to Wallenberg, but the latter sought advice in other quarters, in particular from another Hungarian refugee, W. Boehm. Boehm worked for the British and Olsen reported that he was a "leftist" and "a former minister of war" in Hungary. According to British documents, by the time Wallenberg talked with Boehm, he had a good idea that he would need money from Hungarian sources and a list of Hungarians willing to aid his efforts. Wallenberg also talked of the idea of a special camp for Jews in Budapest under direct Swedish protection. Boehm supplied some of the information Wallenberg required.[62] On

59. Ibid., Box 111, "Summary Report of Activities of WRB with Respect to the Jews in Hungary," no date, p. 9, May 25–26, 1942. Hugo Valentin, op. cit., stated that Dr. Lauer recommended Wallenberg to Olsen on May 15, p. 240–241. Eugene Levai in *Black Book on the Martyrdom of Hungarian Jewry* (Zurich, 1948) made a similar claim, p. 32–33. Gillel Storch has suggested that it was the proposal of the Swedish section of the World Jewish Congress (WJC) to send Wallenberg to Budapest. Gillel Storch, "Insatser av WJC:s sektion," *Judisk Krönika* 31 (1962), p. 137.

60. WRB, Box 111, Johnson to Secretary of State, June 12, 1944, and Box 34, Johnson to Secretary of State, June 9, 1944.

61. Ibid., Box 34, Hungary 1, Memorandum of July 1944.

62. WRB, Box 35, Olsen to Pehle, June 16, 1944. Boehm (Böhm) had indeed been former defense mininster as well as commander-in-cheif of the Red Army. A moderate

June 29, Wallenberg requested that "he would like full instructions as to the lines of activities he is authorized to carry out and assurances of adequate financial support . . ." from the War Refugee Board.[63] How is this request to be interpreted?

At first glance, it would appear as though Wallenberg conceived of himself as an agent of the War Refugee Board operating in Hungary. Olsen certainly believed this to be the case and eventually furnished Wallenberg with a set of instructions and provided 200,000 Swedish kronor from the American Joint Distribution Committee. Wallenberg's perception appears, however, to be considerably different. He seems to have been neither an exclusive agent of the WRB nor a Swedish diplomat sent to aid Jews. Rather, he believed that he had been appointed to do whatever he could for the Jews and that all interested parties in Stockholm relied upon his imagination and initiative. When he arrived in Budapest, he found the Swedish legation already active in trying to help Jews and showing great sympathy for anything that he wished to do. Per Anger, in particular, served with Wallenberg with distinction.

What reasons might the Russians have had for Wallenberg's arrest? Many have speculated on the reasons for their actions. Explanations span a spectrum from reasons related to the Wallenbergs' prominence as the most powerful capitalist family in Sweden to bureaucratic error. A number of neutral diplomats were arrested in Eastern Europe in the wake of the forward thrust of the Soviet armies. Wallenberg also seemed to have been involved in discussions for postwar reconstruction of Hungary which may have roused Russian suspicions. Most of the non-Hungarian monies used by Wallenberg were funneled through Olsen in Stockholm to special accounts in Switzerland.[64] Olsen's primary responsibility in Stockholm was neither as a representative of the U.S. Treasury nor of the WRB but as an agent for the American intelligence organization, OSS. Olsen's intelligence work apparently involved him in much activity in the Baltic area where the Russians were very displeased by U.S. and Swedish policies.[65] Did the Russians know of Olsen's OSS connections and Boehm's British

socialist, Boehm presumably had sought refuge in Sweden because of his Jewish ancestry. See Arno J. Mayer, *Politics and Diplomacy of Peacemaking* (New York, 1967), p. 530.

63. Ibid., Box 111, Johnson to Secretary of State, June 29, 1944.

64. UD 1920, HP 1092, Raoul Wallenberg Memorandum, September 29, 1944, and Grafström Memorandum to Stockholms Enskilda Bank, October 12, 1944.

65. WRB, Henry J. Morgenthau diaries, 712:8, March 20, 1944; Ibid., 50, "OSS," O'Dwyer to Penrose, September 12, 1945; and Ibid., Report of Iver Olsen, November 22, 1944, p. 11.

ties? It is impossible at this writing to know. The Soviet Union has opted to allow the Wallenberg case to fester.

As the Hungarian episode ground to its conclusion, a new effort began that was to lead to the rescue of thousands of Jews held in German concentration camps. This effort has been known as the Bernadotte Mission, and it too is the subject of much controversy. Swedes view Folke Bernadotte, who was the king's nephew and vice chairman of the Swedish Red Cross, as a bona fide war hero who saved thousands of Jewish lives, only to be assassinated by members of the Stern gang in 1947 during his efforts to mediate the Middle East crisis for the U.N. The British historian Hugh Trevor-Roper has suggested that Bernadotte deserves none of the credit for the rescue of the Jews in 1945. Trevor-Roper argues that Felix Kersten, Himmler's masseur, deserves primary credit. Bernadotte is accused of being a bureaucratic nonentity and an anti-Semite, uninterested in the fate of the Jews.

Obviously, attempts to understand the Bernadotte Mission have been complicated by the history of Israel and a confusing welter of documents that surfaced in the fifties. No single person deserves the credit for the success of the Bernadotte Mission. It was the product of the efforts of many forces, not the least of which were the driving ambitions of the Norwegian representative in Stockholm, Niels Christian Ditleff. A full analysis of the rescue effort can be found in chapter 4.

To understand why the Bernadotte Mission took the form and shape that it did, it is necessary to follow parallel developments. One main effort — primarily a product of Norwegian initiative and Swedish Foreign Office efforts — was to rescue Scandinavians. The other development — led through the WJC representative in Stockholm, Gillel Storch, and through the offices first of Felix Kersten and then of Bernadotte — was directed toward helping Jews. Both activities had to have the full support of the Swedish government. Both were finally dependent on the larger circumstances of the progress of the war, Himmler's ambitions, the effectiveness of the Swedish Red Cross, and specifically on the abilities of Folke Bernadotte.

The priority given to the rescue of Scandinavians by the Swedish government and the Swedish Red Cross should not be seen as a lack of interest or concern about Jews, but simply for what it was — a sense of priorities. Sweden had continuously placed the interests of its Scandinavian brethren second after Swedish security concerns in its foreign policy priorities. Sweden cared for large numbers of Scandinavian refugees. In April 1945, 128,288 of the 185,000 refugees in Sweden were Scandinavians. The refugee population was nearly 3 percent of the total population. For the Bernadotte Mission what was critical was Sweden's willingness to act with dispatch and with men and materials. The risks were not small.

When it became apparent that Himmler would permit a Swedish Red Cross mission to enter Germany, two serious risks had to be evaluated: the possibility that Himmler's order would be countermanded and endanger the rescuers; and the likelihood that the mission would come under direct Allied fire. During the rescue operations Swedish vehicles were hit and lives were lost.

Both Kersten and Bernadotte traveled to Berlin to negotiate with Himmler. The two negotiations complemented one another and continued attempts were made to coordinate them. Evidence in Swedish archives suggests that Himmler responded to the variety of the Swedish requests and their apparent urgency with ever-expanding concessions. Also, Himmler grew more bold, less afraid of Hitler's retaliation, as Allied armies continued their progress into Germany.

Initially agreements with Bernadotte to allow the collection of all Scandinavian inmates in one camp in Germany and with Kersten to release 1,000 Jews were changed to permit their transshipment to Sweden in unspecified numbers. The exact total of Jews rescued and sent to Sweden is yet to be tallied. Many of these people would have died had they not received the care provided by the Swedes. These latter changes, which were responsible for the largest portion of rescued Jews, were almost exclusively the product of Bernadotte's negotiations and the chaotic conditions at the camps when the Red Cross mission arrived.

One additional effort should be noted. In late April, Norbert Masur, a Swedish Jew, flew to Germany accompanied by Kersten to negotiate with Himmler on behalf of the WJC and specifically to reaffirm Himmler's earlier promises. The meeting, quite dramatic in itself, provided little new, but it certainly must have encouraged Himmler to make concessions. One other person contributed to the success of the Bernadotte Mission: Walter Schellenberg, Himmler's top aide. Schellenberg handled the organizational details on the German side of the rescue attempts. One need not condone Schellenberg's role in Nazi Germany, but to ignore the importance of his work in the face of active attempts of others within the SS to sabotage the mission would be to underestimate the practical difficulties that blocked realization of the project. Bernadotte's gratitude to Schellenberg went so far that he provided Schellenberg with shelter in Sweden immediately after the war and testified on his behalf at his trial in Nuremberg. Many have tried to take these latter activities on Schellenberg's behalf as proof of Bernadotte's anti-Semitism. Reasons for his behavior were to be found in the help Schellenberg provided under precarious circumstances.

The success of the Bernadotte Mission stands alongside the Swedish activities in Hungary and the rescue of the Danish Jews as the most significant efforts of the Swedish government to aid Jews during the war. There were other efforts of a less spectacular nature that deserve mention. Under the leadership of Gillel Storch, large quantities of food were sent to Jewish inmates in German camps beginning in 1944. Some Finnish and Baltic Jews found asylum in Sweden during the war. Private Swedish institutions, most significantly the Swedish Lutheran Church, tried various ways to aid Jews. The various Jewish congregations also sent considerable aid to their co-religionists.

The total number of Jews helped by Sweden can be estimated at approximately 45,000. There were undoubtedly more who were indirectly aided, especially in Hungary. The figure can be seen as either an impressively large one or a pitifully small one. Prior to the war Sweden ignored, or even actively rejected, the possibilities of taking in significant numbers of Jewish refugees. Only after 1942 did Sweden seriously begin to seek ways to help Jews. It was late — very late.

Many factors contributed to a more active Swedish policy. It was partially a question of responding to the values upon which the Swedish state rested, partially a desire to help fellow Scandinavians, and partially an attempt to justify Sweden's non-belligerency to the Western powers by providing "useful services." Swedes knew what had happened. They were not sympathetic toward Nazi Germany and they abhorred the Final Solution. But Sweden was a small country, and its leadership and its traditions did not encourage it to play an active role in the politics of the war. There was a built-in conservatism in their policies. Risk-taking was minimized. Only slowly did Swedes develop a policy for actively aiding Scandinavian and European Jews. The success of this policy once in operation illustrated both that Sweden cared and that something could be done.

Chapter 3

"Between Chairs" — A Case Study of an Institutional Response to the Persecution of the Jews, 1933–1945

To understand the Swedish response to the experience of Europe's Jews, 1933–1945, it is not sufficient to examine government policy alone. Governmental actions related to "the Jewish Question" frequently depended upon the attitudes of major institutions and public opinion within the country. The government, especially individual ministers such as Gustav Möller, minister of social welfare, appeared more willing to help Jewish refugees than the larger body politic or the public in general. Public opinion was a product of cultural and intellectual tradition and preference as well as of contemporary institutional influences such as the press, political parties, the church, etc., and limited the government's ability to respond to the ever-increasing pressure on the Jews. The behavior of these contemporary institutions — in this essay, the Lutheran state church — illustrated how "the Jewish Question" often posed a variety of conflicting issues for institutional leaders. Just as government officials found themselves caught between the supposed security needs of Sweden and a desire to serve humanitarian goals, so too institutions such as the Lutheran church found themselves caught "between chairs"[1] — an attempt to maintain in a period of crisis tradi-

---

1. Svenska Israelsmissionens arkiv (Uppsala) (Known hereafter as SIM arkiv), Volume 37, Pernow to Bishop Ysander, May 4, 1943.

tional attitudes and policies which with regard to things Jewish were hardly affirmative, and a feeling that in the hour of greatest danger for Jews, Christians should condemn and oppose racial violence. One example of how church officials found themselves trying to define a defensible position was two letters written by Archbishop Erling Eidem within a three-week period in late 1942.

The first letter was a response to criticism voiced by a Swedish parishioner of the church's silence in the face of growing evidence that Germany was killing Europe's Jews and evidence that a similar fate now awaited Norway's Jews. Eidem wrote on November 27:

> I can not share your belief that Christians in our country have remained silent when faced with un-Christian anti-Semitism and the results it has produced. . . .[2]

In early December, Eidem received a request from English ecumenical leader William Paton for Eidem to make a public appeal in Germany to stop the persecution of the Jews. Eidem refused and argued in his letter of December 16 to Paton that his silence would serve a greater Christian purpose:

> And for the part of the neutral countries, Switzerland and Sweden, I think it is much wiser, that their voices be spared for the future, for the time when the world war is coming to an end. I may assure you, that this my opinion is not determined by cowardliness but by an honest desire to be an instrument for reconciliation and goodwill.[3]

What follows here is an examination of the response of the Swedish Lutheran church to the "Jewish problem."

Actually, this essay focuses on two elements of the Lutheran church: the behavior of Archbishop Eidem and *Svenska Israelsmissionen* (SIM). As the Lutheran church was not a hierarchical institution, it is formally incorrect to claim that the archbishop's policies represent the church as a whole. Individual believers, individual pastors, had the right to hold their own views without reference to an official church policy. Nonetheless, the archbishop was the single most important figure in the church and a visible public figure. Eidem tried to represent the church to Swedish society. His public behavior was to a great extent conditioned by his perception of the responsibilities of the leader of the state

---

2. Eidems arkiv, Eidem to Hjorth-Andersen, November 27, 1942.
3. Ibid., Eidem to Dr. William Paton, December 16, 1942.

church. In this sense, his views, especially in the context of how the church should respond officially to persecution of the Jews, can be considered representative of "the church's response." Moreover, the examination of Eidem's policies offers a unique opportunity to view the personal dilemmas regarding these questions that a leading Christian spokesman struggled with. *Svenska Israelsmissionen* was even more directly involved in the "Jewish problem." Its sole purpose was to convert Jews to Lutheranism, and it served as the church's "experts" on matters related to the Jews. Both the press and the Swedish government consulted with SIM on the church's policies with regard to the Jews.

The Swedish Lutheran Church was an important Protestant organization. Over 95 percent of Sweden's citizens were members. Its leaders had been active in ecumenical affairs and were intimately associated with the German Evangelical Church. During the war, church leaders served as a conduit for information and attempts at peacemaking between the belligerents. As regards the "Jewish problem," what emerges was a dualism: a clear recognition on the part of most church leaders that Hitler's anti-Semitism challenged Christian faith fundamentally, and a hesitancy to act publicly and forcefully against Hitler. This hesitancy to speak out clearly depended upon a number of factors: the church's traditional attitude toward politics; its ties with the Swedish government; its hostility to the Soviet Union; its connections with the Lutherans of Germany, especially the so-called Confessional Church; and a historic antagonism to Judaism.

Sweden became a Lutheran country in stages beginning in the sixteenth century. Its first modern king, Gustavus Vasa, broke with the Church of Rome primarily for economic and political reasons. Swedes converted less dramatically, and it was only in the seventeenth century that Sweden became a Lutheran bastion. By 1686, a lasting relationship between the church and the monarchy was firmly established. The king served as head of the state church. Even after the process of democratization in the nineteenth and early twentieth centuries, the government — not a religious figure — remained responsible for its activities. The minister of ecclesiastical affairs, Gösta Bagge, leader of the Conservative Party, held primary authority over church matters during most of the war.[4]

---

4. Bagge's influence was primarily financial. The Swedish parliament provided funds for the operation of the church.

The organization of the church itself was complex. No national governing body existed. The country was divided into dioceses, each with its own bishop and internal organization. The archbishop of Sweden 1931–1950, Erling Eidem, also sat as the leader of the Uppsala diocese. The Church Meeting was the highest religious institution of the church. Its annual gatherings had sixty representatives, half ordained officials, including the bishops, and half elected members of the various dioceses. The archbishop sat as chairman. The Church Meeting could propose changes in the laws of the church. Its decisions, however, were not binding on the government. The parliament retained ultimate authority.

Despite limitations on the independence of the church, the archbishop was the spiritual leader of Sweden. It was he who set the tone of the church's behavior. Eidem's predecessor, Nathan Söderblom, had led the church through a period of exciting reformism that included major ecumenical activities and attempts to break some of the formalism which had dominated the church. Eidem sought to continue Söderblom's work and to maintain the traditionally close relationship with the German Evangelical Church during its trials during the Nazi period.

That Swedish church officials drew inspiration and intellectual sustenance from Germany should be hardly surprising. "Until approximately 1933, Swedish theology was unambiguously and one-sidedly German-oriented."[5]

Germany was, after all, the homeland of Luther. In general, Swedish cultural and intellectual life was dominated by German influence and German values. Swedish church leaders had intimate personal and institutional contacts with their German counterparts. Most of them shared the political conservatism of German colleagues.[6] The crisis which Hitler's rise to power produced for the German Evangelical Church in turn challenged the Swedish church, particularly Eidem, to

5. Ingun Montgomery, "Den svenska linjen är den kristna linjen. Kyrkan i Sverige under kriget," in *Kirken, Krisen og Krigen*, ed. by Stein Ugelvik Larsen and Ingun Montgomery (Bergen, 1982), p. 354. (Known hereafter as *Kirken*).

6. Frederick Bonkovsky, "The German State and Protestant Elites," in *The German Church Struggle and the Holocaust*, ed. by Franklin Littell and Hubert Locke (Detroit, 1974), p. 129. Bonkovsky estimated that 80% of the Lutheran clergy belonged to parties of the right. See also Robert Ericksen, *Theologians Under Hitler* (New Haven, 1985) and John Conway, *The Nazi Persecution of the Churches 1933–1945* (London, 1968).

respond in a way that was both consonant with its own doctrines and its desire to sustain a German connection.

Hitler wanted to cleanse the German church of Jewish influence. But he also hoped to avoid open conflict with the other Christian churches. The concordat with the Vatican, signed in July 1933, provided opportunities for Hitler to authenticate his regime among German Catholics who had been less susceptible to National Socialism than German Protestants.[7] In early September 1933, the Evangelical Church of the Old Prussian Union adopted the so-called Aryan paragraph. It meant that clergymen must be of Aryan descent and married to wives of Aryan descent. This attempt by pro-Nazi elements within the German Lutheran churches to cleanse Christian sects of Jewish influence produced an immediate crisis.

Led by Martin Niemöller, clergymen who objected to this type of political intervention in religious matters organized the Pastors' Emergency League. The German Evangelical Church divided. One group, the German Christians, supported the regime and its attempts to rid Germany of Jewish influences. Another group, the Confessional Church, refused to accept the Aryan paragraph. With the Declaration of Barmen in 1934, pastors unsympathetic to the German Christians pledged to uphold traditional Lutheran values and practices. Of the 18,184 Evangelical clergymen in Germany in 1934, approximately 20.8 percent of them sided with the Confessional Church.[8] A third group, the "intact churches," maintained a local autonomy and independence from either organization.

The revolt that led to the creation of the Confessional Church was a religious reaction to a politically-motivated intervention. Clergymen of the Confessional Church were overwhelmingly conservative and patriotic. Niemöller was a decorated war hero who longed for strong nationalistic leadership. He, and others, were anxious to cooperate with the Nazis. Rarely can one find expressions of open hostility to Hitler such as the following by Dietrich Bonhoeffer:

> If we claim to be Christians there is no room for expediency. Hitler is the anti-Christ. Therefore we must go on with our work and eliminate him whether he is successful or not.[9]

---

7. Ernst C. Helmreich, *The German Churches under Hitler* (Detroit, 1979), p. 244.
8. Wilhelm Niemöller, in "The Niemöller Archives," in Littell, op. cit., p. 53.
9. Franklin Littell, "Church Struggle and the Holocaust," in ibid., p. 14.

The reaction of Confessional Church leaders was not purely a response to state intervention. There had been a close relationship between German states and the Evangelical churches. Among most clergymen, it was accepted that the churches had certain state-supporting functions and therefore state decisions could even affect church policy. The Protestant clergy was fully integrated into the political and economic elites of modern Germany. The reaction of the Confessional clergy to the adoption of the Aryan paragraph was more fundamental. They believed that a basic tenet of Christianity — the act of conversion — had been challenged:

> . . . it was the Jewish problem which revealed in inexorable seriousness the incompatibility of Christianity with the new pseudoreligion. Here evasion became impossible. Even the most superficial connection to Christianity could not tolerate the idea that a baptized Jew be excluded from the parish.[10]

It was the fate of the "Jewish Christians" that moved clergymen to found the Confessional Church. There was always to be a distinction between Jews and Jewish Christians. Jewish Christians were estimated to number approximately 98,000 in Germany proper, including a few members of the clergy.[11]

The majority of Lutherans remained with the German Christians since there was a majority of clergymen who stayed loyal to the regime. One should not oversimplify the situation. Hitler's popularity grew in the first years of his rule. Few wanted to appear treasonous. Even when clergymen opposed Hitler on religious grounds, except for Jehovah's Witnesses, they anxiously separated such opposition from political agitation.[12] The Swedish church followed these developments carefully; Archbishop Eidem sided immediately and consistently with the Confessional Church.

As with many other leading Swedish figures, Eidem found himself in an awkward position after January 31, 1933. Closely tied to German culture and the Evangelical Church and politically conservative, Eidem

---

10. Ferdinand Friedensburg, "On Nazism and the Church Struggle," in ibid., p. 249.
11. Helmreich, op. cit., p. 330.
12. Beate von Oppen, *Religion and Resistance to Nazism* (Princeton, 1971), p. 17. Twenty-five percent of the German Jehovah's Witnesses were killed. Resistance to Hitler among some clergy grew in the late thirties. Such resistance rarely took the form of open political agitation.

feared that Hitler's regime would undermine both the position of the church in Germany and Germany's standing in the community of nations. He, like King Gustaf V, believed that Hitler's anti-Semitic activity would isolate Germany. In April 1933, the King visited Berlin to lecture Hitler in front of President Hindenburg on the subject. Eidem waited a year before he, too, visited the German chancellor to warn him of the damage done to Germany by the anti-Semitic policies of the government.[13] Throughout the thirties, Eidem tried to use whatever leverage he had to modify, temper, or eliminate anti-Semitic influences in the German Evangelical Church; yet Eidem also tried to avoid isolating the German church. He accepted the post of chairman of the Luther Academy in Sonderhausen in 1934, and remained in that post until 1943. He received much criticism both in Sweden and within the ecumenical movement on this matter. He was accused of allowing the Nazis to use his position for propaganda purposes.[14]

Certainly, Eidem was not sympathetic to the Nazis. His position within the Swedish church was, however, quite complicated. There were elements within the church that sympathized openly with the New Germany. These groups could be found anywhere in Sweden, but the diocese in Göteborg, the second largest city, seemed to be their center. The diocese journal, *Göteborgs Stifts-Tidning*, argued that Hitler was a good Christian, criticized democratic values, and equated godless Bolshevism with Judaism. Under Ivar Rhedin's editorship, the journal maintained its support of Hitler throughout the war and even into the immediate postwar period. Rhedin's active hostility toward Jews stemmed from a traditional Christian antagonism toward Judaism mixed with measures of sympathy for National Socialism and hostility to Communism.[15] While no scholar has attempted to identify the depth of support such ideas had among the Swedish clergy, Eidem suspected that it was widespread. In 1941, he wrote:

> Something that is even more worrisome and more serious than such a large number of our colleagues who do not understand what is going on . . . I am not thinking about the masses of anonymous letters I receive from different people because of my speeches against racial persecution, a decline in people's belief in God, etc. I am not thinking either of the

---

13. *Kirken*, p. 298.
14. Ibid., pp. 354–355. See also, Helmreich, op. cit., p. 147.
15. *Kirken*, p. 295–296.

showers of criticism that I receive from Nazi newspapers or leaflets. What
really hurts me deeply is that my own colleagues attack me personally in
such bitter tones. Unfortunately it appears the case that a pro-Nazi attitude (including anti-Semitism and worshiping Mars) is not unusual among
the clergy. . . . [16]

If pro-Nazi influences within the church bothered the archbishop,
other elements wanted a more critical policy toward German totalitari-
anism and anti-Semitism. Some bishops, including Gustav Aulén, held
such views. *Kristen Gemenskap*, the journal of the Ecumenical Council
in Sigtuna, often served as their publication. [17] More frequently, pastors
simply spoke out in their sermons. In 1941, for example, Folke
Holmström, the pastor of Linköping's cathedral, gave a sermon, "Christian Duty toward the Jews," in which he minced no words on the need to
help Jews:

> The situation in Europe is now such that those who wish to confess their
> Christianity must in reality demonstrate their belief by supporting the
> interests of the Jews in defiance of what is happening at this moment. [18]

Eidem chose to follow a moderate course. At a general political level,
he argued that politics had no place in the church. He wrote to the
bishop of Lund, Edvard Rohde, in 1939: ". . . the mixing of politics and
Christianity is for me an abomination unrelated to whether the politics
is totalitarian or democratic." [19] As archbishop, he saw it as his duty to
keep party politics outside the church:

> I have tried for my part in my preaching to avoid politicization or party
> positions and instead have kept myself concentrated on Christian reli-
> gious issues. . . . I regret when political speeches are given during ser-
> mons, whether they serve one country or another. Countries are sinners,
> just as individuals. God alone can judge their heart's intent. [20]

Yet like the Confessional Church, he would not tolerate racism.
Examples abound of Eidem's attempt to limit the clergy's anti-
Semitism. In early 1942, for instance, Eidem wrote a parish priest,
Ernst Ålander, that he wanted an explanation of Ålander's anti-Semitic

16. Eidem arkiv, Eidem to Dr. J. Lindskog, September 3, 1941.
17. *Kirken*, p. 356.
18. *Missionstidning för Israel* 69 (May 1941), p. 131.
19. Sweden, Edvard Rohde arkiv (Lund), Eidem to Rohde, April 25, 1939.
20. Eidem arkiv, Eidem to Britta Andersson, January 16, 1941.

sermons. Despite Ålander's claim that he was not anti-Semitic, simply interested in "race biology" and history, Eidem responded, "Race hate is a crime against Christianity. I must clearly criticize anti-Semitic acts as they conflict with our Lord's nature." To reinforce his point, Eidem made a formal visit to Ålander's parish.[21] The episode illustrated Eidem's values, but it was also done quietly and privately.

The archbishop was, after all, a civil servant. He was responsible to the sitting government. Once the war began, Eidem needed to work with Gösta Bagge, whose personal political views probably coincided quite well with Eidem's. The task of the coalition government was to keep Sweden out of the war. All elements of the government were expected to participate in this task, including the church. Eidem played his part in these efforts. For example, in early 1942 during German attacks on the Norwegian Lutheran Church, which produced much resentment in Sweden both among the lay public and the clergy, Eidem tried to dampen public criticism. He wrote to Bishop Aulén that the reason why such comments must be limited was because of the precarious strategic circumstances in which Sweden found itself:

> The situation is really very serious. I believe that it is a patriotic duty for each of us to weigh our words with the greatest care. . . . This does not mean cowardliness, nor coercion against conscience or belief.[22]

When initiatives from Britain and the United States for various forms of intervention in Germany came directly to Eidem, he resisted involvement. The policy of the Swedish government was to tread gently on issues related to Germany. Eidem supported this policy, as can be seen in the Norwegian church struggle.

Yet another political motivation affected Eidem's reluctance to be more critical of Germany: animosity toward the Soviet Union. Fear of Russia was traditional in Sweden. Hostility toward the Soviet Union was endemic among nearly all Swedes. Within the church, godless Bolshevism was seen as the primary threat to Christian Europe. Eidem constantly received letters from laymen and clergy complaining that his public attacks on Germany's racism ignored the greater danger of Com-

---

21. Ibid., Eidem to Ernst Ålander, January 16, February 6, and September 30, 1942, and Ålander to Eidem, January 22, 1942.

22. Gustav Aulén arkiv, Eidem to Aulén, February 28, 1942.

munism.[23] Eidem shared much of these criticisms privately. He feared that Great Britain and the United States had too closely embraced the Soviet Union. He believed that churchmen such as George Bell, Bishop of Chichester, underestimated the threat of Bolshevism:

> With the worst pain possible, do I observe how English and Americans do not keep their eyes open for the deadly danger of Bolshevism.
> One suffers the Balticum under its German occupation, which, however, is by far preferable to the atheistic Soviet regime. My heart cramps thinking of the fate of the Balticum states, if they should again come under the heel of the Russian.[24]

This deep-seated hatred of the Soviet Union led the Swedish church into its most dubious wartime activity, proselytism in German-occupied Eastern Europe. Missionary organizations nominally were independent institutions under the authority of the Church Meeting. They normally had a governing board headed by one of Sweden's bishops. In reality, they were responsive to the concerns of the archbishop. A mission, *Church Under the Cross* headed by Lars Wollmer, had Eastern Europe as its traditional area of activity. A religiously diverse region, the establishment of the Soviet Union and its intolerance of religions restricted the activities of all religious institutions. After the German invasion of the Soviet Union in June 1941 and the initial German successes, new opportunities arose for missionary work. Organizations such as *Church Under the Cross* seized the opportunity to return to their work. But in order to do so, *Church Under the Cross* had to cooperate with the Nazi occupying authorities.

German policy in Eastern Europe after June 1941 can only be described as brutal. "Roving bands" of SS officials followed the troops eastward, butchering Jews and other undesirables. Over one million people were killed within a year. These activities did not occur in isolated areas. They frequently took place near major population centers and were visible to large numbers of people. It would not have been possible for missionaries in Eastern Europe not to know something about these policies. To undertake missionary activity in occupied Eastern Europe might be defensible on religious grounds, but politically it exposed *Church Under the Cross* to attacks in Swedish newspapers and sug-

---

23. See Eidem arkiv for examples, H. Mallgren to Eidem, December 3, 1942.

24. Ibid., Eidem to Dr. Ignas Scheynius, April 6, 1943, and Eidem to George Bell, undated August 1943.

gested that the church (hence, the government) condoned Nazi policies in the region.

These missionary activities became less tenable as conditions in Eastern Europe, particularly for the Jews, grew worse. Attacks by leading newspapers in Uppsala and Stockholm in late 1942 led Archbishop Eidem to warn Wollmer about his work and to advise that "our Swedish aid policy must be held as much as possible clear of the official German policy." Eidem noted that although the church had acted with a "clear conscience," it was necessary to clarify the situation.[25] Things only got worse for Eidem when the Crown Prince, the future Gustaf VI Adolf, privately attacked *Church Under the Cross* on the grounds that it was anti-Semitic. Wollmer responded to this accusation by claiming that *Church Under the Cross* was not anti-Semitic, only attempting to combat the "Jewish-Soviet," "Godless movement from Russia."[26] *Church Under the Cross* continued to function throughout the war and remained a major liability for the church.

Another Swedish church mission, *Svenska Israelsmissionen* (SIM), was even more directly involved in the "Jewish problem." Founded in the nineteenth century, its purpose was to convert Jews to Lutheranism. By the interwar period, its center of activities was Vienna, although its headquarters were in Stockholm. The experiences of SIM between 1933 and 1945 illustrated more clearly than did any other element within the church how the Swedish church responded to persecution of the Jews. SIM was directly, unavoidably involved in daily dealings with the "Jewish problem." Its director, Birger Pernow, functioned as Eidem's adviser on questions related to Jews. It operated longer in German-controlled Europe than any other similar mission. After 1941, when the United States entered the war, it established a special relationship with a number of American Protestant missions to Jews and ran some of their programs. Money forbidden by American law to be sent to German-controlled territories was laundered through SIM. SIM's own major congregation came under Nazi race laws with the *Anschluss* in 1938.

Caught between the traditional enmity of Viennese Jewish organizations and the hostility of the new regime in Austria, SIM tried to save its

---

25. Ibid., Eidem to Lars Wollmer, December 12, 1942.
26. Ibid., Eidem to Wollmer, February 4, 1943, and Wollmer to Eidem, February 20, 1943.

members. It negotiated with Adolf Eichmann, the Nazis' Jewish expert, to permit its members to emigrate to other countries. Marginally successful with its emigration projects, the bulk of SIM's congregation was deported along with the Jews of Vienna into the concentration camp system. Transferring their primary base of operations back to Stockholm, SIM developed a technique for tracing and monitoring, in a crude fashion, the fate of their parishioners. Throughout the war, they tracked the progress of the Final Solution. Their monthly magazine reportéd their activities. It was widely disseminated among leaders and clergy of the Swedish church. Despite public attacks by the chief rabbi of Sweden, SIM cooperated with the Stockholm Jewish congregation to fund the maintenance of approximately 30 Jews in Berlin during the last two years of the war. The experiences of *Svenska Israelsmissionen*, 1938–1945, exposed many of the dilemmas and prejudices of Christian churches when they became directly involved in the "Jewish problem."

Until 1938, SIM functioned in its traditional ways. It owned a number of buildings in the Austrian capital, including a large mission house in the Jewish quarter and an old people's home. Vienna was a fruitful ground for missionary work among the Jews. It was estimated that there were approximately 20,000 Catholics and Protestants in Vienna who were not Aryan.[27] Of these, 7–8,000 were Protestants left in Vienna after March 1938 under the care of *Svenska Israelsmissionen*. Much to the consternation of SIM officials in Vienna, the difference between Jews and Jewish Christians, at least in legal terms, had disappeared:

> The decisive issue is of which race one is a member — religion in this respect has no meaning. Therefore Christian Jews must of necessity leave the country.[28]

The equalization of Jews and Jewish Christians presented SIM with a number of problems. Its relations with Jewish organizations were not friendly. Forbidden to use Aryan facilities such as hospitals, Jewish

---

27. Göte Hedenquist, *Undan Förintelsen* (Kristianstad, 1983), p. 20. Hedenquist wrote this work many years after his service in Vienna. He used the archives of Svenska Israelsmissionen as well as published works. It is quite brief and ignores many of the most critical issues related to SIM activities. For a history of SIM, see Lars Edvardsson, *Kyrka och Judendom* (Lund, 1976).

28. SIM arkiv, "Allehanda," draft of 1939 annual report. For the purposes of this essay, the terms — Christian Jews, Hebrew Christians, and Jewish Christians — have been used interchangeably. The terms defined practicing Christians who were identified by German race laws as non-Aryans.

Christians found themselves caught in a situation where they were
rejected by official Austria and not acceptable to the Jewish community.
For medical treatment, Jewish Christians suddenly became dependent
on the Rothschild hospital. Jewish organizations were not interested in
helping Jewish Christians emigrate. There were more than enough difficulties for Jewish organizations to try to get the approximately 200,000
Jews out of Austria.

SIM in Vienna reorganized itself into three sections: A, B, and C. Section A, headed first by Göte Hedenquist and after 1940 by Johannes
Ivarsson, functioned as the central administrative and religious unit. It
directed individuals and problems to the other sections. And it sus-
tained the religious activities of the mission. Section B was a direct-help
organization. Its primary activity was the operation of a soup kitchen.
Approximately 125 people were cared for regularly, and its financial
demands were covered by the American Board of Missions to the Jews,
headed in New York by Josef Hoffman-Cohn. Section C dealt with emigration. In 1938–1939, the German government wanted the Jews to
leave and established Adolf Eichmann in Vienna to facilitate the process. Already in late 1938, Pastor Hedenquist met with Eichmann to confirm SIM's responsibility to help the Jewish Christians of Protestant
denominations to emigrate. A mission representative, usually a young
man, was placed in Eichmann's offices. They functioned to aid
cooperation between Eichmann and various emigration agencies and
allowed SIM to observe the activities of the much-feared Eichmann.[29]

As Germany encouraged Jewish emigration until the outbreak of the
war, the real problem facing SIM, as well as Jewish organizations, was
where to send their members. What would have been more natural for a
Swedish mission than to send its congregation to Sweden? Sweden was
not interested in becoming a major receiver of Jewish immigrants. Prior
to the *Anschluss*, few refugees viewed Sweden as an attractive homeland. By 1938, however, German, Austrian, and Czech Jews began to
apply for Swedish visas in numbers that frightened both the Swedish
government and certain sectors of the Swedish public. The Board of
Social Welfare and the Foreign Office, which shared responsibility for
the administration of Sweden's immigration policy, organized a number
of concerned organizations into an unofficial advisory group. Representing the Swedish church was *Svenska Israelsmissionen*. In addition,

---

29. Hedenquist, op. cit., pp. 26–29, 35–40.

the Central Trade Union and the Stockholm Jewish congregation were members. The parliament completed revision of the immigration laws in such a way as to discourage immigration into Sweden of refugees unless classified as "political refugees." Jews were not given such approbation. By late summer 1938, Swedish borders in general were closed to Jewish immigrants except those who had received visas.

A system of quotas was established. Different organizations — the Central Trade Union, the Stockholm Jewish congregation, SIM — received certain numbers of immigrant places. If an individual case was not "clear," Pernow reported to Vienna the possibility of immigration into Sweden was "completely useless."[30] The result of Sweden's niggardliness was that only 15 non-Aryans under SIM's care were permitted to immigrate into Sweden in 1938. The next year, 125 children and 150 teenagers were allowed into the country, mostly as "transimmigrants."[31] It is worth noting that the emphasis was placed on young Jewish Christians. Their religious beliefs and their cultural development could be better controlled by the Swedes.

The total number of emigrants aided by SIM between 1938 and 1940 has been estimated at slightly over 3,000 individuals. Great Britain, France, Holland, and the United States took significant numbers. There was an attempt to establish a small colony in Ecuador. Others were sent to Shanghai, Ireland, Switzerland, etc. At the same time, Jewish agencies succeeded in placing approximately 150,000 Austrian Jews.[32]

Until September 1939, German policy supported a policy of Jewish emigration. Once the war began, the "Jewish problem" became much more difficult. Suddenly, Germany controlled one of the largest Jewish populations in the world, and the possibility of emigration for Poland's Jews was minimal. Other "solutions" were tried, including massive, random slaughters of hundreds of thousands of Jews, especially after June 1941, and the creation of Jewish districts within the Central Government. Deportations of Germany's Jews, including Austria, began in the second half of 1940. How much of the details of the treatment of Jews did

---

30. SIM arkiv, v. 3, Birger Pernow to Ivarsson, September 2, 1940. UD 1920, p. 61, Bergström to Bergendahl, April 11, 1939: "You certainly are aware of the fact that certain organizations — Stockholm Jewish congregation, Svenska Israelsmissionen (Pernow), and the labor movement — all have specific quotas for transmigration through Sweden of non-Aryan children."

31. Hedenquist, op. cit., p. 45.

32. Ibid. Also SIM arkiv, "Allehanda," Draft of the 1939 annual report.

SIM know? What conclusions were drawn from their knowledge? What did they report to Eidem and the Swedish church?

SIM not only followed closely the fate of Poland's Jews, they understood what the future held. In the 1939 yearly report, SIM noted the problems of Poland's Jews:

> How many of Poland's circa 3½ million Jews are still there is not known. Those who have died through war and the following so-called cleaning-up activities are certainly in the hundred thousands.[33]

A year later, the annual report predicted the end of Europe's Jewry:

> If changes in a positive direction do not occur soon, then it is likely that the Polish Jewry are doomed to death. The same is true for those that are deported there. . . .[34]

Pernow wrote: "Right in front of our eyes, it appears as though the whole of Europe's Jewish population is doomed to destruction."[35] The SIM journal, *Missionstidning för Israel*, carried numerous detailed descriptions of the plight of the Jews. Some of these stories were taken from other Swedish publications. Some came from missionaries spread throughout Eastern Europe. For example, the Norwegian pastor Solheim reported from Rumania early in 1941, "The place of Jews in this country no longer exists, and they now go to a terrible fate."[36] SIM recognized even before Germany opted for the Final Solution that there was no place for Jews in a German-dominated Europe and that their fate was death and destruction, not emigration.

The clarity of SIM's vision on the fate of Europe's Jews, including of course Jewish Christians, in 1940–1941 is startling. Didn't they believe that the Jewish districts scheme might provide some measure of hope for Jews? Apparently not, for Pernow wrote to Eidem in April 1941, "Poland means a slow, painful demise via illness and hunger." Ivarsson reported from Vienna that all Jews will be sent to Poland "in order that no one can observe what is happening."[37] The term, "sent to Poland," meant in SIM's publications the destruction of Europe's Jews. What did SIM do?

---

33. *Missiontidning för Israel* 68 (Annual Report), p. 6.
34. Ibid., 69 (Annual Report), pp. 6–7.
35. Ibid., 68 (November 1940), p. 307.
36. Ibid., 69 (February 1941), pp. 47–48, and (May 1941), pp. 147–149.
37. Eidem arkiv, Pernow to Eidem, April 28, 1941; and SIM arkiv, "Allehanda," Johannes Ivarsson to Pernow, January 2, 1941.

Until June 1941, they tried to maintain normal operations in Vienna. On June 15, after a second Gestapo raid, their formal activities were ended by German authorities. The policy of deportation had replaced emigration. Germany no longer wanted SIM to operate in the occupied areas. SIM managed to maintain its retirement home. Ivarsson initially planned to follow his pastoral flock into Poland, but returned to Stockholm. In these last months of existence in Vienna, SIM established some interesting relationships with American religious organizations.

SIM's activities in Vienna had received funding already in 1940–1941 from the Quakers and the American Board of Missions to the Jews. This latter organization published an article in its house publication describing SIM's activities, which produced a harsh response from Stockholm. Pernow wrote that such articles endangered the whole mission: "We are running the terrible risk that our whole staff can be taken into prison or concentration camp, and the whole work will be destroyed." He preferred to work quietly.[38] Perhaps as a result of the Board's publication, two other American missions contacted SIM: the Bethel Mission in Los Angeles, and the Board of National Missions of the Presbyterian Church in the U.S.A. In both cases, SIM's ability to continue to function in Eastern Europe even after restrictions were placed upon them contrasted with restrictions placed upon American institutions and encouraged cooperation. The Presbyterians wanted to send money for work in Vienna and Rumania.[39] After June 1941, SIM could do nothing in Vienna, but did receive money for other work throughout the war. The Bethel Mission had a special problem.

Leon Rosenberg, a Jewish Christian, operated the Bethel Mission. Its major activity appeared to center on an orphanage for homeless Jewish and Jewish Christian children, *Kinderheim Bethel*, in Wierznik-Starachowice, Poland. Rosenberg's daughter ran the home, and his wife also was in Poland doing missionary work. Apparently there were approximately 50 children under the care of the Bethel Mission home. On July 30, 1941, Rosenberg telegraphed Pernow:

> do what you can for Bethel Mission will be gratefully repaid by American board due to treasury department restrictions money here cannot be sent to bethel (home). . . .[40]

---

38. Ibid., v. 35, Pernow to Hoffman-Cohn, April 24, 1941.
39. Ibid., Paul Berman to Pernow, October 8, 1941.
40. Ibid., "Polen Brev," Leon Rosenberg to Pernow, July 30, 1941.

Once established, the relationship would last throughout the war. By using a New York branch of a Swedish bank, Rosenberg sent money to SIM to be used to maintain the home. He sent $8,995 between 1941 and 1945. SIM established contact first with his daughter, Helene Ostrer, and later with his wife. SIM could both send money to Poland and maintain postal contact. A cache of partly-censored letters in SIM's archive details the fate of the home. Mrs. Ostrer and her husband, as well as most of the children, were consumed in the Final Solution. Their letters were filled with Biblical references in attempts by the Ostrers to relay their fate. Mrs. Rosenberg survived.[41]

Information about the *Kinderheim* provided SIM with one perspective on events in Poland. Another came from a technique developed in Stockholm to trace the deported SIM congregation in the concentration camp system. By using international money orders, SIM could send either small amounts of money or food packages directly or via Portugal and Switzerland to camp inmates. Initially, what was needed was an address. Since most of the Jewish Christians from Vienna were first sent to Theresienstadt, the problem of accurate addresses was not difficult. In addition, SIM officials had traveled throughout Germany and Poland trying to trace deportees. The result was that SIM established contact with approximately 925 of their former congregation. In some cases, the deportees could only sign the receipt; in others, at least in the beginning, they could send postcards with their addresses and non-political information.

In the summer of 1941, SIM started a system of sending money or food on a regular basis to the deportees. The receipts were collected and compared with other examples from the same individual. An abrupt change in the signature or a deterioration of the clarity of the signature was duly noted. For approximately 20 percent, the money order or food package was returned with a notification that the intended recipient was no longer available at the camp. SIM assumed that such a notation meant the death of the deportee. The whole system was explained to the readers of SIM's journal in its September 1943 edition, including photographs of the deterioration of signatures. The title of the article was "People Who Disappear."[42]

---

41. Ibid., Rosenberg to Pernow, September 6, 1945, and Pernow to Rosenberg, October 15, 1945.

42. *Missionstidning för Israel* 70 (September 1943), pp. 274–278. See also SIM arkiv, "Hjälp till Judar:" a shoebox with the title "Help to Jews" (a misnomer since it was, in fact,

The actual cards that were used to monitor the deportees can be found in an archive in Uppsala. An analysis of the cards indicated the diversity of the system SIM created. The geographical dispersion was world-encompassing:

Vienna: 164
Germany: 62
France: 6
Italy: 3
Prague: 3
Oslo: 1
Buchenwald: 2
Bergen-Belsen: 10
Theresienstadt: 500 ±
Poland: 146 of which
   23 not identifiable
   23 Lublin district
   19 Lubelski district
   18 Kielce
   20 Warsaw
   33 Lintzmanstadt
    6 Birkenau
    3 Auschwitz
    1 Sobibor
Brussels: 2
Shanghai: 20
Slovakia: 1
Amsterdam: 1
Hungary: 2
Czechoslovakia: 1

Of the 178 cards which have the specific notation "no longer in residence," nearly 70 originated from Theresienstadt. A few specific dates had unusually large numbers of such notification:

    January 25, 1943: 25, mostly from Poland
    January 23, 1943: 15, almost exclusively from Poland

---

help to Christians who had converted), containing cards approximately 4 × 6 inches. Each card represented one person. Although the author can not be entirely certain, it appears likely that this collection of cards has been kept intact from the war.

August 10, 1943: 15, mostly from Theresienstadt
June 30, 1943: 12, mostly from Poland, especially Lublin
August 25, 1944: 9, mostly from Theresienstadt
April 4, 1943: 7, almost exclusively from Theresienstadt
June 16, 1943: 7, almost exclusively from Theresienstadt

A very high percentage of the 146 cards on Polish deportees have such identification and are concentrated to early and mid-1943. However, some contact with Polish deportees continued into 1944, especially with those at Birkenau and Auschwitz.

The average number of times a person received a dispatch varied greatly. 25–30 percent got only 1–3, yet a few were sent as many as 31. Most received between 5 and 7. The values were quite disparate, too, ranging from 5 to 300 Swedish kronor, with the normal sum usually 5 or 10 kronor.

This contact system provided SIM with a steady source of information, albeit not totally clear. On some occasions, deportees from one camp, especially Theresienstadt, surfaced in another. These instances were apparently few. The concentration of undelivered orders on specific dates were viewed by SIM officials as ominous signs: "A returned or undeliverable order corresponds to the modern Jewish obituary."[43] The system permitted SIM to confirm the differentiation of treatment of internees at Theresienstadt from Poland: "The information from Theresienstadt is not so terrible as from, for example, Poland. One must believe that these people, even in such great need, can perhaps get over this difficult period."[44]

As fascinationg as this system was, the critical question was how was the information used? SIM was not reticent to write about it, either in their journal or in private letters. For example, the Quaker headquarters in Philadelphia received a description of the technique in February 1943:

> We have been able to send food parcels to all deported in Poland whose addresses we have received. All those thousands of parcels have been sent via Portugal because it is only permitted persons living in Sweden to send food parcels from here to relatives in Poland.[45]

---

43. *Missionstidning för Israel* 70 (Annual Report), pp. 28–29.
44. SIM arkiv, "Jellinek?," Johannes Jellinek to Ella Stenbäck, May 13, 1943.
45. Ibid., v. 7, Pernow to Mary Rogers, February 23, 1943.

Yet one should not treat this information in isolation. It was only part of a flood of information that both SIM and Archbishop Eidem had about the fate of the Jews.

Another important source of information about German treatment of Jews was the Swedish church in Berlin. The church existed to provide religious sustenance to Swedes living in Berlin. Its pastors were appointed by the Swedish archbishop. Two men, Birger Forell and Erik Perve, held the post of pastor of the Swedish Berlin congregation for most of the war. In addition, there were Swedish seamen's churches in a number of German ports. Forell, who headed the Berlin church until 1942, was close to the leaders of the Confessional Church. He was also politically more progressive than most of his German and Swedish colleagues. He actively involved himself in anti-Nazi pursuits that eventually led him to be *persona non grata* with the German government. Perve was more moderate. Eidem feared some incident if Forell's political activities continued so openly. Yet Perve, too, shared a deep distaste for the Nazi regime and played an important role in aiding a group of Jews in the last years of the war.[46]

Although Forell even before the war had been concerned about persecution of Jews, his reports after 1939 referred constantly to their plight, especially the fate of the Jewish Christians. He complained of his feeling of helplessness when so many "non-Aryans" stood in need of support. And he realized that it would be nearly impossible for a Swede to understand fully what had happened to them in German society: "Their [non-Aryans] fate is not comprehendible for a person who continues to live in a society based on principles and laws like our own." Like SIM, he recognized by the end of 1941 that Jews were doomed in Europe: "It is difficult to tend the souls of people who are doomed to death when death will come in such a form. . . . Forgive me that I expose my attitudes but I cannot keep quiet, even if I do not write any details."[47]

Before the inauguration of Germany's systematic campaign to murder all of Europe's Jews, the individuals in the Swedish church most knowledgeable with regard to Jews and the highest officials had concluded

---

46. See Leonard Gross, *The Last Jews in Berlin* (New York, 1982). This popular account has no citations. Gross had access to Perve's diary. The study exaggerated Perve's role in Berlin. There are a number of inaccuracies. No Swedish study of Forell exists. See Harold Koenigswald, *Birger Forell* (Berlin).

47. Eidem arkiv, Forell to Eidem, December 4, 1941, and Annual report, Svenska Victorialförsamling 1940, March 21, 1941, pp. 3–4.

that Hitler would, in one way or another, seek to destroy European Jewry. The year 1942 witnessed the beginning of the fulfillment of that prediction. What and when did the Swedish church learn of the details of the Final Solution?

Materials in Swedish church archives do not provide conclusive evidence for pinpointing exactly when religious figures in Sweden accepted the news of a terrible new policy begun by the Germans, although an approximate time can be fixed. Part of the problem of interpreting the evidence is the nature of the issue. To predict that Germany would kill all of Europe's Jews was one matter; to believe that a civilized and religious people had committed all of its bureaucratic and technological skills to the task was another. Certainly, the initial reports that came from Polish underground sources in Stockholm and London in May–June 1942 would not persuade the skeptical. Many viewed Polish and Jewish reports as not credible.

George Bell, Bishop of Chichester, visited Sweden in May 1942, primarily to reaffirm contact with the Confessional Church and to explore possible mediation efforts to end the war.[48] While in Sweden, Bell met with "A Swedish expert" on the Jewish question, Birger Pernow. Pernow told Bell that there was "no future for Jews in Europe" and that a return to Germany in the postwar period was not a good idea. Pernow believed that only Palestine and Transjordan were suitable sites for massive Jewish immigration.[49] None of these documents suggest knowledge of Germany's new policies. A month later, Bell received very specific information about the Final Solution from Polish underground sources, including the use of gas and identification of Auschwitz as "the largest camp for men":

> Massacres of the Jewish population constitute one of the grimmest chapters in the history of the German occupation. Those massacres are being kept secret by the Germans and it is only lately that some news has begun to come through.[50]

An exchange of letters between Eidem and Ragnar Bring, influential Professor of Religion at the University of Lund, in late August suggested continued lack of clarity. Bring had just visited Germany and in his

---

48. See Ronald Jasper, *George Bell* (Oxford, 1967).
49. Great Britain, Lambeth Palace, George Bell archive, "Sweden 1942–1950," Bell to William Paton, June 24, 1942, and Press Conference, June 15, 1942.
50. Temple archive, "Polish Research Center" to Temple, July 8, 1942.

report touched upon "secret" information received from a German pastor about treatment of the Jews. This information as reported by Bring focused on the concentration camp at Theresienstadt and the tone of Bring's letter gave no indication of knowledge of the extermination campaign. Eidem's response indicated that he viewed Germany more critically than Bring, but on the Jewish Question, he referred Bring to SIM.[51]

In August 1942, the Swedish government received its first independent, reliable descriptions of the new policy. At least one of them was widely circulated within the Swedish Foreign Office. Whether these reports reached Eidem is not clear. Jewish organizations, including the Stockholm Jewish congregation, also had confirming evidence on the Final Solution by August, and in September began to publish stories of the new atrocities.[52] Swedish Jewish publications were closely examined by SIM and were often quoted in SIM's journal.

Whatever small doubts lingered in Eidem's mind about the German policy were eliminated during a visit to Germany in early November 1942. The official purpose of the trip was to participate in the anniversary of the victory of Sweden's Gustaf II Adolf at Lützen during the Thirty Years' War. Eidem took advantage of the trip to meet secretly with leaders of the Confessional Church and to speak out against racial persecution in his sermon. In his discussions with Otto Dibelius, he was told in explicit detail about the new German policies. The information was totally reliable: an undercover agent of the church had penetrated the SS and actually participated in the killing process.[53] Eidem's knowledge was a heavy burden.

The Swedish government viewed information about the campaign to destroy the Jews as a potential security threat. There had been a fear among some leading Swedish officials in September that German unhappiness about anti-German Swedish press reports would lead to a German invasion. These same officials understood that confirmation by the Swedish government or the church of the reports of a new phase of

51. Eidem arkiv, Professor Ragnar Bring to Eidem, August 25–27, 1942, and Eidem to Bring, September 1, 1942.
52. See *Judisk Krönika* 117, pp. 101–102.
53. Friedlander, op. cit., p. 136. See also Sweden, Sigtuna, Nordiska Ekumeniska Institutet, "A," "Action and Work for the Jews and Non-Aryan Christians in Germany," March, 1943: "Church leaders like Bishop Wurm or the Roman Catholic Bishop Preysing have entrusted special collaborators with the task to be informed as fully as possible and quickly as possible about any actions against Jews or non-Aryan Christians." Eidem arkiv, Eidem to Wollmer, November 23, 1942.

Germany's Jewish policy would incite even harsher criticism of Germany in the Swedish press. Therefore, government policy was designed in such a way that Allied, Polish, or Jewish reports were neither confirmed nor denied. In addition, officials often masked what they knew by the use of deliberately imprecise language or statements to the effect that absolute proof was still not available.

Eidem and SIM followed the same policy. Eidem resisted any temptation to repeat the graphic reports he had received in Berlin. In a letter to the Swedish explorer Sven Hedin in April 1943, he used the term "severe measures" to describe what he had learned from Dibelius.[54] In his exchanges of letters with the Archbishop of Canterbury, William Temple, in February–March 1943, the contrast between Temple's direct reference to "intended extermination of the Jews" and Eidem's "persecution of the Jews" was not only illustrative but deliberate.[55] SIM opted for similar tactics.

SIM had already in 1941–1942 made it clear to the readers of its journal that European Jewry was doomed. The means reported in the journal were a combination of deportation, disease, and starvation, with outbreaks of random violence. The potential for survival was seen as slight but still possible: "Shall those who decided to completely destroy the Jewish people in Europe succeed? We do not know."[56] A contrast to SIM's publishing policy could be found in another Swedish journal, *Israels Väktare*, which also represented a Christian mission, albeit not aligned with the state church, to the Jews. Throughout the fall of 1942, *Israels Väktare* reproduced reports from Jewish sources about German treatment of the Jews, French Catholic condemnations, and the December Allied official protest of the killing policy. "It is undeniable that steps have been taken for the systematic killing of deported Jews," *Israels Väktare* concluded in December.[57]

The difference between *Svenska Israelsmissionen* and *Israels Väktare* was not accidental. In February 1943, Pernow justified SIM's policy on the basis that the publication of graphic details would only produce "bitterness and hate," whereas the duty of Christians was to spread the gospel, and besides the details could not be proven "absolutely":

54. Eidem arkiv, Eidem to Sven Hedin, March 31, 1943.
55. Ibid., William Temple to Eidem, February 24, 1943, and Eidem to Temple, March 29, 1943.
56. *Missionstidning för Israel* 70 (Annual Report), pp. 6–7.
57. *Israels Väktare* 7/11, November 1942, p. 8, and December 1942, p. 11.

We have also received details of cruelty that you referred to, but we have
decided not to publish such details partially because we cannot yet prove
absolutely their veracity, and partially because we did not think that it was
right in these disturbed times to publish such things, all the least in a mission journal. Such could only produce additional hate and bitterness in
the soul, and therefore we Christians should not contribute. Our Christian duty is instead to spread evengelical salvation to all, both those persecuted and those who persecute.[58]

Even in private letters, SIM officials used euphemisms to describe
what was happening to the Jews, "their fate is the most terrible one can
imagine."[59]

Eidem showed great loyalty to the government policy in the face of
rising religious pressure for a more open, critical response to German
policies. A scheme evolved in Great Britain in February 1943, initiated
by the Church of England Committee for Non-Aryan Christians, to
attempt to rouse the German churches to protest the killing of Jews,
including Jewish Christians. The Archbishop of Canterbury asked
Eidem to "be the channel" to make the request of the Evangelical
Church to appeal to the "Christian conscience of Germany." Eidem
refused because he claimed that it would have no effect. "It is most dis-
tressing to be unable to do something of real use in this matter." Yet
Eidem was anxious that Temple did not confuse his refusal with lack of
sympathy. Eidem noted the Swedish bishops' condemnation of racial
persecution in Norway in November 1942 (see below) and that many
Germans, too, condemned the Nazis' anti-Semitism:

> I know quite sure from Germans whom I have met that there are *many*
> Germans who are strongly condemning and abhorring the frightful meas-
> ures against the Jews. . . . They suffer deeply under this crime of their
> people.[60]

Eidem himself was not comfortable with his response to Temple. Two
days later, he decided to try another tack. He asked Sven Hedin to
intervene privately in Berlin on behalf of the *mischlinge*, i.e., Jewish
Christians or those with mixed ancestry. The letter carrying this request
underlined Eidem's preference to use "trustworthy" people to approach

---

58. SIM arkiv, Pernow to Sundgren, February 10, 1943.
59. Ibid., Jellinek to B. Agardh, January 30, 1943.
60. Eidem arkiv, Eidem to Temple, March 29, 1943, and Temple to Eidem, February
24, 1943.

Germans privately rather than public protests and the urgency of the situation because "the severe measures already taken against the full Jews would be extended to so-called half and quarter Jews." Eidem had also talked with the German minister to Sweden.[61] Hedin's response was a combination of incisive analysis of Hitler's Germany, of anti-Semitism, of recounting of past failures on his part to aid Jews, and an expression that his intervention with Hitler on behalf of the Jews would weaken his value as a guarantor of Sweden's security.[62]

Eidem's dilemma about how to act in the face of what he called privately "Germany's monstrous blood guilt" did not even in 1942 lead him to refuse to act in all cases or to do so exclusively through trustworthy channels.[63] In the case of the application of the Final Solution to Norway in November 1942, Eidem supported a more active interventionist policy. The Norwegian episode should be compared with Eidem's responses to English proposals to become more active within Germany.

Resistance to Quisling and the Germans extended deeply into the universities and the Norwegian State Church, which was also Lutheran. Relations between the church hierarchy and the Quisling government deteriorated until the leading Norwegian bishop was held in house arrest and many other church officials found themselves under constant harassment and in danger of imprisonment. This church struggle was closely followed in Sweden, and great sympathy developed for the Norwegians. Eidem advocated in this matter a policy of careful public intervention. In the third quarter of 1942, there was a series of violent resistance incidents and reprisals culminating in the decision to apply the Final Solution to Norway.

On November 22, the Norwegian bishops, despite their restricted freedom, issued a joint protest against persecution of the Norwegian Jews. Their protest detailed acts against Jews in Norway and demanded their cessation. News of the Norwegian bishops' action added to the continuing unhappiness in Sweden about the state of affairs in Norway and led to a massive outpouring of public support against German action on the Jews. Among the most outspoken critics in Sweden were churchmen who used their pulpits to attack German policy. Perhaps the most vocal was chief pastor of the Stockholm congregation, Olle

---

61. Ibid., Eidem to Sven Hedin, March 31, 1943.
62. Ibid., Hedin to Eidem, April 2, 1943. Hedin was a famous explorer whose pro-German sympathies were well known. See Document Collection.
63. Ibid., Eidem to Perve, April 1, 1943.

Nystedt, whose sermon, "If we remain silent, the stones will cry out," was quoted in full length by numerous Swedish newspapers.[64] Eidem and the other bishops immediately found themselves under considerable pressure to act.[65]

On November 30, Eidem decided to issue a public statement on behalf of all Sweden's bishops. It was made public on December 2. A recent church historian called the appeal "an important church expression," partially because certain conservative elements criticized the declaration as "political" in nature and partially because nearly all Christian churches attached themselves to it.[66] While both of these observations are correct, of more interest was the specific text of the declaration and its relationship to other action on the part of Eidem.

A comparison between the texts of the Norwegian and Swedish bishops' appeals indicated that the Swedish text was more vague and less critical than the Norwegian despite the fact that the Norwegian bishops were taking greater risks. The Swedish version attacked "race prejudice" but avoided any specific commentary on Jews. Eidem told the secretary of another Protestant sect that the appeal "would be made on strict religious grounds."[67] Nystedt's speech had asked:

> What has happened to France's Jews, what has happened and what is happening, what awaits Norway's Jews?[68]

Nothing of this kind of reference to a larger consistent German policy was included in the Swedish text.

Privately, Eidem felt much closer to Nystedt's views than the bishops' appeal would suggest. He wrote on November 28 to Marcus Ehrenpreis, the chief rabbi in Sweden:

> I cannot express myself adequately how deeply disturbed I am over the terrible developments in Norway. It is terrible and there is a monstrous blood guilt which these heartless persecutors bring on themselves. With dread have we learned of the inhuman activities which have befallen members of the Jewish people in other countries of the earth. But it is clear that which is happening near our borders fills us with such guilty

---

64. *Nordiska Röster Mot Judeförföljelse och Våld* (Stockholm, 1943), pp. 13–14.

65. The pressure came from various directions: laymen, other church officials, and from Jews. Eidem arkiv, Rabbi Marcus Ehrenpreis to Eidem, November 27, 1942, Bishop Rohde to Eidem, December 1, 1942, among others.

66. *Kirken*, pp. 50–51.

67. Eidem arkiv, Eidem to Ansgar Eeg-Olofsson, December 1, 1942.

68. *Nordiska Röster*, op. cit.

terror that it is something of a higher order. That something of this nature could happen in one of our Nordic countries is of course so terribly puzzling.[69]

What becomes clear is that Eidem in constructing the bishops' appeal continued to believe that he must be circumspect in official pronouncements. At the same time, his horror drove him to more direct action to try to aid the Norwegian Jews.

Already on November 30, Eidem had sought out Foreign Minister Günther with regard to some initiative on the part of Sweden to help the Jews not deported from Norway in later November. Günther was ill, and therefore Eidem turned to the prime minister:

> The subject that I wish to discuss concerns those Jews still remaining in Norway. My sincere and earnest wish is that the Swedish government must take some step that is possible to help those unhappy people through the provision of visas for transit to Sweden or by some other method.[70]

Although it is not entirely clear what specific effect Eidem's letter had, Hansson reported back to the archbishop that Sweden had indeed taken steps to try to help Norway's Jews.[71]

The Norwegian case illustrated many facets of the behavior of the Swedish church. It should be compared with the simultaneous British inquiry for an appeal by Eidem in Germany, which he rejected. The public response in Sweden to events in Norway and the outrage among certain elements of the ministry demanded a formal pronouncement on persecution of the Norwegian Jews. When it came, however, it was moderate and formalistic. But behind the public façade of moderation, Eidem tried to use his influence to initiate a more active Swedish policy. Eidem's concern focused on the fact that it was Norwegians, *Scandinavians*, that were being persecuted and, in some cases, doing the persecution.[72] The circumstance was too close to home to ignore officially as the church had done with regard to their knowledge of murder on the Continent. The Norwegian situation also demonstrated Eidem's understanding of what was happening south and east of Sweden. Bishop Ysander, chairman of the board of *Svenska Israelsmissionen*, noted suc-

---

69. Eidem arkiv, Eidem to Ehrenpreis, November 28, 1942.

70. Ibid., Eidem to P.A. Hansson, December 3, 1942.

71. Ibid., P.A. Hansson to Eidem, December 7, 1942.

72. Ibid., Eidem to Forell, January 18, 1943. See also speech of Bishop Aulén in *Nordiska Röster*, p. 12.

cinctly in an article in June 1943 that the church was under no illusions: "The terrible things that have happened to Norway's Jews are only a detail. What has happened to French and Norwegian Jews and what is happening in Poland we cannot be sure of, but we have heard enough to know that it is terrible and exceeds anything humanity has previously done."[73] The Swedish church would make no further formal pronouncements on persecution of the Jews, even when confronted by the details of experiences at Auschwitz and the attempts to destroy Hungary's Jews in 1944.

The Hungarian episode in 1944 must be considered in a context different from earlier developments. By 1944 no well-informed person doubted that Germany would lose the war, or that Germany had killed most of the Jews within its territories. The Swedish government did not fear a German attack, although it remained steadfastly committed to a policy of nonbelligerency. When Adolf Eichmann arrived in Budapest in late March and began the deportation of Hungary's Jews to Auschwitz, his activities were monitored closely in the West and widely reported in newspapers. Church officials in Sweden and Great Britain were aware of events in Hungary, but their reactions were quite different.

On April 3, 1944, the World Jewish Congress (London) appealed to Bishop Bell to make some public statement about persecution of the Jews in Hungary. The Archbishop of Canterbury, William Temple, immediately approached the BBC and the Ministry of Information about the idea.[74] The European Division of the Political Warfare Executive and the Foreign Office liked the idea but worried about an appeal based exclusively on persecution of the Jews. Instead, Temple was asked to speak "so as to include other victims of Nazi oppression."[75] The appeal was broadcast, but there was no specific mention of Jews or Jewish persecution.[76] Two months later, Temple received information about Auschwitz. Temple turned once again to the government and requested a second appeal to Hungarian Protestants, this time specifically about the Jews: "If the result were the saving of one Jew, it would be worth it."[77] The second appeal, broadcast on July 8, specifically dis-

73. *Missionstidning för Israel* 70 (June 1943), p. 173.

74. Temple archive, WJC (London) to Bell, April 3, 1944; Temple's secretary to Carter, April 5, 1944.

75. Ibid., Francis House to Temple, April 6, 1944.

76. Ibid., Temple speech, not dated.

77. Ibid., Temple to House, June 28, 1944.

cussed "the wholesale roundup of Hungarian Jews" and Auschwitz.[78] In the case of the English response to events in Hungary, Archbishop Temple demonstrated a determination to make a clear public statement, and it was only the political considerations of the British government which had led Temple to postpone a direct appeal on the Jewish question until July. In Sweden, the circumstances were almost completely reversed.

The Swedish government showed a concern about events in Hungary almost as soon as news reached them about Eichmann's activities. Their initial response was one of frustration based on the belief that there was nothing that they could do. The Swedish legation in Budapest, however, began in May to provide transit visas and "protective passes" for a few Hungarian Jews that had some contact with Sweden. Valdemar Langlet began to devise schemes to aid Jews via the Red Cross. After receiving the Auschwitz protocols, the Swedish king, Gustaf V, made a direct appeal to the Hungarian head of state, Admiral Horthy, to stop the persecutions. Raoul Wallenberg was dispatched to Budapest in early July to work exclusively at the Swedish legation to aid Jews. Sweden played an important role in the saving of Budapest's Jews in 1944.

The Swedish church got involved directly in the events in Hungary at an early date. In July, the chief rabbi of Jerusalem, Isaac Herzog, asked Eidem to make a public appeal along the lines of Temple's broadcast. Eidem's intuition was to respond negatively, but he inquired at the Swedish Foreign Office whether they felt he was correct. The reply was in the affirmative.[79] Yet the same day that Eidem wrote to the Foreign Office, Per Anger, the political officer at the Swedish legation in Budapest, telegraphed to Stockholm that he thought that it might be a good idea for Eidem to make a direct appeal to the Hungarian Protestant bishops.[80] On July 24, Eidem telegraphed Herzog that he had decided not to make an appeal and referred to the rescue activities of Langlet.[81]

No evidence exists that suggests that Eidem felt as acutely as Temple about the necessity to speak out on the Hungarian situation. This differ-

78. Ibid., Temple speech, July 8, 1944.

79. UD 1920, HP 1096, Eidem to Grafström, July 20, 1944; and Grafström to Eidem, July 21, 1944.

80. Ibid., Per Anger to Swedish Foreign Office, July 21, 1944.

81. PRO, FO 371, 42816, Eidem to Rabbi Israel Herzog, July 24, 1944. The reader should note that this telegram was intercepted by the British censor and sent to the British Foreign Office.

ence cannot be explained by the security circumstances of their respective countries. Nor does the policy of their respective governments adequately explain their differences. Eidem seemed determined to avoid
specific, public involvement in the Jewish Question after the appeal in
Norway and to maintain the position that politics and religion should not
mix.

Indeed, Eidem had received some criticism about the Norwegian
appeal from a few Swedish pastors and laymen. The tone of the letters
combined anti-Semitism with hostility toward the Soviet Union. Later
in the war, when the Allied powers were about to be victorious, Eidem
resisted proposals to remove pro-Nazi clergy.[82] Within the church
institutionally and in public, Eidem remained consistent: he opted for a
low profile policy on questions related to the Jews. Undoubtedly one of
the main considerations in this policy, as security issues related to
Sweden receded, was Eidem's continuing desire to protect his German
counterparts from Western criticism. His defense of the German clergy
remained steadfast throughout the war. For example, he wrote to the
Archbishop of Canterbury in August 1943 that he had on a recent trip to
Berlin "gained the impression that in numerous circles of the population
one did not at all approve of the persecutions of the Jews:"

> But whatever is said from the pulpits or printed in clandestine leaflets, is
> never printed in the newspapers. This might in other countries create the
> impression that our faithful Christian brethren in Germany quietly have
> given in to all this, but they are, in fact, far more brave than one from
> outside gives them credit for.[83]

In the last three years of the war, it was *Svenska Israelsmissionen* that
would serve as the primary institution within the church when direct
action was taken to aid Jews. SIM's activities had three foci: Berlin,
Rumania, and refugees in Sweden. Yet at the same time that SIM
worked in these areas, serious questions were being raised within the
mission and outside it about its very existence and purpose. The dilemmas SIM experienced during the period illustrated the continuing problems Christian churches struggled with when confronted with the Jewish problem.

---

82. Eidem arkiv, Eidem to Folke Ellioth, December 13, 1943; H. Mallgren to Eidem,
December 3, 1942; E. Österling to Eidem, December 27, 1942; and Nils Stahre to Eidem,
December 3, 1942.
83. Ibid., Eidem to Temple, August 8, 1943.

First, there was the whole issue of what SIM should do if Germany actually succeeded in the destruction of all of Europe's Jews. What would be the purpose of a mission to the Jews if no Jews existed? This question, asked with great frequency among mission officials, was answered in a variety of ways. In part, the aid activities of SIM offered some justification. But SIM could be, and was, criticized by pastors for becoming "a branch of the Red Cross." It was necessary for a Christian institution whose purpose was proselytism of Jews to maintain an active policy. SIM sent a missionary to New York to work under cover in the "vast and potentially great field of American Jewry."[84] In the final days of the Polish ghettos and amidst the refugees who fled to Sweden, SIM attempted to sustain an ambitious religious program. All these activities reinforced the hostility between SIM and Sweden's Jewish leaders.

On April 16, 1943, chief rabbi Ehrenpreis made a public attack on SIM in a speech in Malmö. The criticism bothered SIM officials more than would have been the case in normal circumstances. The reason for their discomfort is not difficult to understand: given what nominal Christians were doing to Jews, was it morally valid to continue their work? Pernow did not want to get into a public debate with Ehrenpreis and felt caught "between two chairs."[85] Already in May, he proposed to Ehrenpreis that a meeting between himself, Ehrenpreis, and Bishop Ysander be arranged "in order to avoid eventual misunderstanding."[86] By January 1944, Pernow had decided that the name of the mission itself "is not suitable and rather it is more an unnecessary hurdle in our work." He preferred something like "Christian Approach to the Jews:"

> I have more and more come to believe that our name, Svenska Israelsmissionen, is not good; too many Jews, especially educated ones, have difficulty with the word mission. I would therefore like to find another name, but have not succeeded.[87]

The issue was more significant than simply a name change. Pernow exhibited little charity to Jewish organizations.

An example of Pernow's unwillingness to draw too close to Jewish

---

84. Hedenquist, op. cit., p. 22. Also, SIM arkiv, v. 38. Pastor David Granquist to Pernow, June 6, 1944.

85. SIM arkiv, v. 37, Pernow to Bishop Ysander, May 4, 1943.

86. Ibid., Pernow to Ehrenpreis, May 28, 1943.

87. Ibid., v. 38, Pernow to Perve, March 1, 1944; and Pernow to Ysander, January 28, 1944.

organizations occurred in June 1943. Two months earlier, *The New York Times* ran an article on extermination of Jews in Poland in which SIM specifically was cited as the credible "Aryan" source. Probably as a result of this article, the World Jewish Congress wrote Pernow requesting information. Pernow responded that WJC could get better information from Jewish sources. The same day, Pernow wrote Berman a detailed letter about conditions of Jews, including the identification of Auschwitz as the destination of the deportation of Norwegian Jews.[88]

Pernow never lost his ambivalent attitude toward Jews. In December 1945, he wrote to Bishop Ysander to recount a meeting at a church with a woman who was Ehrenpreis's maid. The maid reported to Pernow that a rabbi in England had telegraphed Ehrenpreis to have SIM's attempts to baptize Jewish refugees in Sweden stopped. Pernow's response to this information shed interesting light on his mentality:

> He [Ehrenpreis] is so afraid that we might push our way into Jewish camps with the Christian gospel; yet he, himself, has a practicing Christian as a maid! In the future, when one of us visits Ehrenpreis, it will be a Christian woman in his home who serves him and us![89]

Officially, SIM and Jewish leaders remained at loggerheads, but privately they found it desirable to cooperate. The place of their greatest successful cooperation was in Berlin.

Some Jews and *mischlinge* managed to avoid the successive sweeps of Berlin between 1941 and 1943. They went into hiding. Various individuals and organizations supported them. One such institution was the Swedish church in Berlin. The main problem after the finding of a safe locale for these refugees was money for their support. On September 1, 1943, Erik Perve, pastor of the Swedish church, wrote to Pernow to request funds both from SIM and from the Stockholm Jewish congregation. He reported that there were an unknown number of people, "who for well-known reason [were] threatened by destruction, have by one way or another hidden."[90] By September 14, SIM and Ehrenpreis had agreed to provide a thousand kronor apiece for the following two months. Ehrenpreis requested, however, to know how many of those hidden were practicing Jews in contrast to those who were Jewish Chris-

---

88. SIM arkiv, v. 7, Pernow to Berman, June 22, 1943; and v. 37, Pernow to Leon Kubowitzki, June 22, 1943.

89. Ibid., v. 39, Pernow to Bishop Ysander, December 7, 1945.

90. Ibid., v. 37, Perve to Pernow, September 1, 1943.

tians.[91] No distribution of refugees by religion was available. Aid continued to be forwarded from Stockholm for the remainder of the war. One
estimate had the total number of those hidden "in the hundreds." Perve
had named in his September 1 letter the figure of twenty.[92] In any case,
the cooperative efforts bore fruit, and little tension developed between
SIM and Ehrenpreis. The same cannot be said for the Rumanian experience.

The involvement of Swedish religious institutions in developments in
Rumania began in February 1944. SIM had assumed titular responsibility in 1940 for a Norwegian mission to the Jews operating in Rumania
and headed by a Pastor Wurmbrand. In early February, Wurmbrand
wrote to Pernow and described the release of suffering Jews in
Bessarabia as Russian troops moved westward. The description moved
Pernow:

> We have received many upsetting letters before, even relating to our fel-
> low believers' suffering, but nothing has affected me so deeply as this.[93]

Pernow forwarded Wurmbrand's letter to Eidem and Ehrenpreis and
announced that he had sent ten thousand kronor to Rumania immediately and intended to send a similar sum shortly. Ehrenpreis wanted to
publish the Wurmbrand letter, but Pernow, following well-established
precedent, responded negatively. Pernow, however, later changed his
mind and had it published in *Svenska Dagbladet* without any indication
of whence the information had come. Pernow hoped that publication
would lead to more financial support.[94] SIM support to Rumania
escalated dramatically in 1943, 1944, and 1945, far exceeding in financial
terms any other activity of the mission. Pernow also sought support from
American sources and received generous contributions. Problems
developed when Ehrenpreis personally went to Bucharest.

The source of the difficulty was as usual the conflict between Jews and
Jewish Christians. Jewish organizations tried to help Jews; their concern about Jewish Christians was quite small. Christian institutions
talked of helping "Jews," but they used the term as the Nazis defined it,
that is, both Jews and Jewish Christians. In reality, they were most concerned about the latter. One of the most important ways to aid those

---

91. Ibid., Pernow to Perve, September 14, 1943.
92. Ibid., Pernow to Perve, September 1, 1943. See Gross, op. cit., pp. 285–286.
93. Ibid., v. 38, Pernow to Eidem, February 8, 1944.
94. Ibid., Pernow to Ysander, February 29, 1944.

suffering in Rumania was the provision of a Palestine certificate for emigration to Palestine. Ehrenpreis told Pernow that Jewish Christians would not be given any of the Palestine certificates because of the Jewish belief that the English, when they realized the situation, would provide special passes for "Christians in mortal danger."[95] Pernow tried to use the goodwill of the American legation in Stockholm to influence the British for the Jewish Christians. He also wrote to the Bishop of Chichester. As the political struggle over Palestine certificates was fought out in London, Pernow began to receive information from Rumania suggesting that Wurmbrand was more involved with Baptists than with Jews. Nonetheless, his reaction to the British decision to allow only practicing Jews to use the few available certificates was bitter:

> . . . the Jews do not want to have anything to do with the Hebrew Christians, neither the orthodox nor the unbelieving Jews. Consequently they are eagerly watching so that no Hebrew Christian will enter Palestine. . . . I suspect the Jews to be behind that discouraging decision.[96]

Relations between SIM and Jewish groups remained strained throughout the war. Hitler's program of destruction intensified the tasks of both groups in attempts to provide aid and comfort. Sometimes, as in Berlin, these efforts led to cooperation; but the cooperation was strictly a product of a set of unique circumstances. SIM sought to help Jewish Christians, while Jewish organizations aided Jews. In Vienna, Rumania, and among the various refugees that fled to Sweden, antagonisms and hostility marked their relationship. Jewish leaders viewed SIM and its activities historically as anti-Jewish, and in the context of the persecutions, as taking advantage of the situation to seek further converts. SIM's leadership, partially aware of and concerned about the awkwardness of their position, nonetheless never controlled their evangelical fervor. The continuation of hostility, therefore, was hardly surprising. They competed for the souls of the same group of individuals, even when those individuals were being murdered systematically.

The position of the Swedish Lutheran Church as represented by the archbishop cannot be clarified so easily. Eidem's involvements in events in Germany was extensive from the beginning of Hitler's regime. His

---

95. Ibid., Pernow to Iver Olsen, May 10, 1944. The WRB gave money to SIM for their Rumanian work.

96. Ibid., Pernow to Foquett, December 13, 1944; see Pernow to Eidem, September 6, 1944, and Jellinek to Olsen, May 13, 1944.

great concern was not the dictatorial nature of the Nazi government but the challenge that it presented to the German Lutherans. The challenge was the official anti-Semitism of the regime. Anti-Semitism denied a fundamental tenet of Christianity: the act of conversion. Christians in Germany faced the dilemma of how to protect their religious beliefs and remain loyal to the government. Most compromised the former. Eidem sympathized with those Lutherans who tried to sustain their religious commitments while not actively opposing Hitler. Eidem believed that this policy chosen by Confessional Church leaders was a difficult one, and he saw his task to remain sympathetic to it and to protect German Lutherans within the ecumenical movement. He appreciated, however, the burden of anti-Semitism and consistently rejected it. In Germany, he warned Hitler of its dire consequences, and even during the war, was willing in his sermons to criticize it. When confronted with the policy of systematic destruction of Europe's Jews, Eidem's response was less precise.

Eidem learned of Hitler's policy during the fall of 1942. He personally confirmed it on his visit to Germany in November. There is no doubt that he abhorred the policy and, indeed, the regime, and spoke frequently thereafter of "the terrible blood guilt" the Germans were bringing upon themselves. The questions are how did Eidem respond in policy terms to this information and why? What this essay has suggested is that Eidem took a low-profile position. Except in the case of the Norwegian Jews, Eidem maintained a public silence. He did not share his knowledge in any official manner, which had he done so, would have given much more credit to the circulating press reports on the Final Solution. In fact, a clear, forthright statement about the existence of such a policy from Eidem might have had a dramatic effect both in Germany and in the Western countries. His word as a non-belligerent, non-Jewish, Germanophile would have been difficult to ignore. The "terrible secret" would not have been so secret.

Why did Eidem choose to remain silent? Motivation for his choice stemmed from a variety of sources. For Eidem, the greatest danger to Christianity was the existence of the Soviet Union. Its aggressive atheism and attacks on Christian institutions reinforced his traditional Swedish fears of Russia. Germany stood in his mind as the bulwark against the Soviet onslaught. He worried that the Anglo-Saxon powers, involved in the effort to defeat Hitler, would underestimate the danger of godless communism. Yet Eidem rejected the argument made by some clergy-

men and laymen that the threats posed by the Soviet Union justified
uncritical support of Nazi Germany. He saw the danger of Nazi
Germany because it undermined the ability of Germany to stop the
spread of communism.

Eidem opted to remain silent primarily for political and social reasons. As a high-ranking figure in Sweden's government, he felt a responsibility to support the government's foreign policy. The church in political terms was an institution of the state. His public silence reflected a
policy that reinforced what the Swedish government hoped others
would do. The government feared that too much public criticism of
Germany might provoke a German military response. Only once did
Eidem initiate an action that broke with this policy — in the case of the
Norwegian Jews. This exception, however, was done in the most moderate of terms and never repeated.

No evidence has been found that suggests that direct government
pressure was put on Eidem to follow government policy. Any serious
strategic concerns dissipated progressively after December 1942. It
would be difficult to argue that the government bore responsibility for
the church's silence. It was self-imposed. To speak out, however, would
undoubtedly have raised considerable problems within the church. The
clergy was divided on the question of Nazi Germany. For those of a pro-
Nazi orientation, persecution of Jews was either a question of the lesser
of two evils (the Soviet Union being the greater) or acceptable as part of
their own anti-Semitism. To remain silent allowed the church as an
institution to continue to be nominally unified.

It was the priority Eidem assigned to the protection of the church as
an institution both within the political arena and as a social institution of
Swedish society which led him to be publicly silent on the plight of the
Jews. He understood the moral dilemma that the question raised for the
church. He had no sympathy for those who persecuted or aided in the
persecutions. But he would not take the moral leadership in public for
which his office provided the opportunity. There was no physical danger
to his person, as there was to religious leaders in Germany. Eidem rele-
gated his own beliefs to be something of less importance because he
thought that a particular political position would sustain the interests of
the church better.

When faced with the dilemma of defending the church as a social-
political institution or sustaining the role of the church as the moral
leader of society, Eidem chose to be a bureaucrat rather than a religious

figure. How many other churchmen made the same decision?[97] The pressure on the clergy in all modern societies is to conform to a set of given political and social realities. For those churchmen who represent dominant national religious institutions, especially state churches, this pressure is even greater. It was easy to appreciate that Hitler's attack on the Jews was anti-Christian as well as immoral. It was much more difficult to take responsive action to stop it.

---

97. Grafströms anteckningar, November 5–6, 1942, pp. 57–64. A striking contrast to his public silence in Sweden was Eidem's speech in Germany in November 1942. Eidem deliberately made reference to the values of God and German culture before loyalty to the Hitler regime. The Swedish diplomats present at one of his speeches were shocked by the archbishop's outspokenness.

Chapter 4

"No Truck with Himmler": The Politics of Rescue

Whether the Swedish government should involve itself in an active attempt to rescue Jews became a policy issue only after November 1942 in conjunction with the mass arrests and deportation of Norway's Jews. Prior to this time, virtually no one in Sweden proposed Swedish intervention on the Continent on behalf of Jews, and no evidence exists to suggest that the government considered it in any case. After November 1942, suggestions for rescue efforts came from a variety of sources, both domestic and international. No proposals originated from within the government, but the government had to decide whether to embark upon a rescue effort and how much priority such efforts should receive. Sometimes proposals were rejected as impossible, some as undesirable, while others were attempted halfheartedly, or with little hope of success. A few were pursued with vigor and determination. The successes of Swedish policy in the latter cases were impressive: with regard to Danish Jews; in Hungary; and with the Red Cross rescue mission of 1945. Why did Swedish policy vary? Why were some efforts successful, or partially so, while others failed? The answer to these questions must be found in a careful analysis of each attempt at rescue. This chapter examines one case, the Red Cross mission in 1945. Chapter 5 attempts to place the lessons of this case into a perspective of the other efforts and to ask the questions: could more have been done and if so, why wasn't it?

On March 9, 1945, the first section of the Swedish Red Cross rescue mission embarked for Germany. It eventually consisted of 75 vehicles and 250 people and carried its own supplies, fuel, and medicine; its official task at that moment was to organize a camp inside Germany at

Neuengamme for all Danish and Norwegian citizens held in German concentration camps. For nearly eight weeks, the Swedes worked within Germany, exposed to attacks from the combatants and in fear that the operation would be canceled at any moment. By early May 1945 German-held internees from over twenty countries had been transported to Sweden. It was by far the largest and most successful rescue effort in German territory during the war. Yet its history has been largely ignored by scholars. Who initiated this mission? What goals did it have? Who was responsible for its direction? Why was it so successful?

The impetus for the rescue mission came from the conditions of 1944. Most importantly, Germany was losing the war. The defeat of Germany was no longer in question, although the nature and extent of the defeat remained open. European governments, especially neutrals such as Sweden and Switzerland, worried about their place in the postwar order. Sweden feared that German Baltic hegemony would be replaced by a Russian sphere of influence. Sweden wished, while maintaining its neutrality, to build goodwill and understanding in the Anglo-Saxon countries for its independent position and to ensure that Britain and the United States would maintain a lively interest in the future of Northern Europe. Sweden wanted the restoration of free and independent Denmark, Norway, and Finland. It was also anxious to demonstrate to its Scandinavian neighbors that Swedish neutrality could serve their interests as the war drew to a conclusion. The primary question for the Swedish government was how to aid its Scandinavian brothers without being drawn into the conflict.

Possibilities for Sweden to help its neighbors had been few. Finland found itself caught in an increasingly uncomfortable war with the Soviet Union in which Germany was a "co-belligerent." Sweden tried during 1944 to mediate between Finland and the Soviet Union. Denmark and Norway were occupied by German forces. Sweden believed that the Allies might attempt a landing on either's west coast, thereby bringing the war to Scandinavia in much more direct fashion and endangering Sweden's non-belligerency. The likelihood of such an occurrence decreased significantly after the Allied landings in France. What remained to be done was to ensure that at war's end the remaining German troops would not put up a last-ditch struggle within the Scandinavian states and to try to find ways to aid and comfort Danes and Norwegians that had been arrested by Germany and sent to the concentration camps.[1]

---

1. See Carlgren, op. cit.

The desire of the Swedish government to help its Scandinavian neighbors undoubtedly had broad public support. The successful rescue of the Danish Jews in October 1943 produced pride among the Swedes as well as goodwill in the Western countries. As underground activities increased in Denmark and Norway in 1944, German authorities reacted with expectable harshness. Many of these incidents were reported in the Swedish press. A broad consensus existed in Sweden that as much as possible should be done to aid other Scandinavians as long as such activities did not lead Sweden into the war.

Sweden's attitude was not the only factor that contributed to the circumstances surrounding the rescue mission. The Norwegian government-in-exile was anxious to try to mount a rescue effort for imprisoned Norwegians as soon as possible. Its representative in Stockholm, Niels Christian Ditleff, was energetic in proposing and organizing such a mission. By September 1944, Ditleff had convinced the Swedish foreign office that a rescue effort might be possible and began to organize it.[2] Ditleff's proposals concerned only Norwegians held in Germany. The Danish government also began to prepare lists of Danish prisoners, including the approximately 500 Danish Jews incarcerated at Theresienstadt.

The Jewish Question also figured prominently in the rescue mission. By 1944, it was broadly recognized that Germany was conducting a campaign to murder systematically all of Europe's Jews. But the United States and Great Britain refused to give helping Europe's Jews a high priority.[3] Jewish organizations such as the World Jewish Congress (WJC), the American Joint Distribution Committee, and the Jewish Agency, in conjunction with sympathetic individuals in politics, religious institutions, and the media, found themselves trying to influence various governments, all of whom had other, more pressing concerns. Throughout 1944, these groups, or individuals within them, devised various schemes. Many of them involved either Switzerland or Sweden.

Of course, the main problem for any rescue effort was Germany itself. As long as Adolf Hitler exercised absolute authority in Germany, rescue missions had little chance of success. However, it was possible to save people in occupied countries as the Danish Jewish episode had demon-

---

2. See *1945 års Svenska hjälpexpedition till Tyskland* (Stockholm, 1956), pp. 6–7; and Friberg, op. cit., p. 204.

3. See David Wyman, *The Abandonment of the Jews* (New York, 1984), and Bernard Wasserstein, *Britain and the Jews of Europe, 1939–1945* (Oxford, 1979).

strated. German civilian and military officials in Denmark had been in
general unsympathetic to the application of the "Final Solution" to
Denmark and therefore contributed to the escape of most of Denmark's
Jews. By August 1944, after the attempt on Hitler's life in July, Hitler's
authority even among leading Nazi officials became easier to doubt, if
not yet to challenge. Hitler's determination to see Germany destroyed
along with his regime led some high-ranking Nazis, especially Heinrich
Himmler, to question the wisdom of the Füehrer. Himmler's doubts
did not immediately lead to action, but they provided a base upon which
others could build. Two individuals who proved adept at manipulating
Himmler in the last phases of the war were his adjutant, Walter
Schellenberg, and his masseur, Felix Kersten.

Felix Kersten was a Balt who during the war carried Finnish citizenship. Educated in Berlin as a physical therapist, Kersten became
Himmler's masseur prior to the war. As the conflict progressed, Kersten
established his home in Stockholm and commuted to Berlin to care for
his famous patient. Kersten did not share Himmler's political beliefs and
tried to use Himmler's dependence on his treatment to aid various individuals and groups. In October 1944, for example, after consultation
with Christian Günther he successfully interceded with Himmler on
behalf of Swedish businessmen condemned to death for espionage in
Poland. Earlier, he had shown a particular interest in trying to help
Jews.[4] Kersten's problem was that he was viewed equivocally in the
West and in Sweden. Sir Victor Mallet, British minister to Sweden,
thought that he was thoroughly tainted by his contact with Himmler:

Kersten is known to me as a Nazi and a thoroughly bad man. He has a

---

4. Kersten remains a controversial figure. Hugh Trevor-Roper believes him to be an
important figure in a variety of rescue activities and attempts to moderate Himmler's
behavior: *The Last Days of Hitler* (New York, 1947); "Kersten, Himmler, and Count
Bernadotte," *The Atlantic* 44 (February 1953); and *The Kersten Memoirs, 1939–1945*
(London, 1956). Kersten himself produced his memoirs in Swedish, German, and English. The former two differ considerably from the latter. Felix Kersten, *Samtal med
Himmler* (Stockholm, 1947). He also forged documents in the fifties: Gillel Storch arkiv,
Storch to Fleming, April 6, 1976, and Fleming to Storch, September 10, 1976; also, Storch
to Koblik, March 29, 1983. Two Dutch scholars, Posthumous and de Jong, disagree about
his role in helping Dutchmen. Norwegian Professor Didrik A. Seip gives Kersten credit
for convincing Himmler to have German troops in Norway capitulate. Finnish scholars are
also divided in their views of his role in German-Finnish relations. Kersten's role in the
release of the "Warsaw Swedes" is not controversial. *1945 års*, pp. 228–229.

home in Stockholm to which he has brought a big collection of pictures. They are reported to be Dutch, but I have little information on this point.[5]

Swedish opinion of Kersten varied sharply. Günther's experience with Kersten's help in the matter of the "Warsaw Swedes" convinced him that Kersten could be of great value. On February 2, 1945, Günther's top aides considered recommending Kersten for Swedish citizenship. Two voted in favor, while three voted against. One of the negative voices underscored the difficulty Kersten faced in trying to establish his credibility: "Kersten is, according to my opinion, a war criminal, nothing more and nothing less."[6] It would be eight years before Kersten received Swedish citizenship.[7]

The remaining figure who was to play a conspicuous part in the rescue mission was Count Folke Bernadotte. In 1944, Bernadotte served as vice chairman of the Swedish Red Cross. As nephew of King Gustaf V, and chairman of the Swedish Boy Scouts, Bernadotte was a prominent figure in Sweden. During the war, the Swedish Red Cross maintained a broad range of humanitarian activities, including large-scale aid to Greece, prisoner-of-war exchanges, and aid to Scandinavian children. The Swedish Red Cross had been involved in an attempt to help Norwegian Jews in 1942. The Swedish government used the Red Cross for various diplomatic purposes when conventional diplomacy seemed inappropriate or likely to be ineffectual. When Hungary's Jews found themselves in the maelstrom of the Final Solution in 1944, suggestions were made in Hungary that the Swedish Red Cross and Folke Bernadotte should lead an expedition to Budapest to help the endan-

---

5. PRO, FO 371, 48026, Mallet to Foreign Office, February 25, 1945.

6. Sven Grafströms anteckningar, February 2, 1945, pp. 4–5.

7. The issue of Kersten's Swedish citizenship is one of the major reasons for Kersten's behavior in the post-1945 period. It also contributed to the inflamed relations between Trevor-Roper and Bernadotte. Günther tried to get Kersten Swedish citizenship on numerous occasions after the war. He had, however, little influence on the postwar Social Democratic governments who decided the matter. Trevor-Roper's attack on Bernadotte — post-mortem — in 1953 claimed to be based on the injustice suffered by Kersten at the hands of the Swedes. Bernadotte did not mention Kersten's role in the rescue mission in his popular memoir, Slutet (Stockholm, 1945), published in English as The Curtain Falls (New York, 1945). Bernadotte also failed to mention Kersten in some of his briefings with Swedish officials during the actual rescue effort. See Informationsstyrelsens arkiv, v.7, Diskussionsprotokoll, April 16, 1945. His wife, Estelle Bernadotte, has claimed that her husband was fully aware of his memoirs' shortcomings but had been convinced to publish them. Sweden, Arvid Richerts arkiv (Göteborg), Estelle Bernadotte to Richert, May 3, 1956.

gered Jews.[8] Bernadotte himself was eager to play a role in world events. In his capacity with the Red Cross, he traveled abroad frequently and in 1944 met many individuals in London and Paris who had ideas about how to rescue people caught in German concentration camps. Bernadotte appears in the light of the events of 1945 to have been a resourceful negotiator and administrator, pro-Western but sensitive to Germany as well, and a little naive.[9]

These conditions and personae provide the background for the Red Cross mission. Three sources actually initiated the rescue effort: Ditleff; the World Jewish Congress; and Bernadotte. Each had a different goal. None were mutually exclusive. The main problems were diplomatic and organizational. The key was Himmler's willingness to permit such a mission. What becomes clear in the following account is that there were no fixed agreements between Himmler and those representing the Swedes: Bernadotte, Kersten, Norbert Masur, and Arvid Richert. As the war progressed through its final weeks, Himmler granted a series of concessions. The ability of the Swedes *in Germany* to capitalize on those concessions made it possible for the rescue to succeed.

Ditleff's role has already been indicated. It was he as Norwegian representative who constantly pressed the Swedes for action. Already in the summer of 1944, the Swedish government deliberated making a formal démarche in Berlin to request that Germany either release the Norwegians outright or send them to Sweden. On September 6, the

---

8. Per Anger arkiv, Valdemar Langlet to Swedish Red Cross, July 28, 1944. Also, Levai, op. cit., p. 275.

9. Personal characterizations are always difficult. Trevor-Roper's work on Kersten unfortunately included vindictive attacks on Bernadotte. Trevor-Roper accused him of being an anti-Semite, "a transport officer no more," and a bad judge of character — most importantly of Walter Schellenberg. Besides previously mentioned works (see note 4), see Storch arkiv, Trevor-Roper to Storch, February 9, 1949. Trevor-Roper provides little documentation for his conclusions about Bernadotte and his essays are riddled with factual errors. Henrik Beer, a Swedish Red Cross official, wrote a rebuttal to Trevor-Roper, "Sanningen om Folke Bernadotte," *Vecko-Journalen* 14 (1956). Sven Grafström characterized Bernadotte as something of a boy scout — Grafströms anteckningar, February 11, 1945, pp. 8–9. This author has found no indication of anti-Semitism in Bernadotte's behavior or attitudes. Gillel Storch in his 1962 article, op. cit., drew the same conclusions. Trevor-Roper and Bernadotte corresponded with each other when the former wrote his *Last Days*. Bernadotte objected to certain sections of the work and sent copies of his objections to influential friends in Britain. *Kersten Memoirs*, p. 7. Trevor-Roper was clearly embittered by Bernadotte's attacks. They disagreed over Walter Schellenberg's part in the rescue effort. Bernadotte was assassinated in Palestine by the Stern gang in 1948 while serving as the United Nations mediator. Yitzak Shamir, among others, has been implicated in the planning of Bernadotte's assassination.

Swedish minister in Berlin, Arvid Richert, was requested to inquire on behalf of Günther for release of the Norwegians. Richert reported back that some possibilities existed.[10] From early September, then, the Swedish government believed that it might be possible to effect a rescue of the Scandinavians held in German camps. It remained unclear, however, exactly how to manage such an enterprise. By October–November, the idea of utilizing the Red Cross instead of regular diplomatic channels had crystallized. Günther in particular was enthusiastic about the project. Every relevant foreign office document from November to March 1945 showed that the mission was perceived to be one to rescue Scandinavians, of all religious persuasions. The man who was expected to lead the expedition, if and when it could be mounted, was Count Folke Bernadotte.

During 1944, Bernadotte indicated an active interest in trying to find ways to aid Scandinavians.[11] He shared the predispositions of Günther and others that helping the Norwegians and Danes was of highest priority. But he was not uninterested in other groups. Bernadotte had taken a trip on behalf of the Red Cross, October 29–November 14, to London and Paris. Its primary purpose was to identify what Sweden could do with regard to postwar reconstruction, but at the same time Bernadotte met with representatives of various organizations who hoped to engage the Swedish Red Cross in a variety of activities. The General Secretary of the WJC, L. Zelmanovits, talked with him about the possibility of a rescue mission for Jews.[12] In Paris, Bernadotte met with Raoul Nordling and others who encouraged him to aid a large number of French women at Ravensbrück. Bernadotte found the idea of helping the French women appealing and promised to investigate the possibilities:

> Count Bernadotte promised to investigate the possibilities about reaching an agreement with the Germans (about the 20,000 French women at Ravensbrück) and examine the resources which the Red Cross had for such a rescue mission.[13]

---

10. UD 1920, HP 1616, Cabinet to Richert, September 6, 1944, and Richert to Günther, September 7, 1944.

11. For example, see ibid., von Post to Kumlin, January 7, 1944.

12. Ibid., HP 1050, Swedish Legation (London) to Lundborg, January 17, 1945. Zelmanovits had written Bernadotte as well and as of January had received no response.

13. Sweden, Riksarkivet, Swedish Red Cross archive, Folke Bernadotte, II:7, v. 32, Memorandum of Folke Bernadotte's trip, October 29–November 1944, undated but certainly November 1944.

This notion remained with Bernadotte throughout the following months. When the opportunity developed to expand the mission to aid Scandinavians, Bernadotte's interest led the expedition to Ravensbrück, but the chief beneficiary of this twist was to be Polish Jewesses, not huge numbers of French women.

The Jewish aspect of the rescue mission has been in many ways the most confusing part. The little international literature that does exist on the expedition emphasizes aid to the Jews, although Trevor-Roper accuses Bernadotte of not having been sensitive to the Jewish Question. Actually, the initiative for the Jewish part of the expedition came last. It emanated from the WJC. Gillel Storch, WJC representative in Stockholm, had been very active throughout the war in trying to help Jews on the Continent. His greatest success was to develop a large-scale aid program in the form of food and medicines for Jewish internees in German concentration camps. The Swedish Foreign Office had received a number of schemes to aid Jews from him.

Storch had been involved in an unsuccessful plan to rescue 2,000 Latvian Jews in July 1944. The incident was of interest because of the reactions it produced. Iver Olsen, WRB representative in Stockholm, fully supported the idea and offered funding. The U.S. State Department had a less optimistic view and believed the effort was primarily intended by the three Germans involved to make some money. Mallet reported that the Swedish Foreign Office believed the idea had originated with Himmler, who was attempting to "gain credit for himself in Sweden and elsewhere for more humane policy toward Jews. This is no doubt with an eye to saving his own skin later."[14] The Swedish Foreign Office itself was surprised by Olsen's attitude, believing that the whole scheme was not credible, and indicated a continued preference for trying to rescue "a relatively few Jews" for which numerous attempts had been made in Berlin.[15] The Swedish Foreign Office remained skeptical in 1944 of the chances of success of a direct effort to rescue Jews, but was not unwilling to try.

In late January 1945, the WJC once again urged Sweden to take action on behalf of the Jews.[16] An inquiry was sent to Richert in Berlin for opin-

---

14. UD 1920, HP 1050, Memorandum to Erlander, etc., July 7, 1944; and PRO, FO 371, British Embassy (Washington) to Foreign Office, July 6, 1944, and Mallet to Foreign Office, July 12, 1944.

15. Ibid., Memorandum to Erlander, July 7, 1944.

16. Ibid., HP 1950, Swedish Legation (London) to Lundborg, January 17, 1945;

ions about what might be done. Richert advised against any Swedish action on the grounds that it would be a "shot in the dark" because the Germans would never agree.[17] By February 3, the Swedes were pursuing the idea of a joint Swedish-Swiss-Vatican démarche in Berlin for the Jews. Richert reported on February 7 that all neutral representatives and the Papal nuncio were against the idea of a joint démarche. The Swedish minister in Berne, Westrup, informed Stockholm that Switzerland agreed in principle with the idea of a démarche but preferred not to do it jointly.[18] At the same time, Westrup reported that the former Swiss President, Musy, had negotiated with Himmler about the release of Jews to Switzerland. The success of Musy likely stimulated both the decision to launch the Red Cross mission to aid Scandinavians and the issuance of a formal démarche on the Jewish Question in Berlin.[19]

On February 10, Richert was instructed to make a spectacular offer: Sweden was willing to receive all Jews in German concentration camps, "especially those at Theresienstadt and Bergen-Belsen concentration camps."[20] Simultaneously, a decision had been taken to send Bernadotte to Berlin to negotiate with Himmler over the release of the Scandinavians. There exists no evidence to suggest that the Swedish Foreign Ministry actually thought that the German government would respond positively to their démarche. On numerous other occasions when a formal request had been made to the German Foreign Office on behalf of single Jews or large groups, the replies had always been negative. Richert's attitude reflected the frustrations of three years of failure in this area. In fact, there is good evidence that suggests that the Swedish Foreign Office worried that any intervention on behalf of the Jews might hurt efforts to aid the Scandinavians. Wrote one leading Foreign Ministry official:

Boström to Foreign Office, January 21 & 23, 1945; and von Post to Richert, January 25, 1945.

17. Ibid., von Post to Richert, January 25 & 27, 1945, and Richert to von Post, January 29, 1945.

18. Ibid., Richert to von Post, February 7, 1945, and Westrup to Foreign Office, February 8, 1945. Westrup also telephoned on the same day to say that the Swiss believed that further rescue actions to help the Jews were possible with "Himmler's support."

19. Ibid., "PM om diplomatisk aktion i Berlin till förmån för judarna," February 19, 1945.

20. Ibid.; See also, Cabinet to Richert, February 12, 1945. A German agent in Stockholm, Dr. Kleist, had informed the Swedes that there were good possibilities to rescue 2,000 Jews in Bergen-Belsen.

My heartfelt thanks for your letter of the seventh with Kleist. I would like
to inform you however that while we are indeed interested in the possibility of Jews coming to Sweden, the most pressing issue at the moment is to
use all possible means to expedite the repatriation of the Norwegians from
Germany to Norway. I am sure that you fully understood that but I
wanted to write these lines so that you might get an opportunity to underscore our great interest in the return of the Norwegians — especially if the
Germans tried to block the Norwegian issue with the excuse about
investigating the possibility of the Jewish effort.[21]

On February 10, the Foreign Office decided to try to launch the rescue mission.[22] The months of preparation, the interests of Ditleff, Günther, Bernadotte, and the WJC served as a base. The success of Musy in
negotiating with Himmler the release of approximately 1,500 Jews
seemed to have been the deciding factor in sending Bernadotte to
Germany. On February 12, Bernadotte received formal instructions
from the chairman of the Red Cross, Prince Carl, to fly to Berlin to negotiate with the Germans about "civilian prisoners in Germany . . . their
internment and their possible removal."[23] It was understood that the
success of the mission depended upon Himmler. Therefore, Günther
once again sought out Felix Kersten.[24]

Kersten had not been involved with the rescue mission until Günther
asked him to telephone Himmler to smooth the way for Bernadotte.[25]
Richert was also asked to seek out Himmler's adjutant, Walter

21. Swedish Berlin Legation arkiv, v. 73c, von Post to Nylander, January 9, 1945.
22. UD 1920, HP 1618, Cabinet to Richert, February 10, 1945; also, Sven Grafströms
anteckningar, February 11, 1945, pp. 8–9.
23. SRC, Folke Bernadotte, II: v. 2, Prince Carl to Bernadotte, February 12, 1945.
Note that neither Scandinavians nor Jews were mentioned specifically in Bernadotte's
instructions. See also PRO, FO 371, 48046, Mallet to Foreign Office, February 6, 1945.
24. Grafströms anteckningar, pp. 8–9; PRO, FO 371, 48046, Mallet to Foreign Office,
February 11, 1945; UD 1920, HP 1682, Günther to Engzell, November 4, 1948; and FO
371, 48026, Mallet to Foreign Office, February 25 & 27, 1945.
25. Trevor-Roper claimed in his *Atlantic* article, op. cit., and in the introduction to the
Kersten Memoirs that Kersten had already negotiated with Himmler about both the
release of the Scandinavians and the Jews. *Kersten Memoirs*, p. 14. and *Atlantic*, p. 44. He
even used the word "treaty" to describe the arrangement. Not only was Kersten incapable
of signing a treaty (not to mention Himmler) but Kersten apparently was working with the
Swiss for release of the Jews. *Samtal med Himmler*, pp. 231–233. It very well may be that
he talked generally with Himmler about the potential goodwill to be achieved by the
release of the Scandinavian prisoners. Kersten presented the Swedish Foreign Office with
a memorandum on all his humanitarian activities dated June 12, 1945, UD 1920, HP 1050,
(known hereafter as *Kersten PM*). This summary conforms rather closely with *Samtal* but
has important discrepancies from his English memoirs.

Schellenberg, for the same purpose.[26] Schellenberg had proved to be a useful contact for the Swedes since he was anxious to see Himmler distance himself from Hitler. On February 16, Bernadotte flew to Berlin to begin negotiations.

The negotiations proved awkward and difficult. Hitler exploded when he learned of Himmler's deal with Musy; Himmler temporarily became more cautious. Himmler insisted consistently that whatever arrangements were agreed upon would have to be kept completely out of public view. The success of the Swedish government in minimizing publicity about the mission contributed greatly to Himmler's willingness to make concessions later in the mission.[27] During these first negotiations. Himmler refused to allow any transfer of internees to Sweden. He did approve of the general idea of a Red Cross mission in Germany that would gather all Scandinavian prisoners and place them in one camp, Neuengamme, near the Danish border.[28] Bernadotte had taken the first critical step, but no details had been arranged. The actual operation of the mission depended on the development of events in March.

Bernadotte returned to Stockholm prepared to lead the mission into Germany to rescue Scandinavians. At the same time, the issue of helping Jews also had to be addressed. On February 19, Storch had written to Bernadotte, asking him to enlarge his activities to include aid to Jews.[29] Bernadotte replied that he, too, thought something might be accomplished for the Jews:

> As you yourself know, Swedish authorities have made very serious attempts, and given permission, for some Jews to come to Sweden. . . . even in this Swedish action (i.e., the Red Cross mission) some positive results should be achievable.[30]

---

26. *1945 års*, pp. 18–19. Kaltenbrunner reported to the Swedish Legation in Berlin that it would be easy to arrange a meeting between Bernadotte and Himmler. UD 1920, HP 1618, Brandel to von Post, February 14, 1945.

27. Censorship worked efficiently in Sweden. It was mostly self-imposed by the newspapers themselves. One newspaper, *Dagens Nyheter*, broke ranks on the rescue story apparently as a deliberate challenge to the authority of *Informationsstyrelsen*. It was a symbolic act and the newspaper published little information about the rescue after a brief story in early March 1945.

28. Ibid., Folke Bernadotte Memorandum on visit to Germany, February 16–21, 1945, 17 pages. Bernadotte met with Kaltenbrunner, Ribbentrop twice, Schellenberg, three times, and Himmler. He was unimpressed by Ribbentrop. The meeting with Himmler apparently was quite cordial. Bernadotte tried to establish a positive relationship with Himmler. Himmler talked about the Bolshevik threat. No mention was made of the Jews. The impression of the report is of a skillful negotiator who is attempting to build the basis for further agreements.

29. UD 1920, HP 1050, Storch to Engzell, February 19, 1945.

30. Storch arkiv, Bernadotte to Storch, February 26, 1945.

This positive response was a personal opinion only; no change in the rescue effort had been made by the government. Storch decided to expand his efforts. He sought out Kersten.

Kersten and Storch had never met. The latter used a German banker in Stockholm as intermediary in arranging a meeting "in late February."[31] It was agreed that Kersten on his next visit to Germany scheduled for early March, would attempt to get Himmler to accept a four-point program:

1. To grant permission to send food and medicine to the camps.
2. To put all Jews in a few camps and call on the International Red Cross to run them until the World Jewish Congress could take responsibility.
3. To free certain persons specified on lists carried by Kersten.
4. To free certain numbers of Jews to Sweden and Switzerland. The number for Sweden was estimated at 5–10,000.

Kersten left for Berlin on March 3. He had been also requested by Günther to help with Bernadotte's efforts.[32]

The events of March occurred amid increasing confusion. Communication between Germany and Stockholm deteriorated; understanding of who controlled what in Germany lessened; and the diplomatic channels between Stockholm and London and Washington and the Allied command under General Eisenhower proved incapable of providing information and advice in time to be pertinent. Once committed, the Red Cross mission in Germany depended on the skill of its leader, Bernadotte, and his staff, along with the important aid he received from Kersten with regard to Himmler. Decisions were frequently reached "on the spot" and Kersten and Bernadotte had to try to ensure that they would not be countermanded by Himmler or his aides. Schellenberg remained a steadfast support to both throughout the next two months.

On March 1, Eric von Post, head of the Political Department of the Swedish Foreign Office, provided details of the mission to the British minister in Stockholm. He asked Mallet to suggest how the mission could be managed safely. It intended to work within areas under intense air attacks from Allied aircraft. The same request was made to the Americans.[33] Two days later, the British approved the idea of the mission but

---

31. Kersten, *Samtal*, p. 231; and *Kersten PM*.
32. Ibid.
33. PRO, FO 371, 48046, Mallet to Foreign Office, March 1, 1945.

warned that no guarantees of safety could be given. A suggestion to paint the buses white was made. It was hoped the such marking would be easily distinguishable from the air.[34] The United States asked for more time to study the Swedish inquiry. It responded positively in early April, in the middle of the mission itself.[35] Despite efforts to warn SHAFE, British Foreign Office officials worried about the ramifications if Allied military forces attacked the Swedes either in air or sea operations.[36] They understood that there was indeed a great likelihood that such incidents would occur.

For a brief moment, it appeared as though the whole mission would be scrapped. A report to Stockholm from the Swedish legation in Berlin said that the Germans had already begun to move the Scandinavians to Neuengamme and that there was no need for the Red Cross mission. Mallet wrote to London: "It is thought doubtful whether any of Bernadotte's schemes will ever materialize."[37] Uncertain of the situation, Bernadotte was sent back to Berlin, March 6–8. His visit overlapped with that of Kersten, who continued his treatment of and discussions with Himmler.

Kersten's negotiations initially went poorly. Although Himmler promised to maintain the concentration camps until the Allies liberated them, he wanted to trade the release of all Jews held in Germany for a 2–3 week pause in the Allied bombing campaign. Himmler stalled on most of the specific proposals that Kersten carried with him, just as he had done earlier with Bernadotte. Kersten fully understood that the Allies would not bargain with Himmler about a bombing cessation and that Himmler was procrastinating.[38] Bernadotte was slightly more successful with his negotiations; final approval was given on March 7 to begin the Red Cross mission. Its official purpose was to establish a camp at Neuengamme for all German-held Scandinavian internees. Still, doubts existed in Stockholm about the possibilities of the mission.

---

34. Ibid., Foreign Office to Mallet, March 3, 1945.

35. UD 1920, HP 1619, Memorandum from von Post, April 5, 1945. Although the Americans approved the rescue effort which had already been at work nearly a month, they refused to promise that Sweden would receive more food as a result of the rescue effort.

36. PRO, FO 371, 48046, Mallet to Foreign Office, March 5 and 12, 1945, and Halifax to Foreign Office, March 22, 1945.

37. Ibid., Mallet to Foreign Office, March 3, 1945; SRC, Folke Bernadotte, II:7, v. 2, Brandel to Bernadotte, March 1, 1945.

38. *Kersten PM.*

Indeed, there had been considerable opposition to the whole idea of dealing with Himmler within the Swedish governmental bureaucracy. Sven Grafström, assistant director of the Political Department of the Foreign Office and one of its more pro-Allied members, had tried to stop the mission in February. He called it a "light-headed notion," and feared the ramifications for Sweden of negotiating with "Hitler's Number 1 thug." The chief of the Swedish secret service, General Ehrensvärd, also opposed it. But the leadership of the Foreign Office — Günther, Boheman, and von Post — remained enthusiastic. Grafström complained that the Foreign Office "has become a sub-section of the Red Cross and nothing else."[39] The criticism had little effect; Günther wanted to take the risks and hoped that Kersten would serve as a form of insurance in case something went amiss.[40]

On March 9, the mission began its departure from Sweden. Its size had been reduced as a result of Bernadotte's negotiations with Himmler and Schellenberg.[41] A base of operations was established at the Bismarck family estate at Friedrichsruh, not far from the camp at Neuengamme. The support given by the grandson of Germany's Iron Chancellor to the mission impressed the Swedes:

> . . . can you believe that *Otto Bismarck himself*, [!] along with a Russian, worked with his own hands for a whole day helping unload a railroad car of Norwegian packages. . . .[42]

The mission's activities concentrated solely on bringing the Scandinavians to Neuengamme. Sachsenhausen, near Berlin, was the first camp to be visited. As many as 349 Scandinavians were released. The Swedes made the same nine-hour trip to Sachsenhausen five more times. Another column drove south, reaching Dachau and Mauthausen. The Scandinavians were put into the regular camp at Neuengamme, which the Swedes did not view as acceptable. The general conditions of the camp, which held approximately 50,000 inmates, were deemed extremely unhealthy. As the Scandinavians had received better treatment in general, the Swedes wanted to maintain their relatively privi-

---

39. Grafströms anteckningar, February 11 and March 3, 1945.
40. UD 1920, HP 1075, Cabinet to Richert, March 14, 1945.
41. SRC, Folke Bernadotte, II:7, Bernadotte to Schellenberg, February 24, 1945; see also Åke Svensson, *De vita bussarna* (Stockholm, 1945), p. 10.
42. UD 1920, HP 1618, Richert to von Post, March 4, 1945. Underlining was done on the original by the reader (von Post?).

leged circumstances with a specially created "Scandinavian camp" alongside or within Neuengamme where the Red Cross personnel could move freely. They were not permitted inside the regular camp.[43]

By March 27, 4,800 Scandinavians had been relocated to Neuengamme. Still to be aided were 1,400 Danish policemen, 800 Scandinavian Jews at Theresienstadt, and approximately 1,000 "mental patients."[44] The policemen and the Jews were believed to be the groups most difficult for the Germans to release. Therefore, their rescue had been placed last.[45] Bernadotte also reported that he expected the Scandinavian Jews to be somewhat reluctant to move from Theresienstadt:

> As far as the Jews were concerned, both the Norwegians and the Danes felt that the Jews would be rather unwillling to be transported to Neuengamme, a piece of information that came as a surprise to me. In discussions with the Danes and Norwegians, it was agreed to get permission [from the Germans] to bring the Jews to Neuengamme and even here, I achieved positive results. One must expect however that the Jews will not have much enthusiasm for the idea, at least in the beginning. In a longer perspective, however, we are convinced that it will be their advantage.[46]

The reticence of the Jews, if it existed, was probably caused by the combination of fear of what any transport from Theresienstadt usually meant and the relatively mild treatment the Danish Jews had experienced since their arrest in 1943.

Retrieval of the outstanding Scandinavians was not the only remaining problem. Conditions at Neuengamme were still not acceptable. Himmler refused to concede the main objective of the mission — the transferral of the Scandinavians to Sweden. Bernadotte and Kersten continued to try to convince Himmler to be more generous. The latter worked for acceptance of the WJC proposals. In late March, both returned to Stockholm. Kersten carried a remarkable offer.

Himmler offered Kersten on March 21 the opportunity to free 10,000 Jews and send them to Sweden. Himmler indicated that he was willing to *negotiate* with a representative of the WJC on the matter.[47] The

43. Svensson, op. cit., pp. 57 ff.

44. UD 1920, HP 1619, Memorandum on Red Cross mission, March 27, 1945.

45. Ibid., HP 1618, Swedish Legation (Berlin) to von Post, March 10, 1945.

46. Ibid., Folke Bernadotte to SRC Board, March 16, 1945. This report underscored the close cooperation that existed between the Norwegian and Danish officials in Germany and Bernadotte.

47. Ibid., HP 1050, Storch to Adler-Rudel, March 27, 1945.

immediate Swedish response was very positive. They were "very interested in freeing Jews even if we must provide compensation. . . ." The Foreign Office had received other indications that a large-scale rescue of the Jews might be possible.[48] However, Richert reported on the 21st that Musy was back in Berlin on behalf of the Jews and that Hitler had expressly forbidden Himmler to negotiate with anyone.[49]

It was amidst these contradictory pieces of information that the Swedes formally considered their strategy for the following weeks. Despite Richert's news of Hitler's intervention, there was considerable optimism about the future of the mission.[50] On March 26, Bernadotte, Erik Boheman, and von Post met. The meeting produced a much broadened agenda for the mission. A memorandum of the meeting listed the Swedish goals:

A. Most importantly, that all Scandinavians currently held at Neuengamme be permitted to be moved to Sweden.
B. Request that Swedish Red Cross personnel be permitted to move throughout the whole of the Neuengamme camp.
C. Offer to use Swedish Red Cross buses to transport non-Scandinavians, particularly 25,000 French women, to Neuengamme.

The memo ended with the following note:

> Today the above was complemented with instructions to Bernadotte that when he found it suitable and did not threaten the above points, he could request that a number of Jews be sent to Sweden.[51]

What appears to be the consequence of this meeting was both the reaffirmation of the priorities of the mission as they had developed prior to February and its extension in the direction of Bernadotte's concern for the French women and the Jews. The primary goal remained the transfer of the Scandinavian internees to Sweden. Yet the Swedes had enough confidence to try to expand their activities within the whole of Neuengamme and to attempt to rescue non-Scandinavians as well. No

---

48. Ibid., HP 1051, Engzell to Richert, March 22, 1945.
49. Ibid., Richert to Foreign Office, March 21, 1945.
50. Ibid., Nylander to Engzell, March 26, 1945, and Engzell to Richert, March 22, 1945. See also, HP 1692, Richert to von Post, March 22, 1945.
51. Ibid., HP 1619, Memorandum of March 27, 1945. This document was sent to Trevor-Roper in 1955. It apparently had no effect on his writing despite its great importance.

indication exists that there were any differences of opinion between the three Swedish policy-makers.

Adoption of an expanded policy did not mean that it would be accomplished. Much negotiation lay ahead in Germany with Bernadotte and Kersten serving as chief negotiators. Storch sent Himmler's offer westwards with a request that he be given permission by the WJC to negotiate with Himmler on the offer of the release of 10,000 Jews.[52] This request, which was sent via the Swedish diplomatic dispatches as well as through the British and U.S. legations, produced some special problems for the Western countries.

Both Western legations in Stockholm doubted the wisdom of permitting Storch to negotiate with Himmler:

> . . . in no circumstances must Storch be allowed to go to Germany. . . . Storch is a Latvian stateless Jew. Very rich, self-important and very nearly a lunatic in some respects (e.g., 17 of his family were murdered by the Germans but he asked Wilhelmstrasse for a testimonial of his good work for the Jews and then asked U.D. for a similar document).[53]

The most awkward aspects of Storch's request came in London. Some of the Foreign Office officials in London who received the Storch request plainly viewed the idea of rescue of the Jews as bad policy for Britain to be involved with.

A minute was prepared for Winston Churchill in which it was noted that the British had decided not to forward Storch's telegram to the Jewish Agency and suggested that Britain not get involved with the scheme in any way. Sweden, it was noted, could manage the situation alone. The minute introduced Kersten to Churchill, argued that Britain should not be involved in negotiations with Himmler in any fashion, and that "Jewish societies" were willing to insist on the rescue of Jews "at any price."[54] Anthony Eden supported these recommendations and passed them on to Churchill. Churchill's response typified the man: "I agree. No truck with Himmler."[55]

---

52. PRO, FO 371, 51194, Mallet to Foreign Office, March 27, 1945.

53. Ibid., FO 188, 525, Intelligence commentary in British Legation (Stockholm), March 25, 1945.

54. Ibid., FO 371, 51194, Minute for Churchill on Kersten/Himmler, April 1, 1945.

55. Ibid., FO 954, 23, Eden to Churchill, April 1, 1945. Churchill's comment is dated April 5. There is no evidence that Churchill agreed with the Foreign Office comments on "Jewish societies." His main concern was obviously not being involved in negotiations with Himmler.

In fact, the continued fate of the Red Cross mission and its ability to extend its activities became more intertwined in Himmler's efforts to negotiate a separate peace with the Western powers. Indeed, his initial offer to Kersten on March 21 might have been an attempt to open direct negotiations with the West, even through the WJC. When Bernadotte returned on April 2 to his negotiations with Himmler, the separate peace question was the issue Himmler wanted to discuss most earnestly. Bernadotte was to serve as a conduit for Himmler to make "peace feelers" to the Western powers. Himmler's proposals fell on deaf ears. The Swedish government was under no illusion about the probability of these efforts succeeding. Rather, they were concerned about two matters: (1) control and disposal of the German troops in Norway and Denmark; and (2) using Himmler's dependence on a neutral power to forward his offers to widen the activities of the Red Cross mission.[56]

Himmler's concessions came slowly. In late March, he allowed the Swedes to move freely within Neuengamme.[57] On April 2, he refused Bernadotte a blanket request to permit all Scandinavians at Neuengamme to leave for Sweden. However, he did accept the idea of some leaving, including all women, those ill, and a few specific political prisoners.[58] He rejected any transfer of non-Scandinavians to Neuengamme. Almost immediately, Scandinavian internees began their journey across Denmark to Sweden.

Without any publicity, the streets of the Danish cities were filled with crying, flag-waving Danes, as the white buses passed by. The Swedes were greeted as heroes. On April 9, 1945, five years to the day of Germany's attack on Denmark and Norway, the first wave of internees arrived in Hälsingborg. Preparations for their arrival had been underway for over six months. Yet no one in Sweden had imagined that

---

56. UD 1920, HP 1619, Bernadotte notes about discussions, March 29–April 6, 1945; Carlgren, op. cit.; and Informationsstyrelsens arkiv, v. 7, Discussion of April 16, 1945. This latter document provided the clearest insight into Bernadotte's negotiating techniques. Bernadotte appeared in front of the *Informationsstyrelsen* board to explain his activities, ask for cooperation, and answer any questions that they wished to pose. Asked for his personal impression of Himmler, Bernadotte explained how he tried to reinforce the impression of Himmler that Himmler had something to gain by cooperating with the rescue efforts. He described Himmler as a romantic and had given him a book on Nordic runestones. He also agreed that Himmler would not have responded positively to such a rescue effort if Himmler had not already concluded that the war and the Third Reich were lost.

57. Ibid., HP 1619, Memorandum from Foreign Office, March 29, 1945.

58. Ibid., Bernadotte to Hansson, April 3, 1945.

this first contingent of 132 women from Ravensbrück would be the beginning of a flood of 20,000 refugees, most of whom were ill-nourished, sick, and in need of instant care. Before a month had passed, nearly every available space in southern Sweden had been commandeered to care for the internees. It was a remarkable effort — partially planned, partially spontaneous.

News of the new arrivals was almost completely blacked out. Himmler insisted upon total silence so that Hitler would not stop the mission. Some stories appeared, but they were few until late April. The physical conditions of the internees, especially in terms of malnutrition and disease, shocked the Swedes and confirmed the worst stories that had been circulating in Swedish papers since 1942. The silence aided Bernadotte and Kersten in their efforts to expand the mission beyond the Scandinavians.[59]

By early April, there remained only two issues related to the Scandinavians: to get an agreement from Himmler for the release of all Scandinavians to Sweden, and to pick up the Scandinavian Jews at Theresienstadt. This latter operation represented the longest journey of the mission: four days were needed to complete it. On April 12, 35 buses left Friedrichsruh for Theresienstadt via Belzig, Zweikau, Hof, Bayreuth, and Eger.[60] On April 16, the Scandinavian Jews were in Lübeck. The group consisted of 423 people: 215 men, 185 women, and 25 children. They arrived in Malmö on April 18.[61] Resolution of the former problem came unexpectedly on April 19.

Red Cross officials in Germany suddenly received orders from Berlin: remove all Danes and Norwegians from Neuengamme and transport them to Denmark. Within 24 hours, all Scandinavians were removed from Germany.[62] These orders from Himmler's headquarters forbade, however, further movement to Sweden unless war broke out in Denmark. On April 24, Bernadotte got Himmler to agree to permit all internees to be taken to Sweden. The circumstances of the war were

59. SRC, Folke Bernadotte, II.7, v. 2, Richert to von Post, April 10, 1945.

60. UD 1920, HP 1619, Memorandum of Tamm, April 2, 1945.

61. Ibid., Telephone message from Captain Melin, April 17, 1945. See also Marcus Melchior, *Darkness over Denmark* (London, 1973), p. 147. Melchior had been appointed by the Swedish government as rabbi for the Danish Jewish refugees. A controversial figure in prewar Denmark, Melchior became chief rabbi in Denmark after the war. The book offered many interesting insights into Scandinavian Jewish life.

62. Ibid., Brandel to Boheman, April 20, 1945, and Bernadotte to Grafström, April 22, 1945.

rapidly changing the conditions of the mission. Himmler grew more bold as Hitler further isolated himself in his Berlin bunker. Allied aircraft attacked some of the Red Cross convoys. By the end of April, the question was no longer what Himmler would allow, but rather what was feasible, given the military conditions.

The threat of Allied attack had always existed. SHAFE could not guarantee the safety of the Red Cross buses. The British warned the Swedes on April 10 of the increasing risks:

> Air Ministry had pointed out that the tactical battle zone was approaching the area in which the Bernadotte expedition was operating, and the danger from Allied aircraft to all road movements was likely to increase. I imagine that this is no news to you.[63]

The mission was hit three times by Allied planes, with sixteen internees killed and many more wounded. One Swede died.[64] These incidents no doubt hastened the desire of the Swedes to conclude the mission as soon as possible with as little loss of life as possible.

At the diplomatic level, difficulties continued to exist over the idea of sending a diplomatic representative of the WJC with Kersten to Berlin to negotiate with Himmler. The idea of using Storch had encountered resistance among the Allied legations in Stockholm, the British had washed their hands of the whole adventure, and Storch himself had misgivings.[65] The priorities of the WJC apparently differed slightly from the question of the release of 10,000 Jews. They wanted Himmler to fulfill his promise to keep the concentration camps intact, especially Bergen-Belsen and Buchenwald.[66] At this juncture in the war, more Jews could be saved by keeping them in the camps than by exposing them to forced marches.

On April 13, two seats under the name "Kersten" were requested for transport to Berlin.[67] Three days later, special "passes" were written for Storch and Kersten, while on the 19th, another similar document was

---

63. SRC, Folke Bernadotte, II:7, v. 2, Labouchère to von Post, April 11, 1945.

64. PRO, FO 371, 48047, Mallet to Foreign Office, April 19 and 26, 1945.

65. Storch has claimed that he decided not to go to Berlin because it was feared that Himmler would try to use Storch to have Stephen Wise, president of the WJC, request of FDR that Allied bombing of Germany be stopped. Storch to Koblik, March 29, 1983.

66. SRC, Folke Bernadotte, II:7, v. 8, Storch to Bernadotte, April 4, 1945. Storch arkiv, F. Bernadotte to G. Storch, April 17, 1945. Norbert Masur, *En jude talar med Himmler* (Stockholm, 1945), p. 5.

67. UD 1920, HP 1057, von Essen to Aerotransport, April 13, 1945.

written for Norbert Masur, a German-Swedish Jew and prominent figure in the Stockholm congregation.[68] Masur learned that day that Himmler would receive him and Kersten outside Berlin on the following day.

The drama of Himmler's negotiations with a representative of the WJC has been captured in Masur's memoir, *A Jew Talks with Himmler*. His report to the Swedish Foreign Office of his meetings with Himmler and Schellenberg on April 20–21 confirms the details of Kersten's version provided in his memorandum of April 23, 1945. The primary purpose of the negotiations was to ensure that no more Jews were killed and to reaffirm that the remaining camps would be left intact for the Allied armies. On these points, Himmler conceded. On the matter of releasing internees, especially Jews, Himmler apparently was far less pliable. While Himmler agreed to free certain people on lists provided by the Swedes and 1,000 French Jewesses from Ravensbrück, there was no mention of the release of 10,000 Jews. In substance, the Masur-Himmler-Kersten meeting served to reinforce what had already been on-going for a month and even in its limited success did not guarantee anything. Masur warned the Swedes in his report as he urged immediate action to help the Jews: "Himmler's word is naturally absolutely nothing to depend upon. Even during our discussions, he told many lies."[69]

Bernadotte, too, returned to Germany to negotiate with Himmler. Himmler received him on April 21, just hours after Masur and Kersten had departed. Himmler now conceded that the Swedes could take all the internees at Ravensbrück. In their last meeting on the night of April 23–24, Himmler gave his permission for Bernadotte to take anyone he wished without limitation.[70] Himmler's concessions were caused by his increasingly frantic attempts to open communications with the Western powers. He gave Sweden carte blanche.

By April 25, the first 4,000 women from Ravensbrück were on their way to Sweden. Approximately 7,000 would be moved from the camp. The number rescued far exceeded anyone's expectations. The luck of

---

68. Ibid., HP 1692, April 16 and 19, 1945.

69. Ibid., HP 1050, Norbert Masur memorandum, April 23, 1945, and Kersten to Günther, April 23, 1945. There are discrepancies between these two contemporary documents and books written by both men after the war.

70. *1945 års*, p. 30.

finding a usable train allowed the Swedes to move far more internees
than their buses could manage.[71] In total, nearly 21,000 internees from
a variety of camps were transported from Germany through Denmark to
southern Sweden before the end of the war. An American consular official in Stockholm expressed the amazement of nearly everyone at the
success of the mission: ". . . the job being done by the Swedes in caring
for far less fortunate people is nothing short of miraculous."[72]

Who were those rescued? A Red Cross document listed 20,937 internees divided into the following nationalities:[73]

> Danes and Norwegians: 8,000
> Poles: 5,911
> French: 2,629
> stateless Jews: 1,615
> Germans: 1,124
> Belgians: 632
> Dutch: 387
> Hungarians: 290
> Balts: 191
> Luxembourgers: 79
> Slovaks: 28
> British: 14
> Americans: 9
> Rumanians: 6
> Finns: 5
> Italians: 4
> Spanish: 3
> Others: 9

How many were Jews? This question was impossible to answer definitely. Sweden had stopped registering refugees by religion in 1943.
The WJC compiled two lists of "Liberated Jews arrived in Sweden in
1945." Comparing these lists with Red Cross materials taken from specific camps at the time of rescue indicated only an approximate 50 percent overlap. The refugees often had little reason to indicate their religion when Swedish officials showed no interest in it. After all, they had
just experienced unimaginable terror as a result of their Jewishness.

---

71. UD 1920, HP 1619, Telephone from Friedrichsruh, April 25, 1945. See also
Svensson, op. cit.
72. PRO, FO 371, 51193, Whisler to Johnson, May 4, 1945.
73. SRC, II:1, v. 506.

More than one Swede has recorded how fearful and uncertain the refugees were when they reached Swedish soil. When they arrived in
Sweden, officials asked them to take off their pest-infected clothing and
enter showers to clean themselves. "I am so old, you do not need to gas
me," one Jewish woman cried in Trelleborg.[74]

Gillel Storch estimated that the Red Cross saved approximately 6,500
Jews. Hugo Valentin, an economic historian and active Zionist in the
Stockholm congregation, has suggested approximately 3,500, "mostly
women from Ravensbrück." Masur indicated that approximately 50 percent of the 7,000 women from Ravensbrück were Jewish. Clearly,
Valentin's estimate was far short of the actual number. Approximately
500 Scandinavian Jews and 1,615 stateless Jews were registered by
Swedish or Scandinavian authorities. 50 percent of the Poles seemed to
have been Jewesses. Storch's figure of 6,500 seemed quite reasonable.[75]
Whatever the actual count, the Red Cross mission represented one of
the most successful efforts to aid Jews during the war.

Taken as a whole, the success of the Red Cross mission should not be
credited to a single individual. One can understand the frustration of
Felix Kersten for not getting his share of the credit and for having his
citizenship held up for eight years. The internal inconsistencies of his
publications chronicle his rising disappointment. The excesses of a professional historian, i.e., Hugh Trevor-Roper, are more difficult to
appreciate. His attempt to deny the key role that Bernadotte played in
the rescue mission ignored both the reality of the experience and the
evidence. The personal partisanship that has so long played a part in the
understanding of the Red Cross mission has only distracted historians
from the key issue: the politics of rescue itself.

Was Germany willing to barter for Jewish lives, under what circumstances, and in what time periods? How far were the Allies willing to go

---

74. *Judisk Krönika* 14 (5–6), May–June 1945, p. 88. Professor Birgitta Odén reported
similar expressions of fear when she aided arriving Jews in Malmö. May 24, 1984.

75. Masur, p. 34; Storch, "insatser," p. 31; Valentin, "Rescue," pp. 224–251; SRC, II:7,
v. 33, has a variety of lists of Jews rescued. There are many problems related to attempting
an estimate of the number of Jewish refugees. What definition of Jew is one to use? If one
used the Nazi terminology, the number of rescued was likely to be considerably higher
than Storch's estimate of 6,500. If the definition includes only people who are practicing
Jews or born of two Jewish parents, the Storch estimate is probably reasonable. Valentin's
and those of the WJC underestimate the number by nearly half. Leni Yahil, "Scandinavian
Countries to the Rescue of Concentration Camp Prisoners," *Yad Vashem Studies* 6 (1967),
pp. 181–220, underestimates both the total number of individuals rescued and the Jewish
totals.

to help Jews once it was apparent that they were being systematically slaughtered? Could Jewish groups in Allied countries have brought more pressure on their own politicians to give high priority toward helping the Jews? If so, why was it not done? What could the neutrals like Sweden and Switzerland have done to save more Jews? The history of the Red Cross mission, despite its peculiar circumstances, suggests, like other successful rescue operations, that if there had been a more determined effort on the part of the democratic countries to intercede on behalf of the Jews, countless additional lives could have been saved.

Chapter 5

"Too Little, Too Late": The Politics of the Abandonment of the Jews

In 1946, the Swedish parliament commissioned a study of Swedish immigration policy prior to the war. Chaired by Rickard Sandler, the former foreign minister and a critic of the wartime government's foreign policy, the committee represented all of the parliamentary parties. Hjalmar Mehr, the highest-ranking Jew in the Social Democratic Party, also was a member of the committee. The report issued by the committee did not directly condemn prewar policy but indicated in a number of specific cases related to Jewish immigrants in the period 1938–1940 that the negative decision reached at the time could have been a positive one. The more positive, open borders to Jews, policy after 1941 was labeled "too little, too late."[1] Even in the postwar era, it was difficult for Sweden to confront its own behavior. Forty years after the war, only one study, an examination of Swedish immigration policy 1936–1942, has touched on Sweden's treatment of the Jews.[2]

Swedish immigration policy was niggardly in the period prior to the war. It was to Sandler's and his Foreign Office staff's credit that when Germany's persecution of the Jews began, Swedish policy sought to participate in an international resolution of the problem of Jewish emigration from Germany. The limits to Swedish participation in these efforts were also clear — any resolution should be a joint international effort

---

1. SOU, *Flyktningars Behandling*, p. 325.
2. Lindberg, op. cit.

and outside Swedish territory. As long as Jews did not try in any significant numbers to emigrate to Sweden, this policy both conformed to Sweden's humanistic values and did not endanger Sweden's domestic tranquility. Swedish hostility to immigration in general and by Jews in particular was made clear in the revisions of the immigration laws in 1937–1938. When Jews tried to get to Sweden between 1938 and 1940, they found the country closed to them.

The remarkable aspect of the unwillingness of Sweden to accept Jews in this critical period was the breadth of consensus on the correctness of this policy. Few critics existed, but no major institutional opposition was voiced. Two agencies immediately involved in efforts to help Jews — the refugee committee of the Stockholm Jewish congregation and *Svenska Israelsmissionen* — accepted the policy. The reasons for the consensus no doubt varied. A general suspicion of foreigners, fears of economic competition, anti-Semitism, and fears of an increase in anti-Semitism all contributed to a desire to maintain the contemporary racial balance in Sweden. Yet an opportunity was missed. Sweden could have accepted tens of thousands of refugees had it so desired, as it was to do during the war. In the late thirties, Sweden closed its borders; only a few countries did otherwise.

The war changed the situation. Germany no longer sought to have Jews emigrate; instead, they opted to kill all the Jews that they could get their hands on. Sweden, as a small state isolated geographically particularly after April 1940, existed only precariously as an independent country. Germany's needs vis-à-vis Sweden and Hitler's whims placed limits on Sweden's freedom of action. The neutrality that Sweden declared was aimed at staying outside the war, not at trying to maintain an even-handed foreign policy. Public opinion and the government politically favored the democracies. Swedish policies recognized Sweden's dependency on Germany. Between 1939 and 1942, Swedish concessions to Germany extended primarily into military and transportation matters. It was these areas that mostly concerned Germany. Economic ties had grown as a natural development of the war. Still, the government and the public were restive over the relationship between Sweden and Germany.

Public hostility to Germany grew in 1942. The most direct cause of this change was German occupation policy in Norway. German brutality was brought closer to home; it was no longer so easy to ignore. Press criticism increased, and many groups, including the trade unions and some church leaders, began to take more openly hostile positions. In some subtle way, German cultural dominance ebbed, and the country emotionally drifted toward the West. Those responsible for Swedish foreign policy, in particular Günther, Hansson, Boheman, and Richert, worried in 1942 that the growing hostility toward Germany, whose expression could be most dramatically seen in the press, might lead Germany to invade Sweden. It was within these contexts that the Swedish government dealt with the growing evidence of the policy of extermination that Germany had embarked upon with regard to the Jews.

There exists a large body of international literature that has examined and debated what could have been done to avoid the Holocaust. On some points, such as the importance of early, credible information about the policy, there is general agreement. On other issues, such as the feasibility of rescue, there is much controversy. The most important questions with regard to Sweden are:

1. When did Sweden learn of the new policy and what did they do with the knowledge?

2. How would people in German-controlled areas have responded if the Swedish government had shared the information it had on the extermination of the Jews?

3. Were there additional possibilities for rescue and other forms of aid from Sweden?

4. Under what circumstances would Sweden have been more active in trying to help Jews?

Any attempt to answer these questions must keep in mind both the real and imagined limits on Swedish foreign policy in general.

The Swedish Foreign Office learned of the dramatic change in German policy toward the Jews at approximately the same time as Jewish groups did. Only the Poles seemed to have clearer information earlier. In this context, there remains an interesting question: how much of the information smuggled to the London Poles did Sweden get as well? Swedish businessmen served as couriers between the Polish resistance and the Polish legation in Stockholm. Did these same Swedes offer the data to their own government? Certainly some of their intelligence material reached appropriate Swedish officials. In addition, the Swedish secret service had broken the code used by the Poles in their transmissions. What did the Swedes learn, and what was done with that information? The secret service provided information to the Foreign Office only as it saw fit.[3] We do not know. The first fully credible information came the third week of August 1942.

The issue of credibility as it relates to the Final Solution has two different aspects: the reliability of the information itself, and the ability of individuals to comprehend the magnitude of what the Germans were attempting. The Swedish Foreign Office materials provide ample evidence that even when an individual had assured himself as to the reliability of the information, there was a far more difficult step to comprehend the full implication of the data. This problem was hardly unique to Sweden, and therefore makes the issue of suppression of early, reliable information so important. The more information that would have been made public about the Final Solution, the more likely that different policies would have been enacted.

The existence of "a plan to exterminate all Jews from Germany and German-controlled areas in Europe after they have been concentrated in the east (presumably Poland)" had been voiced by Gerhart Riegner, secretary of the World Jewish Congress in Geneva to Howard Elting, the American vice consul in Switzerland, on August 8. Riegner admitted to Elting that the idea of such a policy had at first seemed "fantastic" to him, but evidence gathered over the summer had convinced him of its reality. Elting maintained a reluctance to accept fully Riegner's conclusions but thought "that the report might well contain an element of truth."[4] As is well known, the State Department tried to block transmission of this information to Stephen Wise, president of the World Jewish Congress, and refused to confirm its accuracy until November.

The Swedish Foreign Office did the same thing with the intelligence that they received from the Continent. The report from the Swedish consul general in Stettin on August 20, in its section on the Jews, began as follows: "The picture which my informant has given about the treatment of the Jews in Poland is such that it can hardly be repeated in writing." He continued by providing "some brief pieces of information," including a remarkably accurate description of the killing process and the use of a number of words that the Germans had decided to use in an attempt to hide what they were doing. Vendel had no doubts about the accuracy of the report. Vendel made clear that whatever the specific

---

3. Carlgren, *Svensk Underrättelse*, pp. 89–90 ff.
4. United States, National Archives, State Department, 862.4016/2234, Howard Elting, Jr. to Secretary of State, August 8, 1942. See Document Collection.

treatments were of Jews in Poland at the time, the long-term goal was to "exterminate them." Two days later, Vendel's observations were confirmed by von Otter's report on his meeting with Kurt Gerstein.

No evidence exists from August 1942 to indicate exactly what von Otter reported to his colleague, Eric von Post, in Berlin, nor exactly how much of his report reached Stockholm and in what form. The one document extant indicated that Gerstein provided von Otter with a remarkable set of material:

> [Gerstein] had just returned from a short assignment to the extermination camp in Belsec, near Lublin. He gave a detailed account of the goings-on (the gas chambers, the reaction of the SS personnel, the saving of gold teeth, and so on). He also showed documents, identification cards, and orders from the commandant of the camp for the delivery of hydrocyanic acid.[5]

Von Otter confirmed the reliability of Gerstein's information with Otto Dibelius. Certainly Richert received all this information when he returned to Berlin in late August. He may have kept the details to himself, but by September there seemed little doubt in the Foreign Office that Germany had embarked on an extermination campaign.

Throughout the fall, reports poured into the Foreign Office about the ever-extending circles of violence. As a November 14 report from Vienna put it, "it doesn't seem possible any longer to have any doubts about the masses [of Jews] who have been killed by gassing, machine gunning, and suffocation (the means by which the victims are placed in hermetically sealed railway cars). . . ."[6] Top officials of the Swedish Foreign Office had by the end of 1942 understood that Germany had begun a European-wide extermination campaign.[7] What did they do with their knowledge?

5. UD 1920, HP 1052, Aide-Mémoire, August 7, 1945.

6. Ibid., HP 325, Ytterberg to Richert, November 14, 1942. Gösta Engzell told this author in 1982 that officials in the Swedish Foreign Office had become convinced of the German extermination policy by the summer of 1942. He referred to the von Otter-Gerstein meeting and to reports from the Swedish military attaché in Berlin, Curt Juhlin-Dannfelt. None of the materials in the Juhlin-Dannfelt archive provides clear support for Engzell's contention. The archive, however, does not contain all of Juhlin-Dannfelt's reports.

7. Only Richert seemed to be unwilling to admit that a new policy had been established. Despite the fact that he had received all the reports regarding the extermination campaign including von Otter's report and confirmation of Gerstein's authenticity by Dibelius and Eidem, he wrote on November 18 that information about the extermination

Official Sweden remained silent, totally silent. At no time during the
war did the Swedish government inform the Swedish people of what
was occurring. Swedish newspapers carried stories of the extermination
campaign from 1942 onwards. The government did not deny the stories
or support them. Swedish attempts to aid Norway's Jews were never
mentioned during the war. The government statement of October 2,
1943, offering Denmark's Jews safety in Sweden was not accompanied
by an explanation of why such action was necessary. Of course, the
Swedish public had become aware by the fall of 1943 that something terrible had been happening to Jews in German-held territory. They knew
that Jews had been moved to Poland, where they lived in horrible conditions, dying of malnutrition, disease, and ill treatment. Probably most
had read by that time of German use of various means of execution of
Jews.[8] But did the Swedish public fully comprehend the systematic,
total nature of the Final Solution? When the refugees from the concentration camps arrived in late March 1945, their physical appearance and
the true horror of Germany's policies finally reached a general consciousness. The government had not wanted the public to know.

There is overwhelming evidence available to demonstrate that the
government, especially the Foreign Office, actively sought to delay,
confuse, and refuse to confirm news of the extermination campaign. The
primary purpose of such a policy was to avoid complications in German-
Swedish relations. There was a fear within the government that a public
discussion of the "Jewish problem" would damage German-Swedish
relations. Richert tried to stop information from reaching his own colleagues.[9] The von Otter-Gerstein case was only one example. When the

---

campaign should be taken with "all reservation." Ibid., HP 1589, Richert to Kumlin,
November 18, 1942. Yet, in another commentary about German fears that if Germany
loses the war, there will be reprisals, he wrote: "That blood guilt which is born witness by
the mass extermination of the Jews is not accepted by the Germans generally who blame
the Gestapo, a state and a power in itself which perhaps it is." Berlin arkiv, HP 1 CT, v. 71,
Richert to Kumlin, December 4, 1942.

8. Informationsstyrelsens arkiv, Stabsorientering Högkvarteret, Försvarstaben,
November 19, 1943. "Conditions in our occupied neighboring countries, policies toward
the Jews, and Germany's military losses have led the great majority of Swedes to be
immune to Nazi propaganda for a considerable time." See also, v. 459, "Översikt över
propaganda i Sverige, Februari 1–Oktober 1, 1943," where the report suggests that Swedish reaction to "persecution of the Jews" has been of importance in the pro-Western attitudes of the Swedish public. This latter report was written before the attack on Denmark's
Jews. Swedish newspapers had carried stories continuously. See Nordiska Röster, op. cit.
A careful study of Swedish press coverage remains to be completed.

9. Harald Edelstam, a young diplomat, in Berlin in 1942 accused Richert in 1974 of

Foreign Office asked Richert to confirm the existence of the extermination campaign in late November 1942 because of requests from Swedish Jews, Richert responded that information of such a campaign had reached him in Berlin as well but had not been definitively proved.[10]

Yet Richert knew, probably better than anyone else, what had occurred. Not only did the Berlin legation provide most of the most positive intelligence on the campaign, but all other reports received in Stockholm were forwarded to Berlin for Richert's information. In addition, the Berlin legation had tried to help without success a few Swedish Jews caught in Germany. The plight of the *mischlinge* burdened not only the legation but the Swedish church in Berlin, which eventually hid a number of Jews upon its premises, as well as stashed some others throughout the capital city. Finally, Richert consistently doubted the likelihood of success of every Swedish rescue effort because from his vantage point it appeared that the situation was totally hopeless. All proposals from the Adler-Rudel scheme, to the Danish Jews, to Hungary, and finally the Jewish aspect of the Red Cross mission — all were labeled as "a shot in the dark." In the fall of 1942 Richert worried initially about the government's likely response. Richert knew that Boheman felt keenly about the Jews and that his sister was married to one of Sweden's most influential Jewish leaders. More importantly, he feared that the Swedish press would use the subject to embitter Swedish-German relations.[11] The government tried to limit the damage done by the news of the extermination campaign in the Swedish press.

---

withholding information about the extermination of the Jews, and of someone destroying material on the extermination campaign in the Swedish Foreign Office files after the war. Richert denied the allegations. Richert arkiv, Richert to Edelstam, April 17, 1974, and Richert to Carlgren, June 17, 1974. In addition, Edelstam wrote to this author that he had proposed in 1942 to Richert that the Swedish Legation in Berlin establish "safe houses" in Berlin to protect the Jews. "I had read how the Chilean legation during the Spanish civil war had in an impressive manner helped tens of thousands of needy. They had rented houses and hotels and declared them part of the territory of Chile. . . . My thought was to try to do the same thing in Berlin, something which Raoul Wallenberg managed in Budapest. . . ." Harald Edelstam to Steven Koblik, August 20, 1982. Richert's rejection of the idea is not hard to appreciate, but the issue of suppression of information remains. Gunnar Hägglöf has observed, "During my visits to Berlin I was in constant communication with the Swedish legation but I never heard any member of the staff giving any information about the persecution of the Jews." Gunnar Hägglöf to Steven Koblik, September 10, 1982. See also, Gunnar Hägglöf, *Samtida Vittne* (Stockholm, 1972).

10. UD 1920, HP 1589, Richert to Kumlin, November 18, 1942.

11. This fear plagued Richert throughout the entire war. Sven Grafströms anteckningar, December 6, 1939: " . . . perhaps Richert is right . . . that Sweden is far too

The first full-scale public information of the extermination campaign came from the Polish government-in-exile in London. A book of German atrocities was released in July in English. The Swedish translation was confiscated by the Board of Information. Yet the English version circulated freely.[12] When the press questioned the government about what it had done to aid Norway's Jews, they were apparently told that Sweden was attempting to help the Jews but that the success of these efforts depended upon the press not publishing any information about government activities.[13] The press supported this silence. It was to be repeated in 1943 and 1944. Only one newspaper in 1945, *Dagens Nyheter*, broke this self-censorship to publish one story at the beginning of the Red Cross rescue effort.[14]

The behavior of the Swedish press deserves special attention. A small section of the press actively opposed both Hitler and the coalition government's policy toward Germany. Led by Torgny Segerstedt in Göteborg and supported by a small but vocal socialist group, these critics seized upon persecution of the Jews as primary evidence of the evil nature of Hitler's regime. Even before the war, the German minister in Stockholm claimed, no doubt with some exaggeration, that the greatest problem in Swedish-German relations was the Jewish Question. Governmental attempts at quieting these critics was only partially successful. There is evidence that one of the most frequent reasons why certain issues of newspapers and magazines were confiscated was just because they spread "horror" stories about belligerent behavior — frequently, German treatment of Jews. Still, the credibility of the oppositional

---

little and too poorly equipped to have the luxury in the current situation to have its press write openly in the name of humanity and out-of-date principles. . . ." UD 1920, HP 324, Richert to Kumlin, November 9, 1942. Richert reports that v. Grundherr said "that Sweden did Denmark a great favor by keeping the Swedish press quiet during the current German-Danish conflict [telegram crisis]. Unfortunately the same could not be said for the situation in Norway, and Mr. v. Grundherr said confidentially that Sweden's attitudes had contributed toward the sharp treatment of Norway." Berlin arkiv, HP 1 Ct/AD, v. 73c, Richert to Söderblom, October 1, 1943. In this letter, Richert defended his argument against issuing a démarche on the Danish Jews in Berlin by noting that a new wave of Swedish public indignation about German policies would have no positive effect in Berlin. See also Carlgren, op. cit.

12. Statens Informationsstyrelse, v. 459, Propaganda Report #5, July 31, 1942.

13. *Dagens Nyheter*, December 20, 1942, p. 3, editorial. UD 1920, HP 1070, Thorsing to Westring, December 29, 1942.

14. *Dagens Nyheter*, March 10, 1945. "Red Cross Expedition on the Way." See Informationstyrelsen arkiv, v. 9, Meeting of March 12, 1945, for unhappiness with *DN* for breaking the silence.

papers was not clear. They represented only a fraction of the Swedish newspapers. The behavior of pro-government newspapers was more instructive.

Swedish newspapermen were not unaware of what was happening to the Jews. A number of papers had reporters stationed in Germany. Their reports were, of course, censored in Berlin, but the reporters traveled home to provide additional information that could not be sent by wire or post. Once in Stockholm, they wrote for their own papers in a more honest style, but the papers continued to maintain self-restraint with regard to Jewish policies. Sometimes the Berlin-based journalists wrote books about their experiences and views of Germany. Attempts to restrict freedom of expression were less in book publishing than in the popular press. One of the best examples of such a work was *Bakom Stålvallen* (Behind the Wall of Steel) by Arvid Fredborg, *Svenska Dagbladet's* correspondent in Berlin 1941–1943, published in 1943.[15]

The book was remarkable in many ways. It attempted to be a complete analysis of Nazi Germany during the war, its organization, its successes, its failures, and the opposition to it. The work was both highly informative and highly critical of the Hitler regime. The author left no doubt as to the outcome of the war. His comments on Hitler's domestic opposition were fascinating. His final concern was that the victorious Allies did not make the same mistake that had been made in 1918. He feared that all Germany would pay for Hitler's crimes. Among the crimes, treatment of the Jews figured prominently.

Fredborg's comments made the fate of the Jews quite clear. They were first mentioned with regard to a new anti-Semitic campaign in September 1941 to rid Berlin of its Jews. A brief description, which pointedly denied that the Jews presented any security risk, of the removal of Jews and their shipment "to the east" was followed by the comment: "The fate which awaited them there or on the way there is generally known."[16] Every time he noted the harshness of German occupation policy in Holland and Belgium, he referred to the persecution of the Jews. The two major sections on the Jews came, however, toward the end of the book. The first long passage (over three pages) was part of a section on the mood in Germany in the spring of 1943. It was a highly personal description of the removal of the last Jews from Berlin. It

15. Arvid Fredborg, op. cit.
16. Ibid., pp. 86–87.

underscored the public nature of the Jewish policy and the disquietude it produced. Nonetheless, this section gave no concrete indication of what happened to the Jews or the extent of the policy beyond ridding Berlin of its Jews. The franker details of German Jewish policy were placed into the section on the analysis of the SS: "There is much which the SS organization has to answer for. These groups have above all been used to remove the Jews from Germany. In this context they have developed an almost unbelievable brutality."[17]

The description of that policy which followed these opening comments was based upon materials Fredborg had been able to gather himself. He estimated that over 2 million Jews had already been "executed." He gave some specific figures for areas in Eastern Europe and continued:

> Many Jews have taken part in partisan activities, carried out sabotage, etc. But that is no excuse for the cold-blooded mass murders, the extermination.
>
> The mass butchery has been performed in ways which encourages one to avoid describing. Sometimes they have brought men, women, and children together and let these unfortunate people dig graves whereafter machine guns are turned on them. On other occasions, they have used gas in special chambers or in special trains, and sometimes have these people, who should have been executed, had to walk by a hole in the wall with goose-steps, whereby a soldier shot one shot against every head.[18]

Fredborg concluded by discussing how he received the preceding descriptions. Toward the end of the book, in a discussion of Germany's relations with its allies, he equated the poor relations with Hungary and the good ones with Rumania as dependent to a considerable extent on their respective treatment of their own Jews: "The Rumanian mass executions of Jews — according to unofficial German sources, 17,000 in one day — can be compared in all regards with what the SS further north has managed to achieve."[19]

What Fredborg's book described had already been printed in other versions by the daily press, but rarely were such stories given important placement in the papers, and the pro-government papers ran such material infrequently. At the meetings of the Board of Information and

---

17. Ibid., pp. 285–288, 340.
18. Ibid., p. 340.
19. Ibid., p. 400.

the newspaper editors, it was continually stressed by government spokesmen, including the foreign minister, that Germany followed Swedish newspapers with great care and warned that frequent stories could increase the danger of a German attack on Sweden. The majority of the Swedish press followed a policy of self-censorship advocated by the government. The result was not complete avoidance of the issue, simply a haphazard policy that allowed readers to avoid confronting the brutal reality.

The official silence was defended on the basis that by remaining silent, Sweden could do more to help the Jews. This view was not entirely incorrect; it was clear, for example, that the success of the Red Cross mission in 1945 depended on a veil of secrecy in order that Hitler did not involve himself in the matter. In the case of Norway's Jews, the success of Swedish policy did not depend upon keeping Swedish activities secret. Germany showed little interest in Norwegian refugees resident in Sweden, Jews or non-Jews. The rescue of the Danish Jews was well covered in the international press, yet no German protests were made in Sweden. Moreover, Swedish attempts to help the Jews in 1943 were limited. Gustaf V's appeal in June 1944 to the Hungarian president, Horthy, was published in July. There was hardly any effort to keep Sweden's activities in Hungary quiet. Sweden, after all, was working with the War Refugee Board and benefited from the publicity.

The government's silence cannot in sum be explained because of its desires to be more helpful with regard to the Jews. The real reason was fear of a negative German response if Sweden became a center for anti-German "propaganda." The government's policy not only stopped the Swedish public from fully comprehending the plight of the Jews, it also contributed to a general international silence whose effects were probably helpful to the success of the Final Solution.

When Gerstein met von Otter in August 1942, the reason why Gerstein said that he was giving this information to the Swede was in order that it come to public attention. "He was firmly convinced that if the knowledge of this extermination was spread amongst foreigners, the German people would not for a moment continue their support of the Nazi regime."[20] Whether Gerstein was correct is rather doubtful. The German people understood what was happening to their Jews. Fredborg's descriptions, for example, make it amply clear that there

---

20. UD 1920, HP 1052, Aide Mémoire, August 7, 1945.

were no doubts about the fate of the deported Jews. It seems unlikely that more information about the persecutions would have changed German behavior. However, the impact of such information on other groups is much more open to question.

Rudolf Vrba, one of the men who escaped from Auschwitz and produced the so-called "Auschwitz protocols" for the Western powers, said decades after the war, "Would anybody get me alive to Auschwitz if I had this information? Would thousands and thousands of ablebodied Jewish men send their children, wives, mothers to Auschwitz from all over Europe, if they knew?"[21] The problem Jews faced, particularly in the early phases of the Final Solution, was the lack of certainty. Rumors abounded; a general sense of the horrors that awaited them existed. But it was still possible to believe that the stories were exaggerated and that somehow one's own loved ones would avoid the fate of so many others. The Allies failed to provide much information on the persecutions. Sweden offered none. Jews could not be absolutely certain what awaited them, and they knew that few of their fellow citizens were willing to help them. The experience of Denmark's Jews gives support to Vrba's theory.

While a couple of Denmark's Jewish leaders refused to believe the news that the Final Solution was about to be applied in Denmark in late September 1943, the majority of Jews and their fellow Danish citizens understood the gravity of the situation and took improvised steps to avoid capture. Only 500 of Denmark's 8,000 Jews were taken. The rest made a successful flight to Sweden. In many ways, the Danish example is interesting. Not only did the Jews resist, but so did the Danes as a whole. And the Danish attitudes were so clear in advance on this issue that German authorities in Denmark — both civilian and military — did little to ensure the failure of the operation.

The Danish example was not unique. As early as December 1942, evidence existed that publicity about the mass executions of the Jews coupled with Allied threats of reprisals had some effect in German-occupied areas where locals were cooperating with the SS. Much of the intelligence about the extermination campaign received in Washington and London from its own operatives came via Stockholm. OSS officers gathered intelligence from Germans in Sweden and from various East European refugees. Bruce Hopper, an American agent based in Stockholm, sent a wide-ranging report to Washington sometime in early 1943 on conditions in Poland. He commented upon the "extermination of the Jews" and noted "throughout Ostland the extermination of Jews is being carried on with unabated vigor." He did not give any direct details on the killing centers, but did have some statistics on deaths in the Baltic areas:

> The Lithuanians have a form of autonomous government, and their Defense Guards are being used by the Germans for exterminating Jews and carrying on a generally anti-Polish activity. On the 8th of December, 1942, the BBC issued a warning in Lithuanian to the effect that Lithuanians actively cooperating with the Germans would, after the war, be tried by an international tribunal. This warning has not been without effect.[22]

Hopper's belief that the public warning had had some effect was not what the Allied governments wanted to hear. They avoided as much as possible linking the Allied cause with persecution of the Jews. Even in 1944, members of the State Department continued to argue that publicity hurt rather than helped the Jews:

> Mr. Pell [Special Assistant to the Director of European Affairs, State Department] took the view that the effect of such a propaganda program would be that the Germans would kill the Jews off faster than the Germans would desist from their program of extermination. He stated that when he was in Germany, he had talked with some of the Jewish leaders who had stressed the fact that we should not give any publicity to Germany's persecution of the Jews. Mr. Pehle [head of the War Refugee Board] indicated that he was in thorough disagreement with this point of view.[23]

Pell's views were so patently false that it was remarkable that he would voice them so late in the war. Just as the State Department needed to justify its failures, the Swedish Foreign Office used the rescue efforts to mask their failure either to pass what information they had to the Allies or to speak out themselves.

In November 1942, Pastor Olle Nystedt gave a well-publicized sermon on the deportation of Norway's Jews. It was entitled, "If we remain silent, the stones will cry out." The Swedish government remained silent, as did other countries. It has often been argued after the war that

22. United States, National Archives, OSS, Regular number 266, 40247, "Extracts from Secret Report on Conditions in Poland," no date (early 1943), by Bruce Hopper.

23. WRB, 27, "Memorandum on Film," Meeting in Secretary Stettinius's office, March 2, 1944.

there was nothing that could have been done to help the Jews anyway. The Western powers struggled to win the war. They did not have the resources to help the Jews. The neutrals like Sweden sought desperately to remain outside the conflict; there was little they could do to help persecuted peoples. The success of some rescue efforts between 1943 and 1945 demonstrated the falseness of the latter premise. But it is difficult not to avoid the conclusion that the worst mistake of all was the wall of silence which greeted the Final Solution. This silence depended not on ignorance or disbelief, but on deliberate policy. By remaining silent, Sweden and the other governments supported the hope among Jews that things were not quite as bad as they had heard and among the public that perhaps the newspaper stories were exaggerated as they had been in World War I. The silence also confirmed German suspicions that other states tacitly approved of their Jewish policies. The issue of remaining silent was not a resource question, nor was their evidence that it posed a security threat to Sweden.

Richert and other officials consistently overestimated the import of German hostility toward the Swedish press. It is understandable why he overreacted. German criticism of the press remained a consistent subject in the official relations between the two countries. It was appropriate for the Foreign Service officers of both countries to discuss it. Yet real authority for German policy toward Sweden lay outside the German Foreign Office. Hitler, too, was bothered by Swedish press criticism, but his anger never boiled over into a decision to do something about it. German silence on the Danish rescue suggested that Hitler had no intention of letting the Jewish Question spoil an advantageous relationship (from Germany's viewpoint) with Sweden. The same can be said about events in Hungary in 1944.

How could Sweden have made public information about the extermination campaign and not endangered Swedish security? A variety of alternatives were possible: (1) a direct statement about the persecution of the Jews; (2) a general statement condemning persecution by race or religion by any of the belligerents; (3) deliberately leaking specific information to various Swedish publications and encouraging them to publish the materials; (4) passing information to various international Jewish groups represented in Stockholm; and (5) forwarding information as von Otter had promised Gerstein to London and Washington. Given Sweden's general foreign policy, alternative #1 was highly unlikely in 1942, perhaps even in 1943. Security and other foreign policy interests might have been endangered. A credible statement would demand proof and perhaps expose intelligence sources. Gustaf V's appeal to Admiral Horthy in June 1944 came closest to a direct statement. By then the extermination campaign was well known. Any combination of the other options was possible. Swedes outside the government also kept most of their knowledge to themselves. The policies of Archbishop Eidem and *Svenska Israelsmissionen* have already been examined in Chapter 3. Eidem rejected pleas from English church sources in 1942 and Jewish institutions in 1944 to make an explicit public statement. He claimed that the ability of Sweden and the Lutheran Church to play an effective role as mediator and bearer of goodwill after the war would be damaged by such actions. Similar explanations can be found in the *SIM* materials. One is struck by the attempts even in private letters of these officials not to discuss what they knew. Expressions such as "too horrible to recount" or "should not be repeated" or "beyond imagination" frequently preface information about the Jews in personal letters. A kind of self-censorship existed that allowed these individuals to live with their knowledge. There was also a passiveness when faced with the problem — a passiveness that was a product of fears for Sweden's security, anti-Semitism, a belief that nothing could be done, and a lack of imagination. There is no reason to think that church officials were unique in this regard. Another Bruce Hopper memorandum, March 3, 1943, reported on the "views of Sweden's most influential banker." The banker who had recently returned from a trip to Germany gave Hopper various kinds of information, mostly military. Part of their discussions, however, touched the postwar future of a democratic Germany. The banker reportedly said, "The Germans do not want the Jews back, no matter how much they condemn the Nazi persecutions of Jews."[24] The banker must have been Jacob Wallenberg.

Nor does it seem very convincing that a Swedish confirmation of the extermination campaign would have endangered Sweden's non-belligerency. Germany's unhappiness with Sweden decreased as the war progressed, as did its capacity to do anything about it. The real effects of such a Swedish confirmation would have been in occupied areas and in Britain and the United States. American newspapers liked to cite Swedish newspaper stories about Germany because they were seen as more credible than those emanating from Washington or

---

24. OSS, Op. cit., Bruce Hopper Memorandum, March 3, 1943.

London. Swedish confirmation on the Final Solution would have been major news in the United States. It would have made it more difficult for the State Department to brake efforts to help Jews, and it would have helped to bring the issue into the consciousness of America's Jewry. It could also have been used by those in the American and British governments who wanted to spread information about the Final Solution. Sweden's credibility in the occupied countries was high. There was no reason to suspect that Sweden would spread malicious lies about German activity. Perhaps such propaganda would have encouraged greater resistance, indeed even given some Germans second thoughts as Gerstein had suggested.

But the stones did not cry out. The world remained relatively silent. Only in 1944 did the brutal truth begin to spread into a broad Western consciousness. The pictures from the concentration camps and killing centers in 1945 jolted those who had not wanted to believe. In the vacuum, six million Jews were murdered. The Western powers and the neutrals, including Sweden, played a part in the success of the Final Solution.

For those who wanted to help and met with unwillingness among governments to mount a propaganda campaign, the remaining alternative was to try to rescue or aid Jews directly. Sweden frequently came to mind when rescue efforts were discussed. And the Swedish government was not unwilling to respond positively to proposals. The unanswered questions with regard to rescue efforts are: could more have been accomplished from Sweden? And if so, why wasn't it?

The first issue that needs to be addressed is what were the limits placed on rescue opportunities by Germany? It seems obvious that any rescue effort, at least from the point of view of Swedish possibilities, was directly related to what Germany would permit, either openly or by ignoring what was happening. Attempting to define German attitudes is neither easy nor simple. Hitler and the "radical" anti-Semites showed little interest in anything other than killing Jews after 1940. There were attempts to trade Jews for money or for goods such as trucks, etc. None of these efforts bore fruit. It also seems unreasonable to expect either the Western powers or Sweden to reallocate scarce resources during the war. The American Jewish community had an ability to provide certain levels of funding, and some Jewish institutions supported attempts at barter trade. Nonetheless, Germans seemed to use the barter negotiations as a test of the strength of the others' convictions and to see how far the representatives of the Jewish organizations or Western powers were willing to go.

Another form of direct negotiation that seemed hopeless was any effort made through the German Foreign Office. The Swedes had much experience in this arena. Richert and his staff consistently failed in their efforts to help the thirty or so "Swedish Jews" caught in wartime Germany. Their failures were not for lack of effort, but because the German Foreign Office had so little power where the "Jewish Question" was concerned. Sweden found that the Foreign Office responded either with the comment that Sweden should not involve itself in things that were solely German domestic affairs or by procrastination on the requests made by Sweden as it pertained to Jews. Examples of the former response were made in the case of Norway's and Denmark's Jews, while the latter technique was used with regard to the "Swedish Jews" and the Adler-Rudel scheme. It certainly is of interest that the German Foreign Office did not immediately refuse to negotiate on the idea of placing 20,000 Belgian and French Jewish children in Sweden. Still, it is difficult to imagine that much could have been gained by using normal diplomatic channels. The possibilities for rescue, at least with regard to Sweden, lay elsewhere.

As German armies swept eastward in the summer of 1941, they occupied areas along the Baltic that had large numbers of Jewish residents. Most of these Jews suffered the fate awaiting their brethren in the West. Yet many succeeded in fleeing from their persecutors and found refuge in the countryside or with non-Jews in the city. A similar situation already existed in Poland. What were the possibilities of rescuing Jews in this area?

From the perspective of German authorities, some flexibility seemed possible. The first wave of mass executions in this area were conducted by SS squadrons and their local allies. Often their activities produced revulsion among regular German military units and other Germans in the area. Much of the information Sweden received in 1941 and 1942 came from German sources critical of SS behavior. While these Germans did little or nothing to help Jews themselves, it is likely that they would not have hindered others from doing so. The rescue of Denmark's Jews depended partially on the willingness of the German occupying authorities to look the other way as the Jews fled. Some help to the Baltic Jews should have been possible. Were any efforts made?

Gillel Storch, the main figure in the Swedish section of the World

Jewish Congress, was himself a Baltic refugee who had come to Sweden in 1940. He was a wealthy businessman, and most of his family remained trapped in the Baltic countries. Most of his initial efforts at rescue were directed at the Baltic area. None succeeded.

The problems facing Storch were threefold: the situation in the Baltic itself; the attitudes of the German authorities; and Swedish policy. The extent of collaboration between the Balts and the Germans made rescue activities difficult. Storch bitterly accused Iver Olsen, the Stockholm representative of the War Refugee Board, in the summer of 1944 of not doing enough to help Baltic Jews. Olsen defended himself by claiming that the remaining Jews were difficult to locate because they feared capture by involving themselves in the clandestine rescue operations that were operating across the Baltic. Storch felt that some of the Balts working with Olsen had collaborated earlier with the Germans and now sought to flee from the Russians. Laura Margolin of the American Joint Distribution Committee arrived in Stockholm in the late summer of 1944 and found herself caught in the middle of this squabble. She sided with Olsen, defended his Baltic activities, and labeled Storch's ideas as "fantastic."[25] Storch did indeed have fantastic ideas about rescue. He was unwilling to leave any stone unturned. He and his colleagues in the Swedish section of the World Jewish Congress had a stronger sense of urgency to participate directly in rescue efforts. That many of their schemes led into dead ends did not stop them from creating new ones. It was precisely this spirit that was needed; it was sadly lacking within the larger Jewish community and within the Swedish government.

Storch tried to find a German official who would help him. Perhaps in 1943, certainly in 1944, he thought he had made the right connection, Heinrich Himmler. Storch did not have direct contact with Himmler; rather, he negotiated with a mysterious figure who frequently visited Stockholm, Dr. Kleist. Kleist had been a German civilian official in the Baltic in 1941–1942. He was rumored to be Himmler's agent in Sweden during the last years of the war.[26] In 1944 and 1945, Kleist and Storch discussed terms by which some Baltic Jews would be permitted to escape to Sweden. The terms were primarily financial, and Storch

---

25. WRB, Box 16, "James Mann," Laura Margolin to James Mann, January 12, 1945.

26. Ibid., Box 70, "German Proposals Through Sweden," Paraphrase of telegram received from His Majesty's minister at Stockholm, July 14, 1944. See also, PRO. FO 371, 42867, Washington to Foreign Office, July 6, 1944. UD 1920, HP 1075, Richert to Söderblom, May 29, 1943.

seemed confident, especially in the summer of 1944, that a deal would be consummated. Its collapse left him embittered, and for reasons which are not entirely clear, he blamed Olsen partially.[27]

If the actual situation in the Baltic made rescue difficult but not entirely out of the question, what about the attitude of the Swedish government? Little evidence exists to suggest that the government was concerned, interested, in the Baltic Jews. The main interest of Sweden in the Baltic were the so-called Estonian Swedes, a group of people who inhabited islands off the Estonian coast and were linguistically and culturally tied to Sweden. Major efforts were made to help these people, both by the government and other Swedish institutions, not the least the state church. The result was that many of them were successfully rescued and brought to Sweden. It is hard to judge what Sweden could have done in the Baltic for the Jews had it wanted to, which it did not. One suspects possibilities existed.

At one extreme, it probably would have been possible to establish some form of smuggling operation. This kind of activity the Swedish government refused to partake in with regard to any other country. Therefore, its possibility in favor of the Baltic Jews need hardly be considered. Another alternative would have been to offer to Germany via various channels that Sweden take specific numbers of Baltic or Polish Jews. In fact, Sweden did opt for this policy under the circumstances described below. An option between these two choices would have been to encourage third parties — Jewish groups, Baltic resistance groups, the WRB — to undertake rescue efforts with a clear understanding that they were tacitly supported. After 1942, the government did not stop such efforts — as far as one can tell — but except for the WRB, they did not encourage them either. Indeed, the Swedish attitude toward the WRB indicated the nature of government support for non-Scandinavian Jews.

When the idea of the first major effort to help non-Scandinavian Jews was discussed within the government, those favoring such a plan — the Adler-Rudel scheme — defended it, especially Gustav Möller, on the basis that it would gain goodwill in the United States and Britain. Its opponents argued that the idea was hopeless because Germany would never agree. Whether Möller used this argument primarily to convince

---

27. WRB, Box 16, James Mann to John Pehle, January 13, 1945, and Laura Margolin to James Mann, January 12, 1945.

his reluctant colleague, or whether Bagge, from whom we find reference to the discussion, wanted to justify the policy with an appeal to
greater issues, cannot be clarified entirely. Möller wanted to help Jews
— Adler-Rudel himself was impressed by Möller's receptiveness, especially in contrast to leading figures within the Stockholm Jewish community.[28] Nor is it unlikely that Möller had all along great reservations
about Sweden's immigration policy with regard to Jews. But the cabinet
contained individuals like Westman who did not hide their anti-
Semitism, Bagge whose foreign policy concerns were either involved
with Sweden's neighbors or the great powers, and of course the prime
minister, who resisted all efforts in any direction that might increase
Swedish risk-taking in foreign policy.[29] Möller's use of the great-power
argument guaranteed broader support in the cabinet than otherwise
would have existed. Within the Swedish Foreign Office, however, there
appeared to be a growing willingness to help the Jews.

The Danish case is difficult to analyze because it was a foregone conclusion that Sweden would be willing to help any group of Danes
seeking refuge in Sweden in 1943. The group in October–November
happened to be Jews. Yet certain aspects of the rescue of the Danish
Jews indicated the growing flexibility of the Foreign Office staff. As soon
as martial law had been declared in Denmark, officials at the Swedish
legation in Copenhagen and in the Foreign Office in Stockholm began
discussions about how they could help Denmark's Jews. There was little
doubt that sooner rather than later, the Final Solution would be applied
to Denmark. Stockholm instructed the legation to offer visas and protective passes to any Jews who had the least connection with Sweden. A
surge in Jewish applications occurred. Still, the same officials believed

---

28. See PRO, FO 188, 405, Minute to Mallet, March 11, 1943, and Minute in
Stockholm, April 15, 1943.
29. Contemporary British observers argued consistently throughout the war that the
division between the "pro-German element" in the Swedish government, i.e., Bagge,
Günther, Richert, and the remainder of the cabinet, was a false dichotomy. Typical of this
view was a report from the British minister, Victor Mallet, which denied that Günther was
pro-German: "The fact that he is a career diplomat rather than a politician exposes him to
the criticisms which diplomats often receive from newspaper men and politicians. His
training no doubt qualifies him to be a faithful interpreter of the policy of the Prime Minister, who wields the real power in the government." Ibid., FO 371, 37077, Mallet to Eden,
December 28, 1942. Andreen, op. cit., suggested that in 1940 Günther and Bagge wanted
a "German friendly" neutrality. p. 50.

in late September that there was not much else that could be done.[30] When news of the pending round-up of Jews reached Stockholm, the government — in this case, Günther and Hansson — decided to approach Germany directly in an attempt to aid the Jews. Richert disapproved of the idea and fought it for 48 hours. The disagreement focused less on what could be done for the Jews — Richert was told that the government had little hope that their efforts would help — than on the politics of the situation. Richert believed that such a démarche would hurt German-Swedish relations without helping the Jews, while Stockholm argued that Sweden must show solidarity with Denmark even if it had little practical results. Germany never replied formally to the démarche. Sweden opened its borders.

The Swedes learned in the context of the Danish rescue that efforts on behalf of Jews did not endanger Swedish-German relations. Sweden also received widespread praise in London and Washington. A special "Thanks to Sweden" was arranged in Madison Square Garden to celebrate the rescue of the Danish Jews.[31] For the remainder of the war, the Swedish Foreign Office showed an interest in the "Jewish Question." The interest was not simply a cynical way to protect Sweden in the eyes of the Western powers; it reflected a genuine concern and willingness to help. The Hungarian episode would demonstrate the sincerity of Swedish interest. What government officials lacked was imagination and "fantastic ideas." In the case of Hungary, two outsiders, Raoul Wallenberg and Valdemar Langlet, would provide both.

Swedish policy in Hungary has already been discussed in Chapter 2. What is of consequence in our discussion is the consistent willingness that the Foreign Office and the legation in Budapest showed in trying to devise ways to help Hungarian Jews. They created documents that had no legal meaning and attempted to use them to protect Hungarian Jews. Only in the case of Eidem's refusal to issue a plea to his Hungarian colleagues do we have evidence of a hesitancy to get involved in Hungary. There was also evidence that some "influential politician" had advised the Swedish WJC not to approach the government in April about the idea of an appeal.[32] It is unclear who gave the advice and whether it was

30. UD 1920, HP 1056, Engzell Memorandum, September 10, 1943.

31. Wyman, p. 154. P. A. Hansson arkiv, v. 18, Isaac Grunewald to Hansson, October 3, 1943, PRO, F0 371, 42752, American Legation to Department of State, February 13, 1944.

32. WRB, 34, Hungary 1, Memorandum, July 1944.

good advice. When the "Auschwitz Protocols" arrived in Stockholm in late June, it did not take the government and Gustaf V long to decide to make just such an appeal. The appeal seemed to have some effect in stopping the deportation of Jews. What would have happened if the appeal had been made in April instead?

The first person to use unconvential ways to try to help the Jews in Hungary was Valdemar Langlet. A Swede resident in Budapest, Langlet was an academic with a warm regard for things Hungarian. He responded quickly to the persecution of the Jews. He had no official position initially and therefore was hamstrung in his ability to do anything. He suggested in May that the International Red Cross or the Swedish Red Cross should somehow intercede to protect the Jews.[33] Discussions on the plan went so far that Folke Bernadotte, Gustaf's nephew and vice-president of the Swedish Red Cross, was named the likely leader of such an expedition. The Swedish Foreign Office approved of Langlet's ideas in general and commissioned him to serve as official representative of the Swedish Red Cross. The appointment was made simultaneously with that of Raoul Wallenberg.

What is of interest is that the Langlet and Wallenberg appointments were made without any clear idea in Stockholm of exactly what either could accomplish. In effect, the Foreign Office launched two novices into the game of international politics in Budapest. Both would prove their mettle beyond anyone's preconceived imagination. Langlet did not work with the Swedish legation in Budapest. He established his own operation, including the printing of "protective passports" that bore a seal which was supposed to represent Sweden. Per Anger, the regular diplomat at the legation involved in the rescue of the Jews, had great difficulty in monitoring Langlet's activity. More than once, he complained to Stockholm that Langlet was out of control.[34] The Swedish Red Cross even formally warned Langlet to cooperate more closely with the legation. The warning had little impact. Stockholm was far removed from Budapest. The exigencies of the day, not orders from Stockholm, carried the most weight. There was no evidence that Langlet had any difficulties with the other Swedish effort to help the Jews, the one led by Raoul Wallenberg.

---

33. V. Langlet, op. cit., pp. 45–49. UD 1920, HP 1094, Engzell to Danielsson, April 20, 1944.

34. Anger arkiv, F. Bernadotte to Langlet, August 9, 1944, Prince Carl to Langlet, August 17, 1944, and August 29, 1944, and Danielsson to Engzell, September 10, 1944.

Wallenberg's activities have been lionized elsewhere. The willingness of the legation and eventually the Foreign Office to support his unconventional activities illustrated the genuineness of Sweden's commitment to help Jews. The history of his appointment and the fact that he also represented the War Refugee Board should not confuse either the fact that Wallenberg's activities were a reflection of Swedish policy and that Sweden fully approved of what he did. Unlike the case of Langlet, there were no complaints from the legation staff about Wallenberg's unorthodox style. Quite the contrary, they not only aided him when they could, but placed themselves in danger of losing their lives by trying to carry out his rescue efforts. The decision of the legation staff to stay in Budapest during the last weeks of Soviet attack was an important support for the successful rescue efforts. Without it, Wallenberg would have lost his cover.

As for Wallenberg himself, what kind of person could have thought of the idea of a special camp for Jews under the protection of the Swedish flag *before* he even arrived in Budapest? He certainly was not a staid diplomat who followed the conventional rules. His ability to organize elements in the Jewish community and coordinate them with the legation was remarkable. His success in penetrating the political morass of a collapsing Hungary and sustaining it was critical to building the necessary domestic support to save the Jews. Finally, the personal bravery he showed in challenging Eichmann, SS officials, and the Arrow Cross bullies gave inspiration both to Jews and other neutral organizations active in helping Jews. "Fantastic schemes" were possible in 1944 and 1945, but they needed men willing to pull them off.

Another Swede who had managed a fantastic scheme was the Swedish consul general in Paris, Raoul Nordling. Nordling has been credited with convincing the Germans not to use the streets of Paris as a battleground and leave the city untouched for the advancing Allied armies.[35] In November 1944, Folke Bernadotte visited Nordling and discussed with him Nordling's views about the possibility of rescuing people from German concentration camps. Nordling thought that a way might be found and specifically pointed out that a large number of French women were being held at a camp at Ravensbrück. Bernadotte returned to Stockholm anxious to explore ways to lead a rescue mission to Germany.

35. SRC, Folke Bernadotte II:7, v. 32, Memorandum of Bernadotte trip, October 29-November 14, 1944.

His enthusiasm found common ground with the Norwegian Ditleff and the Jew Storch. The success of their actions was examined in Chapter 4.

Full credit should be given to the Swedish government and those additional individuals who were responsible for the successful rescue of Jews and other peoples in 1943–1945. Tens of thousands of lives were saved. Yet the question has to be asked if more help could have been provided? It is a difficult question. The Swedish government demonstrated that much could be accomplished, particularly in the last two years of the war. But the initiative for these actions came from outside the government, often from outside the country. Why did the Swedes have to wait until they learned specifically of the German decision to deport the Danish Jews before making Sweden a haven? Why wait for an American-Jewish initiative before sending special representatives to Budapest? Why was it necessary to wait for pressure from Norway, Denmark, and the WJC before interceding in Germany in 1945?

If anti-Semitism played a part in the shortcomings of Swedish policy in the late thirties, it seemed of little import toward the end of the war. The lack of initiative that characterized Swedish responses to the plight of Jews depended more on the general thrust of Swedish foreign policy during the war. Particularly in the post-1942 period, Hansson and Günther did not want to see Sweden's policy swing too quickly and too violently in a pro-Allied direction. They would help the democracies, but they preferred that the British and the United States pressured them for concessions. If the Western powers had placed a higher priority on Sweden helping the Jews, there is much evidence to suggest that Sweden would have acted more vigorously even in 1943. The failure of the Western powers has been chronicled by others. Should Sweden have depended upon their encouragement? When it came to issues related to their Scandinavian brothers, there was little hesitancy to act.

Sweden is a small state. In World War II, most of the small states of Europe were occupied by one or another of the belligerents. A few managed to stay out of harm's way. Sweden's independence swayed in the balance as Germany established its hegemony over the Baltic. Sweden accommodated itself to living inside a German sphere of influence. Sweden opted not to take any unnecessary risks. Helping Jews in 1942 appeared potentially risky. After that, Sweden cautiously developed programs to aid Jews. More could have been done. Then again, what obligations did Sweden have toward the Jews?

Between 1939 and 1945, over six million Jews were killed, most of them murdered in a systematic campaign to eliminate all Jews from Europe. No country, not even Germany, should be given full blame for the extermination of so many people of the same faith. If Germany provided the active ingredient that ignited the political chemistry that destroyed millions, it would not have been possible without the aid of people of many other nationalities, bound together by anti-Semitism and fascist ideologies. The silence of the democratic world played its part, too. The silence left doubts, allowed its citizens to avoid confronting the reality, and permitted the refusal to offer any real hope save winning the war. Sweden contributed to the silence. Sweden, too, bore a responsibility.

Documents

The study of history depends upon documents. Documents provide the basis for all historical research. Historical interpretation combines the evaluation of documents with the historical perspectives of the historian himself. Some historical problems are more difficult to interpret than others. The difficulties can arise from the nature of the documents and/or from the nature of the problem. The study of Sweden's response to persecution of the Jews, 1933–1945, is not an easy task. Documents are often unclear in their meaning and a proper historical perspective is difficult to maintain. Many facets of the study are highly emotional issues which touch people alive today. Therefore I have decided to include a selection of documents in this volume.

Unfortunately, the demands of space forced me to be highly selective in the choice of specific documents and to edit them. My selection of specific documents depended upon three principles: general representativeness; interest; and significance. I edited the documents in such a way as to attempt to preserve the context of the original text while eliminating superfluous words. There is always great danger in such an exercise. Serious students of history should consult the original texts. I have asked other scholars to examine the original texts and my edited ones to insure their accuracy. While these scholars approved of my editing, I alone bear responsibility.

The documents are arranged chronologically. Each document is identified. In the case of important documents, references are given to materials in the interpretative section of the book.

Document 1: Memorandum from Einar af Wirsén, April 20, 1933.
This memorandum reports the response of German officials including Hitler to Gustaf V's criticisms of contemporary German policy. It provides insight into the attitudes of Gustaf V.

His Majesty the King telephoned . . . to find out my opinion of how the German Government had taken his conversation with the Reich

President, the Reich Chancellor, the Vice Chancellor and the Foreign Minister, at the Legation on the 21st of this month. His Majesty wondered whether any displeasure might have been observed because of the frankness of his remarks.

. . . the Foreign Minister . . . assured [me] that what His Majesty had said had been very beneficial and useful. The Chancellor always appreciated it when one spoke plainly with him, and it was likely that the King's views would have a certain effect.

The King then inquired . . . whether one might expect any amelioration in the treatment of the Jews, to which I was able to answer that a certain relief had already become manifest. . . .

The King . . . considered it appropriate that the French Government should be informed of the general content of what he had told the leaders of the German Government. . . .

. . . Mr. François-Poincet . . . declared . . .

Just the fact that it had been the King of Sweden, a monarch of great experience, "*un des Doyens des Souverains européens*" and leader of a country upon whose loyalty Germany felt it could rely, that it was he who had interceded, had given the King's words in this case such a weight that the Ambassador was obliged to regard them as being among the most weighty and most valuable contributions to the effort to further a peaceful development.

. . . A person close to Herr Göring . . . hinted that, in a few months, it might become necessary to soften the Jewish regulations, and this for reasons of foreign policy . . .

. . . Minister of Propaganda Goebbels's undersecretary. . . . Even on the Jewish question he expressed himself in a rather conciliatory way; one ought to consider the actions taken against the Jews not as anti-Semitism but as a reaction against their excessive influence. . . .

Document 2: Letter from Erik Boheman to the Foreign Minister, Rickard Sandler, November 25, 1935.
Boheman became secretary general of the Foreign Office during the war and very influential on Swedish foreign policy. This report, sent from Warsaw, illustrates both the interest and the knowledge of Boheman in the "Jewish Question."

Of all the many problems with which modern Poland has to wrestle, the Jewish Question may be one of the most serious and difficult to solve. The Jewish population probably amounts to around three millions, the overwhelming majority of whom consist of a proletariat residing in cities. . . . This great mass is strictly orthodox and lives under the burden of a religion which has grown rigid in custom and in practice, and which has surely contributed to preventing all assimilation between the Jewish population and the nation's real inhabitants, and to holding the Jewish population down at a low cultural and material level.

. . . That anti-Semitism is on the upsurge in Poland should not be doubted. It is fostered by the German example. Here as in other countries it is nourished by the economic crisis, which calls forth discontent that must find expression in some direction and easily turns against the Jewish shopowners and money-lenders. Finally, it is strengthened by the fact that Communism, without the least doubt, has its strongest foothold among the lower layer of the Jewish population.

The Government in power has suppressed all expressions of anti-Semitism with great rigor. In the last few days, anti-Semitic riots have broken out at Warsaw's university and institutes. . . . Because of these riots, the university and institutes have been closed until further notice.
. . .

How the Polish Jewish problem shall ever be solved, probably no one can foresee. I have not found a single constructive idea among those leaders with whom I have discussed this issue. Once they have pointed out the serious nature of the problem, generally they have declared, with a shrug of the shoulders, that it really was insoluble. If a greater emigration cannot be achieved, or if Poland's economic situation cannot be improved in some presently unforeseeable way, then the latent tension is going to be released, sooner or later, in some way that will be serious and painful for the Jewish population, no matter how firmly the Government may intend to prevent such a development by every means.

Document 3: Letter from Folke Malmar to Foreign Office Director of the Political Section S. Söderblom, April 4, 1938.
Malmar was Swedish envoy in Prague. His reports on Jewish interest in immigration to Sweden were critical of what he felt to be an all too open-handed policy on Sweden's part. The opening lines of this document

illustrate the kind of hostility toward Jews expressed by high-ranking diplomats.

The rats are leaving the sinking ship. "Non-Aryans" are standing in line on our stairs to inquire about chances of being allowed into Sweden.
. . .

Document 4: Comments of Gösta Engzell, Head of the Legal Department of the Ministry of Foreign Affairs, to the Conference in Evian, June 29, 1938.
President Franklin D. Roosevelt initiated a special international conference at Evian, France, to discuss the problems of political refugees. Although it had been the issue of Jewish refugees which lay behind Roosevelt's actions, the discussion at the conference failed to touch on the Jewish Question directly. Indeed, virtually no positive steps were adopted by the attending countries. Engzell's speech is of interest because it identifies the real issue — the problem of Jewish emigration — and because it indicates that one of the difficulties with a discussion of Jewish emigration is that Jews were not always classified as political refugees. Many countries including Sweden refused to recognize Jews as political refugees. Sweden wanted the conference to find a general solution to the Jewish Question in Europe.

. . . According to the invitation, the purpose of the conference was to facilitate the emigration from Austria and Germany of political refugees.
In the view of the Swedish Government, in dealing with this question one cannot avoid also touching on a much wider question, which is the Jewish emigration problem in Europe as a whole. A larger and larger portion of the emigrants from Germany and Austria is composed of Jews, not always falling under the rubric of political refugees. . . .
It is clear to the Swedish Government that a solution of the Jewish emigration problem . . . must be sought in emigration to countries outside Europe, and the requirements of such an emigration ought to be studied carefully. In this connection, it appears necessary to direct our efforts first toward seeking to procure one or more areas for colonization, where the Jewish emigrants would be able, through the agency of an international organization, to find a common refuge and create for themselves a new homeland. . . .

However, we must search for an immediate solution to the pressing refugee cases. . . . Sweden, which does not apply any quota system* in its immigration policy, presently considers herself unable to declare any specific number of refugees whom Sweden is prepared to accept. . . .

Document 5: Sigfrid Hansson to all passport control officers, September 9, 1938.
Hansson, brother to Prime Minister Per Albin Hansson and general director of the Bureau of Social Services, instructs border stations to protect Sweden against undesirable immigration. The term "Jew" never appears in the text, but it is clear that the purpose of the instructions is to make clear that Jews without special permission of Swedish authorities abroad should not be permitted into the country.

Aliens who arrive in the Kingdom without having an entry visa or a residence visa, or a residence permit or working permit, may be turned back. . . .

The official edict, which has come out because of the increased immigration from Central Europe, should be applied primarily to holders of the German passport. . . .

The official edict concerns aliens who have emigrated or are about to emigrate from their home country. No distinction is made between persons who wish to remain in Sweden and persons who wish only to pass through the Kingdom. . . .

Finally, in this connection, the Bureau of Social Services would like to remind you of the great responsibility which, in the present situation, rests upon passport control officers who, like a first line of defense, have the duty of protecting the Kingdom from undesirable immigration, although without applying the current refusal regulations with greater harshness than is called for.

The content of this communication must not become known to unauthorized persons and so should be filed accordingly. . . .

Document 6: Memorandum concerning control of aliens with respect to Germany, October 7, 1938.

---

* Strictly speaking, Sweden had no quota system. With regard to Jews, however, at least after 1937, an informal quota system did exist.

A Foreign Office summary on the problem of controlling Jewish emigra-
tion from Germany to non-Germanic countries. Germany had begun to
stamp a large "J" in all German passports whose holders were classified
by German law as Jews. Germany began this policy after pressure first
from Switzerland and then from Sweden.

1. Now that the German Government has issued orders that German
citizens who are non-Aryan should receive passports with special mark-
ings, an opportunity presents itself for the Swedish side to introduce
controls over Jewish immigration, without applying general visa
requirements. . . .

3. It does not seem likely that the difficulties concerning the immigration of German refugees into Sweden would cease completely, even
if an agreement were reached similar to the one which has been concluded between Switzerland and Germany. . . .

The question then remains, whether it can be considered appropriate, given the Swedish conception of justice, to accept an arrangement
which actually means placing the Jews in a special class. . . .

Providing one considers the German proposal acceptable in principle, then from an objective standpoint it will not make any difference
whether we follow Switzerland's example or establish ordinary visa
requirements. From an administrative point of view, the latter arrangement seems preferable.

Document 7: Letter from Professor Eli Heckscher to Brita Dahlman,
November 27, 1938.
Heckscher, Sweden's most distinguished economic historian, was a
member of the Stockholm Jewish community. Assimilated and respected
widely, he found himself caught between the demands of Swedish Zion-
ists and growing anti-Semitism in Europe.

. . . Indisputably it cannot be denied that all existence weighs upon
me as never before in my life. It is not so much a question of German
Jewish appeals for help as of the total devastation of what one regarded
as an inalienable heritage of Western Man, perhaps of Mankind in general. As a historian, I continually look for parallels with earlier times and
attempt to gain perspective over what is happening around us; and
whether or not it is due to the difficulty of seeing one's own objectively,

my conclusion usually is that what is happening exceeds almost every-thing that has ever occurred. Perhaps the main reason is not a worse deprivation than ever before, but instead that the means of effecting destruction have increased to an almost fantastic extent through the development of technology, especially the *concentration* of power over both soul and body, both outer and inner things. To what extent the specifically Jewish has been decisive for me is difficult to say. Of course, it is so, in the sense that the problem thereby touches me more closely, just as you have written. Yet, on the other hand, I cannot discover in myself, despite everything, any of the Jewish nationalism which is now conquering all of the Jewish youth and many of their elders. It is a daily and unremitting anguish to think about the Jews' sufferings, yet they do not stand any closer to me personally than they have ever done, which is to say, very little. All my roots connect me partly with Western culture as a whole, and partly with Sweden. Sad to say I do not belong to those who believe that Sweden is going to escape the consequences of Germany's overpowering force and the Western allies' powerlessness, and in Finland you have just had a rude reminder of this through the resignation of Holsti; the reminder probably will not become weaker because it concerned a man whom hardly anyone greatly valued.

What you write about Russia is entirely true, and of course you in Finland have a special reason to think about it. Whether the German or the Russian dictatorship's record of sins is longer, I think only God the Father can say. Yet, given that, one can probably find certain reasons why people in our countries occupy themselves more with the German spiritual destruction. Probably the chief reason is (as you too suggest) that we know another Germany, a country which has been in the van-guard of the whole culture in which we live, while Russia has been nearly insignificant for us, both under the Czarist and the Bolshevist regimes. Simply in terms of power politics, too, the difference is immense. Russia is practically unable to accomplish anything outside her own borders, she has an unbroken series of political defeats to cata-logue, while Germany's power now looms over Europe. Yet of course that is no reason to forget what is happening in Russia. . . .

Document 8: Letter from Sven Grafström to the Foreign Minister, December 19, 1938.

A typical report from a Swedish Legation in Europe on the new laws against Jews; this one came from Poland.

. . . The periodical *"Zespol,"* close to Agriculture Minister Poniatowski, has presented a proposal for a Jewish Law for Poland.

Even if this proposal may not reflect a unified government viewpoint on the Jewish Question, it cannot be denied a certain significance, since it probably coincides with the attitude of large portions of the Polish people.

It should be noted that the definition of Jew has been based on profession of faith, making the proposal less rigorous, in this respect, than the German laws. . . .

According to the proposal's Article 11, the Jews would be deprived of voting rights for Parliament and municipal offices, and forbidden to occupy national or municipal government positions, as well as being prevented from occupying positions of trust in professional associations, besides which, *numerus clausus* would be introduced for certain independent professions.

Of interest is the proposal in Article 111 for forcible emigration. According to this, within 10 years the number of Jews in Poland would be diminished by half. Should the emigration quotas fixed by the proposal not be fulfilled, the Jews would be subjected to retaliatory measures, including extra taxes for all Jews, a minimum percent of non-Jewish employees in Jewish shops . . . and so forth . . .

Document 9: Letter from Arvid Richert to Erik Boheman, December 21, 1938.
The letter reports on the attempts of Hjalmar Schacht, German minister of finance, to arrange a deal with the Americans for massive Jewish emigration from Germany.

The U.S.A.'s current Acting Chargé d'Affaires, Mr. Prentiss Gilbert, has given Gisle the following information, in the strictest confidence, concerning Dr. Schacht's London discussions about the Jewish emigration matter. . . .

Mr. Gilbert stated that he had worked for a number of months toward bringing about direct negotiations on the question . . . of accepting the Jews.

. . . However, Mr. Gilbert himself could not look optimistically on the chances for this, because, in the first place, it was uncertain that the foreign powers concerned were prepared for a settlement on the basis of the German conditions and, in the second place, it was not at all certain that the German authorities would show themselves willing to continue the discussions initiated. While the "nicer" elements (Göring and Schacht) really wished to give the Jews at least some advantages to ease their chances of emigrating, the extremists (Goebbels, Himmler, Ribbentrop) were decisive opponents of affording the Jews any relief whatsoever. Which tendency was going to win out, it was impossible to foresee just now. . . .

Document 10: Letter from Arvid Richert to Rickard Sandler, December 30, 1938.
A year-end summary of the position of German Jews by Sweden's most influential envoy, Arvid Richert. General conditions of Jews had worsened in November 1938.

. . . Concerning the excesses of November 10 . . . the whole operation was directed by certain party authorities, who called out their members, and also the police had orders not to interfere. That Messrs. Goebbels and Himmler belonged to those forces within the Government and party leadership who initiated the excesses, can be taken for granted. . . .

The attitude of the people toward the operation against the Jews appears, overall, to have been a surprise and an annoyance to the regime, seeing as it showed that a comparatively large part of not only the educated classes of society but even the working people had expressed disgust with what happened in these outrages. . . .

It was also striking, how Germans in official positions dealing with members of the Mission either avoided mentioning the subject or spontaneously expressed their disapproval. . . .

Evidently the operation against the Jews has caused sharp clashes of views within the highest leadership of the Reich. It would chiefly seem to be Göring who took the part of moderation and common sense against the extremists Goebbels and Himmler, with whom Mr. von Ribbentrop, too, is said to have been most inclined to join. Which tendency will gain the upper hand in the long run, probably cannot yet be inferred. However, judging by many indications, Mr. Goebbels's authority appears to have been appreciably undermined during these last few months, which certainly need not mean, though, that the Führer is prepared to sacrifice him. . . .

Document 11: Memorandum by Gösta Engzell, April 21, 1939.

A Foreign Office memorandum which illustrates the informal system of consultation used in deciding which potential immigrants would be permitted into Sweden. The attitudes of the representatives of the Stockholm Jewish congregation are of import.

As summoned, the following persons were present to discuss certain refugee matters:

Bergström, Head of Division, Foreign Office

Josephson, director of the Jewish congregation

Brunberger, chief accountant of the Jewish congregation

Nysted, former City Veterinary Officer, representing *Svenska Israelsmissionen* (Swedish Mission Among the People of Israel)

Granath, secretary of the refugee aid operation of the Workers' Movement

Also Nylander of the Foreign Office attended.

Messrs. Nylander and Granath wished to see what position we would take on the question of possibly accepting into Sweden a number of refugees from Poland, either for forwarding or for permanent residence.

According to reports . . . about 75% would be Jewish emigrants, often less desirable ones. Therefore, the difficulties chiefly concerned this category, while Granath possibly would be able to accept a number of political refugees. . . .

Great hesitation was expressed concerning the Jews. Up to this point, cases had been treated individually, with a decision dependent upon our ability to evaluate the person concerned. There had been so many that had tried to get in but for whom there had been no approval, that it would be a misfortune if Sweden now were going to be forced to accept persons they didn't know. Only if guarantees of forwarding could be obtained should such [admitting of refugees] be considered. There was very little chance of getting entrance permits to other countries from here. Beside, it would surely be unfortunate for our refugee policy if we should accept larger groups of Jewish refugees, a negative attitude toward such [people] could so easily gain momentum.

No inquiry concerning these refugees had been received by the Jewish congregation. Apparently they were very upset there at the prospect of any major action on the matter. If individual cases were found who might be considered suitable for Sweden, they would not oppose it. The congregation was already so heavily committed that one could not count on any significant support from them. . . .

Document 12: Letter from Professor Eli Heckscher to Docent Hugo Valentin, May 30, 1939.
Heckscher and Valentin were both economic historians and active in the Stockholm Jewish congregation. Valentin was a leading Zionist and critical of Heckscher's assimilationist preferences.

. . . First, concerning the Hebrew language in Palestine. I cannot and dare not dispute your historical account, and willingly concede that you are right about it making much of the action explainable which, without it, would be inexplicable. . . . Your positive defense for this way of acting, however, is one of the expressions of what I regard as an unfortunate error of judgment. You make a very characteristic parallel with the Swedes changing to a foreign language because it would be more practical. But that parallel misses reality completely. I presume you cannot mean to say that Hebrew has been the normal language for as much as one single percent of those Jews who now find themselves in Palestine or are expected there. Probably for most of them the language has been Yiddish, for others, the various national languages. Hebrew has been a scholarly language, in which the original religious texts are written, also, to some extent, a language in which later Jewish authors and bards have written. How many Jews have even been able to stumble through a Hebrew text adequately? I recall Glück's joyous amazement, a few months ago, when that more-than-usually zealous Zionist heard one of the pupils at Svartingstorp express himself fluently in Hebrew over the telephone: there was not a moment's doubt that he had not expected it. All the Hebrew teaching at Svartingstorp, as well as in other places, is really sufficient proof in itself that learning a foreign language is what is going on. If you wish to draw a parallel with the Swedes, which is a comparison entirely *too* favorable to your point of view, then you would presume that they, no longer able to use their former language, would choose Old Icelandic instead of one of the major languages. I would have advised them, without a moment's hesitation, to choose the latter — because I am not a nationalist.

Then you ask whether I believe that assimilation "solves" the Jewish problem. The positive part of my answer is, that I do not believe in the "solution" to that kind of question. But the negative side is, in my opinion, much more important, and it goes: does *Zionism* solve the Jewish problem? Even if Palestine really had any prospects within the foreseeable future of becoming a Jewish state (something I doubt to the highest degree, no matter what the significance of the Balfour Declaration's expression "national home"), it would not solve more than a small fraction of the problem. You have, at least earlier, not closed your eyes to the fact that the entirely overwhelming majority of Jews are going to remain in different countries, and thus, at least in a numerical sense, the chief question must become how should they conduct themselves *there*. So far as I can see, nothing is more vital than letting our thoughts now revolve around that problem, and I turn now to that.

I read your essay in the *Judisk krönika*, probably the one you refer to in your letter and admit that it made me more than antagonistic. You spoke there of a Jewish national feeling as the first priority, contrasting those Jews — even, unbelievable but true, in Palestine — who spoke of how things are *"bei uns,"* by this, meaning in Germany. I did not notice a single word about how things looked to those Jews who find themselves neither in Germany nor in Palestine, but beg your pardon in case I overlooked something. In our country as in a number of others, [Jews like myself who are] members of a severely shrunken cultural circle are citizens like any others, taking part in their material and spiritual work, having 99% of their roots firmly fixed. For all such Jews their country is truly theirs. To ignore that fact, and, through your silence on the question of the difference between the natural attitude toward such a country and toward one like Germany, to inspire the idea that loyalty to one's country approaches treason — this, I must admit, my dear Hugo Valentin, seemed to me to prove how far you had slipped into decline. Yet once again I beg your pardon if I should have overlooked something in the article. And the phenomenon — still providing that I saw correctly — became all the more striking because of the fact that the article was written in Swedish and so *only* could reach Jews in those countries I am speaking of. Forgive me for shaking my head.

All of this would have been merely a rather academic discussion if we did not have the immigrants [here]. Because, for them this kind of doctrine is a practical reality. They have not yet melted into Swedish society and they have an *a priori* tendency to look with contempt upon things Swedish, something for which the Svartingstorp pupils have given me clear evidence. For those who are going to come out [of Germany] as for those [immigrants] to whom I just referred, of course this attitude is going to cause temporary difficulties that should not be made light of, but anyhow these [difficulties] will pass away. Yet can you calculate with the least certainty that all the Jewish immigrants, and nearly all the 500 children, too, are going to get to Palestine? (And yet all of these poor children must toil through Hebrew.) For my part, I have accommodated myself to our having to keep them, should the face of the world not be radically changed; whether I wish this or do not wish it is rather immaterial. And we have thereby come to the heart of the problem. As I see it, this is the question: whether or not we shall create a colony of Jewish aliens in Sweden. I know or at least I believe that you do not wish this, yet, once more, that is *not the question*; the question goes like this: are your (and many others') efforts encouraging or opposing this tendency? This is a question for the conscience and a very practical one.

For what I have seen (mostly of the children) absolutely gives an impression that, not only do they *themselves* gravitate, for reasons easily explained, toward those who speak German, but also that *others* do everything to keep them together with one another and with their mutual Jewishness, with — to put it mildly — indifference toward their melting into Swedish society. Our boy, who in every respect seems to be one of the most successful of all, obviously comes from an assimilationist home and turns a deaf ear to all the invitations he gets to the many clubs and inspirational meetings; but we see some small part of it. Two years in a row he received long mimeographed handbills from some youth organization, which included in its program the creation of a *"Weltanschauungsarbeitsgemeinschaft"* — I am sorry that this had not come, when I wrote about how the problem with the immigrants is not that they are Jews but instead that they are Germans, for you must concede that the Hitler Youth could not have done this better. As best we can tell, the boy is getting on very well in the automobile mechanics' department of the Stockholm Municipal vocational school and is becoming, so far as one can foresee, a really good Swedish skilled workman; his one real friend is Swedish. Yet all those we have seen in other places are of the opposite type. Gunnar tells me that Jan Waldenström has told him directly that their foster child is not allowed to go to everything that is offered her — if I remember rightly, it is a girl — because he disapproves of the tendency. Here is the problem, and I would very gladly present it for general discussion. That we who hold this view of the matter are going to become deaf to all appeals, if they should lead to sacrificing the position of the Swedish Jews, is absolutely certain; yet, despite everything, I am convinced that basically you hold the same view. *Say it, then,* for heaven's sake; no one has greater opportunities than you, whose Jewishness stands above all suspicion.

To this last, which I earnestly wish you to take to heart, I will only add a personal reminiscence. In your delightful writings about the Israelite Youth Club you seemed to me to be establishing with satisfaction how the club gradually moved from German — or perhaps it was Yiddish — to Swedish and became one of those factors which made immigrants' offspring into good Swedes; I directed special attention to that page of the work in my reference to the book in the *Historisk tidskrift.* Did I misunderstand you, or have you subsequently changed your mind? Dear friend, the question is much too important to be evaded.

Under such circumstances I shall express myself with comparative brevity about the rest. In my opinion, the struggle is not between the Jewish values and Nazism. On the contrary I see, with daily mounting sorrow, to what a great extent the Jewish practices are becoming (translated into their own language) like the Nazis. The struggle, instead, is between those who put the common Western heritage of civilization first and in its name fight against all forms of nationalism, and on the other side, those who are nationalists of all shades and nationalities. Whether the Jewish problem gets "solved" or not depends essentially upon how the struggle *there* turns out.

Finally, just a word about K.O. Bonnier. All of your construction of his unpopularity as a product of his assimilationist tendencies I must reject; it is based on completely different factors, without my wanting to call it more justified for that reason.

It is almost superfluous to close this letter with emphasis on how highly I esteem your unselfish idealism, your willingness to live as you teach; but perhaps it does not hurt to say so. Alas, idealism does not prevent one being able to do harm even without at all wishing to. . . .

Document 13: Letter from Gunnar Josephson to the Ministry of Foreign Affairs, June 3, 1940.
A request from the refugee committee of the Stockholm Jewish Congregation for help with regard to Jewish transmigrants.

The Aid Committee of the Stockholm Jewish Congregation takes the liberty of respectfully applying for the assistance of the Royal Ministry of Foreign Affairs in the following matter. . . .

Because of the German occupation of Denmark it has . . . been regarded as advisable that . . . of the German-Jewish children . . . so many as possible get the chance to leave the country as soon as possible. Intending to bring this about, the Jewish Agency has placed 270 certificates for immigration to Palestine at the disposal of the children in question. . . .

The issue has then arisen, how the children's passports could most safely be carried from Denmark to Sweden and back again. . . .

. . . whether the possibility exists for the passports to be conveyed in Swedish courier mail despite the fact that no Swedish interest is involved in the matter. Provided such an arrangement could be effectuated, a reassuring security would be achieved for the children's identification papers, which would not, on the other hand, be the case should the passports be entrusted to a private traveler. . . .

Finally, the Committee dares to express the respectful hope that the Royal Ministry of Foreign Affairs will consider itself able to assist the Committee, which obviously would be of the greatest value to the work for Jewish refugees.

Document 14: Memorandum of M. Hallenborg, November 18, 1940.
A Foreign Office review of American policy toward Jewish immigration to the United States. The lack of flexibility in the American refugee policy discouraged Sweden from much openness of its own.

Because of those difficulties in obtaining American immigration visas which have arisen, for Jewish and other refugees from Central Europe who have temporarily been accepted into Sweden for further emigration to the United States of America, the undersigned has, as requested, had a conversation with the official in the local American Consulate General who is chiefly responsible for the matters in question. . . .

. . . The extensive limitations on immigration from Europe to the U.S.A., which were adopted during 1940, have resulted in a rigorous sifting of the applicants. . . .

The restrictions have come to pass because of, among other things, a fear of spies and, on the whole, because of observations which had been made that many Jewish refugees from Europe have difficulty in adapting themselves to the American environment. They have learned, with respect to German Jews, that despite everything they have remained more German than Jewish or American.

The stiffened regulations have most severely affected the refugees from Germany, Poland and Czechoslovakia who have applied for immigration before the first of October, 1938.

. . . It is correct that the applicants, and especially those who belong to the aforementioned category, are often told to obtain further documents and certificates, and that such instructions are often repeated time after time, though without immigration visas being granted. But it should be noted that, at least in many of these cases, Mr. Washington orally advised the parties concerned that their prospects for approval would be slight or, practically speaking, none.

. . . The Poles who are in Sweden, too, have hardly any chance to get over to America, even if they should obtain American visas. . . .

. . . I showed Mr. Washington the notes we had received, partly from Josephson the bookseller — 86 persons — and partly from the Labor Movement Refugee Aid — 24 persons, though only a few for the U.S.A. I asked if he could tell me anything concerning these persons' chances. As expected, the answer was negative. . . .

. . . All American consulates in Europe had similar instructions with respect to the issuance of immigration visas. . . .

Document 15: Letter from Th:son Pihl to Dr. Sven Hedin, December 12, 1940.
Pihl, Berlin correspondent for Syd-Svenska Dagbladet, *like other Swedish journalists received information regarding Jewish persecution and sought ways privately to help the Jews. Hedin was a famous explorer and very pro-German.*

On the evening before Dr. Hedin's departure for Stockholm, the following information, and the request that I deliver it, came to me (though, unfortunately, too late for me to deliver it personally):

Minister Goebbels, in collaboration with the chief of the SS, Heydrich, plans on his authority as Gauleiter of Berlin to banish and deport from the capital some 75,000 persons who are identified as undesirables. Among them are found not only Jews but also a substantial number of foreigners. . . . According to my information, this action is to be initiated around the 6th of January next year.

A corresponding banishment from Vienna is also anticipated. In that city around 45,000 persons are affected, for the most part Jews. Inquiries have been made both in Vichy and in Bratislava to ascertain whether the French or the Slovakian governments, respectively, would like to accept the persons in question, either all or part. Both Vichy and Bratislava have responded in the negative. . . .

. . . All that remained as a place of exile was the General Government of Poland. . . . In Berlin circles interested in the fate of these persons, they are pointing out that exile to Poland — in the middle of winter, to boot — is about the same as a death sentence.

These same circles, of whom I spoke during Dr. Hedin's stay in Berlin, have been in touch with the Red Cross in Geneva, as Dr. Hedin knows, and with the Red Cross representative who was recently in the Reich capital. That person must quickly return to Geneva, to negotiate with the French Minister of War, Huntziger, and with Ambassador Scapini, who, as is well known, is attending to the issue of French prisoners of war.

In connection with the proposal concerning those interned in southern France, which I had the opportunity to present in a preliminary way to Dr. Hedin, these circles have asked me to convey that the Red Cross is exceedingly worried because of this new deportation plan. That is, the Red Cross feels that all such actions ought to be postponed until the war has been brought to an end. Only then could an effective assistance effort be begun in earnest, so that the entire refugee problem could be solved in a unified context. This is the Red Cross's very firm opinion.

Therefore, in Geneva as in Berlin, people have asked themselves what could be done to bring about a similar postponement in the case of the 75,000 from Berlin and the 45,000 from Vienna. Once again their thoughts turned to Sven Hedin. They emphasize that Reich Marshal Göring is not informed of Minister Goebbels' intentions and that perhaps much could be gained were the Marshal informed of the matter.

Then, perhaps, he could bring his influence to bear. Since it is known that Dr. Hedin has good personal relations with Hermann Göring, it is hoped, according to the account I was given, that Dr. Hedin might be willing to inform the Reich Marshal in writing of the information I have just now conveyed, so that he could have the circumstances investigated and then take those actions he found appropriate.

This proposal, that Dr. Hedin should get in touch with Reich Marshal Göring in this matter, with the intention of bringing about a postponement of the deportations, was what I was asked to present by means of this letter. . . .

Document 16: Letter from Birger Pernow to Archbishop Erling Eidem, April 28, 1941.
Pernow headed Svenska Israelsmissionen. *He became the "Jewish expert" for Eidem during the war. "Judekristna" refers to Jewish converts who were classified as Jews by German race law.*

. . . There is one matter that so greatly burdens my heart. . . .

. . . It concerns our poor persecuted Jewish converts in Vienna. As the Archbishop knows, since the middle of November a deportation to Poland has been going on, and it seems as if the intention now is to move all of Vienna's Jews there. . . . This deportation has evoked an inexpressible anxiety among Vienna's Jews, because they know that Poland means a slow and painful destruction through disease and starvation. Therefore our missionaries in Vienna are completely overrun with despairing persons who plead, weeping, to be rescued. All of them would like to come to Sweden, but of course that is out of the question. We are trying to help in every way and we have even succeeded. . . . I have had repeated negotiations with Bexelius, the department head, as well as Director General Höjer at the National Board of Health and Welfare. They are very well-disposed toward our mission nowadays. Thus we have gotten immigration permits approved for three of our Jewish convert mission workers in Vienna, with their wives, as well as obtained approval for similar applications for 15 of our closest volunteer co-workers. . . . It even seems to be possible to obtain immigration permits for a very limited number of parents (preferably aged) who have children in Sweden. This has spurred me to the idea of trying to make a home for the aged for a group of such Jewish converts, for example

around 15 persons. . . . If the Archbishop could help us with the necessary economic contribution, I am willing to take on the organization of
the aforementioned home. . . .

**Document 17: Letter from Erik de Laval to the B Department of the
Ministry of Foreign Affairs, October 14, 1941.**
*De Laval, stationed in Sweden's Legation in Berlin, tried to monitor the
treatment of Dutch Jews at the concentration camp of Mauthausen.*

Through a verbal note on the 13th of September I made a new request
to the *Auswärtiges Amt* for permission for myself or for Legation Secretary Count von Rosen to visit the Dutch citizens of the Jewish race
interned in Mauthausen. In the verbal note, reference was made to the
great mortality among those interned — at that time around 150 deaths
were known of, among the 680 interned.

A few days ago, I received through private hands intelligence from
Holland that lately the mortality has substantially increased and that the
number of deaths in the beginning of October has risen to somewhat
more than 400, of whom during the last three weeks around 50 men per
week have perished. Official notices of the deaths have been given by
the German police in Holland to the so-called *Judische Rat* in
Amsterdam, which accounts for the correctness of this information
being unquestioned.

No information concerning cause of death nor any details of the circumstances in which they occurred has been given, neither has any urn
with the ashes of the deceased nor any personal belongings whatsoever
been given to the relatives. In Holland it is presumed that the Jews were
forced to work without protective masks in a saltpeter mine, which
causes poisoning that, after two or three relapses, leads to death. It is
striking that, according to the official death list, the deaths are generally
concentrated within certain dates, for example the 5th and 6th of September, which may suggest that in hopeless cases they are accelerating
the death process through active intervention. It should be added that
all those interned are (were) in the prime of life, between 18 and 35
years of age.

On the basis of this latest intelligence, Minister Richert yesterday
visited *Geheimrådet* Albrecht at the *Auswärtiges Amt*, put the case
before him, and made an especially serious request that within

Auswärtiges Amt they should allow investigation of the conditions in Mauthausen and correct them, as well as carry through the requested permission for a visit to the camp by a representative of the Mission's B Department.

At the same time, Minister Richert also stated that if the mortality of these last weeks continues, after about five more weeks all those Jews interned in Mauthausen will have died. *Geheimrådet* Albrecht appeared to be very much surprised and very unpleasantly affected by the news of the great mortality in Mauthausen, which he seemed not to have known about earlier. As concerns the Minister's statement, he promised to try to force through a prompt treatment of the matter by the authorities concerned.

Document 18: Memorandum by Arvid Richert, October 26, 1941.
After Germany's attack on the Soviet Union in June, Germany began a new policy of direct extermination of captured Jews through the use of special SS-units. Reports of their activities like this one reached Stockholm. This stage of German policy toward the Jews was quickly followed by the more systematic and efficient "Final Solution."

As an example of the harshness which is being displayed in the war on the Eastern Front, I can relate what was told to me recently by an absolutely truthful German air force officer. My informant, who on the 15th of last month had to land with his machine at an air field near one of the larger towns between Lemberg and Kiev, already noticed when he was above the air field that there was a tremendous stream of people on the broad avenue that led from the town in question out to the airport.

When he had landed and climbed out of his plane, the ground personnel asked him if he had noticed what was going on at one edge of the airfield. When he answered that he had not looked so closely, he was informed that, over there, *"werden heute 3 bis 4000 Juden hingerichtet."* Then my informant looked through his field glasses at this mass execution, which was carried out like this: the victims, without any sign of attempting escape, but instead in a kind of apathetic resignation, were driven together into a column about 35 feet across and fed forward to the edge of pre-prepared mass graves and, there, men from the *Waffen-SS* ended their lives with machine pistols so that the bodies fell directly into the graves.

My informant, who remained at the air field for an hour, during that time had heard the firing of automatic weapons continuing without interruption, and when he once again took off, he had flown over the execution site at a low altitude, from which he could plainly distinguish seven of these mass graves, in size at least 65 by 35 feet, filled with dead, as well as the never-ceasing stream of new condemned prisoners, among whom were women and children, too.

To my comment that the Russians, for their part, commit the cruelest acts against German prisoners, he answered that the aspect of what he had described above, which upset him and his fellow officers so much was, that Germany in its propaganda describes itself as the defender of civilization, while at the same time the *Waffen-SS* are permitted to commit such mass murders, which after sober reflection he believed could only originate in sadism or in a desperate food shortage situation.

My informant continued that, in the prisoner camps built by the Germans for those Russians who had not been sent to workplaces in Germany, the Russians for their only dwellings are reduced to digging themselves dens in the earth. On the other hand, the Russians are said to shoot immediately all German prisoners of officer rank, while, in contrast, they take good care of all prisoners of lower rank, who with good treatment are conveyed to prisoner camps east of the Urals, where they are supposed to be taught Soviet lessons, for the future requirements of Communistic propaganda in Germany after the war.

Document 19: Letter from Arvid Richert to S. Söderblom, October 31, 1941.

Richert received much information about persecution of the Jews. What he did with that information is not entirely clear. The tone of this letter — especially when compared to his previous memorandum (see Doc. 18) — is instructive.

Herewith I beg leave to transmit a memorandum concerning the deportations of Jews from Berlin. If the information given therein is correct — it originates, in any case, from a reliable person — during the last few weeks a total of about 4,800 of Berlin's 70,000 Jews have been evacuated to a camp in the vicinity of Litzmannstadt.

Of course it is not so easy to form any conception of the tempo with which the deportations are going to be carried out in the future. One cannot exclude the possibility that these deportations are going to be spread out over a significant period of time, in part because of the transportation problems with which the German railroads must contend. Many places on the trains are taken up by transport of troops and war materiel to the Eastern Front as well as the return home of wounded and furloughed from the Front and, because of this, for months past the number of trains accessible to the general public has been curtailed. According to the bulletin issued by the *Deutsches Nachrichtenbüro* enclosed herewith, further limitations on travel have taken place, so that passenger trains are now available only to those who make trips on official duty or in the practice of their profession. In a commentary on the bulletin, the *Deutsche Allgemeine Zeitung* states that the withdrawal of a number of passenger trains does not require any further explanation, since the action was imperative. It demanded a sacrifice of everyone, a sacrifice which would benefit everyone, especially the armed forces and the supply effort.

What the reasons for these deportations of Jews may be is not easy to say; probably they are part of a general plan whose intention is to transport most and perhaps all Jews resident in the German Reich gradually to a suitable area of settlement to the east. Earlier, it has been said that an area south of Lublin would preferably be reserved for Jewish settlement. However, Litzmannstadt, where the deportations now seem to be going, has been incorporated into the German Reich; thus, either the plans have been changed or the stay in Litzmannstadt is only considered to be a temporary arrangement. According to a number of accounts, the Jews are presently being assembled within the General Government of Poland, especially in Litzmannstadt and in Warsaw. While the Jews in the latter city, before the outbreak of war in 1939, were supposed to have amounted to around 400,000, it is said that the number of Jews in the ghetto now amounts to 750,000. Among others, all the Jews in the factory town Zyrardow are said to have been brought there.

In certain places, the deportations of Jews from Berlin is being connected with the evident shortage of apartments, which has made itself felt for a long time and to an increasing extent. It is also possible that the authorities believe they ought to evacuate Jews so as to make apartments available. In any case, I know that the demand for the apartments that have become available is especially heavy.

As you know, around the 20th of September it was required of all Jews in Germany and the protectorate to carry in full view on the left side of

the breast the six-pointed so-called Star of David, upon which has been
stitched the word "Jew." With a claim to reliability — though the information cannot be considered confirmed — it has been made known
from Party quarters that the German armed forces demanded that the
Jews be furnished with some sign which would make them easily recog-
nizable. The chief reason for this was an incident that took place a couple
of months ago at a late hour on the Kurfürstendamm, in which a German
officer had knocked down a diplomat from a southern country and afterward tried to excuse his actions by the other having "looked like a Jew."
According to another story, among the reasons the peculiar decoration
was introduced was to make it easier for shopkeepers to tell Jews from
Aryans; that is, they say that it has happened widely that Jewish women,
who unlike the Aryan are not engaged in any public service of one sort or
another, used their abundantly free time to make unreasonably large
grocery purchases of unrationed goods in many stores. However that
may be — on several grounds this reason seems to be not altogether
convincing — it appears that the placing of the Jews in a special class has
not entirely brought with it the intended defamatory result. The Star of
David is a national Jewish symbol, which at least in Polish synagogues is
generally evident. A German Party member said, a while ago, not without resentment, that the bearing of the Star of David gave the Jews a
certain satisfaction related to the joy of martyrdom. "It is like forcing us
Germans to go around with the swastika on our breast," he said, "and we
would never be ashamed to do that."

According to unanimous reports from different directions, both in
Berlin as in the larger provincial cities with sizable Jewish elements, the
Jews nowadays, since they got their "decoration," are being treated with
noticeable courtesy, in some places with friendliness, too, by the German people. Many are said actually to disapprove of the regulation
about wearing the Star of David. You can add to that an important opinion, which anyone can now confirm through his own observations on the
streets and in public places, that a large number of the Jews do not present any striking Semitic feature but actually look as people generally do.
It has been reported from a couple of different directions that the action
with the Star of David has actually failed, just for that reason; therefore it
was even more urgent to remove from the public as soon as possible the
sight of the "decorated" Jews, which would have been a contributory
reason for initiating deportations. To avoid misunderstanding, I beg
leave to add here that, even if many Germans disapprove of the draconic

actions against the Jews, anti-Semitism still seems to be deeply rooted in the people.

The conditions just described might possibly have a certain interest as background to the deportation question. How the evacuation is going to affect most Jews in Germany in the near future is, as has already been stated, uncertain, but the fear of the Damoclean sword, which can strike the one as easily as the other, of course brings many to the brink of despair.

A transcript of this is being sent to Hellstedt simultaneously.

Document 20: Memorandum concerning entry visas for Jewish refugees, by Svante Hellstedt, October 23, 1941.
A summary of Jewish applications for permission to enter Sweden in 1941 and the response of the government.

During the period January 1–August 31, 1941, the foreign passport office authorized visas for 167 Jewish refugees, the overwhelming majority from Germany and from areas occupied by Germany.

During the period September 1–October 21, 1941, 52 such authorizations have been issued. During the same period, some 170 applications have come in. Of these, the National Board of Social Welfare has supported 66 and withheld support from 34, while opinions on the remainder have not yet been issued. (In two cases, the visa has been issued without an opinion being asked of the National Board.)

Of those 34 applications refused support by the National Board, all except three (a family) concerned persons with children, sisters or brothers, or parents in Sweden. After the Foreign Ministry refused them, new petitions for a number of them have been made to the Ministry, generally, through well-known persons as their spokesmen.

With a few isolated exceptions, the applications supported by the National Board concern parents, children or brothers and sisters (in three cases, a niece — a refugee — in Sweden; in one case, a granddaughter in Sweden). In three cases, the persons in question have no relatives in Sweden and no other connection with Sweden: (1) a 48-year-old lawyer in Vienna, spokesman, *Svenska Israelsmissionen* (The Swedish Mission to the People of Israel); (2) a 70-year-old female doctor (granted); (3) a 21-year-old gardener ("since the applicant represents a profession in which a shortage of manpower prevails here, the National Board of Social Welfare will not oppose approval.")

Among those applications supported by the National Board, but not yet decided by the Foreign Ministry, there are some applicants with very close relatives still in Germany. For the sake of security, it appears extremely doubtful whether they ought to be approved.

It is also highly doubtful whether the favorable recommendation of the National Board should be followed with respect to a 55-year-old sister of the Hungarian journalist Faludi, who, during her stay in Sweden, has repeatedly given the Swedish authorities a great deal of trouble because of her lack of loyalty.

To complete the information tendered in the memorandum of October 23, 1941, concerning entry visas into Sweden for Jewish refugees, it should be mentioned that during the period of September 1 to November 4, around 460 applications have come in.

During the same period, 140 applications have been approved and 165 refused. (As concerns around 140 applications, opinions are awaited from the National Board of Social Welfare. Concerning 15 applications, which were supported by the National Board, it appears very doubtful whether they ought to be approved.)

Document 21: Letter from Colonel Juhlin-Dannfelt to the head of the Intelligence Department of the Defense Staff, October 30, 1941.
Juhlin-Dannfelt was Sweden's military attaché in Berlin and an excellent source of information about German military matters. Inadvertently he also learned about German treatment of the Jews.

From a journalist who has just returned from a long trip to the Ukraine, traveling Lemberg-Kiev-Uman-Nikolayevsk-Odessa by bus and from Odessa through Bucharest to Berlin by train, a number of interesting reports on the situation have been received. The essential parts of these reports are given below. . . .

The Jews were gone, everywhere. Either they had fled with the Russian troops or they had been sent away later. In some places a full-scale hunt for Jews had been arranged. In a smaller town, a Russian of German nationality had been encountered, who related that he had now shot 37 of the town's 38 Jews and that he was hunting for the 38th. . . .

Document 22: *Göteborgs Handels- och Sjöfartstidning,* July 11, 1942.
The Polish Government-in-exile released the first information about a systematic campaign to kill Poland's Jews in June–July 1942. This information sent from the Polish underground via Stockholm to London was available in Stockholm but the Swedish Board of Information stopped publication. It reached print as a story from London. A white book on German atrocities also suffered the same fate. The Swedish version was confiscated and the English version was allowed to circulate.

The Germans are executing about 6,000 Poles in Warsaw every week, members of the Polish Government in London related yesterday. The systematic methods of exterminating and terrorizing the Polish people are increasingly effective, and the Polish Government insists that the Allies must do everything necessary to open a second front as soon as possible, otherwise the Germans will have time to exterminate the Polish people before victory can be achieved. Between September 1939 and July 1941, 80,000 Poles were executed; between July 1941 and July 1942, no less than 320,000. One of the Polish ministers related how 30,000 Jews from Hamburg were brought to Minsk and killed and how others were forced to dig their own graves before they were executed.

Brendan Bracken, in the British Government, promised the severest imaginable punishment for those responsible. The Polish Government's horrific descriptions can not be made public in the Swedish press.

Document 23: Unsigned memorandum. Ministry of Foreign Affairs, February 11, 1942.
Even after the campaign to destroy Europe's Jews had begun, representatives of the Stockholm Jewish Congregation showed reticence to press for a more active Swedish policy.

A Danish representative of the Women's International League for Peace and Freedom, Mrs. Fanny Arnskov, has called on Director General Höjer of the National Board of Social Welfare and Legation Counselor Hellstedt to obtain permits for entry into Sweden of 187 Jewish youths in Denmark, stateless emigrants from Germany, who have learned farming for emigration elsewhere. In Denmark, they were now threatened with being sent to *Ostlande.* . . .

Director Josephson of the Jewish Congregation says that it is out of the question to accept so many as 187, there is not enough money. But they are willing to commit themselves to 20 or 30 boys.

Höjer thinks that they are welcome in farming, where we have earlier placed two to three hundred, who have turned out very well. Thinks that only these ought to be considered, should anything be done.

One must assume that what is intended here is straightforward immigration. They are going to stay in Sweden. The question, then, is whether one should — primarily out of consideration for Denmark — take the lesser number. Thereby, certain ones are given preference, the other unfortunates left to their fate.

Document 24: Letter from Herschel Johnson to U.S. Secretary of State, July 21, 1942.

U.S. Legation, Stockholm, reports on information about persecution of Jews. An example of the nature of information available about Jewish exterminations in Stockholm.

I have the honor to refer to the Legation's telegram No. 1831, dated July 16, 1942, in which information was communicated to the Department in regard to the Jewish situation in the areas in Eastern Europe which are at present under German occupation.

As was stated in the foregoing telegram the information in question has been obtained from Mr. Wieclav Patek, who is in charge of the consular section of the Polish Legation at Stockholm.

In a conversation on July 9, 1942, Mr. Patek informed a member of the Legation's staff that he had been informed that the following figures in regard to the number of Jews in Vilna and in Riga before and after the German occupation might be considered to be reliable:

Number of Jews

	Before Occupation	After Occupation
Vilna	70,000	6,000
Riga	25,000	300

Mr. Patek likewise said that the figures next given represented the number of Jews who had been executed by the Germans in Eastern Europe. He added that the figures had been received from foreign newspaper correspondents in Stockholm and that, although they were probably correct, he had as yet not been able to confirm them:

Number of Jews Executed by the Germans

Vilna	60,000
Latvia and Estonia	40,000
White Ruthenia	84,000
Kiev	100,000

The Legation has been in touch with a further reliable source who considers the foregoing figure for Kiev to be correct and the figure for Latvia and Estonia to be very nearly correct.

Mr. Patek likewise furnished the Legation the following information concerning the execution of Jews at Riga which had been received at the Polish Legation at Stockholm. This information had originated with an Estonian officer who had been in the service of the German occupation forces in the Ostland. One of the officer's assignments had been to take a group of these Jews in Riga, they had at once been placed into prison.

Mr. Patek said that the Estonian officer described at a later date a scene, which he had witnessed while in Riga, of the execution of 400 Jews. The unfortunate persons had been marched out to an open field and ordered to dig their own mass graves. Thereupon the men had been ordered to remove all of their clothing, while the women were required to remove their dresses. They had then been executed by firing squads and buried at once. The clothing had, however, been taken up and made use of for other purposes.

From the above-mentioned independent source, it has been learned that precisely the same procedure in respect to the execution of Jews was followed in Kiev and in an instance at Pernau, Estonia, where thirty-five Jews had been executed by the Germans.

Mr. Patek stated that the executions at Riga had taken place under the direction of the German SS. In the execution squads there had been individuals belonging to the local Quislingites. The latter statement was also confirmed by the independent source mentioned above. Moreover, while in Riga, the Estonian officer had been told that as many as 40,000 Jews had been executed in Riga alone. He had also heard that similar mass executions had taken place in Vilna.

In speaking of Vilna, Mr. Patek said that the local Polish residents, despite the inhuman treatment they had received at the hands of the

Jewish commissars during the period of the Soviet regime, had protested to the Germans and to the Lithuanians in favor of the Jews. By the above-mentioned independent source it was stated that in Estonia, similar protests against executions of Jews had been made by the Estonians. The German authorities had, however, responded by introducing even more rigorous measures against the Jews than those that had formerly existed.

In conclusion Mr. Patek said that after his return to Tallinn, the above-mentioned Estonian officer had told the story of the Jewish mass executions at Riga to persons who, in turn, had communicated it to Helsinki from where it had reached Stockholm.

Document 25: Letter from A. Richert to M. Hallenborg, July 22, 1942. *A number of Swedish businessmen in Poland were arrested in July by the Gestapo and charged with various forms of espionage. Richert speculates on the timing of their arrest. Note that Richert sent his reflections to the chief of the Foreign Office press bureau and they were forwarded to Professor Sven Tunborg, director of the Board of Information. Was Richert trying to encourage censorship of "greuel" stories of German atrocities especially regarding Jews?*

In connection with the Mission's official document No. 903 of yesterday (especially as regards Envoy Albrecht's information that the police actions against certain Swedes operating in Warsaw constituted one link in an investigation that had been set in motion by suspicions that Swedes were conveying intelligence between elements of the opposition in Poland and Polish circles in Stockholm, possibly even in London), I hereby beg leave to direct your attention to the fact that the arrest of Mr. Berglind, the engineer, on the 10th of July, closely coincided in time with certain public disclosures in London of information about the conditions in Poland.

As evident from the Damgren-Grafström texts of the German semi-official position (disseminated through the *Deutsches Nachrichtenbüro* on July 11, forwarded on the 13th of this month) the English Cardinal Hinsley, in a radio talk (probably on one of the days immediately preceding the 11th of July) spoke of German "*Greuel*" in Poland and, among other things, that 700,000 Jews had been executed in the General Government since the beginning of the war, and similar stories were also given out at a press conference specifically called for that purpose in London by the British Information Minister, Brendan Bracken. Moreover, judging by the introduction to the lead article, "Reconciliation Prevented," in the July 11 *Göteborgs Handels- och Sjöfartstidning*, just before the 11th of July the Polish Government in London made public information on the treatment of the Polish people under the German occupation, when a death-count of a half-million people was reported.

It is undeniably striking that Director Berglind's arrest thus coincides almost to the day with that moment when people in Berlin would seem to have learned about the disclosures in London, concerning the conditions in Poland, mentioned above.

Document 26: Memorandum of conversation with Gerhard Riegner by Howard Elting, Jr., August 8, 1942.
This document is one of the most famous pieces of evidence relating to knowledge of Germany's Final Solution. Elting, U.S. vice consul in Geneva, interviewed Riegner who as Secretary of the World Jewish Congress had the job of trying to monitor German policy. Riegner had concluded reluctantly that Germany had now embarked upon a campaign to kill all of Europe's Jews. The U.S. State Department tried to hide the information in this document. They were not successful.

This morning Mr. Gerhart M. RIEGNER, Secretary of the World Jewish Congress in Geneva, called in great agitation. He stated that he had just received a report from a German businessman of considerable prominence, who is said to have excellent political and military connections in Germany and from whom reliable and important political information has been obtained on two previous occasions, to the effect that there has been and is being considered in Hitler's headquarters a plan to exterminate all Jews from Germany and German controlled areas in Europe after they have been concentrated in the east (presumably Poland). The number involved is said to be between three-and-a-half and four millions and the object is to permanently settle the Jewish Question in Europe. The mass execution if decided upon would allegedly take place this fall.

Riegner stated that according to his informant the use of prussic acid was mentioned as a means of accomplishing the executions. When I mentioned that this report seemed fantastic to me, Riegner said that it had struck him in the same way but that from the fact that mass deportation had been taking place since July 16 as confirmed by reports received by him from Paris, Holland, Berlin, Vienna, and Prague it was always conceivable that such a diabolical plan was actually being considered by Hitler as a corollary.

According to Reigner, 14,000 Jews have already been deported from occupied France and 10,000 more are to be handed over from occupied France in the course of the next few days. Similarly from German sources 56,000 Jews have already been deported from the Protectorate together with unspecified numbers from Germany and other occupied countries.

Riegner said this report was so serious and alarming that he felt it his duty to make the following requests: (1) that the American and other Allied Governments be informed with regard thereto at once; (2) that they be asked to try by every means to obtain confirmation or denial; (3) that Dr. Stephen Wise, the president of his organization, be informed of the report.

I told Riegner that the information would be passed on to the Legation at once but that I was not in a position to inform him as to what action, if any, the Legation might take. He hoped that he might be informed in due course that the information had been transmitted to Washington.

For what it is worth, my personal opinion is that Riegner is a serious and balanced individual and that he would never have come to the Consulate with the above report if he had not had confidence in his informant's reliability and if he did not seriously consider that the report might well contain an element of truth. Again it is my opinion that the report should be passed on to the Department for what it is worth.

There is attached a draft of a telegram prepared by Riegner giving in his own words a telegraphic summary of his statements to me.

Document 27: Letter from Vendel to Richert, August 20, 1942.
Vendel as Swedish consul general in Stettin had excellent sources for information about Polish developments. This document is the first Swedish Foreign Office correspondence that describes carefully the killing process. The section on the Jews was only one paragraph in a long

report. Richert forwarded it to Stockholm which in turn sent it to Sweden's European Legations.

. . . The picture which my informant gave me concerning the treatment of the Jews in Poland is such that it can hardly be expressed in writing. Therefore I will confine myself to a few brief notes. The treatment is different in different towns, depending on the number of Jews living there. In certain cities there are Jewish Quarters, in others, ghettos, the latter surrounded by a high wall which the Jews may only cross at the risk of being shot; finally, in others the Jews are allowed a certain freedom of movement. However, the intention is to exterminate them eventually. In Lublin, they estimate the number of Jews who have been deprived of their lives at 40,000. The extermination especially strikes Jews over 50 years of age and Jewish children under 10 years. The others are allowed to live so as to fill the labor shortage, and as, gradually, they are no longer needed they are gotten rid of. Their property is seized and ends up, for the most part, in the hands of the SS men. In a city, all the Jews were assembled for what was officially announced as "de-lousing." At the entrance they were forced to take off their clothes, which were immediately sent to "The *Spinstoff* Collection"; the de-lousing procedure, however, consisted of gassing and, afterward, all of them could be stuffed into a mass grave that had been prepared in advance for the purpose. The source from whom I obtained all this information on the conditions in the General Government is such that not the slightest shade of disbelief exists concerning the truthfulness of my informant's descriptions.

Document 28: Aide-Mémoire, August 7, 1945.
One of the most controversial incidents related to knowledge of the Final Solution relates to a meeting between a Swedish diplomat, Göran von Otter, and an SS-officer, Kurt Gerstein. The only document in Swedish archives heretofore discovered is that which follows, dated August 7, 1945. The meeting actually occurred on the night of August 21–22, 1942. According to verbal testimony of von Otter, he reported immediately to his Swedish superiors in Berlin the contents of his discussion with Gerstein which included both a more graphic and more accurate description of the Final Solution than anyone including Riegner had received in the West. Apparently no written report was

*sent to Stockholm. Von Otter reported verbally in January 1943 to
Söderblom. What did von Post and Richert do with von Otter's original
report? Is von Otter's claim credible that he kept no written record of
his conversation with Gerstein? If so, how was the following document
constructed?*

Aide-Mémoire concerning Kurt Gerstein, civil engineer, member of
the "SS-Sanitätsabteilung," Giesebrechtstrasse, born probably
Braunschweig 1907(?), address in 1943: Bülowstrasse 49, Berlin.

In August 1942 Gerstein established contact with a member of a neutral legation in Berlin and told the following story. He had just returned
from a short assignment to the extermination camp in Belzec, near
Lublin. He gave a detailed account of the goings on (the gas-chambers,
the reaction of the SS-personnel, the saving of gold-teeth and so on). He
also showed documents, identification cards and orders from the commandant of the camp for the delivery of hydrocyanid acid. Gerstein said
his endeavor was to bring these happenings to the knowledge of neutral
observers. He was firmly convinced that if the knowledge of this extermination was spread amongst the German population and the facts cor-
roborated by impartial foreigners, the German people would not for a
moment continue their support of the Nazi regime. He further said that
he had spoken in the matter with a high German church dignitary
belonging to the oppositional group, Superintendent Dibelius. (This
was later confirmed by Dibelius himself who vouched for Gerstein's
reliability.)

Later some light was thrown upon the reasons for Gerstein's actions.
Gerstein, who had never taken part in any political activities and was not
a Nazi, had presented himself to the SS and asked to be given a job in the
"Sanitätsabteilung" — the particular branch who organized the extermination camps — because he was anxious to get confirmation of his suspicions regarding the abnormal death rate in the German lunatic asylums
in the years 1941–42. During that time a near relative of Gerstein whom
he loved dearly had also died in such an asylum. What he later learned
in the extermination camps convinced him that his suspicions had only
been too well founded.

Half a year later Gerstein again paid a visit to the same neutral diplomat and asked him if it had been possible to do anything. That was the
last time he was heard of.

His grief and sense of shame over the goings on in the extermination camps seemed to be both genuine and deep, and his wish that the outside world ought to know about it so as to be able to stop it seemed sincere enough.

Document 29: Telegram from Kumlin to Richert, November 13, 1942.
By this date, information about the German extermination campaign had spread internationally. Marcus Ehrenpreis, chief rabbi of Sweden, asked the Swedish Foreign Office to confirm the information. Stockholm turned to Richert.

Chief Rabbi Ehrenpreis had inquired of us whether a report that has reached him, that nearly all the Jews from the Warsaw ghetto will be deported, corresponds with the true situation. I see by Captain von Schwerin's report (No. 828) on the ninth of this month, which was sent here by you, that, according to what he has learned, the number of Jews in the Warsaw ghetto, which formerly came to 400,000, has now dropped to about 30,000. This in itself indicates that a large-scale deportation has taken place. I would now like to ask you whether you think that the figures given could be confidentially communicated to Ehrenpreis, in response to his inquiry, or if some other, possibly more clarifying information is available.

Document 30: Letter from Einar Ytterberg to Arvid Richert, November 14, 1942.
Ytterberg, Swedish consul general in Vienna, also had gathered information about persecutions of Jews. Richert forwarded this report to Stockholm.

Ever since its incorporation into the German Reich (*Heimkehr ins Reich*, according to German terminology), *Ostmark* has lived under a mounting terror.

In the beginning the new possessors of power trod quite lightly and only a very few supporters of the ousted regime as well as a few socialists and communists were deprived of their lives. Yet within a short time the Gestapo seriously set to work on the important chapter of the new order which is called the annihilation of the Jewish population. Pogroms were set in motion with the willing collaboration of the Hitler Youth, Jews were murdered irrespective of age or sex, the plundering of shops and robbery of homes were sanctioned, property was seized and many were deprived of their dwellings. However, the storm quickly passed and thousands of Jews succeeded, partly with the consent of the Gestapo, in leaving the country.

The outbreak of the war brought with it a new wave of terror. It now was directed not only against Jews but also against other so-called enemies of the state, though the communists, in consideration of the entente with Russia, were generally left in peace. Gradually the persecutions of the Jews accelerated in the form of mass deportations, and this procedure has just recently come to an end, since practically all of the at least 300,000 individuals amounting to the Jewish population in *Ostmark* have been sent to Poland and Russia. One has no reliable knowledge of the fate of the deportees, but many things indicate that a very large part of them have already perished or been killed. It seems no longer permissible to doubt that great numbers have been deprived of life through gassing, machine-gun fire and suffocation (through the shutting up of the victims in hermetically sealed railroad cars) and that many have perished through disease and deprivation.

All the while, though, the Gestapo has not neglected its other duties. The prisons have been filled with socialists, monarchists, separatists and priests or persons who incautiously expressed their opinions, listened to foreign radio, practiced smuggling, etc., as well as with communists, especially since the friendship with Russia came to an end. According to what a reputable lawyer told me, the terror is now raging worse than ever. The reactions to the events in Africa have especially contributed to sharpening it. According to my informant, one can get an idea of the extent of the terror by considering that presently around 300 persons in Vienna are waiting for their death sentences to be confirmed on the highest level. He added that the official suspension of legality brought with it an increase in the number of victims. It was now the Gestapo who, unopposed, had the final say concerning the administration of the law (if one must now honor administrative arbitrariness with that term). A consequence of this has been that judges who have delivered judgments according to the letter and spirit of the law and not according to the intentions of those in power have been fired. Poles, Czechs and others belonging to "lower" races (despite their Aryan descent) were usually hopelessly lost, if they, even through no fault of their own, came in contact with the executive authorities. It was therefore the Gestapo and

not the so-called enemies of the state whom public opinion regarded as
the enemies of national order. The Gestapo's ravages are also regarded
as indicating weakness in a regime which was obliged to resort to such
methods.

Document 31: Letter from Richert to Kumlin, November 18, 1942.
Richert's response to Kumlin's inquiry about Ehrenpreis's information.

In reply to your letter of the 13th of this month, concerning Jewish
deportations in Poland, may I say that no reliable information in this
regard is available to me. I recommend that Chief Rabbi Ehrenpreis be
told that reports have also reached the Ministry of Foreign Affairs about
evacuation, to a greater or lesser extent, of the ghetto in Warsaw, but
that it has not proved possible to check the accuracy of this information,
so that it must be reported with all reserve.

I thank you for the consideration you have shown in not letting the
reports from the Mission be passed on to Ehrenpreis without first making inquiry here with me, and I am encouraged to see in this a guarantee
that those reports on the treatment of Jews, and so on, which may be
sent in by the Mission, will not be passed on to outsiders.

Document 32: Letter from Richert to Söderblom, December 5, 1942.
Richert reports on his Legation's efforts on behalf of Norway's Jews.

In connection with my personal letter of the first of this month, I beg
leave to inform you that today von Post presented to Envoy von
Grundherr the same views concerning Swedish-born persons on the
"Jewboat" from Norway as he presented several days ago to Envoy
Albrecht. Mr. von Grundherr had already spoken with Dr. Albrecht on
the matter, but promised to try again; however, he doubted that Jews
who were not Swedish subjects would be allowed to depart for Sweden.
In this regard, von Post stated that such an insignificant number of persons was involved that, in the interest of Swedish-German relations, and
so as not to provoke further irritation in the Swedish public, they on the
German side ought to make a concession in this matter.

On the occasion in question, von Post told Mr. von Grundherr privately that Sweden was prepared to accept Norwegian Jews who had not

yet been deported. Mr. von Grundherr informed him that he had just received a telegram from the German mission in Stockholm, in which he was told that Söderblom had very cautiously sounded out Dankwort on this question. As it happened, Foreign Minister von Ribbentrop himself had given orders to the German mission that should anyone on the Swedish side wish to take up any domestic Norwegian issues, they were to refuse all discussion of such matters, as outside interference; Dankwort had answered in accordance with this. For his own part, Mr. von Grundherr wished to express the hope that those on the Swedish side would not make any official representation on the matter. The outcome could only be negative and a Swedish intervention would, in general, injure rather than benefit the Norwegian Jews.

Document 33: Letter from Prince Carl to Director F. Heyerdahl, December 9, 1942.
The Swedish Government decided not to make a formal request in Berlin to take the remaining Norwegian Jews, but, instead chose to use the Swedish Red Cross as a vehicle to help the Jews. Prince Carl and Heyerdahl were chairs of their respective Red Cross organizations.

Since it has come to my knowledge that a deportation of Jews from Norway has been planned and has been partially carried out, we have discussed within the Swedish Red Cross the possibilities of helpfully interposing in this matter, in fulfillment of our humanitarian mission. We have learned that the Swedish authorities concerned would probably raise no obstacle to immigration permits for a number of, or perhaps all of the Jews remaining in Norway. The Swedish Red Cross, for its part, is prepared to look after these Jews in Sweden and would be glad to assume this humanitarian task.

I would be very grateful to you, Director Heyerdahl, if you would be so kind as to present this offer of the Swedish Red Cross to the German or Norwegian authorities, an offer to which the Board hopes to receive a favorable reply.

Document 34: Letter from Claus Westring to Gösta Engzell, December 12, 1942.
Diplomatic report from Oslo.

Yesterday I conveyed H.R.H. Prince Carl's letter to the president of
Norway's Red Cross, Director F. Heyerdahl. He was more than a little
hesitant concerning how the action could be managed. His first hesitation concerned the political consequences which he thought the matter
could have for Sweden, since from the German side they had told him
that *"die Judenfrage war eine kompromisslöse Frage"* and that they on
the German side could not allow any interference in this question. I
assured him that he need not concern himself with this, but should leave
it to Swedish authorities. In accordance with His Excellency's instructions I emphasized, however, that the initiative came entirely from the
Swedish Red Cross, and that the Swedish Government took no part in
the matter except insofar as the authorities concerned would not raise
obstacles to the entry of the Jews into Sweden. He was further hesitant
whether he should convey the offer to the German or the Norwegian
authorities, this hesitation arising from the fact that these authorities
blamed each other: a complaint had come from the direction of the Norwegian Government over the measures and over their having been
forced to participate, and from the German side (though from another
direction than the one mentioned above) they had complained of the
striking lack of judgment Quisling had shown by starting these Jewish
persecutions. However, a favorable circumstance was the concil-
iatoriness and willingness to negotiate that Terboven had shown at a
strange supper at Skaugum on the 8th of this month, where Heyerdahl
had been the principal guest. However, he wished to sleep on the matter.

Today Heyerdahl got back in touch, and he informed me that he felt
he had been able to establish that the measures against the Jews pro-
ceeded on Himmler's orders and that carrying them out lay entirely in
the hands of the German security police, which meant that the Quisling
government had no influence at all in the matter. Before he undertook
anything, though, he wanted to check further on whether any new
deportation of Jews was intended. It is true that around 170 Jews were
sitting in jail, but he entertained certain hopes — perhaps based especially on the oft-mentioned dinner — that further deportations would be
possible to avoid. He would give me more information on Monday.

One has to wait for Heyerdahl's soundings and deliberations, but
from other parties I have learned, for one thing, that they don't look so
optimistically on the effects of the dinner, and, for another, that yesterday the first arrest of a half-Jew took place, which they interpret as

meaning that the persecutions are not over at all, but, on the contrary, may be intended to be widened to both half- and quarter-Jews. They also point out that Quisling recently declared in a speech the Norwegian Government's position on the Jewish Question to be uncompromising, too, stating that the only possibility was for the Jews to leave Europe, as well as characterizing even quarter-Jews as real Jews, in whom the Jewish element dominated. They believe that these sentiments were received ready-made before they were delivered and consider it best to be prepared for further measures. I am pretty much inclined to endorse the latter view and shall not stop pressing Heyerdahl to take a position. The possibility should not be excluded, though, that, considering his own and the Norwegian Red Cross's position, he will not consider himself able to present Prince Carl's démarche, which, because of the urgency of the matter, I have wished to convey to you, since in that case some kind of presentation by Richert or myself might come up. I have been advised from the direction of the leading "Jössings"[1] that they expect a Swedish initiative.

As concerns the individual cases, it has proved necessary to go through each case on its own, before any presentation to the authorities is made, since many of those in question have not identified themselves as the regulations require, and a démarche for their benefit would be equivalent to a denunciation. There are more than a few Swedish-born and others with some connection to Sweden, besides the list I received from the Foreign Office. However, I plan on Monday to look up both Minister of the Interior Hagelin and the chief of the security police and feel their pulses and present at least a provisional list.

I am proceeding on the understanding that it conforms with our intentions that I issue provisional passports and request exit permits in the usual way for those who have signed naturalization applications, and perhaps a few others who are stateless.

P.S. on the 14th of December:

Today Heyerdahl has informed me that his remaining hesitations have been dispersed, because the Swedish newspapers have published a bulletin on H.R.H. Prince Carl's initiative. Therefore he has now visited *Oberregierungsrat* Dr. Schiedermair in the Reich Commissa-

---

1. Jössing: After the British seizure in February 1940 of the German support vessel *Altmark* in the Jøssingfjord, the word was first used by the Nazis as a name for their opponents but was soon used by Norwegians loyal to the government in London as a term for a Norwegian patriot.

riat, to whom he had been referred, as well as given him a translation of
the letter from the Swedish Red Cross. He also said that he had spoken
warmly in favor of the matter and that he received the promise of a decision within a few days.

Document 35: Letter from von Post to Engzell, December 14, 1942.
*Report from Berlin about the German Foreign Office's response to the
Swedish initiative for Norwegian Jews. Note how von Grundherr com-
ments on the Swedish press. German officials constantly complained to
Swedish Foreign Office representatives about the biases of the Swedish
press.*

Referring to your personal letter of the 7th of this month, concerning
permission for the widow Leimann and other Jews deported from
Norway to travel to Sweden, I beg leave to inform you that I have had a
conversation on the subject both with Envoy Albrecht and with Envoy
von Grundherr, speaking with the latter for most of an hour. . . . Was it
not possible, in the interest of Swedish-German relations, to release the
fifteen Jews who were on the list delivered to the *Auswärtiges Amt*?

Mr. von Grundherr declared, among other things, that the retrieval
of their Swedish citizenship by a couple of the people concerned must
give the German authorities reason to suppose that "typical Jewish
manipulations" of persons identified for deportation were involved;
therefore it could hardly be expected to make a sympathetic examination of the matter by the authorities any easier. "Do you really imagine,"
Mr. von Grundherr said, "that the German authorities would be willing
to allow Jews with Swedish connections, who have already been
deported, to leave for Sweden?" Mr. von Grundherr then said he realized that the deportation of the Jews in question must affect the atmosphere in Sweden unfavorably and also make trouble for the Swedish
Government. However, through the attitude of the Swedish press,
especially in the treatment of news from Norway . . . a situation had
been created that one might describe as the Swedish press having . . .
burnt its boats. I pointed out here that, in the matter under discussion,
it was not a question of the attitude of the Swedish press, but instead of
the honest convictions of practically every Swede. . . .

From Mr. von Grundherr's remarks I was able to understand that he
considered it to be unwise, from the Swedish point of view, to draw

attention unnecessarily to the Swedish-connected Jews who had not yet
been deported. . . .

Document 36: Memorandum by Engzell, December 18, 1942.
Germany rejects Sweden's attempts to aid Norway's Jews.

Consul General Westring has informed me today by telephone that
Director Heyerdahl has received an answer from the Reich Commissa-
riat to the proposal from the Swedish Red Cross concerning the Jews in
Norway.

The answer had the following content (allowing for inaccuracies in
transcribing it by telephone):

*Die Übersiedlung der Juden aus Norwegen nach Schweden würde
nicht den Zielen entsprechen, die von dem deutschen Reich und der
norwegischen Regierung in der Judenfrage verfolgt werden.*

*Ich empfehle Ihnen nahe zu legen den im Schreiben vom Presidenten
des Schwedischen Roten Kreuzes gegebenen Vorschlag nicht weiter zu
verfolgen.*

Document 37: Eli Heckscher's notes in a calendar.
End of the year 1942.

In spite of everything, the year 1942 has offered a ray of hope, completely unlike the two preceding. It is true that I do not belong to those
who believe the war will soon be over, and true that it is best to be ready
for new setbacks, but that a turn for the better has begun does not seem
to be an expression of unjustified optimism. It is becoming even clearer
that I feel myself, first of all, a citizen of Western civilization and a servant of the free search for truth, next, a Swede and, in the third place, a
Jew. Were it not so, the mass murder of the Jews that Hitler has now
begun would not be bearable, but would haunt me night and day, as is
probably the case with Hugo Valentin. Now I think that, in spite of
everything, there is something grand in the Jews being martyrs for the
salvation of the world. That role, Sweden is not willing to assume and
therefore I cannot now feel any pride in being Swedish, no matter what
good is accomplished here at home. That a victory for the right side will
also introduce new troubles is certain. [Such a victory] is, in any case, an

indispensable prerequisite for anything other than the real downfall of the West.

What new cruelties Nazism may come to perpetrate on its way down remains to be seen. Whether Sweden will be involved is doubtful, I do not think they can afford what it would cost them and would gain utterly dubious advantages. On the other hand, the outrages in Norway have increased lately, and Denmark's fate — *a fortiori* our Danish relatives' fate — being in the hands of such a voluntary traitor as Erik Scavenius may perhaps give the most anxiety — despite everything, despite everything! . . .

Document 38: Memorandum Concerning the Jews in Norway, by M. Hallenborg, February 25, 1943.
A summary document of events in Norway. Note the information about the locality of Norwegian deportees and the German denial of an extermination campaign. By this time, information about the Final Solution had been spread widely.

Ever since the beginning of 1942 it is possible to identify measures of the occupation power and the Quisling government aimed at placing Jews in Norway on a special footing. . . .

Consul General Westring . . . warned Jews of Swedish nationality of anticipated coercive measures, and advised them to warn their co-religionists and recommended that they place themselves in safety in time. However, most of them did not heed this advice since they did not expect that things would go so badly as they later did, and because they would not willingly abandon their homes, their businesses and their property. . . .

After the deportation of November 26, all the Jews who could do so attempted to flee to Sweden. It is estimated that, as of the present moment, around seven hundred have come over the border. The number of Jews at liberty in Norway is now thought to be insignificant, surely less than a hundred. . . .

Until very recently, no word had been received where the Jews deported on the steamer *Donau* had been conveyed. However, just recently Swedish relatives have received letters from several such persons. It has turned out that a number of these, all of them male Jews of an age capable of work, find themselves in the work camp Monowitz,

Ost-Oberschlesien (that is, within formerly Polish territory). A few find
themselves in the work camp Birkenau in *Oberschlesien*. An official in
the Jewish Congregation here, who works on keeping track of the Norwegian Jews, has informed me that, as far as he has been able to learn, it
would be less probable that Norwegian Jews have been conveyed in
large numbers to the General Government of Poland. The older and less
able to work have been conveyed to Theresienstadt near Prague. . . .

Judging by information from the Consulate General in Oslo, one must
be prepared for the possibility that operations will be extended to half-
Jews and quarter-Jews, even though there is nothing pointing to such an
action being immediately impending. Should such an operation begin,
obviously it can come very suddenly. . . .

Consul General Westring's personal letter of January 8, 1943, concerning a conversation with *Sturmbannführer* Neumann, who is said to
direct the execution of German policy toward Jews in Norway, can be
cited. Westring writes:

"In contrast to other German authorities, Neumann did not attempt
to conceal that the deportations and other actions against the Jews took
place in accordance with orders from the German side, and in concord-
ance with Germany's general policy toward them. This was especially
intended to remove them from all influence in Europe but not at all to
annihilate them — as Mr. Eden had said — but rather to put them to
useful work in suitable areas of eastern Europe. [The Germans] had
been unable to accommodate the Red Cross's démarche, since Sweden
surely had no chance to keep them interned and render them harmless
even during the war now going on. [The Germans] had experiences with
the Swedish press that were too bad to want to allow the Norwegian
Jews the chance to set off in Sweden a new propaganda storm against
Germany, or to create the basis for new attacks from the German-hating
press. The Jews were, in general, an element with which the German-
hating circles in Sweden should not be strengthened."

Document 39: Letter from Archbishop Erling Eidem to Sven Hedin, March 31, 1943.

In an extraordinarily difficult and painful matter, may I turn to you. I
do so with all frankness and in certitude that you, Doctor, shall not be

offended at my appeal or misinterpret my honest purpose. My appeal
has nothing with political viewpoint or position-taking to do.

The matter concerns the so-called *mischlinge* in Germany.

As early as the beginning of last November, when I made a visit to
Berlin, various reliable persons conveyed to me serious apprehensions
that the severe measures carried out against the Jews would be
extended in the immediate future to the so-called half-Jews and quarter-
Jews.

Information is coming to me from trustworthy sources in Berlin that
these fears have now come true, and that operations are now beginning
against these poor people.

In Christian German circles, great despair prevails. But there is no
possibility of their making their voices heard.

A wish has been expressed by the Christian Germans that a public
campaign should be started by the Swedish Church. However, it is my
conviction that such expressions of opinion are not worth much in
waking up the authorities concerned. It seems to me that a better and
more effective way is for someone who enjoys great trust among the
Germans to intercede for the distressed. One difficulty with this is that
these measures against the *mischlinge* take place without mention in the
press. The unfortunates simply disappear without any mention of the
matter being allowed into the newspapers.

For my own part I wish honestly to declare that I consider all of anti-
Semitism both un-Christian and inhuman, even if I willingly and unre-
servedly admit that in the German Reich they have had something
which can be called a Jewish Problem. These measures against the
so-called *mischlinge* seem to me to be even more frightful and, if possible, more agonizing.

I would willingly have directed a personal plea to leading persons in
Germany, but I know that my name has no particular resonance nor
does it elicit any trust at all. I know in my heart that I have always loved
and to my last breath always will love the German people, even if I have
never been able to admire the National Socialist Party's philosophy with
its proclamation of the totalitarian position of the state.

On repeated occasions I have conveyed my worries to the Prince of
Wied, who has always been very friendly to me. In the same way, I have
had occasion, right from the beginning, to present to both the leaders of
the German Reich and the leadership of the official German Evangelical

Church my profound anxiety over the regime's anti-Semitism and its relationship with the church.

In my deep distress I make bold to turn to you, Doctor, with the plea that you make an attempt, should it in any way be possible, to influence those who hold the power in this matter.

Document 40: Sven Hedin's reply to Erling Eidem, April 2, 1943.

Your letter, so friendly, manly and humane, has deeply moved me and stirred both gladness and sorrow in me. It pleased me to read in your open and honest words the confidence you have in me, and it saddened me that, out of the experience of several years, I know the tremendously sharp limitation of the influence I may, to some extent, have on Hitler — for, on all the great questions of principle, the decision rests exclusively with him personally. Especially on the Jewish Question, he does not tolerate anyone, whoever they may be, trying to disturb his rock-solid and once-and-forever crystallized decision. It is for this reason that the position of the Jews and also the *mischlinge* in Germany is so tragically hopeless. During the years 1939 and 1940 I visited Hitler several times and expressed in earnest and insistent words the necessity for Finland to be rescued — not least for Germany's own sake. So long as the German-Soviet pact was in force, his hands were tied. On the 4th of March, 1940, when Finland's military strength faltered, I pleaded with the Führer, as with Ribbentrop, Göring and Goebbels, to apply pressure in Moscow for peace. On the 20th of March I received from my old friend Field Marshal Milch the news that my conversation had had a decisive influence on the events that followed. One can understand that, since my statements coincided with their political and strategical points of view.

The Jewish Question is a completely different and much less favorable matter. As Your Grace says, it is not of a political kind, but it affects all the more intimately National Socialism's fundamental principles and *Weltanschauung*. Hitler and his men regard the Jews and their closest descendants in mixed marriages as vampires and parasites, who have sucked German blood and through their positions of power in the banking industry, the press, film, radio and literature have attempted to lower the morals of the German people, to cripple and weaken them.

Without in any way endorsing the National Socialist philosophy, I must regard these apprehensions and complaints as fully justified.

I understand, too, the new Germany's psyche and the ways and methods its leadership has taken. The goal of the Entente was to crush Germany and its goal is the same this time, as well. But Germany *does not want* to go under, and if its leadership considers that certain foreign elements constitute a hindrance in the struggle for victory, it considers that these foreigners must be removed.

How often during these years have I not been stormed with pleas from Jews who begged for my help for themselves or for their families, through personal visits or by letter, and it troubles my conscience *not to be able* to rescue them. Especially with Funk, Himmler and Frick I have talked and presented prayers and pleas both for Norway and the Jews, yet always in vain. The only success in respect to the Jews I have been able to note is very insignificant and cost me long letters and personal visits. That concerned my old school friend Professor Philippson in Bonn, who was moved last summer to Theresienstadt and was separated from his library and his extremely deserving uncompleted manuscripts. Finally I succeeded in getting his books and writings sent to him, which he confirmed by a letter in his own hand from his new location. That is all.

When I turned then to the same authorities in new Jewish cases, I was requested in private, yet from an official quarter, not to mix too much into the Jewish Question since that could damage my standing in Germany. At the same time I was told that the new steps which were then being taken occurred by orders from the highest level and that every appeal to other authorities was excluded.

All the steps which now were undertaken by the top leadership of the Swedish Church, by private quarters — yes, by the King himself, were mere shots in the dark. Several times, for reasons of conscience and on purely humane grounds, I have jeopardized the rare position of power I hold, both with Hitler and with the German people. As soon as I came home from Asia in 1935, and after, I expressed to German friends in positions of leadership my fears that the German Jews who had moved to England and America would constitute a constantly growing threat which unconditionally and at the first legal opportunity *must* lead to a new war against Germany, an unforgiving war of revenge, cruel, brutal, ruthless. In practically every case, they admitted that I was right and that a looming threat was called forth through the Jewish Laws.

My beloved Mother, who died in 1925, always had a soft spot for the unhappy Jews, who had been persecuted by other people for two thousand years. If I were *able* to help them I would by so doing please her now. It would also be a great pleasure to me to be able to grant Your Grace's Christian and humane plea. But I have no chance to do so. Every step in that direction would be met with the same unforgiving rejection Your Grace experienced in Berlin.

For me it is also of great importance, for the sake of our country, not to disturb through hasty acts the limitless trust I now enjoy both with Hitler and with the German people. For, just as my statements in 1939–40 worked, at least to some extent, toward the rescue of Finland from a very dangerous situation, it is conceivable that Sweden, before this war is over, could get into a situation where it is advantageous that there be one Swedish man who has access to the Führer at any time and enjoys his full confidence. However, of this we can know nothing. Our fate rests, like that of others, in the hands of God. I cannot think that thought through — and I have a sense of suffocation if I simply imagine the possibility of an end to Sweden's shining history and the loss, if only temporarily, of our people's freedom. About this thought and about Sweden's past and its greatness I have spoken, deeply and warmly, with Hitler, and at such times stirred his warm understanding, his friendly and sympathetic smile, and his assurance, expressed with great force, that in the new Europe our people shall not lose one iota of their freedom and that no constraint shall be imposed on their individuality.

Yet now I have taken up far too much of Your Grace's time. I have done so in full certainty that Your Grace will understand my position and my way of thinking.

Document 41: Diary of Gösta Bagge, April 15, 1943. *Re: Adler-Rudel Scheme to negotiate release of 20,000 Jewish children.*

The Minister of Health and Social Affairs informed us that he had received a petition, from a representative of the Jewish Society, for Sweden to address a direct and public request to Germany for the transfer to Sweden of Jewish children. Hansson felt that there were very few prospects for achieving any result. Möller supported a request, his motive being, partly, that we would gain the good will of England and America thereby. I declared that the latter point did not interest me but that it was clear to me we ought to make an attempt, for the sake of our conscience, even if there were only one chance in a thousand to succeed. Also, if the Jewish Question was the bee in Hitler's bonnet, I believed that there was no great risk for us in making such a proposal and, in any case, we ought to investigate whether we would be able to do it. Since Rasjön agreed with me entirely and Bramstorp opposed the whole thing, it was decided to investigate.

Document 42: Letter from Birger Pernow, Director of *Svenska Israelsmissionen* (The Swedish Mission to the People of Israel) to the Rev. Paul Berman, American Board of National Missions, June 22, 1943.
SIM *had received considerable monetary support from American Christian groups to help Hebrew-Christians. Pernow wrote two letters to Americans on this day. The second to the World Jewish Congress stated that* SIM *had little information about the fate of Europe's Jews and the WJC should contact the Stockholm Jewish Congregation for further information.*

Thank you very much indeed for your kind letters of March 26th, which I received June 5th, and of April 30th, received June 19th. On the latter day I even had the great pleasure of receiving your promised gift, $300 for which I enclose a receipt. I was very glad indeed to hear from you again and to receive this kind sign of your readiness to assist us in our endeavours to bring our suffering Hebrew-Christian brethren support in their great distress. And I wish to bring you my own as well as my organisation's most humble thanks for this most valuable contribution. Please forward these our thanks to your organisation and supporters.

According to your wish for further information I will give you the following details:

Although our blessed missionary work in Vienna was closed up in the summer 1941, we have still been able to continue our relief work, especially amongst the Hebrew-Christians, of course on a successively reduced scale as a result of the deportations. Together there are now scarcely 5,000 Jews left in Vienna, all of them in mixed marriage. This relief work is carried out by a Swedish lady, still remaining in Vienna.

With a heavy heart I even must tell you that our blessed relief work amongst the deported of Poland has been reduced in consequence of the tremendously high mortality. A year ago there existed about 55 ghettos in Poland, and some of them were very great. The Warschau ghetto, for instance, had about half a million inhabitants. That ghetto is now destroyed and all its inhabitants are dead. The same applies to most of the large ghettos. Other[s] are emptied by epidemics, so that we fear that only very few ghettos still exist. As a result, our relief work has been reduced to less than a third. The inhabitants of the ghettos still left have since September 1942 been prohibited to send a written word to the outer world. The only sign we still can get is their name under the bank receipts for the money we are sending. At present we can communicate only with the inhabitants of the ghetto Theresienstadt in Bohemia. Those we are still able to support both with money and food parcels, while the deported in Poland have been prohibited since last autumn to receive food parcels. All such parcels to Poland have since then been confiscated and neither the adressees nor the senders have got any information. In Auschwitz in Upper Silesia a new ghetto has been erected, to which especially the Norwegian Jews have been deported for work in the mines, but we are not able to communicate with them, because they are absolutely isolated from the outer world.

As you write that you are sending food parcels to Poland, I regret having to inform you that this kind of support work is absolutely in vain. All such parcels will undoubtedly be confiscated by the Nazis.

We have even undertaken the full financial responsibility of the whole Norwegian missionary work in Budapest and Roumania, and the Norwegian missionaries are still at work. Quite recently we even have taken over the support of the starving Hebrew-Christian congregation in Bukarest and even the Finnish missionary in Jerusalem. Further, we are even temporarily sending support to Hebrew-Christian refugees in Switzerland and to the internees in Italy. Here in Sweden we have to bear the responsibility for about 300 refugees.

Regarding your confidential proposal in your last letter, I should very much appreciate if you would kindly give me the name of those people and organisations for which you warn me. You can fully trust me not to misuse your confidence. But it is nicer for me and more convenient to know the names beforehand, and we are saving time, especially on account of the present postal communications.

As soon as I hear from Mr. Stokes, I will inform you.

Document 43: Memorandum of August 17, 1943.
*This summary reflects on the difficulties that the Swedish Legation in
Berlin had in helping Jews who carried Swedish passports or were eligible to be Swedish citizens. Despite considerable efforts after 1944, few
results were achieved.*

During the last few months, the Swedish Mission in Berlin has made
appeals to the German Ministry of Foreign Affairs on a number of occasions, with the purpose of attempting to negotiate releases and emigration permits for those persons of the Jewish race concerning whom the
Mission had earlier issued representations. On this, the Foreign Ministry has continued to display an attitude which was, to a certain extent,
sympathetic toward the cases the Mission had taken up. However, the
decision lay with domestic authorities who, after having deliberated for
a lengthy period, have now taken a position on the representations we
have made. Regrettably, the result of the German authorities' deliberations has, on the whole, been negative.

In a meeting which the Secretary of the Legation, Baron von Otter,
had some days ago with the official designated as spokesman for the Foreign Ministry, the German side declared that, in the opinion of the
domestic authorities, the Swedish requests on the subject of special
treatment for Swedish Jews went significantly beyond what they on the
German side had expected, and that they could not make any further
concession than those exit permits which had already been approved.
This meant that the German response on release and exit permits for
cases still undecided, was negative.

In this connection, the German official informed us that, concerning
the deported Jews, it was almost impossible to determine their whereabouts, since they had been placed in a great number of camps and a central directory was lacking.

In any of the cases taken up with the German authorities, if the relatives should in any way have obtained, or should they in the future
obtain information on the whereabouts of deported persons, information which had not been furnished the Department earlier, the Department expects this information to be provided. In such cases the Department will inform the Mission, so that the Mission may consider whether
new démarches concerning such persons may prove possible.

Document 44: Letter from Gösta Engzell to Envoy von Dardel. September 1, 1943.
This letter illustrates the willingness of Sweden to take Jewish refugees and also the belief that little could be done that would be effective.

Professor Ehrenpreis's secretary, Mrs. Ragna Schiratzki, née Aberstén, has asked us to do whatever we can for some of her Jewish relatives in Denmark. . . .

Those involved are, on the one hand, two Swedish-born sisters of her father as well as their children . . . and, on the other hand, brothers and sisters and nieces and nephews of her Danish-born mother. . . .

It seems incredible to me that all these people could be conveyed to safety in Sweden. Entry permits they could get, but not exit permits. To the extent possible for the furthering of this matter, provisional passports can be issued for the Swedish-born. For those purely Danish, such would seem to be excluded. . . .

I think that the Mission, should it be generally possible, could get in touch with one or a couple of those mentioned and display readiness to help. Much more cannot be asked.

Document 45: Letter from Marla Granat to Birger Pernow, September 26, 1943.
Granat worked for SIM in Vienna.

Some rumors are going around, here, that Theresienstadt is going to be evacuated. The future will have to show whether this is true. In any case, it appears that recently about 5,000 persons have left Theresienstadt, some to Birkenau in Silesia, a labor camp. Some bits of news are coming from Birkenau and you can even send packages there. From Auschwitz, in Eastern Silesia, too, come some sparse reports. You cannot send packages there. Margit Weiss with Hannes came to Auschwitz at the end of March this year, as I wrote earlier. She has not written. She came not to the concentration camp but to the labor camp. One hears nothing from Poland. Not from Litzmannstadt, either. They say that most of the Jews have been sent away from there. Just now, no sizable transports are going out of here. During the last few weeks, smaller transports have been sent — 20 to 25 persons to Theresienstadt and, in more serious cases, to the concentration camp (Auschwitz). The largest part of those who are evacuated are brought from the prisons, where they are kept because of various offenses such as, for example, omitting to wear the star, etc. Those with Aryan relatives are still exempted from being carried off, so long as no punishable crime is involved for which there is a risk of deportation. At present, in Vienna, there are only 200 to 250 Jews without Aryan relatives and around 7,000 with such relations.

Document 46: Telegram from von Dardel to Stockholm, September 29, 1943.
Confirms information already received in Stockholm about round-up of Danish Jews.

According to reliable report 6,000 Jews are expected to be collected on Friday or Saturday morning and sent by boat to Germany.

Document 47: Telegram from Boström (Washington) to Stockholm, September 29, 1943.
Intelligence related to Germany's plans for Danish Jews had also reached America. Henrik Kauffmann represented Denmark in the U.S., but he operated with a great deal of latitude. His proposal to intern Danish Jews in Sweden was underlined by the reader in Stockholm.

In a note to Hull, Kauffmann has informed him of German steps for deportation of 6,000 Danish Jews and he assures him that aid measures which the American Government is in a position to take have his full and unconditional support. Kauffmann guarantees reimbursement to American or any other government from Danish funds under his control for all costs for steps to help Danish Jews or other Danes persecuted by Nazis. I learned that Hull is telegraphing the note to the London Committee for Help to the Jews and presume they are going to try to interest the Swedish Government through the American Legation in Stockholm. Kauffmann has conveyed to me that, should the Swedish Government consider itself able to make same appeal to Berlin as in case of Norwegian Jews, prospects may exist for it to be accepted, provided offer is made for Danish Jews to be interned in other countries to end of the war. Kauffmann's financial guarantee covers such a case as well. Have you planned any action and may I tell Kauffmann anything about it? Has Kruuse taken up the matter?

Document 48: Letter from Richert to Söderblom, October 1, 1943.
Richert's reaction to his government's instructions to make a démarche in Berlin. In a second letter of the same day, Richert wrote to Söderblom: ". . . For my part, I cannot help but persist in having grave misgivings about a Swedish démarche in today's situation, as I have already expressed. One should not suppose that a reference to the indignation which would be provoked in Sweden, were Jewish deportation to come about, would make any serious impression on the German leadership. Countless Swedish publications are considered here to have gone so far in their hatred of Germany that the gunpowder has more or less already been fired off, so that a further sharpening in tone could hardly persuade the Germans involved to take any special notice. . . ."

In connection with my dispatch in code and my personal letter earlier today concerning the démarche based on the rumors of impending deportations of Danish Jews, I beg leave to inform you that, on my return from my visit to Steengracht, to whom I presented myself at 4:30 P.M. (German summer time), I received a non-coded telegram from Dardel with the following contents: "Very urgent démarche be made today."

Whatever is involved, the situation is such that, either they are still considering the possibility of getting out of martial law or they have definitely given up the thought of this and decided to take the path of sheer violence. With the first alternative, it seems unreasonable to imagine that they would take a step which would unfailingly make impossible what they intended — which, of course, does not at all keep them from spreading rumors or even taking preparatory steps with intimidation in mind. If and when the latter alternative should occur, I cannot imagine that they would throw out possible intentions to deport Danish Jews because of a reference to the reaction in Swedish public opinion; among the decision-makers, Swedish public opinion may already be so regarded that doing a little more or less is not accorded any great importance, and Hitler's and Ribbentrop's reaction to our démarche is surely not going to be as good-natured as Steengracht's.

So, even though I still have to adhere to my own opinion of the usefulness of the démarche, I want to say that I understand very well that one must make it, even so, especially since I now have understood — through Svenningsen's telephone conversation today with Mohr and through Dardel's telegram — how pressing they have been in Copenhagen for us to do something.

Document 49: Letter from Söderblom to Richert, October 2, 1943.
Announcing the decision of the government to go public with a communiqué. According to Sven Grafström's diary, Söderblom and Grafström on the morning of October 2 had urged "immediate publication" of the Swedish démarche to Günther, who agreed to discuss the final form of the communiqué. In a second meeting between the three Swedish officials they were joined by Nils Bohr, the Danish physicist, who had fled 2 days earlier from Denmark. The communiqué fails to mention the idea of internment for the Jews in Sweden.

According to a telephone report from the Mission in Copenhagen, the action against the Jews in Denmark is now a fact. A first ship with 1,600 Jews aboard is said to have departed. From the statements of refugees who have arrived here, it appears that the preparations for the action in Copenhagen were taken in such a way that they were apparent to everyone. It is surprising that the Counselor of the Danish Legation in Berlin has not been better informed of what has gone on.

Our intention is to issue, this afternoon, the communiqué enclosed herewith. We have regarded it as wisest to get it out without delay. That is, we must expect that a storm will break out in the press and among the public, and we consider that the papers' commentaries will be lifted to a higher plane and be on a more solid basis if they are able to connect with the Swedish Government's announcement.

Document 50: Speech by Christian Günther, October 18, 1943.
The official version of events prior to October 2, 1943.

. . . Lately the resentment against the occupying power has increased further because of the persecution of Jews. As early as August, concern arose that the Germans would eventually proceed with measures against the Danish Jews. At that time, the Mission in Copenhagen was instructed to undertake those steps which might be possible to take privately, to rescue Jews living in Denmark by bringing them over to Sweden. By this was chiefly meant those who were Swedish-born and their closest relatives. If anything could be accomplished by issuing provisional Swedish passports, the Mission was authorized to do so. Besides that, the Mission was authorized to issue immigration visas for the Jews in question without advance inquiry to the Foreign Ministry.

From the beginning, it was clear that neither a Swedish provisional passport nor a newly acquired Swedish citizenship would always save those concerned from measures that might be planned. In another connection, the German side had already explained that they did not consider themselves able to recognize a change of nationality that took place under such circumstances. On the other hand, when steps against the Jews in Norway were involved, it had actually turned out that the Swedish Consulate General in Oslo succeeded, at least in certain cases, in getting into Sweden a number of Jews who were considered to have close connections with our country. When the danger of deportation of the Norwegian Jews became acute, in the fall of 1942, the Swedish Red Cross made an offer through the president of the Norwegian Red Cross to the Reichs Kommissariat, to take charge in Sweden of all the Jews whom they intended to deport from Norway. On December 15, that offer was declined in writing, on the basis that the transfer of the Jews from Norway to Sweden would not be in keeping with those purposes which the German as well as the Norwegian Governments pursued on the Jewish Question. A similar Swedish offer was conveyed privately in Berlin through diplomatic channels, without a positive result being achieved. In this situation, we tried to help at least the interned Norwegian Jews who had special connection with Sweden, for example through their place of birth or having relatives here. Concerning such cases, the Swedish Consul General in Oslo, as instructed, inquired of the Norwegian as well as the German authorities whether they might be allowed to travel here. Also the Mission in Berlin was ordered to take up the matter privately with the German authorities. A certain result was achieved by these representations, even though, as mentioned above, only in a fairly minor number of cases, where it was a question of persons who had not had Norwegian citizenship. However, as you know, during the late fall of 1942 upwards of 800 Norwegian Jews, that is, about half the total, succeeded in fleeing to Sweden.

When, on the evening of September 29, the Mission in Copenhagen reported that, according to reliable sources, it was feared that the Danish Jews were about to be sent to Germany, the same evening the Mission in Berlin was ordered to inquire at the *Auswärtiges Amt* whether the rumor might have any basis in fact. At the same time, the Mission was to point out the extraordinary indignation such a step would provoke in Sweden. The following day, the Mission was also instructed to convey the Swedish Government's offer to accept all Danish Jews into Sweden. In the instructions, it was further emphasized that the German authorities should have explained to them the serious reaction in Sweden to the persecution of Jews in Denmark. On the Swedish side, we were willing to take measures to prevent the Jewish refugees from carrying on any activities harmful to Germany in Sweden. Thus we were prepared to intern them till the war's end. Simultaneously, the Mission in Copenhagen was instructed to work in the same direction. The démarche was conveyed the following day to the Undersecretary of the German Ministry of Foreign Affairs; the Danish authorities and Dr. Best had already been informed of Sweden's attitude before that, through Envoy von Dardel, who, in a conversation with Best a week earlier, had, on his own initiative, warned against any operation against the Danish Jews. On the second of October, reports came in of a raid against the Danish Jews having taken place during the night. On the third of October, the Mission in Berlin was instructed to propose, in connection with the earlier démarche, that, in the first place, the Jewish children in Denmark be sent to Sweden, since, according to a German press bulletin, the German measures were based on the Danish Jews poisoning the atmosphere and it was impossible that this could have any application to the children. . . .

Document 51: Letter from Herschel V. Johnson to James Dunn, U.S. Department of State, January 11, 1944.
The materials that follow are but a small part of a 9-page document related to U.S. intelligence activity in Stockholm. The materials illustrate the lack of coordination and hostility between different U.S. agents in the Swedish capital. The most interesting part of the document is related to Felix Kersten, a person of great interest in this study. It was the first intelligence in American archives on Kersten.

SUBJECT: DR. FELIX KERSTEN

During the first week in October 1943, I called on a Swedish business man who is a close personal friend. He showed me a card reading

Dr. Felix Kersten

Medicinalrat

and remarked that this was a very high title in Finland, there being only two other men living who possess it. My friend added that he had known of Dr. Kersten as early as 1928 in The Hague where he had been "Leibartz" to Henry, the Prince Consort. He was also known to have developed an enormous practice as a nerve specialist and had been retained to treat many of highest government officials and members of royal families, such as Mussolini and Queen Marie of Roumania. After the German invasion of Holland, Dr. Kersten moved to Berlin which he had made his headquarters until his visit to Sweden in October–November 1943. He was known to have treated many of the high German officials, and to be a man of considerable influence in Germany.

At the time I met him, the above were all the facts I knew, except that he had been born a Finn and was still a Finnish citizen.

My friend arranged that the Doctor should call upon me with a view to treating me for some pains in the back which actually did exist. The doctor examined me and agreed to give me a course of manual therapy, which meant treatments for one hour six days a week. These treatments continued until the doctor returned to Berlin about the first of December.

As the doctor spoke no English or French, all conversation was in German. What follows represents a digest of points he made during and after these treatments:

1. He had treated Himmler in 1938 with marked success. When the Germans invaded Holland, he was forced in 1941 to move to Berlin, where he again treated Himmler. After a time he was put under contract to treat twenty-one members of the German Government each year. While he put the matter in this precise way, from other things he said I gathered that most of his time was put in at S.S. headquarters treating Himmler and his staff.

2. Seven Swedish engineers had been caught working with the Polish underground, and had been condemned to death. The head of the

Swedish Match Monopoly in Germany, Alva Möller, who is a friend of mine, went to Dr. Kersten and asked him to use his influence with Himmler to have the sentence commuted. Möller offered to pay a very large sum of money, the doctor mentioned 100,000 Kr., if the lives of these men could be saved. The doctor refused to take the money but said he would see what he could do. He said he discussed the matter with Himmler several times and had two interviews on the subject with Hitler. The sentence of death was commuted and the men confined to a concentration camp. As a reward for his efforts, the Swedish Government invited him to Sweden for two months' holiday.

The above was the doctor's account of how he got to Sweden. What I believe happened was something along the following lines. The Swedish engineers were caught and condemned to death. The money was offered the doctor to get them off. He at once told Himmler, who instructed him not to accept the money, but arranged to have the sentences commuted. He knew the Swedes were bound to offer the doctor some other reward, and instructed him to accept an invitation to visit Sweden, where as a Finn he would have considerable freedom of movement and opportunity to establish contact with Americans.

I believe that it was no accident that he met me, as one of the most influential men in Sweden, whom I see regularly, asked me if I knew the doctor and urged me strongly to talk with him. This man has intimate contacts in Germany, and moves at the highest level. It was plain he wanted to make sure I met the doctor.

3. As time went on, the doctor opened up a great deal. He gave a good many military facts which have been reported elsewhere, some of which have been borne out.

4. He stated that Himmler, since becoming Minister of the Interior had become the most important man in Germany; that all the cells of resistance to Hitler which had been crystallizing had been wiped out. There were now many individuals bitterly opposed to Hitler but no effective organization to oppose him. Even the communications between the generals and other high Army officers had to pass through the hands of the Gestapo or S.S.

5. Himmler himself, however, had reached the point where he knew the war was lost. For the time being he was loyal to Hitler, but the doctor intimated that the time would come when he would not be.

6. As an illustration of this changed point of view, the doctor cited Denmark, where Himmler gave his men orders to let the Jews escape to

Sweden without injury. This statement is borne out by the Danish Jews who have arrived in Sweden.

7. Himmler is fanatically anti-Russian, but is neither anti-British nor anti-American. He is anxious to reach an arrangement with them that will leave something of Germany. He knows that it is impossible for them to treat with Hitler, and is quite prepared to oust Hitler. I asked the doctor if in his opinion Himmler's patriotism was such that he would oust Hitler, make himself responsible for keeping order in Germany for a very limited period, and then retire. He said he thought he would. I pointed out that everyone in America and Britain was convinced we would win the war, and it was useless for Himmler to think about a compromise peace favorable to Germany.

8. The doctor added that in the event no such arrangement proved possible, he had heard considerable discussion at S.S. headquarters about the German plans. When the point is reached where they believe further military resistance is futile, Himmler intends to destroy all the property possible in the occupied countries, and in Germany as well, with a view to taking all property and valuables away from individuals. The purpose of this would be to precipitate a wave of communism. Himmler and his crowd would announce themselves as communists, and count upon riding in on this wave into some sort of collaboration with Russia.

Fantastic as this sounds, there is some possibility that the S.S. crowd would follow this course. It would be an outlet for their known sadism, and give them a gamble for survival with power which would be denied to them in the case of straight military surrender. Further the events in the south of Italy tend to bear out the fact that wholesale destruction in certain circumstances is the German plan.

9. The doctor pressed me on four separate occasions to come to Germany to confer with Himmler at once. I pointed out that I was purely a private citizen and in no way represented the Government of the United States, and that I had no means of knowing what the policies or intentions of the Government were at this time. He then suggested that I go back to Washington, and after getting the general picture there, come to Lisbon, where I would be met and taken to confer with Himmler.

Technical arrangements were made to establish contact in Lisbon in the event that I came there. No promise of any kind was made by me.

10. Peace proposals from Russia were brought to Germany by Prince

Wied, former German Minister to Stockholm, and by von Papen, Minister to Turkey. The first was brought just after Stalingrad, and the second last May. The details of these proposals as discussed at S.S. headquarters and reported by the doctor, were reported fully elsewhere, and I no longer remember them accurately. In general, Russia was to have a free hand in the Balkans, and to extend her territory to Salonika, Constantinople and an Adriatic port, to keep the Baltic provinces, and that part of Poland taken in 1939.

11. Doctor Kersten said that it would be all right if I arrived in Lisbon as late as February 15th 1944.

Since that time word has reached me from Germany that due to the damage wrought by the air raids they are very anxious that I should arrive in Lisbon as soon as possible.

While the value of such a mission from the standpoint of establishing a foundation for peace negotiations appears very small, its value from the standpoint of intelligence is enormous.

Document 52: Telegram from Cabinet (Stockholm) to Swedish Legation, Budapest. February 4, 1944.
Note how early the Swedish Government is willing to help Hungarian Jews.

(Concerning assistance to E. and A. Eisman.) If, in your judgment, prospects thereby for obtaining visas through Germany, provisional passports may be issued in accordance with [Regulation] F. Your communication No. 28.

Document 53: Telegram from Cabinet (Stockholm) to Swedish Legation, Budapest, March 31, 1944.

(Concerning assistance to Hungarian Jews.) On request, visas for three months' stay in Sweden may be issued all Jewish persons for whom, through us, your assistance has been requested.

Document 54: Letter from Norbert Masur to Rabbi Ehrenpreis, April 18, 1944.
Origins of the mission that Raoul Wallenberg eventually undertook.

Referring to our conversation last Saturday, I would like to define the proposal I made:

We should try to find a prominent person, clever, with a good reputation, a non-Jew, who is willing to travel to Rumania/Hungary, there to lead a rescue operation for the Jews. The person in question must have the confidence of the Foreign Ministry, and be equipped with a diplomatic passport, and the Ministry must ask the legations in Bucharest and Budapest to help him to the best of their ability. We must put a large sum of money at this person's disposal, for example 500,000 Swedish Crowns.

His assignment is to help the Jews to leave Rumania/Hungary. In Rumania it is certain that the flight of many (including, by boat) to Turkey could be made possible through bribes. At the same time, however, his operation must be facilitated through Palestine certificates, which we will try to obtain. With the aforementioned Palestine certificates it is probable that a number of persons would be able to get direct exit visas as well as transit visas through Turkey, when a neutral individual, with the authority of his legation behind him, stands ready, intercedes helpfully and, should it prove necessary, with money.

I think that through this plan several hundred people could be saved. The prerequisites are: the right man, support from the Foreign Ministry, the money. The last is probably the least problem, for we can surely get most of it from the U.S.A. Also, the support of the Foreign Ministry should be possible to obtain, considering how ready our authorities now are to help. Obviously, it would be of the greatest importance should the Foreign Ministry simultaneously authorize the legations in question to issue a limited number of provisional Swedish passports, should this be absolutely necessary in order to accomplish the trip through Bulgaria.

According to Barlass's telegram, which you showed me, it was clear that hardly a thousand Jews have been able to escape to Turkey during the last three months. With help from the neutral side, surely more will succeed in saving themselves from destruction. I believe it is worth a try to carry out the plan. But there is no time to waste.

A copy of this letter is going to Gunnar Josephson and Hugo Valentin.

Document 55: Report of *Svenska Israelsmissionen* **to War Refugee Board, Spring 1944.**
Note how the words — "Jews," "Jewish," "Christians of Jewish birth," "Mosaic Jews," "Jewish birth," "non-Mosaic Jewish," "people of Israel," "persecuted Jews" — are used. SIM *spent almost all of its efforts on converted Jews.*

RELIEF WORK OF "SVENSKA ISRAELSMISSIONEN" SINCE 1933.

Without losing sight of the specific aim of "Svenska Israelsmissionen" (The Swedish Mission among the people of Israel) — the preaching of the New Testament among the Jews — the activity of the mission since 1933 has more and more come to comprise relief work also. The objects of this relief work were in the first place Christians of Jewish birth, who naturally could not address themselves to the different Mosaic congregations, but support and help were more and more given to Jews without regard to their confession. Of this relief work we can discern three periods:

1. The beginning of the persecutions 1933–38;
2. The systematizing of the persecutions 1938–40;
3. The war of extermination against the Jews after 1941.

In connection with the report of the last period we have to answer three questions:

a) Which are our experiences?
b) How can the relief work be increased already now in war-time?
c) What relief measures are we planning for post-war time?

I.
1933–1938.

1. After 1933 the first Jewish refugees came to Austria. Our missionary station in Vienna, founded in 1921, started relief work. This work consisted in the first place in spiritual guidance but also in material help, such as financial support, serving out of food, etc.

2. Very soon it became apparent to us that the most effective help would be to assist the refugees to emigrate. We began with modest attempts, and during the last years of freedom for Austria we established an emigration office in contact with all the great emigration centrals and relief offices all over the world.

3. Our missionary station in Vienna automatically became a central

for the Christian refugees of Jewish birth. A Swedish clergyman, two Swedish deaconesses and a staff of about ten voluntary assistants gathered the first experiences for a more and more increasing relief work.

II.
1938–1940.

1. After the conquest of Austria in March 1938, the persecutions of the Jews were put into system. Seeing what happened already during the first days and weeks after the "Anschluss," it became apparent that a boundless catastrophe was threatening the Jewish population not only of Austria and of Germany but perhaps of the whole European continent. In his capacity of president of the International Committee on the Christian Approach to the Jews, the director of "Svenska Israelsmissionen," pastor Birger Pernow, called the council to a conference in London on the 3rd of May 1938. Two resolutions were taken: (1) A representation to the British Government to take the initiative to an inventory of the immigration possibilities of the world and to a conference of the civilized Christian states with a view to discuss the transferring of the threatened Jewish population of the continent of Europe, averaging 3 million people, and a distribution of the costs for this transferring. After the great conference at Evian in the south of Switzerland in the autumn of the same year an executive committee was appointed with the object of carrying on the initiatives thus taken. (2) A special relief work of the missionary societies and the Christian churches. Committees for the reception of refugees were constituted in different countries.

2. Our mission in Vienna immediately increased the work of the emigration office, and the staff of assistants now numbered 30 people. We also appointed a representative at the central for Jews of the secret state police ("Gestapo") and helped hundreds of people to emigrate by facilitating their "via dolorosa" through 16 different offices. It was possible for "Svenska Israelsmissionen" to save in time about a thousand children and about a thousand grown-up Jews and Christians of Jewish birth by getting them out of Austria and Germany.

3. The relief work was concentrated primarily upon the children and the young people. "Svenska Israelsmissionen" obtained the permission of the Swedish Government for a large contingent of our youths to come to Sweden, to go from there to England and America. The outbreak of war made it impossible for several hundreds of them to leave Sweden.

4. Extensive plans for the establishing of agricultural colonies in

South America and in Ethiopia were made but were for the most part frustrated by the growing menace of war.

5. Parallel with all this emigration work a steadily growing work of support for the Austrian Christians of Jewish birth and for many Mosaic Jews was going on. Large consignments of clothes and shoes were sent from Sweden to Vienna. Two clergymen and three deaconesses were working together with a large staff of voluntary assistants to help the Jews during the compulsory removals to the notorious Jew-houses into sickness and poverty.

6. The mission also established the serving out of food, which meant that many people, who would otherwise have been starved to death, could live through.

7. Contact was established with relief works of the same kind in Berlin and in Geneva. Through the connection with the Quakers and with the assistance of our representatives in America, in France, in Switzerland, in the countries of Scandinavia and in Shanghai, "Svenska Israelsmissionen" succeeded in increasing the emigration assistance even after the outbreak of war 1939.

8. The mission also established a home for old people in Weidling near Vienna and in that way was able to keep alive many old men and women, who would otherwise have been starved to death.

9. In Paris a special relief office was established, where a vicar of Jewish birth worked as representative of "Svenska Israelsmissionen" among the German and Austrian refugees.

This struggle for the rescuing of human beings went on intensively until 1941, when the roads to the outer world were inexorably closed and the war of extermination against the Jews began with the deportation to Poland. This entailed a new alteration of the relief work of the mission.

III.
After 1941.

1. Now the important thing was to support in every way the unhappy people, who were summoned for deportation. They needed help with their outfit. Our clergymen and deaconesses and the voluntary assistants helped those who had to set out on the journey of death to Poland to take with them the most practical and necessary articles. Many of them also were without the barest necessities and had no money to buy them with.

2. For many of them the temptation to commit suicide grew very strong, and it stands to reason that "Israelsmissionen" gave them the necessary spiritual support, so that its protégés should get the strength to carry on.

3. For the establishment of a school for non-Mosaic Jewish children in Vienna, "Svenska Israelsmissionen" gave financial support and placed a clergyman at the disposal of the school.

4. After the arrival of the first letters from Poland, describing the unspeakable distress among the deported, an organized relief work was instituted, which sent necessities, food and money to the deported.

5. A spiritual relief work for the deported also was organized, consisting in duplicated letters to each of our protégés, containing information from their native country, a word of consolation and material for divine service in groups in the places of deportation (passages from the Bible, hymns and prayers).

6. In the ghettos of Poland groups were founded by our former assistants of Jewish birth, having experience from the relief work in Vienna, so that in practically every ghetto of Poland we were able to give consolation and help also to such deported who would otherwise have remained unknown to us. Such representatives of ours worked in the Polish ghettos of Opole, Kielce, Modliborcycze, etc.; a vicar of Jewish birth was our representative in Warszawa. Through our representatives we also succeeded in getting in connection with the evangelical and catholic clergymen of the different Polish communities and to get them to help the deported.

7. This relief work began in March 1941. It then comprised 35 people. In the autumn of 1942 it comprised several hundreds of deported. Sums of many thousand crowns have been sent to the different Polish ghettos and to the working camps, which were established in the so-called Warthegau. Thousands of food packages were also dispatched through Portugal.

8. Since June 1941 — when the station in Vienna had to close on the request of the authorities — all this work was done solely from the central in Stockholm. After the liquidation of the Polish Jews in the years of 1942 and 1943, the relief work was mostly concentrated to the ghetto of Theresienstadt, to the remaining Jews in Austria (Vienna) and in Germany (Berlin), to the Jews in the internment camps of France and Italy, to the refugees in Yugoslavia and Hungary, and to Shanghai.

9. In the meantime the work went on among the refugees in Sweden.

Several hundreds of youths and grown-up Christians of Jewish birth and Jews, having been saved through the work of "Svenska Israelsmissionen," are still in contact with our mission and get regular or temporary support. Courses in languages, circles of young people, etc. have been instituted. In a camp, established by "Svenska Missionsförbundet" at Tostarp in the south of Sweden, a number of young men from intellectual circles were re-trained to become farmers.

10. For the Danish refugees, who came to Sweden in the autumn of 1943, temporary homes were established at the expense of "Svenska Israelsmissionen," and about 30 of those refugees have been fully supported by the mission until the 1st of April, when they were taken over by the Danish office for refugees ("Danska Flyktingskontoret"). Several boxes of clothes and shoes were sent to the different cantonments for Danish refugees in Sweden.

11. In 1941 "Svenska Israelsmissionen" took over the costs for the missionary and relief work of the Norwegian Mission among the people of Israel ("Norska Israelsmissionen") in Hungary. Since the German occupation the distress is steadily growing among the 800,000 so that our relief work, having formerly comprised only support to refugees in the internment camps, has now to be increased.

12. In Rumania, where hundreds of thousands of Jews have been deported, the situation is terrible. There "Svenska Israelsmissionen" has also taken over the work of the Norwegian and the Scotch missions. 7000 deported Jews returned in December 1943 to Rumania in rags and as living skeletons. In addition to the sums of money, which had been sent before, "Svenska Israelsmissionen" immediately dispatched several thousands of crowns as a first aid.

The work of support since 1938 amounts to several hundred thousands of crowns; during 1943 alone, the support amounted to more than 100,000 crowns in money and food consignments.

Actual experiences.

According to our experience, our monetary remittances reach their destinations. We get personal receipts, which are very often the only signs of life from the deported. Until the autumn of 1942 we also received many letters, acknowledging our food consignments, and since the establishment of the ghetto at Theresienstadt we get post-cards with thanks for the packages. Receipts also come from the above-mentioned protégés in other countries. In Vienna and in Berlin we have special representatives, who distribute the money from "Svenska Israels-missionen." In Berlin we are able to save through our support even such people who are in hiding from the secret state police. We have reason to believe that the Jews of Theresienstadt may have the Swedish sums, several thousands of crowns having been sent there during the last two years, to thank for their better treatment. Thanks to our well-schooled representatives, we have practically absolute security that our remittances are either given into the hands of the addressee or sent back to us, in the case of the addressee having died.

How could the relief work be increased already now in war-time?

1. The relief work for Theresienstadt could be increased by sending out more food packages. We are without the means of increasing this important help. To be able to do the most necessary in this respect, we should need 1,000 crowns a month in addition to the sums already spent by us.

2. In Vienna about 7,000 Jews are still left, being married to so-called Aryans. Most of these people are baptized. They are all doing compulsory work, and their earnings are so small that they are not able to buy even the few provisions to which they are entitled from their provision cards. For Vienna we should also need a sum of 600 – 1,000 crowns a month in addition to the sums spent by us, if we should be able to ease only the worst distress.

3. In Berlin the distress is especially great among the Jews who are in hiding from the secret police. Everyone of those people, who are leading a subterranean life without residence, without money and without provision cards, is in need of great means. To be able to ease the worst distress and to help precisely there, we should need 1,000 – 1,500 crowns in addition to the sums spent by us.

4. A great increase of the work of support in Shanghai would be sorely needed. To this end we should need 400 – 600 crowns a month in addition to the means which we send out already.

Summing up and counting also the possibilities not especially mentioned here, we should be able, by increasing the food consignments and the financial support by a sum of about 5,000 crowns a month, to save several hundreds of people.

What relief measures are we planning for post-war times?

1. "Svenska Israelsmissionen" is practically the only Christian organ-

ization in connection with the persecuted Jews almost all over the whole European continent. Through our representatives in nearly every country and through our official and private sources we get reliable information and are à jour with the state of affairs. Therefore we will be able to start post-war measures the moment the frontiers are opened.

2. "Svenska Israelsmissionen" has at its disposal a staff of clergymen and deaconesses, who have been excellently schooled for 10 years, having been or being in the relief work and not only being familiar with all organization problems but also having the necessary psychological schooling.

3. "Svenska Israelsmissionen" is going to start very soon a training course for young clergymen and deaconesses, willing to place themselves at disposal for post-war work and to go out to the remaining Jews after the war.

4. As matters now stand, this relief work would in the first place comprise the remaining Jews in Theresienstadt, where we have at present three of our former employees as representatives, in Hungary, where "Svenska Israelsmissionen" pays a clergyman as our representative, in Roumania, where "Israelsmissionen" does missionary and relief work through two clergymen and two deaconesses and through a staff of voluntary assistants, in Berlin, where a Swedish clergyman is working on account of "Svenska Israelsmissionen," in Vienna, where a staff of 10 well-schooled voluntary assistants could immediately be set to work, and in Poland.

5. For the post-war fund, instituted by "Svenska Israelsmissionen," a substantial contribution is needed, if this great and well-prepared work shall succeed. We must be sure to get in good time:

a) money,
b) food,
c) clothes,
d) temporary residences (wood houses or sheet-iron barracks),
e) medicine.

Consequently, we are exceedingly thankful for the prospects of co-operation with the authorities of the United States.

Document 56: Letter from Minister Danielsson to E. Boheman, April 25, 1944.
A proposal from Budapest to import Jewish workers to Sweden. This dispatch was circulated widely within the Government.

I have been told, and I myself have noticed in the Swedish press, that our agriculture is suffering from a striking and, in many cases, very difficult shortage of both male and female labor. In part, much of our male youth has been inducted into emergency service and, in part, both youths and girls prefer to go to the cities, and in our farming it is often said that only he whose own grown children are willing to stay at home may look forward to having the necessary labor properly done.

This being the case, I have found it appropriate to present the idea whether the chance of travel into Sweden from here should not be offered to a certain number of Jewish workers, accustomed to physical labor, who could fill the aforementioned need to some extent. In this connection, a number of younger men who have been conscripted into national labor service for two whole years, would seem to be chiefly in question, for a careful selection of those most suitable for the purpose.

Of course, the question is not a very real one for the time being, since travel permits are not being approved at present. However, I have learned that a decree on emigration may be expected within the rather near future, for which the absolute condition will be fixed, that the persons in question must have entry visas into a neutral country. For this reason, I have wanted to bring up the question now.

If it were possible to authorize the issuing of visas with the condition imposed, that the party in question accept assigned agricultural work and commit himself that, should he wish to leave agriculture, he would make no claim to be allowed to remain in the country, then we have an outstanding expert, in the person of agriculturist Viktor Landhard, who could prove helpful in the selection of applicants.

This commitment to leave the country is not now worth much as a guarantee against leaving agricultural service. But, according to the radio, the U.S.A. is willing to take in refugees from the Axis countries who succeed in getting to neutral countries, and this opens the possibility of "reexport," as soon as traffic across the Atlantic can once again be considered.

Document 57: Memorandum from Swedish Legation, Budapest, May 4, 1944.
Outlines initial Swedish response to persecution of Hungarian Jews.

Memorandum concerning the Budapest Legation's actions concerning persons (Swedes, Soviet Russians, Dutch, Iranians, Argentinians, refugees, Hungarian and stateless Jews and so on) for whom assistance from the Royal Ministry of Foreign Affairs has not been sought.

Every *Swede* in Hungary has received from the Legation for his person, dwelling, automobile and possibly other property a *"Schutzbrief"* with the following contents:

*"Hiermit wird bescheinigt, dass XY schwedischer/arischer Staatsangehöriger ist und sowohl er persönlich wie auch seine Wohnung/*addresse*/ — automobile, etc. — unter dem Schutze der Kgl. Schwedischen Gesandtschaft in Budapest steht/resp. stehen/."* All the protective letters and certificates are provided with the stamp of the Legation and the signature of the Minister.

Swedish enterprises in Hungary, as well as those which are for the most part Swedish-owned, have also received protective letters. Such protective letters have been issued for the following enterprises:

*Szabadkaer Elektrische Strassenbahn- und Elektrizitäts A.-G./*Electroinvest/Offices in Budapest of the Hungarian Export Office in Stockholm/Mr. Meisel,

Zentaer Industrieunternehmungen, Zenta/Electro-Invest,

NIFE Akkumulatorenfabrik und Elektrizitäts A.G. Budapest,

SKF, Schwedische Kugellagerfabrik A.-G., Budapest,

Ungarisch-Schwedische Handels A.-G., Budapest/The Swedish Trading Company's representative in Hungary/,

*Ungarische Autogen Gasaccumulator A.G.'*s office and factories, Office of representative of C.A. Wallenborg & Sons AB/Baron Kruchina Office in Budapest of representative of Höganäs-Billesholm AB/Mrs. Franz Rácz/.

For citizens of countries whose interests are represented by the Legation, the following protective letter has been issued:

"Hiermit wird bescheinigt, dass XY iranischer Staatsangehöriger/arier/und dass sowohl er persönlich wie auch seine Wohnung/address/unter dem Schutze der Kgl. Schwedischer Gesandtschaft in Budapest, betraut mit der Vertretung iranischer Interessen in Ungarn, stehen."

Soviet Russians. Prisoners of war and civilian refugees who have escaped from Germany to Hungary are all interned and seem to have no need to fear for their lives, since they are in camps which are administered by *Hungarian* authorities, who, keeping in mind the Hungarians in Russia, exert themselves to treat them humanely to the greatest extent possible. Other than these persons, there is supposed to be no more than a single Soviet Russian in Hungary, Mr. Gilels Ginzburg, who lives here legally; because of his frail health he has, at the request of the Legation, been freed from internment. Ginzburg, who is of Jewish birth, has subsequently, through the local Palestine Committee, succeeded in getting himself a Hungarian alien's passport for emigration to Palestine, as well as the promise of the necessary transit visas from the legations concerned; however, he has not yet obtained the requisite exit permit.

The *Dutch*/approx. 125 persons/and the *Iranians* /18 persons/ have so far not had any difficulties.

The *Argentinians.* Besides former personnel of the Argentinian Legation, there are three Argentine citizens here; their citizenship is of rather recent date, which is why the Mission has so far not succeeded in negotiating, with the responsible Hungarian authorities, the treatment which is supposed to be due to citizens of countries whose interests are represented by the Swedish Government. . . .

Even though the Mission is all but convinced that the aforementioned identification papers have been forged, after consulting with the Argentinian chargé d'affaires in Budapest, the Mission has issued protective letters, so as eventually to give them a chance for rescue. The protective letters have been formulated in the following way: *"Hiermit wird bescheinigt, dass XY, laut der Bescheinigung der deutschen Sicherheitspolizei in Bochnia, römisch-katolischer argentinischer Staatsangehöriger ist und unter dem Schutze der Kgl. Schwedischen Gesandtschaft in Budapest, betraut mit der Vertretung argentinischer Interessen in Ungarn, steht."* Thereby, the responsibility has been thrown upon the German police in Bochnia.

Of course such a protective letter does not mean any real assistance, since the Hungarian authorities want, above all, to see a regular passport; if such cannot be produced, the person involved is handled thenceforth as a stateless person. The other question which is put by the authorities is, whether the person involved has come into Hungary legally or illegally, which case must be proved by the stamp of the border authorities. Should he have come in illegally, he is inexorably arrested and interned. On issuing the aforementioned protective letters, the Mission has directed the attention of those involved to the fact that neither this issuance nor the Mission can save them from internment in case it turns out that they are staying illegally in Hungary, as well as that the Mission will not intervene for their release in such a case.

Polish refugees. Especially in the beginning, Polish Jewish and non-Jewish refugees have thronged the Legation to place themselves under its protection. In the beginning, they asked for Swedish passports, but later, when they understood that that was not possible, they pleaded for a certificate, of any kind whatsoever, that had the stamp on it. Considering that the situation then was still unclear and the Mission did not want to roughly spurn these people who were looking for help, in certain cases meaningless certificates have been prepared, for example reading as follows: "By this is certified that XY has submitted his application for Swedish citizenship to this Legation"; stamp without signature.

Others seeking help. Besides those for whom the protection of the Legation has been sought through the Foreign Office, certain persons with connection to Sweden, in accordance with the telegraphic authorization, have obtained a *"Bescheinigung"* of the same kind as has been issued for those persons named in the Foreign Office's instructions. An example of that form is enclosed. These persons have proven convincingly that they have relatives or have had business relations since some years back or some other connection with Sweden. . . .

A number of persons have applied for employment at the Legation as chauffeurs, servants or anything whatever, and a few have asked for asylum in the Legation's quarters. All these requests and applications have been declined.

Document 58: Letter from Karl Höjer to Gösta Engzell, May 27, 1944.
The Bureau of Social Welfare rejects justification of immigration of Hungarian Jews on economic grounds but is willing to expedite a Jewish immigration policy on humanitarian grounds if the government decides on such a policy.

Referring to your request for views on certain questions from Envoy Danielsson in Budapest, permit me, after consulting a representative of

the Labor Market Committee, to inform you that the situation concerning resources of manpower in agriculture is not such that it can be cited
as justification for immigration of Jewish labor from Hungary. The lack
of manpower in agriculture generally seems to concern professionals.
More and more unskilled labor is becoming available through the arrival
of refugees from neighboring countries.

Even if the immigration of Jews from Hungary cannot realistically be
justified in terms of the labor market, it does not thereby follow that we
will oppose the matter. Humanitarian reasons advance strongly to the
fore. Despite the fact that the National Board of Health and Welfare
presumes that it must be regarded as more than doubtful whether the
parties concerned will be able to escape from Hungary, the Board, for
such humanitarian reasons, is fully prepared, for its part, to recommend
that the issuance of entry visas be approved in such cases.

**Document 59: Letter from Valdemar Langlet (Budapest) to Gustaf
Nyborg, (Stockholm), June 20, 1944.**
On conditions for rescue of Jews in Hungary.

On the 4th of this month I received your letter of June 2nd. Its contents amazed me. Of course I informed the Dery family immediately, in
the Legation's name, of the authorization to issue visas; this was already
done on the 4th of May. Yet never could we here have dreamed that
your word *"Abwarten"* referred to this simple action? I had asked you,
through my letter to your daughter — whose death I greatly regret —
about the possibility of adoption and could not understand the matter
otherwise than that we should wait for the result of your steps in that
direction. With such an action they would have been saved. An entry
permit alone is of no value without exit and transit permits. Are people
there at home still such wide-eyed innocents that they believe they can
save human lives with nothing more than a gracious permission to cross
the Swedish border? Don't they know that all Jewish people here are on
the way to destruction through deportation from the ghettos and internment camps? You may ask why I have not written earlier? Every day I
waited for your information. And since the 4th of June, when your letter
came, I have not had access to a courier until today when this letter can
be sent. Mr. Dery is sitting in an internment camp, the ladies are going
this week to the ghetto, which is the portal to hell. Should you in the K

Department of the Foreign Office be able to get authority for us to issue provisional passports for these people, then there may yet be a possibility of saving them, or some of them, from fates of which people there at home do not seem to have any real conception. Yet in that case it must take place through telegraphic orders to the Legation.

Document 60: Telegram from Johnson (Stockholm) to State Department, June 21, 1944.
Announcement of Raoul Wallenberg's appointment.

Mr. Boheman has informed me that Mr. *Raoul Wallenberg* will be appointed an Attaché to the Swedish Legation at Budapest for the specific purpose of following and reporting on situation with respect to persecution of Jews and minorities. It is likewise intention of Foreign Office to secure if possible an appointment as representative of other Swedish Red Cross for Professor Maltet, a Swede who is now teaching in University of Budapest. Professor Maltet will not be connected with Swedish Legation but will cooperate closely with Wallenberg (my 2069, June 9, 6 p.m.). As Wallenberg's functions in Budapest will be purely official and he has for time of appointment severed all business connections, Boheman does not anticipate any trouble in his securing the necessary visa. He said if the visa is refused the Swedish Government will simply refuse in turn to receive the Hungarian Chargé d'Affaires. Mr. Boheman made it clear the Foreign Office and his Government are disposed to cooperate as fully as possible in all humanitarian endeavors and the appointment of the Attaché is undoubtedly an evidence of official Swedish desire to conform to the wishes expressed in Department's telegram 1010, May 25, 2 p.m.

Olsen and I are of opinion that War Refugee Board should be considering ways and means of implementing this action of Swedish Government particularly with respect to financial support it may be possible to arrange for any concrete rescue and relief progress which may be developed.

Document 61: Telegram to Budapest announcing appointment of Valdemar Langlet and Raoul Wallenberg, June 21, 1944.

(Concerning rescue of Hungarian Jews:) Your coded telegram No. 179. As proposed by the Foreign Office, the Board of the Swedish Red Cross has authorized Mr. Langlet, until such a time as definite arrangements are made, to act for the time being as its representative in Hungary in questions associated with possible action for rescue of Hungarian Jews therefrom. Board requests Legation issue to Langlet on its behalf credentials necessary for assignment.

(Jewish problem in Hungary:)
Recognizing interest here, desirable Jewish problem be followed with greatest attention so that special reporting continually takes place and proposals be drawn up suitable and practicable humanitarian initiatives as well as necessary postwar assistance measures. American mission here has also devoted great attention to problem. Since we find it self-evident that your present personnel cannot spare manpower this special assignment, we are considering attaching to Legation Raoul Wallenberg who with good connections knowledge Hungary should have prerequisites for this. Telegraph soonest if any problem.

Document 62: Letter from Minister Danielsson to Minister for Foreign Affairs Christian Günther, June 24, 1944.
Legation summary of Hungarian Jewish situation to accompany documents pertaining to conditions at Auschwitz. These documents included the so-called "Auschwitz Protocols" (in German) that provided detailed description of the killing process at Germany's most important extermination center.

The decrees concerning the Jews in Hungary referred to in the last-cited communication have subsequently been supplemented by the Hungarian Interior Ministry with a series of new regulations which it would [take too long] to quote.

Suffice it to say that, according to entirely reliable sources, all Jews, (1) in the area of the country lying east of a line from Kassa in the north through Miskolc and Szolnok to Szeged in the south, and (2) in southern Hungary all the way to the German border, either have been assembled in internment camps with terrible sanitary conditions or have temporarily been assembled in ghettos, in order to be transferred successively from there into such internment camps, as these are emptied. All such imprisoned Jewish persons, men and women, children and aged, would then seem to have been loaded into boxcars and carried away partly to Germany, partly to the General Government of Poland.

According to the latest available information this deportation, up to the middle of last week, amounted to 420,000 persons; those remaining, with the exception of 150,000 men between the ages of 18 and 48, who had been conscripted into military labor in Hungary, appear to amount to about 300,000 persons; according to earlier information, even the latter would be carried off before the end of this month; the date by which Hungary will be completely *"entjudet"* is now given out as the 15th of July.

Those Jews still remaining comprise about ¼ million people, chiefly resident in Budapest and its suburbs. Earlier, it seems to have been planned for the capital's Jewish population to be assembled in three different ghetto districts at the beginning of June. The violent bombardment of some ten Hungarian cities which took place on the 2nd of June appears to have caused, for one thing, some delay and, for another, a certain changing of the plans. Out of fear that Budapest, too, would be subjected to violent destruction, perhaps sparing only these ghetto districts, another arrangement was undertaken. That is, the Jewish population were ordered to move together into certain specified houses, spread out over the whole city. A drawing was made and published showing those houses in which Jews were allowed to dwell, for the time being. These chiefly consisted of such houses as were mostly occupied by Jews. Such houses would be identified by a Star of David painted at the entrance as "Jew houses"; those Jews who lived in other houses were obliged, within a deadline of five days /which later was extended to seven, and expired Saturday, the 24th of June/ to move with what they themselves could carry of their belongings. Since the Jews were forbidden to use anything but a wheelbarrow or a horse-drawn wagon, of which only a few are available in Budapest, they obviously could only carry along an insignificant part of their property.

By this and the preceding measures, the Jews have been robbed of practically all of their property. They have had to manage to live 8 to 10 persons in a single room. Further, a prohibition has been issued against Jews being seen outdoors at any other times than three fixed hours per day /from 2:00 to 5:00 o'clock/ as well as against their receiving visits in their apartments. To avoid the sight which a deportation in broad daylight of a quarter million persons would have to involve, it is said they intend to arrest Budapest's Jews successively, in night raids and house searches and to convey them into internment and deportation, respectively. The Christian houses, too, are to be searched, to the extent that denunciations occur, thereby to arrest the not insignificant number who have hidden themselves with Christian friends. Such denunciations are said to be streaming in by the thousands and are even said to have disgusted the German authorities to whom they have been delivered. To carry out the arrests, it appears they are using a special corps of gendarmes led by the notorious "executioner from Ujvidek," a certain General Zöld, who earlier fled to Germany, but has returned and now taken charge of the execution bureau of Budapest.

The carrying off of the capital's Jews, which, according to the above, is intended to be completed within three weeks, confronts the greatest part of these unhappy people with a terrible fate. It is thought that those who are lucky enough to be capable of needed labor, are going to be transported to German industrial plants, where they have prospects of being treated fairly well. On the other hand, the others, children, weaker women or aged persons, are going to be deported to extermination camps in Auschwitz-Birkenau, near Kattowitz in Poland /see material appended to this report/.

The Mission has, to the best of its ability and with those few personnel who are at its disposal, turned to, first, trying to help persons with connection to Sweden, and then, through telegraphic requests for expanded authorization, trying to gain the possibility of more effective intervention. Its experiences (which are briefly reported in memoranda submitted, the latest, No. 10 on the 23rd of this month) have been of the very worst. Most of those who obtained "protective" papers have subsequently not even had a chance to get in touch with the Mission, and letters have sometimes been returned as undeliverable. Personal visits, which obviously could only by undertaken in extremely few cases, have turned out to be impracticable or without result. Communications, partly to the Ministry of Foreign Affairs, partly to the military authorities, have in many cases been sympathetically received with the promise of decision in a few days, but these promises have practically never been kept. The difficulty of arranging anything important has obviously been increased by the present government's evident anger, partly over commercial relations being broken off, and partly over the fact that normal Hungarian diplomatic representation in Stockholm has not taken place. Obviously, under such conditions, to gain agreement to even the most paltry requests is accompanied with the greatest difficulties. For example, such a request was that at least the Jews here who through the issuance of Swedish passports had been placed on an equal footing with Swedish citizens, should be left at liberty until the possibility could be prepared to convey them to their homeland. But instead of going along with this, the Hungarians involved have said that all foreign Jews shall be interned, starting on the first of July. On inquiring orally at the Ministry of Foreign Affairs, whether these persons might not, at least, be interned in special camps, under the protection and care of the neutral powers, only evasive replies have been obtained.

To shed light on how Hungarian and German authorities in this case blame one another, a couple of recent experiences can be cited.

A German officer — an eyewitness — has recently lamented in the closest confidence for a member of the Mission the unnatural cruelty with which the Hungarian transports of the deported are being carried out; on opening the sealed boxcars /whose small air vents were shut/ when German Red Cross sisters stood ready with refreshments at the border station and passenger cars stood ready for onward transportation, they found in the Hungarian boxcars numerous corpses, between which emaciated white-haired persons were desperately trapped!

In a conversation with a journalist close to the present regime, in which it was declared that if one wanted to get rid of the Jews in Hungary it would be more humane to let them emigrate to some country where they have entry permission rather than to torture and destroy them, the answer was given that "it is no concern of any outsider what the Hungarian government does with its citizens." To this was added the remark that "every people has a natural right to retribution." To the objection that small children could not have sinned against the nation, no other response was obtained than that the two who were conversing obviously did not understand one another, which, without any doubt, was the case.

I must respectfully enclose the following accounts, collected by the Mission, about whose truthfulness I obviously must withhold my judgment, but which would seem to be meant to further illuminate the conditions touched on above:

1. Account of arrests and deportations of the Jewish Council in Budapest.

2. Account of the extermination camp in Auschwitz, written by two Slovakian Jews who escaped from there.

3. Condensed summary of the above.

4. Story of a woman who ran away from the camp in Auschwitz.

Document 63: Part of a Memorandum, July 1944.

The document is among the papers of the War Refugee Board. No signature is on the document, although its author appears to be a member of the Stockholm Jewish Congregation, probably Gillel Storch or Norbert Masur.

TELEGRAM FROM H. M. KING GUSTAF TO ADMIRAL HORTHY
June 30th, 1944

After have been informed of the extremely hard methods, which your Government has initiated towards the Jewish population of Hungary I venture to appky (sic) personally to Your Highness to beg you in the name of humanity to take measures to save those who still remain to be rescued of this unfortunate peopel (sic). This appeal has been dictated by my old feelings of friendship for your country and by my sincere anxiety for the good name and reputation of Hungary in the society of nations.

ADMIRAL HORTHY'S ANSWER

I have received the telegraphical appeal, which Your Majesty has delivered to me. With feelings of the greatest understanding I beg Your Majesty to be convinced that I am doing everything that under the present circumstances is in my power in order that the principles of humanity and rightness may be respected. I highly appreciate the feelings of friendship for my country which inspire Your Majesty, and I beg Your Majesty to maintain them towards the Hungarian people in these days of hard afflictions.

TELEGRAM FROM PROFESSOR EHRENPREIS AND GUNNAR JOSEPHSON,
Chairman of the Stockholm Jewish Congregation, to *H. M. THE KING*, July 20th, 1944.

The Jews of Sweden have with deep movement been informed of Your Majesty's appeal to the Hungarian regent. The address has not been in vain, and the unspeakable thankfulness of a world is streaming towards Your Majesty. In the middle of the worl's (sic) darkness the King of free Sweden has raised the voice of Humanity to the benefit of unhappy Israel, the defenceless people which for one decade has been the victim of an extermination campaign without parallell (sic) in History. The world's conscience, asleep for too long a time, has spoken through Your Majesty's mouth and the stimulating kingly words have arisen a mighty echo throughout the world. They have given to our morally degraded generation feelings of relief and hopefulness.

KING'S ANSWER, July 21st, 1944.
Chief Rabbi Ehrenpreis, Stockholm.
   I send you and the Jewish Congregation my hearty thanks for your so kindly expressed thoughts.

                                                                 Gustaf

SWEDISH ACTIVITY FOR HELP
   Shortly after the German occupation of Hungary in March, we made a plan for the help which could be given by our initiative. This plan was based on the following lines:
   1) To try to obtain an intervention from the Swedish Government or some other influential body.
   2) To find a Swedish person, willing to go to Budapest and work there with support of the Swedish representation there.

   The plan was based on the good-will and interest which our Government and its legation in different countries have shown towards the Jewish case. When investigating the possibilities for the first part of the plan, we became concinved (sic) that an intervention at that moment (April) could not be obtained, and because of that we did not approach the Government. Instead of that, professor Ehrenpreis approached the Head of the Swedish Church to obtain an application from the Swedish Church to the Hungarian Church and to the public opinion with a protest against the persecutions of the Jews. This proposal was placed before the Council of Bishops and though met with the greatest sympathy the Council did not find itself in a position to follow this suggestion.
   When deportations began and based on a telegraphic information on the situation and on a direct demand from the Jewish Agency in Jerusalem, Professor Ehrenpreis could address himself to the Swedish

Government and supplicate for an intervention of the King. This supplication was granted immediately by His Majesty, with a result that is known to you. We are deeply grateful to the King and the Government for the extraordinary help, which the King's démarche has meant and by which thousands, if not hundreds of thousands of Jewish lives have been saved up till now.

In the meantime also the other part of the plan was carried out. We found a businessman, member of a wellknown family with extremely good connections in Hungary, who was willing to place himself at disposal for this work. By intervention of Mr. Salén, a wellknown shippingman, it was arranged that this man was taken in the service of the Swedish Foreign Department as a secretary of the legation in Budapest with the special task to help Jews. Surely this form was the best which could be found, and we may say that our Foreign Department in this manner has gone to the limit of what it possibly can do for helping us.

In the beginning of July Mr. Raoul Wallenberg, the new secretary of the legation in Budapest, began his work. It must be stated that already at once after the occupation of Hungary the Swedish legation in Budapest has begun a valuable work. Many Jews with some connections with Sweden, either by relatives or only by business, had addressed themselves with the legation for protection. With the permission of the Swedish Foreign Department the legation gave to many of them entry-visas to Sweden in a form which can be called letters. . . .

Document 64: Letter from Mr. Labouchere (British Legation, Stockholm) to Haigh (Foreign Office, London), July 3, 1944.
British Intelligence report on Raoul Wallenberg.

You may be interested to know that the Swedish Government have decided to attach to their Legation in Budapest, Monsieur Raoul Wallenberg, whose job it will be to deal with matters affecting the plight of Jews and persons whose lives or property are endangered by the Germans.

Wallenberg is a director of Mellancuropeiska Handels A.B. of Stockholm in which the well-known shipowner Sven Salén and, we believe, Stockholms Enskilda Bank are interested. The firm has done a good deal of business with Hungary during the past two or three years and Wallenberg has visited Hungary several times for his firm's account.

He belongs to the same family as Marcus Wallenberg and has the reputation of being an intelligent, efficient and "rather smart" businessman.

I took the opportunity of a recent conversation with Grafström to ask
why this man in particular had been selected for the job of helping the
Jews and was told that it was because his acquaintanceship with prominent Hungarian officials and businessmen made it likely that he would
be in a position to exert influence on behalf of these unfortunates.

While I have no doubt that there is much truth in this and that the
Swedes are actuated by the best of motives in this appointment, it does
seem on the other hand that Wallenberg's firm will be able to profit by it
to facilitate their business with the Hungarians.*

**Document 65: Letter from Gösta Engzell to Minister Danielsson,
Budapest, July 5, 1944.**
Swedish rescue policy in Hungary before R. Wallenberg's arrival.

The Hungarian agreement in principle you mention in your coded
telegram No. 211, for "repatriation" to Sweden of Jews with connections
with our country is a tiny bright spot in all that misery. However, I take
for granted that it is going to be altogether impossible to obtain German
permission. . . .

Finally, I want to touch on the provisional passports and want to point
out that we must be restrictive with them. Everyone wants one and it
would be a debacle if we went along with this too much. Just now, it is
partly a matter of chance who has gotten them. We do not really know
what good they do. If emigration could be arranged with their help, we
have granted them, but it is not advantageous for such passports to be in
circulation among persons who have no prospects of leaving the country. To a great extent it is a question of judgment, which is difficult to
decide here. I have seen that Langlet complains about our being
bureaucratic and inflexible about this, but it has its reasons. Should you

---

* Comments by London-based British Foreign Office official:

"King Gustav's appeal to Horthy is proof of the Swedes' genuine interest in the fate of
the Hungarian jews (sic). But the Swedes have no opportunity for furthering their business
interests and . . . very much whether this appointment was entirely disinterested.

"I feel sure that Marcus Wallenberg will have done pretty well out of the ball-bearing
negotiations and we know that he has an eye to business with Russia after the war. Raoul
Wallenberg seems to me on a less good wicket if much of his business is with Hungary."

find, in individual cases, that such papers can save anyone, we have not opposed your taking action.

Document 66: Letter from Per Anger to Gösta Engzell, July 5, 1944.
Letter indicates that early forms of the Swedish "protective pass" were being respected by local officials.

Despite our being especially skeptical, at first, concerning the value of the various protective letters the Mission has privately issued to assist persons in need, it has plainly been shown in individual cases that the aforementioned document could be helpful if the holder was lucky, yes, might perhaps mean rescue at least for a time.

A person who had obtained Protective Letter B related as follows: The other day he was on a street where all Jewish persons were halted by the police and taken away, it was said, to help with clean-up after the last air raids. He immediately displayed the Swedish protective letter and because of it was able to go by unhindered. Of the approximately one hundred Jews who were arrested on that occasion, he and a medical doctor were the only persons who went free.

Document 67: Memorandum from Gösta Engzell, July 7, 1944.
Swedish intelligence on Gillel Storch.

Mr. G. Storch, telephone 616015, resident in Sweden since 1940 and formerly a Latvian citizen, a Jewish businessman, has on various occasions visited me, to tell me, among other things, that he is some kind of representative in Sweden for most of the large Jewish organizations in America, England, Palestine and other countries. He is working, here, with Professor Ehrenpreis. Storch has shown especial interest in saving Jews from Latvia. He has had some discussions with the Refugee Attaché at the American Legation, Olsen, in which he raised the prospects of economic support.

1) In order to attempt the rescue of some people from the Baltic States, principally Latvia, Olsen has wished to put funds at the disposal of former minister Salnais. With Storch and a third person he was to sign a contract to manage the money, 200,000 Swedish Crowns, for the

stated purpose. Storch, who has especially wanted to rescue Jews, for various reasons has not considered himself able to participate.

2) Storch, who has earlier been in contact with Dr. Klaus, a German staying in Sweden, and has been offered by him the chance to get his relatives in Riga freed, in return for a certain sum of money, has now through Klaus come in contact with another German here, Dr. Boening. The latter, who has described himself as acting on orders of Dr. Kleist, has raised the prospects of getting about 2,000 Jews free from Latvia in return for a sum of two million Swedish Crowns in foreign currency, on condition that:

1) The Foreign Ministry were involved and that the money were allowed to be deposited in the Foreign Ministry.

2) [The German side] would be allowed to purchase supplies in Sweden for this sum, for export to Germany. They would not ask any "strategic" supplies, but chiefly meant "sanitary" supplies.

3) The Swedish Red Cross would charter a ship to fetch the refugees, whose travel to the ship would be paid for by the Germans.

Dr. Kleist would then present the matter to Himmler.

Emphasizing sharply the dubiousness of the whole enterprise, I have said I was willing to explore the question, as far as we are concerned. I stated that we on the Swedish side were most interested in being able to bring out those few Jews in whom the Foreign Ministry and the Mission in Berlin had taken a special interest. This Storch thought could be accomplished.

According to Storch, Olsen has been willing to cooperate. The position formerly taken by the American Government, that they did not wish to participate in such purchases of human beings, they have now completely left behind them, and now it was only a question of saving people, the means for doing so being of no importance.

On the 26th of June, Attaché Olsen visited me and stated that he found the proposal impossible to realize, since the American Government will surely not wish indirectly to support the German Government. Olsen would willingly bring the money to a German private citizen, and confirmed that the Allied Governments nowadays were not sticking to their previous position.

On the 30th of June, Dr. Boening visited me. Since the spring of 1939 he had been employed in the German Legation's "*Kulturabteilung*" and handled film exchange. He had now left the Legation, since he had not gotten along with Counselor Dankwort. He had returned to Germany, but there had been pressed into service by Dr. Kleist, whom he had known for a long time. He was now in Sweden with Dr. Kleist. They would like to do something to improve relations between our countries and had spoken, among other things, of attempting to rescue Baltic Jews. When B. understood that the American Government could not give the money indirectly to the German Government, B. had hit upon the idea that, outside the quotas, one would be able to deliver simple furniture to those bombed out in Germany, for 200 to 300,000 Swedish Crowns. As for the rest of the money that had been discussed, it could be given to some private person or perhaps to the Swedish Red Cross, to be used for the benefit of those bombed out in Germany.

B. would now like to know whether the Swedish Government would be willing to allow the Baltic Jews to come to Sweden.

I explained to B. that I had no authority to answer in the affirmative but that I could express our general policy that we would like to see the problem solved.

Dr. B. has revisited me later and said that he had met with Olsen and discussed the matter. Dr. B. and Dr. Kleist now wished to try to carry through the plan in Berlin.

When I mentioned that we were more interested in the release of a relatively few Jews for whom several démarches had been made in Berlin, Dr. B. asked to get a list of these. He believed it would be possible to do something in these cases.

Document 68: Letter from B. Åman to Birger Pernow, July 10, 1944.
About Swedish policy toward refugees defined as Jews by German law.

Referring to your letter of May 30, 1944, may the National Commission on Foreigners state the following:

In the forms for residence visas issued by the National Board of Health and Welfare (presently the National Commission on Foreigners) it has not been felt desirable to present any question concerning the race of the foreigner in question, but only concerning his religious affiliation. Not even this question of religious affiliation appears in the Board's application form for the alien's passport. Because of this, we do not always have knowledge of whether a refugee arriving here is of Jewish birth or not. In certain cases, for example when persecution of Jews is explicitly cited as the reason for coming here, information is submitted in this connection.

Those refugees whom *Israelsmissionen* (Swedish Mission to the People of Israel) has taken charge of, are as a rule counted among the Jewish refugees. The fact that a refugee has at that time obtained an entry permit through *Israelsmissionen's* efforts means that the refugee is of Jewish birth.

As concerns the terminology "Jewish" refugees, used in the alien statistics published by the National Board of Health and Welfare, I agree utterly with you that this terminology is not fully adequate. Therefore I think that we ought to consider such a change of terminology as is raised in your letter, but I am fully aware of the fact that every application in official Swedish statistics of a division by race is going to stir up criticism. As recently as the fall of 1943, this matter was the object of polemics in *Morgon-Tidningen*.

In case you have information which would affect the official count of refugees to a significant extent, without question we would be interested in getting information about those additional persons who could be regarded as refugees.

Document 69: British Intelligence report on Wallenberg Mission, July 26, 1944.

Mr. Boehm has now furnished the following details of his discussions with Mr. Olsen of the U.S. Legation of the question of Jews in Hungary and also an account of a meeting he had with Mr. Raoul Wallenberg before the latter's departure for Budapest.

In the second half of May Mr. Boehm received a telephone call from Mr. Cole of the U.S. Legation, who told him that Mr. Olsen, who is in charge of the Jewish question, had received a telegram from Washington advising him to contact Mr. Boehm in order to obtain information about the persecution of Jews in Hungary and to learn whether he had any suggestions to make. Mr. Boehm promised to furnish Mr. Olsen with a report and some suggestions within 8 to 10 days, and early in June this report was submitted and a copy was given to Mr. Parrott a few days later.

Some time later Mr. Olsen asked Mr. Boehm to visit him again and told him that his report had been translated and transmitted to

Washington. Mr. Olsen thought that the report was very instructive and of the greatest value.

Around the same time the representative of the Jewish World Congress, M. Storch, asked Mr. Boehm (whose address he had obtained from Mr. Olsen) and Mr. Olsen for a copy of the report, but Mr. Boehm did not feel justified in complying with the request. Mr. Olsen thereupon asked Mr. Boehm for permission to hand a copy of the report not to M. Storch but to the Chief Rabbi of Sweden, M. Ehrenpreis, who needed it for some action. Mr. Olsen further told Mr. Boehm that the U.S. Government was preparing some action and that, should this succeed, it might perhaps be possible to bring about some alleviation of the position of the Jews in Hungary.

Mr. Boehm pointed out to Mr. Olsen that, according to his information, the suffering of the Jews was indescribable, and he made a number of suggestions for the alleviation of the situation. He drew Mr. Olsen's attention also to the fact that the lives of many thousands of Jews were endangered.

At the end of June Mr. Boehm received a telephone call from the Hungarian composer Lajtay, who stated that M. Raoul Wallenberg wished to see him (Mr. Boehm) very urgently, if possible within a few hours. Mr. Boehm agreed to a meeting after consulting Mr. Parrott, and this took place the next day at the offices of "Salénrederierna," Strandvägen 7A, which is also the address of Mellaneuropeiska Handels A.B.

M. Wallenberg informed Mr. Boehm that he was a partner of the Hungarian businessman, Dr. Lauer, that he had hitherto imported from and exported to Hungary, and that during the war he had twice visited Budapest and knew conditions in Hungary, He emphasized that he was no politician and understood very little of politics. He had been appointed by the Swedish Government as Secretary to the Swedish Legation in Budapest. Officially, his task would be to help Hungarians who had been bombed out, but actually it would be to help the Jews.

After first hinting at the fact, M. Wallenberg eventually told Mr. Boehm quite openly that:

(1) the Americans, particularly Mr. Olsen, had a finger in this pie, and

(2) he as well as Dr. Lauer had read Mr. Boehm's "confidential" report on the Jewish question. The report had been submitted by M.

Ehrenpreis to the King and formed the basis of the King's action. The
report was thought in all quarters to be valuable.

M. Wallenberg hinted also at the difficulties his mission was still
experiencing. The Swedish Government was of course paying him the
salary of a Legation Secretary (according to Dr. Lauer, 2,000 Kronor per
month plus a very high representation allowance). As to other expenses
in connection with the mission, the Americans were to help to discharge
these, but, as Mr. Olsen pointed out, it takes about three months to
obtain sanction from America.

M. Wallenberg asked Mr. Boehm for advice and for addresses of Aryans in Hungary who were reliable anti-Nazis and whom he could contact
in order to get information on the Jewish question, and in reply Mr.
Boehm made the following suggestions:-

(1) to send provisions and possibly also clothes for the Jews in internment camps and in ghettos. Everything is obtainable in Hungary for
money. Corruption is the order of the day; especially with cigarettes,
coffee, cocoa, butter and foreign currency a lot can be achieved. M.
Wallenberg has asked to be supplied with tens of thousands of cigarettes, etc.

(2) to try to get Jews, who possess visas for Sweden and other countries, out of Hungary, even if in sealed railway carriages. An offer should
be made to exchange them for interned or sick German civilians.

In this connection M. Wallenberg thought that economic compensation and goods would be better for bartering, but that the British and
Americans would never agree to this or, if they did, it would take several
months.

(3) to visit the heads of the Church and others who were approacha-
ble and to try to intimidate them should the persecution of Jews continue.

(4) to prevent Jews from being deported.

M. Wallenberg also had a plan of his own, namely that for those Jews
who are under Swedish protection (several hundred persons) a separate
camp should be established and its care taken over by the Swedish Government.

Mr. Boehm supplied M. Wallenberg with a list of reliable Aryan
friends from whom he could obtain information. He also gave him a list
of Catholic and Protestant Church dignitaries, whom he could approach
immediately, and, finally, an address through which M. Wallenberg
could keep in touch with Mr. Boehm. Mr. Boehm did not, however,

give M. Wallenberg any political instruction nor the addresses of any of the "illegal" persons in Hungary as he felt it advisable first to have proof of his reliability.

Some of the foregoing is probably worth reporting to the F. O. as a supplement to what you have already written them about M. Raoul Wallenberg.

Document 70: Report of Raoul Wallenberg, July 29, 1944.

MEMO CONCERNING RELIEF WORK FOR THE JEWS IN HUNGARY

Different forms of relief work

Relief work is possible a) within the framework of agreements with the governments of Hungary and Germany, b) through private channels and c) through propaganda within the country with the aim of inducing the Jews to help themselves and soliciting help from other people as well as informing other nations about the true state of affairs in Hungary.

Aims and means

On account of the continually changing situation it is impossible to lay down any absolute limits for the relief work. The principal thing is to have the necessary financial and organisational means for such steps as may be required at any moment without further sanction.

Steps taken

On the basis of this assumption about 20 persons, mainly volunteers, have been engaged. Most of them are of Jewish birth but exempted from wearing the Star. The Swiss Legation has done exactly the same and it has moreover been impossible to secure Christian employees. Even Gestapo has been compelled to engage Jews. If we had not acted in this way it would have been absolutely impossible to cope with the existing work as the permanent staff of the Legation already when I arrived was almost worn out.

A telephone with 3 apparatuses has been installed in the B-Department building. Several thousand stencilled forms have been prepared. New office material has been bought for about P. 1,000 and besides half a dozen typewriters, desks, chairs, etc. have been borrowed from various quarters.

A bill for these expenses will be presented in the event of the Embassy (*sic*) being sanctioned to pay them.

Indirect contacts have been established with certain authorities in order to obtain correct information about removal e.g. of Jews and the postal communications with deported Jews.

I have rented a very beautiful house as my private residence in order to be able to represent on a suitable scale. Besides a certain person with the most valuable letters of recommendation has arrived here in order to probe the future prospects in the highest German circles.

Official way of negotiations

The negotiations with the Foreign Office in Budapest have as already reported resulted a) in the approval by Hungary of repatriation, b) the Hungarians have expressed their intention of obtaining especially fine houses for our Jews and c) in several cases with provisional passports have already been released from forced labour service and have been exempted from wearing the Star. All this is an immense step on the way towards rescue as the ban on appearing outdoors (Jewish curfew) and the risks in connexion with this ban are hereby eliminated.

Partial German consent seems to depend on whether Hungary agrees to send the remaining Jews abroad as "labour": This will entail tabling of the question of home transportation until a late date. I submit, however, that in spite of everything you try to obtain partial consent in Berlin.

Please also let me know if the Embassy (*sic*) is allowed to issue a provisional passport for instance to a brother, sister, father, mother, husband or wife of a Swedish subject or to a person who has been of great importance for the trade between Swedish (*sic*) and Hungary or for the cultural connections between these two countries.

Private relief work

Relief work has already started, though on a very limited scale. Funds have already been requested from a religious organisation which have been very active in helping the Jews but, however, could not be provided. The same applies to the recently appointed Jewish Board for Christian Jews. It would naturally be desirable if this activity could be pursued either in the form of support to a camp through the agency of the Red Cross or in the form of support to individuals or persons and organisations who have proved themselves useful. It is indeed regrettable that the persons who have been most interested in my journey are (*sic*) apparently failed to understand that the funds are necessary.

Propaganda. Self-help to the Jews

The following opinions have been expressed by certain persons when interviewed and seem to be deeply rooted among the rumours in Budapest. The activity of the post-war tribunals is supposed to have started already especially in order not to lose sight of those reponsible for the persecutions against the Jews. Hungary's policy against her Jews especially in the light of the policy pursued in Rumania would seriously harm the country at the conclusion of a peace treaty.

It is vital to try to overcome the apathy which still characterizes the majority of the Jews. The national indifference to their fate on the other hand has diminished considerably since my last report. The point is to outroot the feeling among the Jews that they are forgotten. The message from the King was of the utmost importance in this respect. Similar messages from other foreign institutions to corresponding organizations here are most valuable in this connexion. I therefor (*sic*) repeat my proposal regarding a telegram from the Archbishop to certain bishops previously mentioned; this suggestion has now also been made from clerical quarters.

The mere fact that the Swiss and Swedish Embassies (*sic*) have received Jews, listened to them and registered them has encouraged both the Jews and those who have been inclined to help. A successful repatriation action on a small scale or the establishment of a Red Cross camp or pecuniary assistance would be of the greatest importance because it would give hundred of thousands of Jews new hope and awaken their at present paralysed instinct of self-preservation.

A few words about the Allied propaganda. In all quarters the Anglo-Saxon broadcasts are criticized as being crammed with general threats of reprisals without offering help, forgiveness or directions about any alternative, practicable policy. The Russian propaganda which speaks magnanimity and love of peace is considered better. If at least some promises about future help could be given those who now help the Jews the propaganda certainly would have a better effect.

Knowledge of the situation abroad

It is quite obvious that the publicity in the foreign press essentially contributed to ease the situation here. Thus, continued publicity is

desirable. In this connection I refer to the enclosed report regarding the
treatment of Jews in Hungary.

Document 71: Telegram from Hellstedt to Danielsson, July 29, 1944.
Attitudes of Swedish Foreign Office toward Langlet's activities.

(Concerning the Jews in Hungary:)

We are wholly convinced here that Mr. Langlet renders the Legation
great service on the Jewish Questions and that, through his knowledge
of local conditions and persons he is of the greatest usefulness, neither
do we doubt that he is doing his best to help the poor distressed people.
However, I have not wanted to neglect directing your attention to [the
fact that] Langlet, in his great zeal, sometimes lets himself be seduced
into writing particularly unsuitable letters to relatives, here, of Jews in
Hungary. I beg to enclose, in facsimile, two samples of his way of writing
which speak for themselves, and would like to ask whether it is not
appropriate, at your first opportunity, to point out to Langlet the altogether unnecessary irritation which his temperamental communications stir up in the relatives, already severely stressed, of victims of the
Hungarian Jewish actions.

Document 72: Letter from Langlet to Governing Board of the Swedish Red Cross, September 9, 1944.
Langlet's first report on his rescue activities.

. . . Our activities now are divided into the following departments:

1. A central office. . . . A freer reception of those seeking help cannot
take place there, since the Hungarian Red Cross is formally prevented
from concerning itself with Jews, and an influx of persons wearing a yel-
low star would risk our cooperation with this sister organization. Therefore I must receive such persons in my own home or they are referred to
the offices of some of our other departments. . . .

2. For taking in and caring for children and youths up to 17 years of
age, agreements have been reached with several convents and similar
institutions, where upwards of 200 places can be provided. . . . Further, agreements have been formally made to rent, without cost . . .
some quarters for children's homes of our own. . . . Of these, we may in

the near future be able to open so many that places can be provided for
another two to three hundred children. These homes are going to be
placed under the direction of Asta Nilsson. . . .

3. To search for Hungarian Jews who have been carried off either
from their homes or from ghettos and internment or prison camps set up
during the worst persecution, an especially spacious place with three
large rooms has been rented (gratis) from the Legation, as I proposed.
Here, a staff of around 30 carefully chosen volunteer co-workers carry
out the receiving, sorting, answering and entering in card indexes of the
tens of thousands of inquiries that stream in.

The office, which is led by particularly suitable and clever persons,
namely, the Belgian subject Count Michael Tolstoy and the Englishman
Mr. Dickinson, and their wives, has now made such progress with its
recording of the persons being looked for — probably amounting to
around a fifth of all those Jews, at least 400,000, who have disappeared
— that, in the very near future, we will be able to put official inquiries to
the appropriate authorities, both here in this country and in Germany.
. . .

4. Another office works on searching for Hungarian prisoners in
Russia. . . . Concerning the Russian prisoners of war in Hungary, they
amount to a very insignificant number. As for the few Russian civilian
internees, they are very satisfactorily taken care of; for our part, we have
contributed with gifts of tobacco, some articles of clothing and a couple
of longed-for musical instruments, which were procured with funds collected by Count and Countess Tolstoy.

5. Through a special unit for which separate quarters have not yet
been set up, a number of those persons now in internment camps have
been able to gain release. . . .

6. To check on the management of resources, and to discuss suitable
ways to procure further necessary resources — money and barter — a
three-person committee has been convened. . . .

We have secured all our 5 office locations, 4 dwellings and 6 children's
homes rent-free and . . . only in an insignificant number of cases [do we]
pay wages. . . .

This report should not conclude without a brief mention of the amaz-
ingly comprehensive work which, in parallel with our own but without
collaboration is carried on by the Legation's B Department under the
leadership of Secretary of Legation Raoul Wallenberg, assisted by several hundred unpaid co-workers. . . .

For my part, lacking all influence on the actions of the B Department and being, in my Red Cross activities, independent of them, I imagine that the Red Cross which, unlike the Legation's support operation, is not at all intended only to help the Jewish population, is going to acquire a rather significant and unique assignment during the occupation that may be impending. Probably the distress will then be intensified still further, as seems to have occurred in Italy and, earlier, in other places, for example in Poland and Greece. Then the chief assignment may change from helping persecuted Jews to trying to aid, as best we can, non-Jewish elements among the population who are threatened by danger and need, who belong to a social group who, from the (domestic and external) bolshevik standpoint, are badly regarded. By this, I mean the higher, educated and well-to-do middle class and, perhaps not least, the highest circles of society. Already fears are evident in these quarters of losing both life and property or, at best, of being subjected to imprisonment, deportation and economic ruin, if occupation from the east should take place, or if a revolution should take place from within. A tangible sign of this is the evident eagerness to put places at our disposal, in return for promises of some kind of protective sign for homes, as well as to get hold of our protective letters (which are, so to say, legalized by the authorities' silent assent) — preferably, they say, with both English and, especially, Russian text!

Document 73: Memorandum of September 12, 1944 about expenditures of monies to help Jews in Hungary.

The first *Kr. 10.000.-* have not as yet been fully used, only ¼ having been distributed. The office expenses of the Jewish action in Budapest have been covered from other sources.

The Legation purposely has refrained from a large-scale humanitarian effort. It has been found, that this distribution of passports up to now constituted a bigger measure of help to the Jews in Budapest, than any distribution of funds or money.

To-day, as the work with the passports has almost been carried to a close, it is planned to start a humanitarian action including the distribution of foodstuffs and money. A first lot of foodstuff at a value of *P. 65.000.-* has been purchased, but has not as yet been delivered.

A small department for the distribution of money to the holders of

protective passports has been opened and a fund of *P. 30.000.*- been put
at its disposal. Rules for the distribution of money and foodstuff will be
worked out on the basis of the experience of the first distribution.

A considerable part of the expenses till now has consisted in giving
dinners and lunches for various influential officials, particularly the officers responsible for the Jewish questions.

During one of these dinners the promise was given to liberate all
those Jews, who were interned and who held Swedish protective passports and to free up to 4,500 Jews who held Swedish protective passports from the Jewish star.

As for the further funds, placed at the disposal of the Jewish action,
none of this money has been distributed, but it will probably in large
part be invested in foodstuff. No money has been used for bribes for
certain gifts of sardines have been distributed. No money has been used
to pay damages to those Jews, who were to have been ousted from their
apartments in Pozsonyi Street, which was to have been transformed into
a Swedish ghetto. This plan was never carried out due to the changes in
the general situation.

**Document 74: Letter from Raoul Wallenberg to Iver Olsen, October 7,
1944.**
Wallenberg reporting briefly to Olsen.

When I now look back on the 3 months I have spent here I can only
say, that it has been a most interesting experience and I believe, not
quite without results.

When I arrived, the situation of the Jews was very bad indeed. The
development of military events and a natural psychological reaction
among the Hungarian people have changed many things. We at the
Swedish Legation have perhaps only been an instrument to convert this
outside influence into action in the various Government offices. I have
taken quite a strong line in this respect although, of course I have had to
keep within the limits assigned to me as a neutral.

It has been my object all the time, to try to help all Jews. This, however, could only be achieved by helping a whole group of Jews to get rid
of their stars. I have worked on the hypothesis that those, who were no
longer under the obligation to carry the star, would help their fellow

sufferers. Also I have carried out a great deal of general enlightenment work among the keymen in charge of Jewish questions here.

I am quite sure, that our activity — and that means in the last instance yours — is responsible for the freeing at this time of the interned Jews. These numbered many hundreds. At first only those were freed who possessed Swedish protective passports, but later all who had not committed a criminal offence, were freed.

I have also received a promise that all "Swedish" Jews in civilian service (Arbeitsdienst) will be ordered back. The number of these Jews is about 500 but I doubt that more than half of them may be brought back from their present assignments, which are situated partly in front-districts.

Mr. Olsen, believe me, your donation in behalf of the Hungarian Jews has made an enormous amount of good. I think that they will have every reason to thank you for having initiated and supported the Swedish Jewish action the way you have in such a splendid manner.

Document 75: Report of Iver Olsen, November 22, 1944.
This document is of great interest because it reflects on all activities of the War Refugee Board in Sweden and was submitted at a time when the fate of many Jews, especially in Hungary, was in great doubt.

As is generally known, the Swedish public is most sympathetic to humanitarian efforts and has made an extremely distinguished record in this field during the war period. A similar attitude is prevalent among the Swedish authorities. . . .

It was rather clear from the outset that the program had to be dealt with in two parts — relief and rescue — and that entirely different approaches had to be made with respect to each of these programs. . . .

The usual obstacles and disappointments were encountered as regards jealousies between local organizations. This was particularly true with regard to the Jewish organizations in Sweden which, it seems to me, have been strikingly ineffective during the past years and contributed virtually nothing to furthering the operations of the War Refugee Board. They seemed much more concerned with personal considerations, personal prestige and jockeying for position vis-à-vis a rival organization, than the desperate fate of their people in Europe. They were openly critical of any efforts of others but quick to claim a participating credit in the more successful efforts. . . .

Approximately 1,200 persons rescued. . . .

. . . The outstanding failure of the Estonian program was the inability to evacuate the Czech and French Jewesses from Tallinn. . . . As it was, I was informed that contact was made with these Jewesses but they were too frightened to risk the journey. I have no way of verifying this statement. . . .

. . . the Swedish Intelligence Service took advantage of this excellent underground connection to run a few excursions of their own for the purpose of checking as to what was going on in Estonia. This would be quite natural, since the Swedish General Staff was most cooperative, even to the point of supplying weapons and forged German identification papers, and it would be quite unlikely that there wasn't some *quid pro quo* somewhere. . . .

Latvian Rescue Operations.

This operation was considerably more difficult than the Estonian, and the results much more obscure. . . .

. . . there were occasional rumors that pro-Nazis or persons participating actively in the slaughter of the Latvian Jews had been brought to Sweden. . . .

In not a single instance was it possible to find a concrete basis for these rumors, and it may be assumed that they sprang from jealousies and ill will between the various Latvian elements in Sweden. . . .

The failure to rescue any Latvian Jews was a great disappointment and even now it is not clear what else could have been done to obtain better results. Several attempts had been made by some individuals here to hire less reliable groups to bring Jews out of Latvia at so much per head. In all instances, however, money was paid out in advance but no results were forthcoming. I am rather convinced that our group would have brought some of them out if possible, since I was constantly reminding Salnais of several rumors I had heard that he was anti-Semitic, to which he strongly protested. However, there is no question but what an important segment of Latvian officials are anti-Semitic and responsible for some of the unspeakable crimes committed against the Jews in Latvia, and perhaps some of the failure was due to the attitude of the underground group in Latvia. Otherwise, and considering the fact that hardly a single Jew has come out of Latvia during the German occupation, there seems to be a reasonable basis for accepting the explanation that the Jews were either out of reach of rescue operations or were in hiding and too terrified to make a break for safety.

These operations received a death-blow almost at the outset and from which they were never able to recover. That was in the loss of the group's key man. . . .

. . . The failure in this instance to rescue any Jews can most certainly be attributed to technical obstacles alone since it is known definitely that several efforts were made to establish the necessary channels. . . .

Criticisms Encountered.

The most active criticism of the Baltic rescue program was initiated in October by the Communist press in Sweden. . . .

Some of the local Jewish organizations were disposed to criticize these operations as having failed to rescue any Jews despite the fact that funds of American Jewish organizations were employed (which was not true). The failure to rescue any Jews was greatly regretted and has been explained, a circumstance that these Swedish organizations should have understood when it is considered that in the past several years the position of the Jews in the Baltic has been most critical and they themselves did not bring a single one to safety nor did they initiate a single step in that direction. Most of the criticism probably originated from the fact that they wanted all funds originating from Jewish organizations in the United States to go through their hands.

Finnish Rescue Operations.

These operations were limited exclusively to bringing to safety the stateless Jews in Finland. . . . This operation involved considerable discussion with the Swedish Foreign Office as to entry visas, with the local Mosaic Community as to maintenance provisions, and with the Finnish Mosaic Community as to evacuation details. All arrangements were finally completed and perhaps 150 eventually arrived in Sweden on a piecemeal basis. The Swedish Mosaic Community was distinctly luke warm towards the whole program, and on occasions needed rather strong prodding.

Arrangements were also concluded with the Swedish Foreign Office, on a preliminary basis, whereby they would undertake to evacuate the Finnish Jews at the same time that conditions in Finland seemed sufficiently dangerous to necessitate the evacuation of Swedes in Finland. . . .

Balkan Rescue and Relief Operations.

Results: Approximately 6,000 Hungarian Jews brought under Swedish protection and segregated in areas of greater safety. Many thousand Hungarian and Rumanian Jews given urgently needed food, medicines and money.

Rescue and relief operations in the Balkans could, of course, be organized and directed from countries in closer proximity to the area than Sweden, which also had representatives of the War Refugee Board. Accordingly, the principal effort from here was to exploit fully whatever Swedish channels appeared particularly strategic. In this connection, Swedish diplomatic representation in these countries seemed the outstanding factor to work on and was in fact explored very actively. As previously stated, the Swedish Foreign Office has at all times been extremely cooperative in these matters and of tremendous assistance. Also, a few of the local Jewish organizations had certain quite effective channels with the Balkan countries, due in part to working channels through the Swedish Foreign Office. . . .

Hungarian Rescue and Relief Operations.

This program went extremely well . . . probably was the most constructive action initiated from anywhere for the relief of the Hungarian Jews. The keystone of the entire operation was the willingness of the Swedish Foreign Office to assign an Attaché to its Legation in Budapest exclusively for the purpose of initiating relief actions for the Hungarian Jews. The Attaché sent, Raoul Wallenberg, was personally known to us and was in fact our choice. Very energetic, great initiative and resourcefulness, and sincerely concerned with the urgency of the problem. . . .

The first major action initiated was to get as many Hungarian Jews as possible under Swedish protection. Such protective papers were issued to all Hungarian Jews who had relatives or close friends in Sweden, or had long established business connections with Sweden. Approximately 6,000 persons were found eligible — out of thousands of applications filed. . . .

Relief and Rescue Operations in Rumania

These were very limited in scope and the results somewhat obscure. Indirect and unofficial pressure was brought to bear on the Rumanian Legation here with respect to the policy of the Rumanian Government towards the Jews, and these approaches were received very sympathetically and perhaps were helpful. Chief Rabbi Ehrenpreis had good working channels through the Swedish Foreign Office and certain officials and religious leaders in Rumania, with the result that several urgently needed relief actions were carried out with the assistance of 25,000 Swedish kronor turned over to him from available W.R.B. funds. Also established working contacts with the Svenska Israels Missionen, an organization of Christian Jews which seemed to be able to move around Rumania with comparative freedom in the more troublesome days. It was engaged primarily in relief operations since they were unsuccessful in obtaining Palestine permits for a group which could have been evacuated. The activities of this group were not extensive, but financial assistance was arranged for them from the United States and there is every reason to believe that their efforts were well worth-while.

Some negotiations were held with the Rumanian Legation in Stockholm with respect to transport facilities for the evacuation of Jews from Rumania to Turkey, but these were dropped upon advice that the War Refugee Board was pushing a similar program from Turkey.

Activities With Respect to the Rest of Europe.

These efforts were not on any organized pattern but were undertaken from time to time when special circumstances suggested a hope that certain approaches might be helpful. For example, channels were found for directing a strong appeal to Goering, on an excellent personal basis, on behalf of the Jews in Theresienstadt, Bergen-Belsen and other well known Jewish concentration camps in Europe. For some unknown reason, Goering replied that he was able to give the highest personal assurances that conditions in Theresienstadt were entirely satisfactory, but that he was powerless to intervene elsewhere. He stated that he had endangered his Party position because of his intervention in behalf of Jews and that he no longer was strong enough in such matters to exercise a controlling influence. On other occasions, certain well connected German authorities were approached informally and unofficially with respect to the evacuation of Baltic Jews, as well as the transport to Sweden of South American Jews. These negotiations were unusual, to say the least, but despite assurances of a reciprocal interest in humanitarian matters nothing concrete developed except perhaps a gain of time.

The food parcel traffic to concentration camps in Europe was explored very carefully and every possible encouragement and stimulant was given to an expansion of this traffic. This became increasingly urgent as the flow of parcels from other neutral countries was interrupted, coupled with the increasing clarity of the fact that the Germans were finding it interesting to experiment with the simple process of just starving the

Jews to death. It was possible to increase the shipments of food parcels from Sweden substantially to such areas as Theresienstadt, Bergen-Belsen, Polish concentration camps and several other areas where conditions were acute. Thousands of packages have now been going forward monthly. Funds supplied by the War Refugee Board have been made available to finance the shipment of parcels for certain to their relatives in Europe.

Through these and other measures, the flow of food parcels, medicines and clothing into Germany, Poland, Czechoslovakia and Austria have been increased to a considerable degree, although still far short of requirements. Shipments to Poland from Sweden were interrupted this week, due to technical difficulties and perhaps will not be resumed.

Document 76: Report from Raoul Wallenberg, December 8, 1944.
Report reflects new dangers to Budapest Jews.

Report Concerning the Situation of the Hungarian Jews
Since the last report, the situation of the Hungarian Jews has worsened further.

Probably around 40,000 Jews, of whom 15,000 are men from the conscript labor service and 25,000 persons of both sexes who have been taken in their homes or on the street, have been forced to march on foot to Germany. The distance is 149 miles. Ever since arrangements have begun for these death-marches, the weather has been cold and rainy. People have slept under shelter or in the open. Most have been allowed to eat or drink only three or four times. Many have died. The undersigned established in Mosonmagyaróvár that seven persons had died that day and seven the day before. The secretary of the Portuguese Legation had seen 42 dead along the march route, and Deputy Minister-President Szöllösi admitted to me that he had seen two dead. The marchers are shot if they cannot walk. At the border they are taken over by Eichmann's SS *Specialkommando*, with blows and lashes, and taken away to hard labor on the border fortifications.

Photos are enclosed of civilians marching away /1 and 2/, of military conscript laborers marching away /3/ and of two girls before and after traveling Budapest-Hegyeshalom-Budapest /4/.

Twenty thousand military conscript laborers have been transported by rail to the border. These are mainly working on Hungarian soil. Photos are enclosed /5/ that show the work of the Swedish Rescue Committee.

Forced labor on trenches and earthworks, which was mentioned in earlier reports, has stopped.

The Jews are assembled in a central ghetto which is intended to hold 69,000 Jews, but probably will contain more, as well as a foreigners' ghetto for 17,000, which already contains 35,000; of these, 7,000 in Swedish houses, 2,000 in Red Cross houses and 23,000 in Swiss houses. Every day, thousands of Swiss and Vatican protectees are taken away from here, for deportation or to the central ghetto. In the ghettos the Jews live four to twelve persons in a room, best in the Swedish houses.

An epidemic, not yet widespread, of the "Ruhr" sickness has broken out among the Jews. In the Swedish houses, health conditions are still good. Only five have died so far. The Department is now having all Jews under Swedish protection inoculated against typhus, paratyphus and cholera. The staff, too, are to be inoculated.

The Jews are now generally very destitute since, during the continual moving around that is now under way, they may only take with them what they themselves can carry. Their economic situation is on the point of becoming catastrophic.

The Arrow Cross men drag great numbers into their places and brutalize and torture them, then take them away to the collection points for deportation.

Rumors are going around that a death brigade close to Minister Kovacs is going to start a pogrom against the Jews but I do not believe this pogrom will reach any great extent since, for example, SS units are said to have received orders not to start any systematic slaughter of Jews.

The Organization

After the staggering blow in October, the Department has once again powerfully expanded. The number employed is 335, to which are added some forty doctors, house captains, etc. All these are living in the Department's rooms, along with an equal number of family members. The number of offices and dwelling houses is 10, of which one is in the foreigners' ghetto.

Two infirmaries have been established, and improvised, respectively, with a total of 150 beds.

A soup kitchen has been set up.

The Jews in the Swedish protective houses turn their food ration cards in to the Department and these are redeemed and the groceries distributed.

A large part of the Department's correspondence has been destroyed.

The food department has now made purchases amounting to about two million pengo.

Results Achieved

The Department succeeded in obtaining from the Minister of Defense [*Honved*] an open order that all Jews in the conscripted labor service who have foreign documents should be returned to Budapest. Since a military person, dispatched in one of the Department's cars, distributed the order, around 15,000 Jews have returned.

The columns being marched toward the border have received a certain distribution of food and medicine for a short time, until it was forbidden. The sick have been taken from deportation collection points in rescue cars, around 200 persons.

Through intervening in one way or another in the shutting up in boxcars or shipping away of Jews, some 2,000 persons have been taken back, including about 500 from Hegyeshalom. However, this traffic has unfortunately had to be interrupted since the Germans in the Eichmann kommando made threats of violence.

So far, the Jews with protective passes have gotten along comparatively best of all those protected by foreign powers. As of the present date, it seems that only eight to ten of them have been shot in Budapest and its environs.

Document 77: Telegram from the Swedish Government to Swedish Legation in Budapest, December 13, 1944.
Sweden decides not to recognize the Szalasi regime in Hungary, but orders its diplomats to continue their work.

Referring your 585 we confirm that Swedish Government does not intend to recognize Szalasi regime. You should try to prevent question being brought to a head, and emphasize particularly regrettable impression made not only in Sweden but in whole world by Jewish evacuation from Budapest, which we presume also intended to include Jews with Swedish protective passes. Should question of break in diplomatic relations come up you may, if appropriate, remind them that Sweden looks after Hungary's interests in eleven countries, including U.S.A., British Empire, Rumania and Argentina.

Document 78: Coded telegram from Danielsson to Swedish Foreign Office, December 15, 1944.
Report that Eichmann ordered Raoul Wallenberg assassinated.

The head of the SS-*kommando* for solution of the Jewish problem, here, General Eichmann, has told an *orskanstld*** that he intended to have the Jew-dog Wallenberg shot. His deputy, Daögger, has made similar remarks with obvious intention of frightening Mission. Raise question whether representations be made in Berlin, in which Germany's guilt in atrocities against Swedish protectees is pointed out. According what is said in another SS quarter, here, Himmler does not wish such atrocities and besides has said he sets great store by relations Sweden-Germany. A Jewish member of Mission staff and three family members of such have been shot so far.

Document 79: Telegram from von Post (Stockholm) to Richert (Berlin), December 18, 1944.
Telegram indicated that the rescue project was identified with Norwegian Minister in Stockholm, Ditleff, and designed to aid Norwegians.

(Aid operation for Norwegians interned in Germany:)
Referring our conversation in Stockholm concerning Minister Ditleff's project for a Swedish operation aiding Norwegians interned in Germany, I beg leave herewith transmit Ditleff's strictly confidential memorandum on subject. Foreign minister would appreciate if you in whatever way you find appropriate would probe possibilities for aiding Norwegians remaining in Germany, upon a German collapse.

---

* Translator's note: Meaning of abbreviation unclear.

Document 80: Letter from Nylander (Berlin) to von Post (Stockholm), January 7, 1945.
This document related a conversation between a Swedish Legation official and a German, Kleist, who was believed to be a Himmler operative.

Last Friday I succeeded in meeting with Kleist, who has had quite a lot of difficulties to endure in the latest bombing attacks on Berlin. He received me in the cellar of the house on *Kurfürstenstrasse*; because of the shortage of coal only a few small cellar rooms could be warmed, while the house is otherwise unusable because of the fierce cold. I relayed a greeting from you, for which he expressed thanks and hoped that you received the little Christmas angel his wife had made.

After having discussed the transfer to Sweden of the Estonian Swedes, here, in whom we Swedes had an interest — a group of about ten persons could, according to Kleist, probably travel this week — the conversation shifted to general political issues. Kleist spoke of an article recently published in a Swedish paper (*Dagens Nyheter?*) in which a bulletin from London was repeated, according to which he had been seized by the Gestapo and liquidated, all this in connection with efforts to arrange peace during an intended visit to Lisbon. Kleist's attention had been drawn to the article through Hilger in *Auswärtiges Amt*. According to Kleist, who stated that naturally articles of that sort were pretty unpleasant for him personally, the purpose of such a bulletin might very well be, that people on the Allied side wanted to make him unusable as an intermediary for eventual serious negotiations toward a settlement.

Kleist expressed himself quite optimistically concerning Germany's future prospects, not in terms of "winning the war," but as concerned chances for the country to emerge from the war without defeat. The powerful German offensives had shown that Germany's resources were far from exhausted; the longer the war lasted, the more probable it became that the belligerents sooner or later had to sit down to the negotiating table to try mutually to achieve an agreement which put an end to the fighting. An active participation on the part of Germany was inescapable for this.

Rather in passing, we came onto Swedish-German relations. I gave the usual views on Norway and Denmark and vigorously deplored that they, on the German side, had up to now done far too little concerning the Norwegian internees. What did 65–80 returned students amount to,

in comparison with all those multitudes of Norwegians in forced internment in Germany? More, more, more must be done, and this as soon as
possible.

After a pause, I asked Kleist (while stating that I had no assignment at
all to do so and that the whole matter represented my own personal
deliberations) whether, in his opinion, there was any prospect, say,
through the Red Cross, of getting a number of Jews out of Germany into
Sweden. I expanded on the significance for Swedish-German relations
of the issue of the Norwegians, where a deeply rooted public opinion
stood behind the Swedish Government, and how a release of interned
Norwegians could seriously strengthen the Swedish position vis-à-vis
the Allies. What was involved was to get the Allies, especially the
U.S.A., to recognize the importance of Sweden's remaining neutral,
and to realize that maintaining Swedish-German relations was even positively in Allied interests. Perhaps, I said, a release of Jews and their
transfer to Sweden would work in a similar direction; in any case, it
seemed indisputable that such an aid operation would have an
extremely strong *"Durchschlagskraft"* on the highest level in
Washington.

Kleist recapitulated the earlier attempts which had been made, by
himself among others, to help Jews get out of the country. On one occasion, he had taken up the matter with Ribbentrop, but the latter had
brusquely rejected the subject before Kleist had time to express his
views. However, during earlier negotiations, there had been talk about
compensation in money, something which Kleist, for his part, wanted to
have nothing to do with. The framing of the question now lay on another
plane. After some deliberation, Kleist declared himself prepared to *"das
heisse Eisen anfassen"* and to sound out both Ribbentrop and Himmler.
He concluded that an operation of that kind, to benefit a limited number
of Jews — to begin with, perhaps seven thousand and, as a suggestion,
the "South American" Jews — could be very appropriate from a directly
German standpoint, since the war must, inescapably, be followed by
mutual negotiations and agreements among all countries.

Document 81: Letter from von Post to Nylander, January 9, 1945.
*This Foreign Office response to Nylander's inquiry underscored the
notion that Swedish rescue priorities began with the Norwegians.*

With hearty thanks for your letter of the 7th of this month, concerning your conversation with Kleist, may I inform you that we certainly are interested in making it possible for Jews to come to Sweden but that, naturally, the highest urgency now is for Norwegians, to the greatest extent possible, to be returned from Germany to Norway. I am sure you are perfectly clear about this but have wanted to write these lines with the thought that eventually you may — in case the Germans should try to paralyze the "Norwegian" action by referring to their exploring the possibilities of the "Jewish" action — find reason to underscore our extraordinary interest in the return of the Norwegians.

Document 82: Telegram from von Post to Richert, January 25, 1945.
Richert asked to comment on WJC proposal for Sweden to demand of Germany a stop of its extermination campaign.

According to what Boström has reported from Washington the World's [sic] Jewish Congress has turned to him with the question whether the Swedish Government would consider it possible to make an appeal to the German Government calling on it to halt Jewish persecutions in Europe, in any event to halt the extermination methods. The representatives of the organization had thought it possible that, seeing the way the war was now going, the Germans might now be more willing than earlier to stop the Jewish operations. Boström adds that the organization had presented the same question to the Swiss and Spanish chiefs of mission, who, similarly, had forwarded this plea to their governments. Finally, Boström says, the people concerned would like to know whether the system with protective passes can be extended to Germany as well.

I would be grateful if you would share your views with me in this matter as soon as possible.

Document 83: Memorandum from the American Minister in Stockholm, January 27, 1945.
This document was discussed widely in the Swedish Foreign Office and sent to Richert for comment.

Well known German practice of exterminating Jews who may survive in any area previous to its evacuation by the Germans focuses once more attention on the danger faced by Jewish survivors in any territory controlled by Germany.

Continued efforts should be made to keep any victims of Nazi persecution who now survive alive during the coming stages of war operations. According to present information the four largest concentrations of Jews in territory controlled by Germany are Lodz with 60,000 to 80,000 internees, Theresienstadt with 40,000 to 60,000, camps in the vicinity of Vienna with 18,000, and Camp Belsen-Bergen with 9,000.

In the opinion of the United States Government extended and frequent visits of Consuls of Sweden to regions and places where Jews have been brought together provide one of the most effective means of preventing their further massacre. In Budapest this method proved its effectiveness and thanks to the presence of Swedish personnel it seems that many lives were saved.

In view of the fact that a considerable number of relief parcels have reached Camp Belsen-Bergen through the good offices of the Red Cross and Swedish Y.M.C.A., these organizations might consider the desirability of having their delegates stationed in or sent on an extended visit to that camp. These delegates might assist in the distribution of the parcels that have been sent and through means of their presence the lives of these 9,000 inmates may be in some measure safeguarded. There is mounting evidence of confusion among local German officials and as to their increasing accessibility to pressure of a psychological nature designed to divert them from carrying out extermination policies ordered by certain German authorities. It would seem that full advantage might be taken of this state of mind in the interest of saving lives, not only through official channels but through unofficial channels.

It would seem from an objective point of view that the measures suggested above should be actively followed as long as the danger exists.

Document 84: Letter from Richert to von Post, January 29, 1945.
Richert advised against a positive response to the American idea for Sweden to request that Germany stop its extermination policy.

Referring to your letter of January 25, concerning Jewish persecutions in Germany, I beg leave to tell you the following.

Actually, the first question in your letter can be considered already

answered by my letter of the 25th of this month, concerning the
so-called *Mischlinge*: such an intervention by the Swedish Government
as has been conceived of by the persons in Washington, would, in my
humble opinion, be only a shot in the dark: it would not be accepted and
would be altogether without effect.

As concerns the question about "protective passes," I want to point
out the great difference between the conditions in Hungary, at the time
Danielsson began with these passes, and the conditions in Germany
today. In Budapest — as in Hungary otherwise — a lot of Jews moved
around freely, and "the protective pass" was intended to prevent their
"liquidation." Here, there are practically no more Jews, now, who are at
liberty; those who are still alive would practically all seem to be in camps
and such. During the last year I have not myself seen a single person
equipped with the Star of David. This is one, and an important, difference. Another is that, so long as the Gestapo has been responsible for
the domestic "law and order" of this country — and it is precisely for that
period the "protective pass" would be needed — I cannot conceive that,
if one can imagine such a case actually occurring, they would give it the
least consideration, if the poor Jew in question were suddenly to present
a Swedish so-called protective pass. Only in case the person concerned
could show himself to be a Swedish citizen (and not only show papers
saying that he had been *made* into a citizen) would one, as far as I understand, expect *any* consideration. In other cases, it probably would even
harm the person involved, if he could be accused of having sought protection of a foreign power.

**Document 85: Telegram from the Cabinet to the Swedish Legation,
Berlin, February 2, 1945.**
*Sweden decided to seek papal and Swiss support for a joint protest
about the Jews.*

Inquire whether Nuncio is willing in concert with you and Swiss minister call upon Undersecretary German Ministry of Foreign Affairs and
orally expand on following, in general:

The article published by Reich Minister Goebbels in *Das Reich* January 21 this year, entitled "*die Urheber des Unglücks der Welt*," has
stirred great uneasiness in neutral countries over fate which can befall
Jews in Theresienstadt, Bergen Belsen and elsewhere in Germany and
dem deutschen Machtbereich. Because of this, Holy See and Swiss and

Swedish Governments wish to direct German Government's attention to utterly unfortunate *falls den Juden etwas zustossen würde*, both from international viewpoint and in interest of German people.

We are directing corresponding inquiry to Swiss Government.

In our opinion, to avoid prestige problems on part of Germans arrangements should be so made that no publicity given to démarche for present.

Background to proposed démarche is deep concern for German violence against still surviving Jews in phase of war when prospects of saving Germany from total defeat seem minimal. Unconfirmed rumors circulate here already of massacres being undertaken against Jews in Theresienstadt. World Jewish Congress has directed insistent apeal to us to try to halt Jewish persecutions through appeal to German Government. American minister here has also presented ideas on measures from Swedish side to protect Jews. All Jewish associations in Argentina have done same. Swedish Jewish circles are also extremely anxious for something to be done.

Document 86: Telegram from Richert to Ministry of Foreign Affairs, February 7, 1945.
Richert reported negative responses of Swiss and papal colleagues and reflected his own view that the pressure for such an act came from "Swedish Jews."

Nuncio declines take part in collective démarche, which he considers solely harmful. Frölicher of same opinion. Only form for presentation of Swedish démarche seems to me, that we offer accept Jews in Sweden. If general warnings of what is thought to be in German people's interest or such are added, there is risk that démarche will not be accepted. In case of publicity, which gives démarche character of a demonstration, risk remains that it will not simply accomplish nothing but will directly harm Jews involved. Swedish Jewish circles should, in my opinion, abstain from pressing Swedish Government to actions which, in best case, will be a shot in the dark.

Document 87: Telegram from Westrup (Berne) to Ministry of Foreign Affairs, February 8, 1945.
Report of Swiss attitude and successful rescue of 1500 Jews.

Primo. As answer to démarche according to your No. 29, presented on morning of fifth of this month, this evening it has been orally communicated that Council of Swiss Confederation wholly in agreement with Swedish Government in this matter, but faithful to its principles does not wish participate in collective démarches. Council has yesterday telegraphically instructed minister in Berlin to contact his Swedish colleague confer with him about matter and about coordinating démarches with him and Nuncio, though separately and independently presented. Further agreed on no publicity.

Secundo. Swiss, who earlier have accepted 1,500 Jews who had been interned in Germany, have yesterday received official communication that further 1,200 from Theresienstadt are on way here, which is regarded as good sign. However, this is most closely connected with private efforts of former Councillor Musy, who has special connections in Nazi circles and recently has visited Germany.

Tertio. Considered probable here that certain SS-circles are favorably disposed toward attempt to save Jews. . . .

Document 88: Telegram from the Cabinet to Richert, February 10, 1945.
Announced decision to send Folke Bernadotte to Berlin to lay the basis for a rescue of Norwegians and Danes. Note last sentence which illustrated the impact of Musy's success on Swedish determination to help Jews.

Intention is to send Folke Bernadotte to Berlin to inspect Red Cross operation, but actually chiefly to try negotiate sending interned Norwegians and Danes to Sweden or Denmark. For this purpose contact should be made with *Auswärtiges Amt* but chiefly with Himmler. Try through Schellenberg discover whether Himmler is willing to receive Bernadotte for discussion questions affecting relations between Sweden and Germany.

Departure ought to take place soonest.

For information. Swiss Musy's successful negotiation on Jewish Question seems to us give certain prospect for consideration our wishes.

Document 89: Telegram from Cabinet to Richert, February 10, 1945.
Swedish decision to make protest about Germany's continuance of its Jewish policy and to offer to take any German-held Jews.

Westrup telegraphs that Council of Confederation agrees wholly with Swedish Government on matter but faithful its principles does not wish participate collective démarches. It has telegraphically instructed Frölicher to contact you and confer about central issue and about coordinated démarches with you and Nuncio though separate and independent.

Provided Swiss minister also presents démarche, you should undertake démarche generally according our No. 26 as well as presenting offer accept Jews into Sweden. Number need not be specified.

1,500 Jews have already arrived Switzerland and 1,200 more are on way after intervention former Councillor Musy.

Document 90: Letters from von Post to Richert, March 1, 1945.
Two letters that reflect on the continuing development of the Red Cross rescue.

Tomorrow, Kersten flies to Berlin, in accordance with his written pledge on the occasion of the freeing of the Warsaw Swedes, to revisit Himmler and work on him. Then Kersten is going to put in a word, to the extent it proves possible, about the transfer to Sweden of the Danish and Norwegian internees, or, in any case, for the successful carrying out of the Bernadotte expedition, and besides that intends to take up a number of special cases, chiefly regarding departures to Sweden.

The Minister of Foreign Affairs told me yesterday that he intended to write to you asking you to render Kersten all assistance, of course not least if he should unexpectedly encounter difficulties. Since I do not know if he did so, and will not have the opportunity to see him before the departure of the courier, I have wanted, with these lines, to let you know of the matter.

* * *

The results of Folke Bernadotte's trip to Berlin must indisputably be considered very satisfactory, since it seemed, initially, to lie beyond the bounds of possibility that Himmler, the first time around, would have allowed the transfer of all the interned Danes and Norwegians to Sweden. . . .

The same day Bernadotte returned — Thursday, the 23rd of February — a press conference was held under the auspices of the Foreign Minister, at which Bernadotte reported on his trip. The importance of nothing being published at this stage was heavily underscored both by the Foreign Minister and by Bernadotte. When information came in yesterday that a couple of papers intended to publish articles even so, a so-called gray slip was dispatched at once. . . .

Document 91: Letter from Himmler to Kersten, March 21, 1945.
Kersten carried this letter back to Stockholm and it was forwarded to London and Washington.

First of all, please accept with these lines my thanks for your visit. This time as always I have been glad when you came and with old friendship placed your great medical skill at my disposal.

During the long years of our acquaintanceship we have indeed discussed many problems, and your attitude was always that of the physician who, remote from all politics, desires the good of the individual human being and of humanity as a whole.

You will be interested to know that during the course of the past three months I have brought about the realization of an idea which we once discussed. Roughly 2,700 Jewish men, women and children were taken to Switzerland in two trains. This is, in effect, the continuation of the policy which my collaborators and I have consistently pursued for many years until the war and the resulting folly in the world made it impossible to carry out. You know, of course, that I in the years 1936, -37, -38, -39 and -40, in collaboration with Jewish American associations created an emigration organization which functioned very fruitfully. The two trains which travelled into Switzerland are the intentional resumption, despite all difficulties, of the fruitful procedure.

From a prisoners' camp at Bergen-Belsen there recently came the rumor that a typhus epidemic of larger proportions had broken out. I immediately sent the Hygienist of the SS, Dr. Mrugrowski, there with his staff. It was a question of cases in the camp of spotted typhus which unfortunately occurs very frequently among people from the East, but the cases are to be regarded as under control thanks to the best medical and modern methods.

I have the conviction that, by eliminating demagogism and superficialities, despite all differences and in spite of most bloody wounds on all sides, wisdom and logic must prevail, and at the same time the human heart and the spirit of helpfulness.

It goes without saying that I, just as I have done throughout all the past years in good times and bad, shall gladly examine requests which you transmit or communicate to me in the humanitarian sphere, and, whenever it is at all possible, shall decide them generously.

Document 92: Letter from Richert to von Post, March 22, 1945.
Report on Felix Kersten's talks with Himmler. The reference to "a list of Jews" relates to a set of Jewish prisoners with direct relations to Sweden.

Kersten, who is returning to Stockholm today, first called on me a couple of days ago. In connection with the conversation I had with him then, we have sent him afterwards, for one thing, our "Swedish" List of Jews with a couple of additions, for another, a list of all Swedes who are under arrest in Germany. Besides this, Folke Bernadotte has turned over to him a couple of special cases (Sapieha among others) for further negotiation.

Folke Bernadotte and Brandel, on the way here to Schönhausen last Saturday, made a visit to Kersten at his country place to deliver the papers in question. Through them, and through his secretary, Mrs. Wacker, who seems to be well-informed about his "business," Kersten has subsequently told me that the "List of Jews" was accomplished, and that the Swedish prisoners would be released, excepting those under death sentence. About these, Himmler had not been authorized to reach any final decision but promised further negotiation in the friendliest possible spirit. Kersten also informed me that most of the special cases were already accomplished. Now we can hope soon to be able to state that the promises given to Kersten will be kept before it is too late.

Concerning the interned Danes and Norwegians, Kersten has apparently worked on those involved, with the purpose of getting the internees conveyed from Neuengamme to Sweden. According to him, Himmler has been won over to this view, however, the realization of it evidently also requires agreement from other parties. But, on this, you must have gotten more information from Kersten himself, by the time you receive these lines, which, like some other letters, are a little bit delayed because of Mrs. Bartel's absence for a couple of days.

Kersten seems to have worked even for other Jews than those on our list, with what he believes will be good results.

Document 93: Letter from Kersten to Gillel Storch, March 24, 1945.
Kersten's report to Storch about his negotiations and the idea that Storch should negotiate directly with Himmler.

With reference to the negotiations of March 3 this year between us and Mr. Ottokar von Knieriem before I left for Germany, I beg to send you a short report on the results of my various conversations with the *Reichsführer SS* Himmler.

You asked me a lot of questions in the course of our conversation, and in a memorandum you wished to make clear the same points to Mr. Himmler.

After having discussed each of these things with the *Reichsführer SS* Himmler, he has arranged a favorable investigation which you will have seen in the letter of March 21, 1945 addressed to me from his Adjutant Brandt, which letter I gave to you. I will let you know as soon as I know anything further about the definite resolutions. At this time about 350,000 Jews are supposed to be living in Germany. I have not discussed the question concerning the eventual liberation of the 8,000 Jews to Sweden who are in possession of Palestine visas because this was not mentioned in your memorandum. A result in this matter may be favorable if the Swedish Government would undertake the necessary steps. I will personally do what I can and will also assist in this matter.

Apart from the last resolution on which we will have to wait, I believe that on account of the utterances made by Mr. Himmler, I can say the following.

The distribution of food parcels sent by you to the various camps, in cases where the addressees are not to be found, will be given to other members of the camps; thus these parcels will reach Jewish members of the camps. Mr. Himmler was especially interested to know that the

Jews arrived in Switzerland had stated this. I also believe that sending of medicines would be permitted. I have particularly and very elaborately considered with Mr. Himmler the question of placing Jews in especially arranged camps, and have met a great understanding. These eventual camps should gradually come under control of the Red Cross and thus the treatment and feeding of these people would be left to the Red Cross.

A new investigation will look into the matter of releasing certain groups of Jews to Switzerland or Sweden. I have discussed with Mr. Himmler the list of single persons I received, and I do hope that I will soon be able to give you a favorable reply. At the same time I wish to draw your attention to the fact that you yourself must arrange the eventual transport.

Concerning the treatment of Jews in camps, I believe that there is a prospect of satisfactory improvement. In my presence the *Reichsführer* gave some orders in this respect and I have seen the written special order saying that cruelties and the killing of Jews are forbidden. Besides, he has claimed that sanitary conditions should be put under a permanent control. To what extent these measures will work out I can not give you any guaranty, you will understand. Herr Himmler has called together all the leaders of Jewish camps for a meeting on March 24 in order to give them new instructions how to treat the Jews in a human way. From now on each leader of a camp will be made responsible for the death of any Jews, and has to report exactly about the cause of death. The eventual relief of Jews, as well as the above-mentioned improvements in their treatment, will be stopped the moment these measures are published in the world press and are told as an example of the weakness of Germany.

It should not be necessary for me to point out that negotiations of this kind which I have had with Mr. Himmler, because of the very delicate material, and because of the many strong contradictories in Germany itself, and, not least, because of the eventual possible utilization of the material as propaganda, have had to be dealt with with the utmost caution and under the strongest discretion. The positive accomplishment of these resolutions may be dependent on various circumstances over which we can not have any influence. But one thing is certain, that all our efforts are condemned to failure if they are not handled with the utmost discretion. It is also certain, however, that through the negotiations we have gained time, which can be of the greatest importance as you will understand on the basis of your personal reasons.

I wish to assure you that I am willing to completely sacrifice myself for those unfortunates as I have done already, for example, for the seven Swedish engineers, as well as for several Jewish Freunds, which was not without fear for myself. However, I consider it to be my moral duty to help where I can, and so far as I can afford it. At last I wish to inform you that the *Reichsführer* SS Himmler, on account of a proposal from me, is prepared to discuss these questions with you personally. Without having submitted this proposal for you I could not go into the matter and would ask you to inform me about your point of view in order that I can undertake the necessary steps.

To sum up, I may say that each of your proposals has found complete understanding by Mr. Himmler, and will be worked out individually and that certain improvements will be undertaken, and that on the part of the *Reichsführer* of SS a readiness to negotiate on these questions exists, and, when possible, to solve the problems.

Document 94: Telegram from Storch to Rabbi Weiss, March 27, 1945.
Storch's report of Kersten's negotiation and request to negotiate for WJC with Himmler.

have 3/3 conferred with doctor kersten masseur who himmlers private doctor 4/3 he departed to himmler doctor kersten has great influence on himmler stop I am negotiating regarding release and cessation murders and permission better treatment stop 22/3 kersten returned with letter Himmler and related that himmler promised consider our desires kindly also prepared release about 10,000 Jews to Sweden or Switzerland I am invited together with Kersten to negotiations with Himmler have been promised free conduct stop Swedish Foreign Office decided permit entrance of the 10,000 Jews also assistance with transport stop Swedish Foreign Office finds my journey important Count Bernadotte who today departed Berlin to negotiate concerning interned 5000 Danish 8000 Norwegians will also negotiate regarding our question but he also considered I must definitely go Berlin stop Kersten declared he supposes Himmler wishes procure alibi stop this must be treated strictly confidential because Himmler declared if this appears in press and is interpreted as weakness on part Germany he will take back his

promise stop sending you these letters through American Minister
Johnson stop cable urgent your opinion.

Document 95: Memorandum of March 27, 1945.
Sweden's rescue policy for Bernadotte's continued negotiations.

In a meeting yesterday with Undersecretary Boheman, Count
Bernadotte and the undersigned, the following guidelines were drawn
up for Count Bernadotte's planned conference with Himmler.

In the first place, permission would once again be asked for the transfer to Sweden of all the Danes and Norwegians interned in Germany
(Neuengamme).

Secondarily, he should:

1) request that Swedish Red Cross personnel be allowed to be in the
whole Neuengamme Camp (50,000 interned):

2) offer for Swedish Red Cross buses to be used for transport to the
Neuengamme Camp, or other suitable camp, of the non-Scandinavians
interned in Germany. Those who should chiefly be brought out were
25,000 Frenchwomen who, in connection with the German retreat from
France, were taken to Germany and there placed in a camp.

Today the above has been supplemented with a message to
Bernadotte that, provided it should prove appropriate and no disadvan-
tage from it could be expected to affect the assignment described above,
he should ask for the transfer to Sweden of a number of Jews.

**Document 96: Letter of Anthony Eden to Winston Churchill. April 1,
1945. Churchill's note dated April 5, 1945.**
*Eden's reflections on Swedish and World Jewish Congress efforts to aid
Jews.*

"A naturalised Finn named Kersten, who has been in Germany for
some years as masseur to Himmler and others, with frequent visits to
Sweden, has just come back to Stockholm with a letter from Himmler
representing the fruits of a negotiation carried on by Kersten with the
knowledge of Sporborch, (*sic.*, Storch) Swedish representative of the
World Jewish Congress, for the release of Jews. Himmler has apparently agreed to let 10,000 Jews go to Sweden or Switzerland and wishes

Sporborch to go to Berlin to arrange the matter. The Swedish Govern-
ment have agreed to receive these Jews and to help get them there.
Sporborch asks, via the British Legation in Stockholm the World Jewish
Congress in London and the Jewish Agency for approval to his visiting
Berlin, and also that they should ask the Foreign Office to support the
proposal with the Swedish Government and allow H.M. Legation at
Stockholm to arrange for the lists of Jews concerned to be handed over
through the Legation."

2. The above message has been passed by Sir V. Mallet (with the
approval of the United States Minister) to the Foreign Office for onward
transmission, and Sir V. Mallet has not accepted any responsibility for
the subject matter.

3. I have telegraphed to Sir V. Mallet informing him that I am not prepared to transmit this message since the proposal emanates from
Himmler. I do not wish to be dragged into this matter. It may be a
Himmler plant and it may have entangling consequences. It is now for
consideration whether a further instruction would be sent to Sir V. Mallet to the effect that it is of course open to the Swedish Government to
transmit the message to the World Jewish Congress if they wish. My
reason for hesitating in doing this is the same as my reason for declining
to transmit the message. The reason, on the other hand, for conveying
such a hint to the Swedish Government would be to re-insure ourselves
against an accusation by the Jews that we were blocking a proposal
which might result in the saving of Jewish lives. All the same on balance
I would prefer to say nothing to the Swedes. Do you agree?

"I agree. No truck with Himmler" W.S.C.

**Document 97: Minutes of a discussion in a meeting with the Swedish
Information Office, April 16, 1945.**
*Folke Bernadotte's report of the rescue effort. He did not mention
Kersten.*

Count Bernadotte gave me an orientation about the Swedish Red
Cross Expedition to Germany. . . . A Swedish expedition to
Theresienstadt had left . . . on the 11th of April. . . . The Swedish expe-

dition to Mecklenburg had departed Saturday the 14th of April. Both expeditions had Neuengamme as their destination — all together, 9,500 Danes and Norwegians in various camps had been brought back by the Swedish Red Cross Expedition. . . .

. . . A portion of the camp was set aside for the Norwegian and Danish prisoners' use, and within that portion the Swedish representatives were allowed to move freely as well as take charge of nursing, social services, and such. . . .

. . . Count Bernadotte had had a discussion with the camp commandant of Neuengamme, Pauli, who had formerly been head of a so-called *Vernichtungslager* at Auschwitz, about what would happen to the prisoners in the camp in case the allied troops should approach Neuengamme. It had come out that evacuation was ordered, but an agreement had been reached that permitted the Scandinavian prisoners to be transferred to Denmark. . . . Concerning the question of evacuation of concentration camps, Count Bernadotte had had a conversation with Himmler on the second day of Easter week. On that occasion, Himmler had informed him that several concentration camps, among others, Theresienstadt and Buchenwald, would not be evacuated but would be handed over intact to the Allies. . . .

. . . Count Bernadotte mentioned a conversation he had had with *Brigadeführer* Schellenberg of the SS, who was among Himmler's closest subordinates, and who had been Count Bernadotte's liaison at Himmler's headquarters. Schellenberg, with whom, Count Bernadotte explained, he had become good friends and who had done much for Sweden during these years, had learned that Hitler had decided that the prisoners in the most outlying concentration camps would be evacuated from them on foot. When Schellenberg learned that, he had protested to Himmler about it and declared that such a course was equivalent to murder. At first, Himmler had been irritated at Schellenberg's objections, but after several hours had changed his mind and issued counter-orders, saying that Schellenberg had been right. . . .

. . . Count Bernadotte's conversation with Himmler had been carried on in a very open spirit. Himmler now regarded the situation very pessimistically. . . . He had . . . been sure that the game was over and with it his own career. Among other matters, questions of surrender had been discussed. . . .

. . . Count Bernadotte related that he had declared before Himmler and Schellenberg that he had no interest in going to see Eisenhower, but that he might possibly consider doing so on certain conditions, namely, the dissolution of the Nazi party and the *Wehrwolf* organization, as well as the transfer of all Danes and Norwegians to Sweden. . . .

. . . One very powerful man at the present time was Gestapo commander Kaltenbrunner. . . . On several occasions, Kaltenbrunner had gone directly to Hitler and complained about various Red Cross actions. Himmler had taken Count Bernadotte aside and earnestly warned him against Kaltenbrunner. According to Himmler, Kaltenbrunner was very irritated by the Swedish Red Cross Expedition and had given orders for special tapping of all of Count Bernadotte's telephone conversations. . . .

. . . On the subject of publicity concerning the Swedish operation, Himmler had emphasized that press coverage would put the entire enterprise at risk. As was known, the operation for the benefit of interned Jews done by the Swiss had been halted by Hitler, because he came to know of it through the international press. . . .

To a question from Mr. Reuterswärd about his personal impression of Himmler, Count Bernadotte said that he had only met Himmler twice and therefore did not feel himself able to give any very definitive judgment. However, he believed that there was something good even in Himmler. At their first meeting Himmler had asked whether, outside Germany, he was the most hated man in existence, and whether they considered him a cruel person — a sadist. Count Bernadotte had replied in the affirmative and added that he himself had also believed that for a long time. However, he had come round to the view that Himmler had no knowledge of many of the misdeeds which his subordinates had carried out in his name. Therefore, to some extent, he had had to suffer unjustly for others' crimes. On the other hand, one had to say that he, as chief of the Gestapo and SS, could not avoid his responsibility.

Count Bernadotte had gotten an impression that Himmler had, to some extent, a romantic tendency. Among other things, he had a lively interest in old Scandinavian ways of life and especially in rune-stones and rune research. Because of this, Count Bernadotte, once his first negotiations with Himmler had yielded results, bought an old book about runes in Latin and Swedish at an antiquarian bookstore in Stockholm. This book, Count Bernadotte had presented as a gift when he made a second visit to Himmler, and he declared that he had seldom seen anyone as touched and grateful for a present as Himmler became, when he received that book.

Count Bernadotte thought the reason Himmler now agreed to facilitate the work of the Swedish Red Cross Expedition to the extent he had, might be Himmler's wish to go down to posterity with at least a few good deeds to his credit. It had even been possible to observe a very marked shift in Himmler's attitude toward the Jewish Question in recent times. Most well-informed persons, however, had been as surprised as Count Bernadotte over the fact that his negotiations with Himmler had reached such a favorable outcome. His general impression of Himmler was that Himmler had considerable intelligence and might be more sensitive than one might think.

Mr. Reutersvärd offered the idea that Himmler's attitude toward the Red Cross Expedition could be explained by his not wishing, once he realized that the game was lost, to commit any unnecessary cruelties. So long as it profited Germany in one way or another to use harshness and terror, he had been prepared to do so, but when Germany's fate was sealed anyway, he wanted to go down in history as a man who had not been guilty of any, even from the German viewpoint, meaningless crimes.

Count Bernadotte thought that this interpretation had much in its favor. . . .

Document 98: Telephone conversation between Brandel (Friedrichsruh) and Crafoord (Ministry of Foreign Affairs, Stockholm), April 20, 1945.
Announcement that all Scandinavians to be moved from Neuengamme to area near Danish border.

1. On the 19th, in the evening, information is received that the camp at Neuengamme is to be emptied of Danes and Norwegians. At 5 a.m. on the morning of the 20th, all Danes and Norwegians there will be picked up by the Red Cross and transferred to a camp which is being readied in the vicinity of Hortens in Denmark.

This news is for internal circulation only.

2. Just before the call came, we were informed from Berlin that Bernadotte is allowed to meet Himmler some time on the 20th. Therefore Bernadotte will travel to Berlin at 5 a.m. on the morning of the 20th.

3. Brandel went on to say that a number of threatening low-level

overflights had taken place during the day just past. A Danish bus had been fired on, among others.

Document 99: Coded telegram from Folke Bernadotte to Sven Grafström, April 22, 1945.

Bernadotte reported Himmler's continuing fear of Hitler's response to a large-scale movement of concentration camp inmates to Denmark and Sweden.

Supplemental to telephone conversation on Saturday with Tamm. Himmler could not allow immediate transport of Scandinavians to Sweden since Hitler had firmly forbidden it. I have worked out with Himmler that the transfer may take place when fighting begins in Denmark. Preparatory orders for this issued.

Document 100: Memorandum by Norbert Masur, April 23, 1945.

Masur's report of his mission.

In connection with various conversations between Mr. Storch from the World Jewish Congress's Relief & Rehabilitation Department in Stockholm, and Dr. F. Kersten, during March Mr. Storch turned over a list of our requests, with respect to the Jewish internees in Germany, to Dr. F. Kersten. The latter was to travel to Germany and present these requests, together with a list which Dr. Kersten received from the Foreign Office, to the authorities in Germany, primarily, Himmler. During the conversation with Himmler, some of Dr. Kersten's demands were granted, but in order to carry out the large outlines of the proposals, Dr. Kersten suggested that Himmler should discuss the questions with some Jewish representative from Stockholm. Himmler went along with the suggestion and through Kersten invited such a representative, with a guarantee of safe passage. . . .

. . . The conversation with Himmler took place on the night between Friday and Saturday, the 20/21 of April. Our demands, in general, were the following:

All Jews still alive in Germany should receive permission to stay in those places where they are, and no new forced evacuations should occur.

Should evacuation to a neutral country still be possible through the Red Cross's or other neutral assistance, such voluntary evacuation should be permitted.

Commanders of camps should receive orders for the good treatment of the Jews and for turning over the camps to the Allies /the American, Soviet Russian or British armies/ if the fronts should approach any camps.

Besides this, we turned over the Foreign Office's detailed lists of those persons whose release was desired. . . .

The result of the negotiations was as follows:

1. Fifty Norwegian Jews on the Foreign Office's list to be released and to be brought by the German authorities in Norway to the Swedish border.

2. Releasing of those Swedish citizens who, according to the Foreign Office list, sit imprisoned at Grini and at other places in Norway shall be given sympathetic consideration and, if possible, be approved.

3. One thousand Jewish women as well as some Frenchwomen, according to the list from the Foreign Office, should be released and should immediately be brought out by the Swedish Red Cross.

4. The release of a number of specifically named persons in Theresienstadt, in accordance with a list from the Netherlands Legation, was approved, yet it is probable that this order cannot be carried out.

5. A firm promise that no Jews are to be shot.

6. A promise that, if possible, no further forcible movements are going to take place, even if the fronts approach the camps.

7. Foodstuffs and medicines may be sent through the Red Cross to all internment camps.

8. Persons named on various further lists should be sought, but such searches are surely completely impossible now.

9. A condition, that our visit and conversation with Himmler remain absolutely secret as well as that nothing be published about the freed Jews' and non-Jews' arrival in a neutral country.

In connection with No. 9 I wish to mention that — as I learned in conversation with the gentlemen around Himmler — Hitler is still absolutely against any release whatsoever of Jews from Germany. . . .

. . . According to information from Counselor Engzell on Sunday afternoon, the Berlin Legation, at the instance of Count Bernadotte, communicated as early as Saturday evening that the transport column was on its way to Ravensbrück. One may expect this transport of 1,000 women to arrive in Sweden on Wednesday.

Should the transport column succeed in bringing home the 1,000 women from Ravensbrück, we are convinced that — should there still be time for it — more women are going to be released to be brought out. . . .

From the conversation with Himmler, I wish only to bring up one point to which he attached special importance: Himmler said that the turning over to the Allies of the concentration camps /Bergen-Belsen, Buchenwald/ was badly rewarded by the descriptions in the press concerning the conditions in these camps, which descriptions he characterized as "*Greuelmärchen.*" This made him hesitant whether it is right to continue on the course they have taken. I told him to his face that one cannot deny that gross outrages have occurred and that, besides, the free press in free countries cannot be stopped even by the governments of those countries. Nevertheless, it is conceivable that these descriptions could carry with them a stimulus for Himmler and *consortes* to conceal every trace completely, through transporting away or exterminating whole camps instead of turning them over to the Allies. Last Saturday, we saw long columns of prisoners from the concentration camp Oranienburg marching north.

In summary, I wish to observe the following:

Of course Himmler's word is absolutely nothing to rely upon. Even in the conversations with us, he told many obvious lies. However, evidently he wishes to do something now, at the last minute, for which reason I believe that he is going to give the orders he has promised. On the other hand, his whole thought-pattern concerns sheer catastrophe theories. If Nazism is to go under, then at least as many as possible in Europe and the rest of the world are going to share its fate. Therefore it is not inconceivable that Himmler or — should power glide out of Himmler's grasp — that some of the other Nazi leaders, at the last moment, would give orders for the murder of all Jews. Because of this, it is so extraordinarily important to evacuate as many Jews as possible in any way to neutral countries or behind the Allied lines, even if one must feel that liberation through the armies is very near at hand. The danger for non-Jews is considerably less. . . .

Of great value were the negotiations we carried on with Schellenberg, Franz Göring and Dr. Brandt. . . . These are younger men, who wish to live. They say they are entirely aware that every act of violence — also against Jews — is a crime, even against the future Germany. We have the firm conviction that they are going to sabotage any possible order from Himmler for acts of violence. . . .

The negotiations described above and the results achieved would have been inconceivable without [Dr.] Kersten's active and wholehearted participation, and one should be especially grateful to him that he, without regard for his own safety, followed me on this dangerous trip in the service of humanitarian rescue.

Document 101: Memorandum by Gösta Engzell, April 25, 1945.
A summary of Norbert Masur and Felix Kersten's meeting with Himmler April 20–21, 1945. Note that the number of women to be released from Ravensbrück was 1000.

When he was visited in March by [Dr.] Kersten, *SS Reichsführer* Himmler had declared that he was prepared to receive Kersten once more, in company with Mr. Gillel Storch (formerly Latvian, now stateless Jewish refugee in Sweden, who as representative for the Worlds (*sic*) Jewish Congress here has worked for assistance to Jews in Germany). When Storch felt he could not travel, the Swedish Jewish merchant Norbert Masur was invited to go along. On Thursday the 19th of April, 1945, Kersten and Masur left and, on the night between the 20th and 21st of April, Himmler joined them at Kersten's estate north of Berlin. There, negotiation took place on, among other things, some general questions about the treatment of the remaining Jews in Germany. A number of special requests were conveyed by Kersten, supported by information he had obtained from the Ministry of Foreign Affairs. A brief summary follows below:

1. K. requested release and return to Sweden of 50 Jews who were interned at Berg near Tønsberg in Norway. A list was presented. Attachment A.

Himmler granted the request, for which orders would immediately be given.

After Consul General Westring had been informed of this, on the 23rd of April, he told us later the same day that the order had reached Oslo and that the matter would be arranged.

2. K. asked for release of Swedish citizens held in Norway, as listed. Attachment B.

Himmler promised an investigation and that the request would be given friendly consideration.

3. The proposal was made that the Swedish Aid to Norway be allowed, through extra rations, to increase the daily rations of the political prisoners at Grini.

Himmler approved this, for which orders would be given to Oslo.

4. Himmler gave permission for gift packages and medicines to be sent to the Jews in German camps. The shipments should go through IRK and the Swedish Red Cross. See the letter in Attachment C.

5. Release of Swedish penal convicts in Germany was requested. This had earlier been conveyed by K. and most of them had been released, among others certain ones condemned to death.

6. The release of some specifically named persons of various nationalities was requested and would be approved to the extent it proved practicable.

7. Release of about 1,000 women of various nationalities from the camp in Ravensbrück was promised, among them about 300 Frenchwomen. This has already been carried out, for the most part.

8. Per the consultation with Minister Ditleff, certain requests for release of Norwegian prisoners in Norway were presented. See Attachment D.

Himmler promised to investigate in a friendly spirit.

Bibliography

I. **Unpublished Documents:**
Denmark:
  National Archive: Copenhagen
    Ebbe Munchs arkiv

Great Britain:
  Lambeth Palace: London
    Papers of William Temple
    Bishop George Bell's papers

  Public Records Office: London
    Minutes of the War Cabinet meetings and papers
    Papers of the Foreign Office including Lord Avon's papers and
      the private papers of Sir Orme Sargent
    Papers of the Prime Minister (PREM series)

Sweden:
  Arbetarrörelsens arkiv: Stockholm
    Per Albin Hanssons samling.

Göteborgs länsarkiv:
  Arvid Richerts samling

Krigsarkiv: Stockholm
  Curt Juhlin-Danfelts samling, and Anders Forsells samling

Kyrkans hus arkiv: Uppsala
  Svenska Israelsmissionens arkiv

Lunds Universitets bibliotek
  Biskop Gustaf Auléns samling, Fredrik Bööks samling, Torsten

Nothins samling, Biskop Edvard Rodhes samling, and Ernest
Wigforss' samling

Mosaiska församlings arkiv: Stockholm
    Materials in this archive were uncatalogued and spread
throughout the buildings of the Stockholm Jewish congregation.
The amount of relevant material is considerable. The congregation
gave their holdings to the National Archive after the author
completed research for this volume. The materials have been
moved but remain uncatalogued.

Riksarkiv: Stockholm
    Gösta Bagges minnesanteckningar, Hermann Erikssons papper,
Sven Grafströms anteckningar, Gustav V's privata samling, Sven
Hedins arkiv, Informationsstyrelsens arkiv, Svenska Röda Korsets
arkiv including Folke Bernadottes arkiv, Utrikesdepartementets
arkiv including Arvid Richerts samling, Pressbyråns arkiv,
Tidningsklipp

Sigtuna
    Nordiska Ekumeniska Institutets samling, and Sigtuna
Stiftelsens Bibliotek Klipparkiv

Uppsala länsarkiv
    Erling Eidems samling

Uppsala Universitets Bibliotek
    Yngve Brilioths papper, and K.G. Westmans papper

Utrikesdepartementets arkiv: Stockholm
    Swedish Legation, Berlin, archive is not listed at the National
Archive but is being held at the Foreign Office. It is uncatalogued.

United States:
    National Archives: Washington
        Papers of the Department of State, and the OSS
        Presidential Library of Franklin D. Roosevelt: Hyde Park, New
York, War Refugee Board archive

II. Journals:
Israels Väktare
Judisk krönika
Svenska Israelsmissionen Missionstidning för Israel

III. Published Materials:
Adler-Rudel, Salomon. "A Chronicle of Rescue Efforts." *Leo Baeck Institute Yearbook* XI (1966), 214–241.
Andreen, Per G. *De Mörka Åren*. Stockholm. 1971.
Anger, Per. *Med Raoul Wallenberg i Budapest*. Stockholm. 1979.
Berlinger, Eliser. *Mosaiska Församlingen i Malmö 100 år 1871–1971*. Malmö. 1971.
Bernadotte, Folke. *The Curtain Falls*. New York. 1945.
Bernadotte, Folke. *Slutet*. Stockholm. 1945.
Boheman, Erik. *På vakt*. Stockholm. 1964.
Braham, Randolph. *The Politics of Genocide*. New York. 1 981.
(no author). *Niels Bohr*. Copenhagen. 1964.
Brehmer, T. *Kriget mot juden*. Örebro. 1943.
Burns, Frank (Gunnar Hägglöf). *Paradis för oss*. St ockholm. 1952.
Böök, Fredrik. *Resa till Jerusalem*. Lund. 1977.
Böök, Fredrik. *An Eyewitness in Germany*. London. 19 33.
Carlgren, Wilhelm. *Svensk underrättelsetjänst 1939–1945*. Stockholm. 1985.
Carlgren, Wilhelm. *Svensk utrikespolitik 1939–1945*. St ockholm. 1973.
Carlgren, Wilhelm. *Swedish Foreign Policy during the Second World War*. London. 1977.
Carlsson, Holger. *Nazism i Sverige*. Stockholm. 1942.
Carparsson, Ragnar. *LO under fem årtionden*. Stockholm. 1948.
Childs, Marquis. *Sweden: The Middle Way*. New Haven. 193 7.
Conway, John. *The Nazi Persecution of the Churches 1933–1945*. London. 1968.
Dardel, Gustaf. *Lyckliga hov, stormiga år*. Stockholm. 1953.
Denham, Henry. *Inside the Nazi Ring*. London. 1984.
Drangel, Louise. *Den kämpande demokratin*. Stockholm. 1 976.
Edvardsson, Lars. *Kyrka och Judendom*. Lund. 1976.
Enqvist, Per Olof. *Legionärerna*. Stockholm. 1968.
Ericksen, Robert. *Theologians Under Hitler*. New Haven. 1985.

Erlander, Tage. *1940–1949*. Stockholm. 1973.

Fein, Helen. *Accounting for Genocide*. Chicago. 1979.

Fleming, Gerald. *Hitler and the Final Solution*. Berkele y, 1984.

Fredborg, Arvid. *Bakom Stålvallen*. Stockholm. 1943.

Fredborg, Arvid. *Destination Berlin*. Stockholm. 1985.

Friberg, Göte. *Stormcentrum Öresund*. Borås. 1977.

Friedlander, Saul. *Kurt Gerstein: The Ambiguity of Good*. New York. 1969.

Fritz, Martin. *German Steel and Swedish Iron Ore, 1939–1945*. Gothenburg. 1974.

Fritz, Martin. "Swedish Ballbearings and the German War Economy." *Scandinavian Economic Review*. 1973.

Gilbert, Martin. *Auschwitz and the Allies*. New York. 19 81.

Gilbert, Martin. *The Holocaust*. New York. 1985.

Gordon, Sarah. *Hitler, Germans, and the "Jewish Question."* Princeton. 1984.

Gottfarb, Inga. *Den livsfarliga glömskan*. Austria. 19 86.

Gross, Leonard. *The Last Jews from Berlin*. New York. 1982.

Günther, Christian. *Tal i en tung tid*. Stockholm. 1945.

Hadenius, Stig. *Swedish Politics during the Twentieth Century*. Borås. 1985.

Hæstrup, Jørgen. *Den gang i Danmark*. Odense. 1982.

Hæstrup, Jørgen. *Secret Alliance*. Odense. 1976–1977 .

Hagberg, Hilding. *Röd Bok om Svart Tid*. Uddevalla. 19 66.

Hammar, Tomas. *Sverige åt svenskarna*. Stockholm. 1964.

Hedenqvist, Göte. *Undan förintelsen*. Älvsjö. 19 83.

Helmreich, Ernst C. *The German Churches under Hitler*. D etroit. 1979.

Hilberg, Raul. *The Destruction of the European Jewry*. C hicago. 1967.

Hägglöf, Gunnar. *Det kringrända Sverige*. Stockholm. 1983.

Hägglöf, Gunnar. *Samtida vittne 1940–1945*. Stockhol m. 1972.

Höjer, Torvald. *Svenska Dagbladet och andra världskriget, september 1939–maj 1945*. Lund. 1969.

Jasper, Ronald. *George Bell, Bishop of Chichester*. Oxfo rd. 1967.

Johansson, Alf. *Per Albin och kriget*. Stockholm. 1984.

Johansson, Alf. "Svensk medgörlighet. Ljus över Günther och Per Albin inför operation Barbarossa." *Historisk Tidskrift*. 4–1984. 391–400.

Jones, S. Shepard. *The Scandinavian States and the League of Nations*. New York. 1939.

Kersten, Felix. *Samtal med Himmler*. Stockholm. 1947.

Koblik, Steven. *"Om vi teg, skulle stenarna ropa"* — *Sverige och judeproblemet 1933–1945*. Stockholm. 1987.

Koblik, Steven. *Sweden's Development from Poverty to Affluence, 1750–1970*. Minneapolis. 1975.

Koenigswald, Harold. *Birger Forell*. Berlin.

Kungliga Utrikesdepartementet. *1945 års Svenska hjälpexpedition till Tyskland*. Stockholm. 1956.

Kungliga Utrikesdepartementet. *Frågor i samband med Norska regeringens vistelse utanfor Norge 1940–1943*. Stockholm. 1948.

Langlet, Nina. *Kaos i Budapest*. Vällingby. 1982.

Langlet, Valdemar. *Verk och Dagar i Budapest*. Stockholm . 1946.

Laqueur, Walter. *The Terrible Secret*. Boston. 1980.

Levai, Eugene. *Black Book on the Martyrdom of Hungarian Jewry*. Zürich. 1948.

Levai, Jenö. *Raoul Wallenberg*. Stockholm. 1948.

Lewandowski, Jozef. *Swedish Contribution to the Polish Resistance Movement during World War II (1939–1942)*. Uppsala. 1979.

Lewin, Leif. *Planhushållningsdebatten*. Stockholm. 1967 .

Lindberg, Hans. *Svensk flyktingpolitik under internationellt t ryck 1936–1941*. Stockholm. 1973.

Lindström, Ulf. *Fascism in Scandinavia 1920–1940*. Stockholm. 1985.

Littell, Franklin, & Hubert Locke (eds.). *The German Church Struggle and the Holocaust*. Detroit. 1974.

Lönnroth, Erik. *Den svenska utrikespolitikens historia V, 1919–1939*. Stockholm. 1945.

Masur, Norbert. *En Jude talar med Himmler*. Stockholm. 1 945.

Melchior, Marcus. *Darkness over Denmark*. London. 1973.

Mendelsohn, Oscar. "Actions Against the Jews in Norway during the war." *Nordisk Judaistik*. Scandinavian Jewish Stud ies. V. 3, no. 2. 1982. 27–36.

Mendelsohn, Oscar. *Jødenes historie i Norge gjennom 300 år*. Oslo. 1969.

Munch-Petersen, Thomas. *The Strategy of Phony War. Britain,*

Sweden, and the Iron Ore Question, 1939–1940. Stockholm.
1981.

Munck, Ebbe. *Sibyllegatan 13.* Stockholm. 1967.

Nerman, Ture. *För människovärdet.* Stockholm. 1946.

Nerman, Ture. *Trots Allt! Minnen och redovisning.* Stock holm.
1954.

Nilsson, Göran B. "Midsommarkrisen 1941." *Historisk Tidskr ift.*
1971.

Nilsson, Torsten. *Människor och händelser i Norden.* S tockholm.
1977.

Nissen, Henrik S. (ed.). *Scandinavia during the Second World
War.* Minneapolis. 1983.

(no author). *Nordiska röster mot Judeförföljelse och vå ld.*
Stockholm. 1943.

Nybom, Torsten. *Motstånd, anpassning, uppslutning — linjer i
svensk debatt om utrikespolitik och internationell politik
1940–1943.* Stockholm. 1978.

Oppen, Beate R. von. *Religion and Resistance to Nazism.*
Princeton. 1971.

Pentkower, Monty. *The Jews Were Expendable.* Urbana. 198 3.

Philipp, Rudolph. *Raoul Wallenberg.* Stockholm. 1947.

Quensel, Nils. *Minnesbilder.* Stockholm. 1974.

Revue Internationale d'histoire Militaire. *Neutrality and Defe nse:
The Swedish Experience.* Stockholm. 1984.

Riste, Olav. *Londonregjeringa II. 1942–1945. Vegen Heim.* Oslo.
1979.

Rustow, Dankwart. *The Politics of Compromise.* Princeton . 1955.

Sandler, Rickard. *Strömväxlingar och lärdomar.* Stoc kholm.
1939.

Scott, Franklin D. *Sweden: The Nation's History.* Minnea polis.
1977.

Segerstedt, Torgny. *I dag.* Stockholm. 1945.

Skodvin, Magne. *Norway and the Second World War.* Oslo. 1966.

Statens Offentliga Utredningar. *Parlamentariska
undersökningskommissionen angående flyktingsärenden och
säkerhetstjänst.* 3 vols. *Flyktingars behandling.* Stockholm.
1946. *Utlämnande av uppgifter om flyktingar.* Stockhol m. 1947.
Säkerhetstjänstens verksamhet. Stockholm. 1948.

Storch, Gillel. "Insatser av WJC:s sektion." *Judisk Krönik a*. 31 (1962).

Svensson, Åke. *De vita bussarna*. Stockholm. 1945.

Sydow, Björn von. "Krisuppgörelsen: man måste betona förändringen." *Politisk Tidskrift*. 1–2. 1983.

Söderpalm, Sven A. *Direktörsklubben*. Stockholm. 197 6.

Thulstrup, Åke. *Svensk utrikespolitik under andra världskrig et*. Stockholm. 1950.

Tingsten, Herbert. *The Debate on the Foreign Policy of Sweden, 1918–1939*. London. 1949.

Torbacke, Jarl. *Dagens Nyheter och demokratins kris 1937–1946*. Stockholm. 1972.

Torell, Ulf. *Hjälp till Danmark. Militära och politiska förbindelser 1943–1945*. Stockholm. 1943.

Trevor-Roper, Hugh. "Kersten, Himmler, and Count Bernadotte." *The Atlantic* 44 (Feb. 1953).

Trevor-Roper, Hugh. *The Last Days of Hitler*. New York. 1947.

Trevor-Roper, Hugh. "The Strange Case of Himmler's Doctor, Felix Kersten, and Count Bernadotte." *Commentary*, April 1957. 356–364.

Uhlin, Åke. *Februari krisen 1942*. Stockholm. 1972.

Valentin, Hugo. *Judarna i Sverige*. Stockholm. 1964.

Valentin, Hugo. "Rescue and Relief Activities in Behalf of Jewish Victims of Nazism in Scandinavia." *YIVO Annual of Jewish Social Science* 13 (1953). 224–251.

Wahlbäck, Krister. *Finlandsfrågan i svensk politik 1937–1940*. Stockholm. 1964.

Wahlbäck, Krister. *Regeringen och kriget. Ur statsrådens dagböcker 1939–1941*. Stockholm. 1972.

Wasserstein, Bernard. *Britain and the Jews of Europe, 1939–1945*. Oxford. 1979.

West, John. *German-Swedish Relations, 1939–1942*. Unpublished dissertation. University of Denver. 1976.

Westman, K.G. *Politiska anteckningar september 1939–mars 1943*. Stockholm. 1981.

Wiberg, Ingrid Segerstedt. *Torgny Segerstedt*. Stockholm. 1955.

Wigforss, Ernst. *Minnen III*. Stockholm. 1954.

Wilkinson, James. *The Intellectual Resistance in Europe*. Cambridge. 1981.

Wyman, David. *The Abandonment of the Jews*. New York. 1984.
Wärenstam, Eric. *Anti-semitism in Sweden, 1920–1945*.
    Unpublished master's thesis. Columbia University. 1955.
Yahil, Leni. *The Rescue of the Danish Jewry*. Philadelphia. 1969.
Yahil, Leni. "Scandinavian Rescue of Prisoners." *Yad Vashem
    Studies* VI (1967). 181–220.
Åmark, Klaus. *Makt eller moral*. Stockholm. 1973.

Index